I0754236

Eng^{d} by H.B. Hall & Sons, N.Y.

Paul Hamilton Hayne.

POEMS

OF

PAUL HAMILTON HAYNE

Complete Edition

WITH NUMEROUS ILLUSTRATIONS

BOSTON
D. LOTHROP AND COMPANY
32 FRANKLIN STREET, CORNER OF HAWLEY
1882

PRESS OF
L. N. FREDERICKS.
31 Hawley St., Boston.

TO

COLONEL JOHN G. JAMES,

PRESIDENT OF THE STATE AGRICULTURAL AND MECHANICAL COLLEGE OF TEXAS,

These Verses,

IN WHICH HE HAS TAKEN SO UNSELFISH AN INTEREST,

ARE

AFFECTIONATELY DEDICATED.

BIOGRAPHICAL SKETCH.

It had little to do with Byron's success as a poet that he was born in the purple of the English aristocracy; or with the quality of Shelley's genius that he was the son of a Sir Timothy, who prided himself on a descent from a long line of British squires; or that Algernon Swinburne's father was a baronet. And yet if our poets have gentle blood in their veins, other things being equal, we prefer that they should have it.

Good birth, as a general thing, argues good breeding, refinement, education, fixed social position, and a wide margin of generous leisures; all of which have much to do with the outcome of a poet's life.

We do not believe that Tennyson would ever have written as he has, if it had been his fortune to labor for his daily bread. Even had the genius all been there, the wide leisures would have been wanting, and he would have produced his poems, not as Goethe, at his "unhasting ease,"—absolutely free from all exigence,—but under the pressure of a goad, which would have destroyed all their beautiful spontaneity.

It is therefore to the advantage of our poet, PAUL HAMILTON HAYNE, that he had ancestors. It may sound somewhat unrepublican perhaps, to hear him wish, as he does in one of his keen sonnets, that these same ancestors had been content to stay in their four-hundred-year-old Shropshire Manor-House, enjoying the positive good England gave them, rather than go sailing over seas in quest of what might be of questionable benefit; but we can forgive him, in view of his antecedents on this side the water, of which he may be proud as well. His English progenitors settled, early in colonial days, in Charleston, South Carolina, and from the first were of importance in the civil affairs of the young State. They furnished noble patriots, who shed their blood in Revolutionary days, for the liberties of their adopted country. The name of the renowned statesman and orator, Robert G. Hayne, who was the poet's uncle, has become the possession of the country. While in the Senate of the United States, he was not afraid to match his strength with Webster's, and he was governor of South Carolina when to be governor of the Palmetto State was an honor worth the winning.

The subject of this sketch is the only child of Lieutenant Hayne, a naval officer, who died at sea when his son was an infant; his mother, recently deceased, was a South Carolina lady, of good English and Scotch descent. He was born in Charleston, January 1st, 1830, and educated at Charleston College, from which he was graduated. Inheriting the prestige of a noble name, high position, and a sufficient amount of wealth, the world was before the youth, and he was free to choose his path. From earliest boyhood his fondness for literature, particularly poetry, was pronounced, and there was everything around him to foster this love. The Charleston of thirty-five years ago was a very different place from the Charleston of to-day. The old Huguenot element, with its aristocratic names and associations, was strong, and the large admixture of good English blood helped to make its people just a little exclusive. Boston herself did not gather the mantle of her self-importance in a more queenly manner about her than did this city by the sea. There was a decided literary element, too, among its higher classes. Legarè's wit and scholarship brightened its social circle; Calhoun's deep shadow loomed over it from his plantation at Fort Hill; Gilmore Simms's genial culture broadened its sympathies. The latter was the Macænas to a band of brilliant youths who used to meet for literary suppers at his beautiful home; and here it was that the love for old Elizabethan lore, and the study of the classics of the English tongue, which has always characterized Mr. Hayne, found one of its best stimulants.

No sooner had he graduated than he threw himself actively into literary life. He became connected with the journalism of the city, and when the enthusiastic group of young scholars established a Literary Monthly Magazine (*Russell's*) Mr. Hayne was appointed its editor.

His first volume of Poems was published by the old house of Ticknor & Co., Boston, in 1855, when he was some twenty-five years old, his second in 1857, and his third in 1860. These all met with such success as encouraged him to adopt fully a literary life as his vocation.

In the meantime he had married Miss Mary Middleton Michel, of Charleston, the daughter of an eminent French physician, who received a gold medal from Napoleon the Third, for services under the first Napoleon at the battle of Leipsic. Of the poet's wife it is but the scantest justice to say that she has been the inspiration, the stay, the joy of his life. No poet ever was more blessed in a wife, and she it is, who, by her self-renunciation, her exquisite sympathy, her positive, material help, her bright hopefulness, has made endurable the losses and trials that have crowded Mr. Hayne's life. Those who know how to read between the lines can see everywhere the influence of this irradiating and stimulating presence.

Then came the disasters of the civil war. Mr. Hayne, whose health, delicate from his childhood, would not allow him to take field service, became an aid on Governor Pickens's staff. During the bombardment of his native city, his beautiful home was burned to the ground, and his large, handsome library utterly lost. Even the few valuables, such as the old family silver, which he succeeded in securing and removing to a bank in Columbia for safe-keeping, were swept away in the famous "march to the sea;" and there was nothing left for the homeless and ruined man but exile among the "Pine Barrens" of Georgia. There he established himself, in utter seclusion, in a veritable cottage (or rather *shanty*, dignified at first as "Hayne's Roost"), behind whose screens of vines, among the peaches, melons, and strawberries of his own raising, he has fought the fight of life with uncomplaining bravery, and persisted in being happy.

Here, then, at "Copse Hill," nested amid his greenery and his pines, our poet has lived for fifteen years,—content with little of this world's gear, happy in his chosen work, writing as his frail health would permit, and in manly independence. In 1872, the Lippincotts published his *Legends and Lyrics*, and in 1873 his edition of his friend Henry Timrod's Poems appeared, accompanied by one of the most pathetic biographical memorials of which literature gives an example. In 1875, *The Mountain of the Lovers* was published. A Life of Gilmore Simms (still in MS.) was also written, with Memorial Sketches of Governor Hayne and Mr. Legarè,—so that these years of seclusion have been well filled up with literary labor; and during the past five years the names of not many writers have appeared more frequently, perhaps, in the pages of our current literature, than that of the recluse of "Copse Hill." Here he has interpreted Nature, we think, with as clear an insight as the poet of Rydal Mount. He has made the melancholy moanings of his Georgia pines sob through his verses. He has given voices to the *Midnight Thunder;* to the *Windless Rain*; to the *Muscadines of the Southern Forests;* to their *Woodland Phases;* to the *Aspects of the Pines*, as has not been heretofore done.

It were superfluous to enter upon any criticism of his poems, nor is this the place for it. They are left with the reader, who, if he cannot, of himself, find therein the aromatic freshness of the woods, — the swaying incense of the cathedral-like aisles of pines, — the sough of dying summer winds, — the glint of lonely pools, and the brooding notes of leaf-hidden mocking-birds, — would not be able to discern them, however carefully the critic might point them out.

MARGARET J. PRESTON.

CONTENTS.

YOUTHFUL POEMS.

SONNETS.

DRAMATIC SKETCHES.

POEMS OF THE WAR.

LEGENDS AND LYRICS.

LATER POEMS.

HUMOROUS POEMS.

POEMS FOR CHILDREN.

LIST OF ILLUSTRATIONS.

HOME OF PAUL HAMILTON HAYNE,
"Copse Hill," Ga.

YOUTHFUL POEMS.

1850–1860.

THE WILL AND THE WING.

To have the will to soar, but not the wings,
Eyes fixed forever on a starry height,
Whence stately shapes of grand imaginings
Flash down the splendors of imperial light;

And yet to lack the charm that makes them ours,
The obedient vassals of that conquering spell,
Whose omnipresent and ethereal powers,
Encircle Heaven, nor fear to enter Hell;

This is the doom of Tantalus — the thirst
For beauty's balmy fount to quench the fires
Of the wild passion that our souls have nurst
In hopeless promptings — unfulfilled desires.

Yet would I rather in the outward state
Of Song's immortal temple lay me down,
A beggar basking by that radiant gate
Than bend beneath the haughtiest empire's crown!

For sometimes, through the bars, my ravished eyes
Have caught brief glimpses of a life divine,
And seen a far, mysterious rapture rise
Beyond the veil that guards the inmost shrine.

"THE LAUGHING HOURS BEFORE HER FEET."

The laughing Hours before her feet,
Are scattering spring-time roses,
And the voices in her soul are sweet
As music's mellowed closes;
All hopes and passions, heavenly born,
In her, have met together,
And Joy diffuses round her morn
A mist of golden weather.

As o'er her cheek of delicate dyes,
The blooms of childhood hover,
So do the tranced and sinless eyes,
All childhood's heart discover;
Full of a dreamy happiness,
With rainbow fancies laden,
Whose arch of promise grows to bless
Her spirit's beauteous Adenne.

She is a being born to raise
Those undefiled emotions,
That whisper of our sunniest days,
And most sincere devotions;
In her, we see renewed and bright,
That phase of earthly story,
Which glimmers in the morning light,
Of God's exceeding glory.

Why, in a life of mortal cares,
Appear these heavenly faces,
Why, on the verge of darkened years,
These clear, celestial graces?
'Tis but to cheer the soul that faints
With pure and blest evangels,
To prove, if Heaven is rich with saints,
That Earth may have her angels.

Enough! 'tis not for me to pray
That on her life's sweet river,
The calmness of a virgin day
May rest, and rest forever;
I know a guardian Genius stands
Beside those waters lowly,
And labors with ethereal hands
To keep them pure and holy.

EVE OF THE BRIDAL.

YES! it has come; the strange, o'ermastering hour,
When buoyant hopes, and tender, tremulous fears
Sway the full heart with a divided power,
The flush of sunshine, and the touch of tears!

Oh! for a spell to charm away thy care,
As I *could* charm, were I but near thee now
To chide coy flickerings of that half despair
Of virginal shame upon thy downcast brow;

A fitful gloom 'mid blushes of bright joy,
Like those transparent clouds in summer days,
That cast their transient shadows of alloy
Across the noontide's else too dazzling blaze;

Yet, from the fair hills of this foreign shore,
I waft thee benedictions on the wind,
Hopes that a peaceful bliss forevermore
May rule the gracious empire of thy mind.

And blessing thus, the dreary distance dies,
And in a clearer than Agrippa's glass,
The enamored fancy, — what pale visions rise,
Brightening to shape and beauty ere they pass?

A room where sunset's glory deep, though dim,
Girds thy rich chamber with luxurious grace,
Rounds the fair outline of each delicate limb,
And crowns with chastened ray thine eloquent face,

In shimmering folds thy raiments soft and rare,
Swell with the passionate heavings of thy breast,
O'er whose young loveliness, the entranced air,
Languidly breathing, seeks voluptuous rest.

Thy hand —(in two brief hours no longer thine) —
Gleams near a gossamer curtain, stirred with sighs,
And the full, star-like tears begin to shine
In the blue heaven of thy bewildering eyes.

Tears for the girlhood, almost past away,
Its innocent life, its wealth of tender lore,
Tears for the womanhood, whose opening day,
May not reveal the untried scene before.

Not bitter tears! for him thou lov'st is true,
And all thy being quivers into flame,
A swift delicious flame that thrills thee through,
Whene'er thy memory lingers on his name.

Ev'n now I see thee turn thy timid head,
Luxuriant-locked, towards a dim retreat,
Where twilight shadows veil thy bridal bed,
And golden gloom and tender silence meet.

MY FATHER.

My father! in the vague, mysterious past,
My boyish thoughts have wandered o'er and o'er,
To thy lone grave upon a distant shore,
The wanderer of the waters, still at last.

Never in childhood have I blithely sprung
To catch my father's voice, or climb his knee;
He was a constant pilgrim of the sea,
And died upon it when his boy was young.

He perished not in conflict nor in flame,
No laurel garland rests upon his tomb;
Yet in stern duty's path he met his doom;
A life heroic, though unwed to fame!

First in vague depths of fancy, scarce-defined,
Love limned his wavering likeness on my soul,
Till through slow growths it waxed a perfect whole
Of clear conceptions, brightening heart and mind.

His careless bearing and his manly face,
His cordial eye; his firm-knit, stalwart form,
Fitted to breast the fight, the wreck, the storm;
The sailor's frankness and the soldier's grace.

In dreams, in dreams we've mingled, and a swell
Of feeling mightier for the eyes' eclipse,
The music of a blest Apocalypse,
Thrilled through my spirit with its mystic spell:

Ah, then! ofttimes a sadder scene will rise,
A gallant vessel through the mist-bound day,
Lifting her spectral spars above the bay,
Gloomily swayed against gray glimmering skies.

O'er the dim billows thundering, peals a boom
Of the deep gun that bursteth as a knell,
When the brave tender to the brave farewell —
And strong arms bear a comrade to the tomb.

. . . . .

The opened sod: a sorrowing band beside —
One rattling roll of musketry, and then,
A man no more among his fellow-men,
Darkness his chamber, and the earth his bride,

My father sleeps in peace; perchance more blest
Than some he left to mourn him, and to know
The bitter blight of an enduring woe,
Longing (how oft!) with him to be at rest.

SONG.

Fly, swiftly fly
Through yon fair sky,
O purple-pinioned Hours!
And bring once more the balmy night,
When from her lattice, silvery bright,
Love's beacon-star — her taper — shines
Between those dark manorial pines,
Above the myrtle-bowers.

Fly, breezes, fly,
And waft my sigh
With love's warm fondness fraught,
'Twill stir my lady's languid mood,
Where, in her verdurous solitude,

She sits and thinks, a moonlight grace
Cast o'er her beauteous brow and face,
Touched by a passionate thought!

Glide, rivulet, glide
With whispering tide,
Through coverts low and deep,
To woo her with the airy call,
The music faint, the far-off fall,
Of fairy streams in fairy climes,
Or pleasant lapse of fairy rhymes,
Soft as her breath in sleep.

Fly, swiftly fly
Through yon calm sky,
O gentle-hearted dove!
And pausing on her favorite tree,
Murmur your plaint so tenderly,
That, born of that sweet tone, a charm
Her very heart of hearts may warm
With rosy bliss of love.

Fly, swiftly fly
Through yon fair sky,
O purple-pinioned Hours!
And bring once more the balmy night,
When from her lattice, silvery bright,
Love's beacon-star — her taper — shines
Between those dark manorial pines
Above the myrtle-bowers!

SONG.

Ho! fetch me the winecup! fill up to the brim!
For my heart has grown cold, and my vision is dim,
And I fain would bring back for a moment the glow,
The swift passion that age has long chilled with its snow;
Ho! fetch me the winecup! the red liquor gleams,
With a promise to waken youth's rapture of dreams,
And I'll drain the bright draught for that promise divine,
Though Death, Death the spectre, should hand me the wine.
'Tis not life that I live, for the blood-currents glide
Through my wan shrunken veins in so sluggish a tide,
That my heart droops and withers; what! *life* call you this?
O! rather, consumed by one keen thrill of bliss,
Would I die with youth's glory revivified round me,
The deep eyes that blessed, and the white arms that bound me;
O! rather than brood in this dusk of desire,
Sink down, like yon marvellous sunset, all fire,
The soul clad with wings, and the brain steeped in light;
Then come, potent wizard! I call on thy might,
Breathe a magical mist o'er the ravage of Time,
Roll back the sad years to the flush of my prime,
And I'll drain thy bright draught for that vision divine,
Though Death, Death the Spectre, should hand me the wine!

BY THE GRAVE.

[Extract from an unfinished narrative poem.]

This is the place — I pray thee, friend,
Leave me alone with that dread grief,
Whose raven wings o'erarch the grave,
Closed on a life how sad and brief!

Already the young violets bloom
On the light sod that shrouds her form,
And Summer's awful sunshine strikes
Incongruous on the spirit's storm.

She died, and did not know that I,
Whose heart is breaking in this gloom,
Had shrined her love, as pilgrims shrine
A blossom from some saintly tomb.

And, ah! indeed, it *was* a tomb,
The tomb of Hope, so ghastly-gray,
Whence sprung that flower of love that grew
Serenely on the Hope's decay.

A pallid flower that bloomed alone,
With no warm light to keep it fair,
But nurtured by the tears that fell,
Even from the clouds of our despair.

She perished, and her patient soul
Passed to God's rest, nor did she know
I kept the faith we could not plight
In honor, or in peace below.

But, Love! at last, all, all is clear.
You see the flame of that fierce fate,
Which blazed between my life, and yours,
And left them both — how desolate!

And well you comprehend that now
My heart is breaking where I stand,
But 'mid the ruin, shrines its faith,
A relic from love's Holy Land.

"Come! come! and seek us here,
In these cool deeps."

SONG OF THE NAIADS.

GAY is our crystal floor,
Beneath the wave,
With strange gems flaming o'er
The Genii gave;
Sweet is the purple light
That haunts our happy sight,
And low and sweet the lulling strains that sigh
While the tides pause, and the faint zephyrs die.

Come! come! and seek us here,
In these cool deeps,
Where all is calmly fair,
And sorrow sleeps:
Thy burning brow shall rest,
Couched on a tender breast,
And, charmed to bliss, thy soul shall catch the gleams
Of mystic glories in Elysian dreams.

Come! ere the earth grows drear,
The tempests rave,
And the fast-failing year
Is nigh its grave:
Thy summer, too, is past,
Wouldst thou have peace at last?
O! here she dwells serenely in still caves,
And waits to woo thee underneath the waves.

LETHE.

A DUMB, dark region through whose desolate heart
Creeps a dull river with a stagnant flood;
Its skies are sombre-hued, and dreary clouds,
No wind hath ever stirred, hang low and dim

Above the barren woodlands; all things droop
In slumber; the little willow stoops to kiss
The waves, but not a ripple murmurs back
Its salutation, and wan starlike flowers
Yield a white radiance to the failing sense,
And odors pregnant with the charms of rest,
And glamour of Oblivion; all things droop
In slumber; for whate'er hath passed the bounds
Of this miraculous kingdom, bird or beast,
Men lured from action, or soul-sick of life,
Weary and heartsore, maids in love's despair,
Or mothers stricken by their first-born's crime —
All sink without a struggle to deep peace.
Prone in the gleam the river casts abroad,
A gleam more pallid than the light of Hades,
Lie those who sought this region ages since;
Their upturned brows are smooth, and tranced with calm.

And on their shadowy lips a waning smile
Fitfully glimmers; round them rest the forms
Of savage beasts; the lion all unnerved,
Drowsy and passionless, his huge limbs relaxed,
And curved to lines of languor: the fierce pard
Tamed to a breathless quiet, whilst afar,
Gloom the gaunt shapes of mighty brutes of eld,
The world's primeval tenants; all things droop
In slumber; even the sluggish river's flow
Sounds like the dying surges of the sea
To ears far inland, or the feeblest sigh
Of winds that faint on lofty mountain-tops.
This is the realm — "Oblivion" — this the stream
Which mortals have called — "Lethe!"

THE REALM OF REST.

In the realm that Nature boundeth
Are there balmy shores of peace,
Where no passion-torrent soundeth,
And no storm-wind seeks release?
Rest they 'mid the waters golden,
Of some strange untravelled sea,
Where low, halcyon airs have stolen,
Lingering round them slumbrously?

Shores begirt with purple hazes,
Mellowed by gray twilight's beams,
Whose weird curtains shroud the mazes,
Wandering through a realm of dreams;
Shores, where Silence wooes Devotion,
Action faints, and echo dies,
And each peace-entranced emotion
Feeds on quiet mysteries.

If there be, O guardian Master,
Genius of my life and fate,
Bear me from the world's disaster,
Through that kingdom's shadowy gate;
Let me lie beneath its willows,
On the fragrant, flowering strand,
Lulled to rest by breezeless billows,
Thrilled with airs of Elfin-land.

Slumber, flushed with faintest dreamings;
Deep that knows no answering deep,
Unprofaned by phantom-seemings,
— Mockeries of Protéan sleep; —
Noiseless, timeless, *half* forgetting,
May that sleep Elysian be,
While serener tides are setting,
Inward, from the roseate sea.

Hark! to mine a voice is calling,
Sweet as tropic winds at night,
Gently dying, faintly falling
From some marvellous mystic height,

Troubled Thought's unhallowed riot
By its wandering glamour kissed,
Feels a charm of sacred quiet
Fold it, like enchanted mist.

"There's a realm, thy footsteps nearing,"
[Thus the voice to mine replies,]
"Where the heavy heart despairing,
Breathes no more its life in sighs;
'Tis a realm, imperial, stately,
Refuge of dethronèd Years,
Calm as midnight, towering greatly,
Through a moonlit veil of tears.

"Though an empire, freedom reigneth,
Kingly brow, and subject knee,
Each with what to each pertaineth,
Slumbering in equality;
'Tis a sleep, divorced from dreamings,
Deep that knows no answering deep,
Unprofaned by phantom-seemings —
Noiseless, wondrous, timeless sleep.

"On its shores are weeping willows,
Action faints, and Echo dies,
And the languid dirge of billows,
Lulls with opiate symphonies;
But beside that murmurous ocean
All who rest, repose in sooth,
And no more the stilled emotion
Stirs to joy, or wakens ruth.

"Thou *shalt* gain these blest dominions,
Thou *shalt* find this peaceful ground,
Shaded by Oblivion's pinions,
Startled by no mortal sound;
Noiseless, timeless, ALL forgetting,
Shall thy sleep Elysian be,
While eternal tides are setting
Inward from that mystic sea."

THE ISLAND IN THE SOUTH.

THE ship went down at noonday in a calm,
When not a zephyr broke the crystal sea.
We two escaped alone: we reached an isle
Whereon the water settled languidly
In a long swell of music; luminous skies
O'erarched the place, and lazy, broad lagoons
Swept inland, with the boughs of plantain trees
Trailing cool shadows through the dense repose;
All round about us floated gentle airs,
And odors that crept upward to the sense
Like delicate pressures of voluptuous thought.
I, with a long bound, leapt upon the shore
Shouting, but she, pavilioned in dark locks,
Sobbed out thanksgiving; 'twixt the world and us,
Distance that seemed Eternity outrolled
Its terrible barriers; on the waste a Fate
Stood up, and stretching its blank hands abroad
Muttered of desolation. Did we weep,
And groaning cast our foreheads in the dust?
So it *had* been, but in each other's eyes
Smiled a new world, dearer than that which rose
Beneath the lost stars of the faded West.
That very morn the white-stoled priest of God
Had blessed us with the church's choicest prayers,
And these did gird us like a sapphire wall
When the floods threatened, and the ghastly doom
Moaned itself impotent; free we were to love
To the full scope of passion; a few suns,
And in the deep recesses of the woods
We built ourselves a cabin; the dim spot
Was fortressed by the tropic's giant growths,
Luxuriant Titans of a hundred years;
And the vines, laced and interlaced between,
Drooped with a flowery largess many-hued.

It was a place of Faëry; songs of birds
That glimmered in and out among the leaves,
Like magical dreams embodied, wooed the winds
To gentlest motion of benignant wings;
And the sun veiled his radiance, and the stars
Peered through the shadowy stillness with a light
So spiritual, the forest seemed to wane
In tremulous lines waved down the silvery aisles.
There lived, there loved we, as none else have lived
And loved, I think, since the primeval blight
Rained down its discords, and death clinched the curse.
No shallow mockeries of a worn-out age,
Effete and helpless, bound young passion round
With the cold fetters of detested forms:
Civilization was not there to set
Its specious seal of custom on our hearts,
Prisoning the bolder virtues; we might dare
To act, speak, think, as the true nature moved,
Untutored and majestic; our souls grew
To the stature of the spirit, that looks down
From the unpolluted regnancy of heavens
That hold no curses; the glad universe
Showered rare benedictions on our path;
Matter was merged in poesy: the winds
From the serene Pacific, the quick gales
From mountainous ridges in the uppermost air,
The eternal chorus of far seas serene,
The harmony of forests, the small voice
That trembles from the happy rivulet's breast,
All touched us with that sweet philosophy,
Which, if we woo the visible world aright,
Blesses experience with new gates of sense
Where through we gain Elysium.

So the years
Were winged and odorous with a thousand joys,
Of which the poor slave to the hollow law
We term society, hath had no dream;
Our love was comprehensive, full, divine,
Rounding the perfect orbit wherein life
Should gravitate to God, even as the spheres
Roll to the central fire; love mastered life
As maelstroms suck still waters, love the one
Electric current through act, reason, will,
Throbbing like inspiration; no vain touch
Of weak, fantastic passion, no thin glow
Of morbid longing, fluttering feebly up
From shallow brains, stirred to a dubious flame,
And tortured with false throes of sentiment—
(That bastard whimperer to the deity, Love—
As a changeling to the Titans)—no red heat
Of base desire, fusing the delicate thought
To chaos; but a steadfast, genial sun,
A luminous glory, gentle as intense,
Making our fate a heaven of warmth, light, rest,
Whose very clouds were halos, and whose storms
Were tempered into music. Thus time stole
On muffled wings through the still air of bliss,
Gathering our ripened hopes, and sowing seeds
Of joy to come. My innocent bud had flowered
To beauty—oh! such beauty as these lips,
Touched though they were with fire, might not profane
With shackles of mean utterance. Oh, God! God!

"We reached an isle
Whereon the waters settled languidly."

Why didst thou take her from me? why
transform
The passionate presence in my shielding arms
To this poor phantom of a broken brain,
Mocking my woe with shadows? On a night
When the still sea was calmest, the bright stars
Most bright, and a warm breathing on the wind
Spoke of perpetual summer, a strange voice
I scarce could hear, said: "It is evening time,"
And a wan hand my eyes were blind to note
Beckoned her far away.
The awful grief
Closed round me like an ocean. I was mad,
And raved my memory from me. When again
The world dawned, as a dreary landscape dawns
Grotesquely through the sluggish mists of March,
I walked once more in a great capital's streets,
A savage 'midst the civilized, a man —
Shattered and wrecked, I grant you, — still a man
Amongst the puppets that usurp the name
And act the fraud so basely, that the Fiend
Wearies to death the echoes of his hell
In laughter at them. I *am* with you still,
Emasculate denizens of the stifling mart,
Where heaven's free winds are throttled in the fumes
Of furnaces, and the insulted sun
Glooms through the crowding vapors at midday,
Like a God, re-collecting to himself
His immortality; where nerveless limbs
Bear nerveless bodies to their separate dens
Of torture, and lean, wide-eyed revellers
Foster the hungering worm that never dies,
And fan the lurid fire unquenchable;
Where stealthy avarice lurks in wait to sack
The widow's house; and license of low minds,
Loaded with prurient knowledge, and no hearts
(Self-worship having killed them), make the world
A Pandemonium. I *am* with you still;
But the hours creep on to a more fortunate time;
A vessel swells her broad sails in the bay,
And the breeze bloweth seaward; I will seek
My island in the southern waves again;
A thousand memories urge me, tones that slept
Waken to invitation; I can feel
The Hesperian beauty of that realm of peace
Flushing my brain and fancy; but through all
The ruddy vision glides a tender shade,
And pauses with mute meaning by a grave.

ODE.

Delivered on the First Anniversary of the Carolina Art Association, Feb. 10, 1856.

THERE are two worlds wherein our souls may dwell,
With discord, or ethereal music fraught,
One the loud mart wherein men buy and sell
(Too oft the haunt of grovelling moods of Hell),
The other, that immaculate realm of thought,
In whose bright calm the master-workmen wrought,
Where genius lives on light,
And faith is lost in sight,
Where crystal tides of perfect harmony swell

Up to the heavens that never held a cloud,
And round great altars reverent hosts are bowed,
Altars upreared to love that cannot die,
To beauty that forever keeps its youth,
To kingly grandeur, and to virginal truth,
To all things wise and pure,
Whereof our God hath said, "Endure! endure!
Ye are but parts of me,
The *hath been*, and the evermore *to be*,
Of my supremest Immortality!"

We falter in the darkness and the dearth
Which sordid passions and untamed desires
Create about us; universal earth
Groans with the burden of our sensual woes;
The heart heaven gave for homage is consumed
By the wild rages of unhallowed fires;
The blush of that fine glory which illumed
The earlier ages, hath gone out in gloom;
There is no joy within us, no repose,
One creed our beacon, and one god our hold,
The creed, the god, of gold;
The heavenward wingèd Instinct that aspires,
Like a lost seraph with dishevelled plume,
Pants humbled in the "slough of deep Despond;"
The present binds us, there is no Beyond,
No glorious Future to the soul content
With the poor husks and garbage of this world;
And are indeed the wings of worship furled
Forevermore? Is no evangel blent,
No sweet evangel, with the hiss and hum
Of the century's wheels of progress? Science delves
Down to the earth's hot vitals, and explores
Realms arctic and antarctic, the strange shores
Of remote seas, or with raised vision stands,
All undismayed, amidst the starry lands:
Man too, material man, our baser selves,
She hath unmasked even to the source of being;
Almost she seems a god,
Deep-searching and far-seeing;
And yet how oft like some wild funeral wail
Which goes before the burial of our hopes,
Emerging from the starry-blazoned copes
Of highest firmaments, or darkest vale
Of the nether earth, or from the burdened air
Of chambers where this mortal frame lies bare,
Probed to the core, her saddening accents come;
"What! call'st thou man a seraph? nay, a clod,
The veriest clod when his frail breath is spent,
Man shows to us who know him; what is he?
A speck! the merest dew-globe 'midst the sea
Of life's infinity;"
Or, "we have probed, dissected all we can,
But never yet, in any mortal man,
Found we the spirit! thing of time and clay,
Eat, drink, enjoy thy transient insect-day!"
Thus Science; but while still her mocking voice
Rings with a cold sharp clearness in our ears,
Her beauteous sister, on whose brow the years
Have left no cankering vestige of decay,

Eternal Art, she of the fathomless eyes
Brimming with light, half worship, half surprise,
In whose right hand a branch of fadeless palms,
Plucked from the depths of golden shadowed calms,
Points upward to the skies,
She answers in a minor, sweet and strange
The while, all graces in her aspect meet,
And Doubt and Fear shrink shuddering at her feet,
"I bring a nobler message! Soul, rejoice!
Rise with me from thy troublous toils of sense,
Thy bootless struggles, born of impotence,
Rise to a subtler view, a broader range
Of thought and aim;
Mine is a sway ideal,
But still the works I prompt, alone, are real;
Mine is a realm from immemorial time
Begirt by deeds and purposes sublime,
Whose consecration is faith's quenchless flame,
Whose voices are the songs of poet-sages,
Whose strong foundations resting on the ages,
The throes and crash of empires have not shaken,
Nor any futile force of human rages.

"Come! let us enter in!
Behold, the portal gates stand open wide!
Only, from off thy spirit shake the dust
Of any thought of sin,
Or sordid pride,
For sacred is the kingdom of my trust,
By mind, and strength, and beauty sanctified."

She spake! and o'er the threshold of a sphere,
A marvellous sphere, they passed;
From the deep bosom of the purpling air
A lambent glory broke along the vast
Horizon line, whence clouds, like incense, rolled
Athwart a firmamental arc of gold
And sapphire; clouds not vapor-born,
But clasping each the radiant seeds of morn,
Which suddenly, clear zenith heights attained,
Burst into light, unfolding like a flower,
From out whose quivering heart a mystic shower
Of splendor rained:
A spell was hers to conquer time and space,
For from the desert grandeur of that place
A hundred temples rise,
The marble poems of the bards of old,
Whereon 'twere well to look with reverent eyes,
Because they body noblest aspirations,
Ethereal hopes, and winged imaginations,
Whether to fabled Jove their walls were raised,
Or on their inner altar offerings blazed
To wise Athèna, or, in Christian Rome
Beneath St. Peter's mighty circling dome,
A second Heaven, the golden censers swing,
The clear-toned choirs those hymns of rapture sing,
Which, on harmonious waves of gratulation,
The outburst of the sense of deep salvation,
Uplift the spirit where the Incarnate Word
Amid the praise no ear of man hath heard,
The peace no mind of man can comprehend,
Awaits to welcome Time's worn wanderers home!

"But look again!" Art's eager Genius cried:
"Thou hast not seen the end,
Scarce the beginning!" As she spake, a tide
Of all the mighty masters, loved, adored,
From out the shining distant spaces poured,
All those who fashioned, through an inward dower,
The concrete forms of beauty and of power;
Whether from white Pentelic quarries brought,
The voiceless stone uprose, a breathing thought,
Or, from the mystic rays of rainbows drawn,
And colors of the sunset and the dawn,
The painter's pencil his ideal fine,
Had clothed in hues divine;
Or, skilled in living words
Melodious as the natural voice of birds
(But each a sentient thing, a meaning grand,
It is not given to all to understand),
The poet from the shade of breezy woods,
From barren seaside solitudes,
And from the pregnant quiet of his soul
Outbreathed the numbers that forever roll
Perennial, as the fountains of the sea,
And deep almost as deep eternity!

Near and yet nearer the bright concourse came,
Their faces all aflame,
As when of yore the quick creative thrill
Did smite them into utterance, and the throng,
Awed by the fiery burden of the song,
Grew reverent pale and still;
O! solemn and sublime Apocalypse
That wresteth, from the dreary death-eclipse,
The sacred presence of these marvellous men!
Yonder the visible Homer moves again,
Moves as he moved below,
Save that his smitten vision
Rekindled at the fount of fire Elysian,
Burns with a subtler, grander, deeper glow;
And yonder Æschylus, with "thunderous brow,"
Scarred by the lightning of his own creations,
Wrapped in a cloud of sombre meditations,
Hath seized the tragic muse, as if to her
He scorned to bend an humble worshipper,
But would extort her gifts;
Then Shakespeare mild,
Blessed with the innocent credence of a child,
With a child's thoughts and fancies undefiled,
And yet a Magian strong
To whom the springs of terrible fears belong,
Of majesty, and beauty, and delight,
To the weird charm of whose infallible sight,
The heart's emotions,
Though turbid as the tides of darkest oceans,
Shone clear as water of the woodland brooks—
He passed with wisdom thronèd in his looks
Attempered by the genial heats of wit;
While close beside him, his grand countenance lit
By thoughts like those which wrought his Judgment Day,
Grave Michel Angelo
His massive forehead lifts,
In a strange Titan fashion, unto Heaven;
Next Raphael comes, with calm and starlike mien,
Fresh from the beatific ecstasy,
His face how beautiful, and how serene!
Since God for him the awful veil had riven

That shrouds Divinity,
And rolled before his wondering mind and eye
Visions that we should gaze on but — to die!

They passed, and thousands more passed by with them;
Again Art's Genius spake: "Lo! these are they
Who, through stern tribulations,
Have raised to right and truth the subject nations;
Lo! these are they,
Who, were the whole bright concourse swept away,
Their fame's last barrier, built the surge to stem
Of chaos and oblivion, whelmed beneath
The pitiless torrent of eternal death,
Would yet bequeath to races unbegot
The precepts of a faith which faileth not;
Pointing, from troublous toils of time and sense,
From bootless struggles born of impotence,
To that fair realm of thought,
In whose bright calm these master-workmen wrought,
Where crystal tides of perfect music swell
Up to the heavens that never held a cloud,
And round great altars worshipping hosts are bowed—
Altars upreared to love that cannot die,
To beauty that forever keeps its youth,
To kingly grandeur, and to virginal truth,
To all things wise and pure,
Whereof our God hath said: 'Endure! endure!
Ye are but parts of me,
The HATH BEEN, and the evermore TO BE,
Of my supremest Immortality!'"

QUEEN GALENA, OR THE SULTANA BETRAYED.

HOLD! let the heartless perjurer go!
Speak not! strike not! he is *my* foe,
From me, me only, comes the blow —
I will repay him woe for woe;
Look in my eyes! my eyes are dry,
I breathe no plaint, I heave no sigh,
But — will avenge me ere I die.

Think you that I shall basely rest,
And know the bosom mine hath prest,
Is couched upon a colder breast?
Think you that I shall yield the West,
The Orient soul *my* nature nurst,
Till the black seed of treachery burst
And blossomed to this deed accurst?

My rival! O! her glance is meek,
Her faltering presence wan, and weak
As the faint flush that tints her cheek.
'Tis not on *her* that I would wreak
My vengeance — sooner would I wring
Life from an insect-birth of spring
Than palter with so poor a thing.

But he — I tell you if he flew,
As it was once his wont to do,
Repentant — pleading — quick to woo,
With all his wild heart flaming through
The glance of passion — it were sweet,
Yea, more! 'twere righteous, just, and meet,
To slay him kneeling at my feet!

He *shall not* wed her; by Heaven's light
He shall not; o'er my lurid sight
Throbs a thick fire; the ancient might
Of a stern race is stirred to-night;
My sovereign claim annul — disown!
I will repay him groan for groan,
Or — stab him at the altar-stone!

THE POET'S TRUST IN HIS SORROW.

O GOD! how sad a doom is mine,
To human seeming:
Thou hast called on me to resign
So much — much! —*all* — but the divine
Delights of dreaming.

I set my dreams to music wild,
  A wealth of measures;
My lays, thank Heaven! are undefiled,
I sport with Fancy as a child
  With golden leisures.

And long as fate, not wholly stern,
  But this shall grant me,
Still with perennial faith to turn
Where Song's unsullied altars burn
  Nought, nought shall daunt me!

What though my worldly state be low
  Beyond redressing;
I own an inner flame whose glow
Makes radiant all the outward show;
  My last great blessing!

THE BROOK.

But yesterday this brook was bright,
And tranquil as the clear moonlight,
That wooes the palms on Orient shores,
But now, a hoarse, dark stream, it pours
Impetuous o'er its bed of rock,
And almost with a thunder-shock
Boils into eddies, fierce and fleet,
That dash the white foam round our feet,
A raging whirl of waters, rent
As if with angry discontent!

A tempest in the night swept by,
Born of a murk and fiery sky,
And while the solid woodlands shook,
It wreaked its fury on the brook.
The evil genius of the blast
Within its quiet bosom passed,
And therefore this transfigured tide,
Which used as lovingly to glide
As thought through spirits sanctified,
Rolls now a whirl of waters, rent
As if with angry discontent.

I knew, of late, a creature, bright
And gentle as the clear moonlight,
The tenderest and the kindest heart
That ever played Love's selfless part,
Across whose unperturbèd life,
A sudden passion swept, in strife,
With wild, unhallowed forces rife.
It stirred her nature's inmost deep,
That nevermore shall rest or sleep,
Remorse, its rugged bed of rock,
O'er which for aye, with thunder-shock,
The tides of feeling, fierce and fleet,
Are dashed to foam or icy sleet,
A raging whirl of waters, rent
By something worse than discontent!

NATURE THE CONSOLER.

Gladly I hail these solitudes, and breathe
The inspiring breath of the fresh woodland air,
Most gladly to the past alone bequeath
  Doubt, grief, and care;
I feel a new-born freedom of the mind,
Nursed at the breast of Nature, with the dew
Of glorious dawns; I hear the mountain wind,
Clear as if elfin trumpets loudly blew,
Peal through the dells, and scale the lonely height,
Rousing the echoes to a quick delight,
Bending the forest monarchs to its will,
'Till all their pond'rous branches shake and thrill
In the wide-wakening tumult; far above
The heavens stretch calm and blessing; far below
The mellowing fields are touched with evening's glow,
And many a pleasant sight and sound I love
Would gently woo me from all thoughts of woe:
Sunlighted meadows, music in the grove,
From happy bird-throats, and the fairy rills
That lapse in silvery murmurs through the hills;

"Gladly I hail these solitudes, and breathe
The inspiring breath of the fresh woodland air."

Great circles of rich foliage, rainbow-crowned
By autumn's liberal largess, whilst around
Grave sheep lie musing on the pastoral ground,
Or sending a mild bleat
To other flocks afar,
The fleecy comrades they are wont to meet
Homeward returning 'neath the vesper star!

Oh, genial peace of Nature! divine calm
That fallest on the spirit, like the rain
Of Eden, bearing melody and balm
To soothe the troubled heart and heal its pain,
Thy influence lifts me to a realm of joy,
A moonlight happiness, intense but mild,
Unvisited by shadow of alloy,
And flushed with tender dreams and fancies undefiled.

The universe of God is still, not dumb,
For many voices in sweet undertone
To reverent listeners come;
And many thoughts, with truth's own honey laden,
Into the watcher's wakeful brain have flown,
Charming the inner ear
With harmonies so low, and yet so clear,
So undefined, yet pregnant with a feeling,
An inspiration of sublime revealing,
That they whose being the strong spell shall hold,
Do look on earthly things
Through atmospheres of rich imaginings,
And find, in all they see,
A meaning manifold;
The forces of divine vitality
Break through the sensual gloom
About them furled,
All instinct with the radiant grace and bloom
Caught from the glories of a lovelier world.

A lovelier world! in the thronged space on high,
Dwells there indeed a fairer star than ours,
Circled by sunsets of more gorgeous dye,
And gifted with an ampler wealth of flowers?
Can heavenly bounty lavish richer stores
Of color, fragrance, beauty, and delight
On mortal or immortal sight,
In any sphere that rolls around the sun?
See what a splendor from the dying day
Through the grand forest pours!
Now, lighting up its veteran-crests with glory,
Now, slanting down the shadows dim and hoary,
Till, in the long-drawn gloom of leafy glades,
At the far close of their impervious shades,
The purple splendor softly melts away!

Now, overarched by dewy canopies,
And awed by dimness that is hardly gloom,
We stand amidst the silence with hushed lips,
Watching the dubious glimmer of the skies
Paled by the foliage to a half-eclipse,
And struggling for full room,
With intermittent gleams, that quickly die
In throbs and tremors, waning suddenly
To the mere ghosts of flame, to apparitions
Impalpable as star-beams in deep seas,
Lost in the dark below the surface-ruffling breeze.

Latest of all these marvellous transitions,
And crowning all with their ineffable grace,
The eyes of the night's empress, witching sweet,
Scatter the shadows in each secret place,
So that, where'er her beamy glances fleet,

Shot through and through, as if with arrowy might,
The dusky gloaming falls before her shafts of light.

THE SOUL-CONFLICT.

Defeated! but never disheartened!
  Repulsed! but unconquered in will,
Upon dreary discomfitures building
  Her virtue's strong battlements still,
The soul, through the siege of temptations,
  Yields not unto fraud, nor to might,
Unquelled by the rush of the passions,
  Serene 'mid the tumults of fight.

She sees a grand prize in the distance,
  She hears a glad sound of acclaims,
The crown wrought of blooms amaranthine,
  The music far sweeter than Fame's.
And so, 'gainst the rush of the passions
  She lifts the broad buckler of right,
And so, through the glooms of temptation,
  She walks in a splendor of light.

THE PRESENTIMENT.

Over her face, so tender and meek,
  The light of a prophecy lies,
That has silvered the red of the rose on her cheek,
  And chastened the thought in her eyes!

Beautiful eyes, with an inward glance,
  To the spirit's mystical deep;
Lost in the languid gleam of a trance,
  More solemn and saintly than sleep.

And, forever and ever, she seems to hear
  The voice of a spirit implore,
"Come! enter the life that is noble and clear;
  Come! grow to my heart once more."

And, forever and ever, she mutely turns
  From a mortal lover's sighs;
And fainter the red of the rose-flush burns,
  And deeper the thought in her eyes.

The seeds are warm of the churchyard flowers,
  That will blossom above her rest,
And a bird that shall sing by the old church towers,
  Is already fledged in its nest!

And so, when a blander summer shall smile,
  On some night of soft July,
We will lend to the dust her beauty awhile,
  In the hush of a moonless sky.

And later still, shall the churchyard flowers,
  Gleam nigh with a white increase;
And a bird outpour, by the old church towers,
  A plaintive poem of peace.

THE TWO SUMMERS.

There is a golden season in our year,
Between October's hale and lusty cheer,
And the hoar frost of winter's empire drear;

Which, like a fairy flood of mystic tides,
Whereon divine tranquillity abides,
The kingdom of the sovereign months divides;

The wailing autumn winds their requiems cease,
Ere winter's sturdier storms have gained release,
And heaven and earth alike are bright with peace.

O soul! thou hast thy golden season too!
A blissful interlude of birds and dew,
Of balmy gales, and skies of deepest blue!

That second summer, when thy work is done,
The harvest hoarded, and the mellow sun
Gleams on the fruitful fields thy toil has won;

Which, also, like a fair mysterious tide,
Whereon calm thoughts like ships at anchor ride,
Doth the broad empire of thy years divide.

This passed, what more of life's brief path remains,
Winds through unlighted vales, and dismal plains,
The haunt of chilling blight, or fevered pains.

Pray, then, ye happy few, along whose way
Life's Indian summer pours its purpling ray,
That ye may die ere dawns the evil day.

Sink on that season's kind and genial breast,
While peace and sunshine rule the cloudless west,
The elect of God, whom life and death have blessed!

LINES.

"Though dowered with instincts keen and high."

"I weep
My youth, and its brave hopes, all dead and gone,
In tears which burn." — PARACELSUS.

THOUGH dowered with instincts keen and high,
With burning thoughts that wooed the light,
The scornful world hath passed him by,
And left him lonelier than the night.

Yes! cold and hopeless, one by one
The stars of faith have quenched their flame,
And like a waning polar sun,
Declines the latest hope of fame.

He longed to sing one noble song,
To thrill, with passion's living breath,
The fools whose scorn had worked him wrong,
And baffle fate, and conquer death.

Dear God! dost thou endow with powers,
Whose aspirations mock the bars
Of time and sense, whose vision towers
Irradiate 'mid thy sovereign stars,

Only to furnish some faint gleams
Of loftier beauty, quick withdrawn,
Leaving a frenzied hell of dreams,
And wailings for the vanished dawn?

The oracles of fancy mute,
Ambition's priests dethroned and fled,
He wanders with a tuneless lute,
Through dreary regions of the dead.

But from that place of bale uploom
The phantoms of unburied years,
The haunting care, the grief, the gloom,
The treacherous hopes, the pale-eyed fears

That stormed his spirit's brave design,
That clogged its wings, betrayed its trust,
Defaced its creed, and dashed the wine
In song's bright chalice, to the dust.

Ah, Heaven! could he retrace his life
From out this realm of doubt and dearth,
He would not court thought's eagle strife,
But clasp the calm that clings to earth.

Above, the threatening thunders wait
For dauntless souls that dare aspire,
But lowly lives are safe from hate,
And peace is wed to meek desire.

Yet, birds that breast the turbulent air
Are worthier than the things that creep,
And nobler is a high despair
Than weak content, or sluggish sleep.

SONG.

O! YOUR eyes are deep and tender,
O! your charmèd voice is low,
But I've found your beauty's splendor
All a mockery and a show;
Slighted heart and broken promise
Follow wheresoe'er you go.

All your words are fair and golden,
All your actions false and wrong,
Not the noblest soul's beholden
To your weak affections long;
Only true in — lover's fancy,
Only constant in — his song.

ON A PORTRAIT.

A widower muses over the likeness of his dead wife.

THE face, the beautiful face,
In its living flush and glow,
The perfect face in its peerless grace
That I worshipped long ago;
That I worshipped when youth was strong and bold,
That I worship now,
Though the pulse of youth grows faint and low,
And the ashes of hope are cold.

The face, the beautiful face,
Ever haunting my heart and brain,
Bringing ofttimes a dream of heaven,
Ofttimes the pang of a pain
Which darteth down like a lightning flash
To the dreadful deeps,
Where the gems of a shipwrecked life are cast,
And its dead cold promise sleeps.

Sweet face! shall I meet thee again,
In the passionless land of palms,
By the verge of Heaven's enchanted streams
In the hush of its perfect calms;
Or, forever and ever, and evermore,
While the years depart,
While the ages roll,
Walk the glooms of a ghostly shore,
Made wild by a phantom-haunted brain,
And a cloud-encircled soul;
By a haunted brain and a cheerless heart,
While the years and the ages roll?

No answer comes to my cry,
Though out of the depths I call:
Not the faintest gleam of a hopeful beam
Shines over the shroud and pall.
My soul is clothed with sackcloth and dust,
And I look from my widowed hearth
With a vacant eye on the tumult and stir
Of this weary, dreary earth;
For my soul is dead and its hopes are dust,
And the joy of passion, the strength of trust,
These passed from the world with *her*.

THE SHADOW.

THE pathway of his mournful life hath wound
Beneath a shadow; just beyond it play
The genial breezes, and the cool brooks stray
Into melodious gushings of sweet sound,
Whilst ample floods of mellow sunshine fall
Like a mute rain of rapture over all.

Oft hath he deemed the spell of darkness lost,
And shouted to the dayspring; a full glow
Hath rushed to clasp him; but the subtle woe,
Unvanquished ever, with the might of frost,
Regains its sad realm, and with voice malign
Saith to the dawning joy: "This life is mine!"

Still smiles the brave soul, undivorced
from hope!
And, with unwavering eye and warrior
mien,
Walks in the shadow, dauntless and
serene,
To test, through hostile years, the utmost scope
Of man's endurance — constant to essay
All heights of patience free to feet of
clay.

Still smiles the brave soul, undivorced
from hope!
But now, methinks, the pale hope gathers strength;
Glad winds invade the silence; streams,
at length,
Flash through the desert; 'neath the
sapphire cope
Of deepening heavens he hails a happier
day,
And the spent shadow mutely wanes
away.

THE WINTER WINDS MAY WILDLY RAVE.

The winter winds may wildly rave,
How wildly o'er thy place of rest!
But, love! thou hast a holier grave,
Deep in a faithful human breast.

There, the embalmer, Memory, bends,
Watching, with softly-breathed sighs,
The mystic light her genius lends
To fadeless cheeks and tender eyes.

There in a fathomless calm, serene,
Thy beauty keeps its saintly trace,
The radiance of an angel mien,
The rapture of a heavenly grace.

And there, O gentlest love! remain
(No stormy passion round thee raves),
Till, soul to soul, we meet again,
Beyond this ghostly realm of graves.

UNDER SENTENCE.

Place — *Scotland.* Time — *Thirteenth Century.*

Off! off! No treacherous priest for me!
What's Heaven? what's Hell? Eternity!
It hath no meaning to *mine* ear,
Unless —— Stay, father! Canst thou
swear
By holy Rood, that I shall meet
Him there, whose crime made murder
sweet?
Him whose black soul I've hurled before?
He's gone! How cold my dungeon
floor!
And the rack wrenches still! This hand,
Which stiffened to a fire-hot band
Of steel, crushing his base breath out,
They've foully mangled! See that gout
Of blood there — there, too! What
care I?
It did its work well: let it lie!

I'd give ten mortal lives, I trow,
As full of sweets as mine of woe,
To feel that quivering throat once more;
To view the blue-tinged, strangling gore
Spout from his lips! To watch the dim
Film o'er those cruel eyeballs swim,
And the black anguish of his stare,
Dashed blind with horror! Lords! beware
Much trifling! We are dogs, ye ken,
Who yet may rise, and smite like men.

What's this? Ah, yes! the flower I took
From *her!* I think her dying look
Baptized it, for it keeps so fair.
I wonder if they decked her hair
With other flowers like this, ere yet
They lowered her beauty to the wet,
Dark mould? If maiden dust to flowers
(Some say so) turns, not all the bowers
This spring shall warm will equal those
To blossom from her pure repose!

My nuptial night! God's blood! what
right
Had *I* to nuptials? To the bright

Keen joy that burns on wedded lips?
My life-star could not break the eclipse
Wherein 'twas born! So that dark doom
Which hounds me to a shameful tomb,
Ordained that the fiend's trick they used
Should trap me! Faith, love, peace abused,
I woke to find my heart bereft
Of its *one* treasure! What was left?
What, but that mandate Vengeance, hissed
With hot tongue thro' a seething mist
Of passion; the fierce mandate, "Kill?"
Aye! but *she*, too, lay blanched and still.

Blanched on the couch I dreamed would be
My wedding couch! Oh, infamy!
His outrage smote her to the heart;
It crashed the gates of life apart,
Where through her shuddering soul took flight!
But ere the death-dew dimmed her sight,
She gave me, as I said, this flower,
And — one long smile! To my last hour
I've shrined her smile! If, if somewhere
There *be* a heaven, benign and fair,
Its saints, I feel, must smile so there!

Dread God! couldst thou have marked my wrong,
Yet sheathed thy lightning? I was strong
And lusty as the hillside roe;
Could wield the brand and bend the bow
So deftly, that his lordship deigned
To show me favor! Was it feigned?
I know not! His *last* kindness took
A strange shape truly; for it shook
My hopes to atoms! Yet *he* fell
Prone with them! Shall we meet in hell?

I ask again. Ha! if we do
And there's a single nerve, or thew,
Or muscle left to naked soul,
I'll strangle him once more; enroll
My ruthless arms round breast and throat,
And wring from out his gorge that note
Of palsied fear! I'll do 't, tho' all
The devils should pull me back, and call
Fresh torments on my anguished head:
Doubtless they'll take *his* part instead.

Of *mine*, being devils, and he the worst;
A prince amongst their tribes accurst
By this time; for a month has sped,
Beshrew me, since he joined the dead,
The damned dead! Full time I trow,
For all the bounds of hell to know
That Satan's rivalled! Hark without!
The gathering tramp, the approaching shout
Of thousands! Well, their scaffold's high;
Fair chance for all to see me die!

THE VILLAGE BEAUTY.

The glowing tints of a tropic eve,
Burn on her radiant cheek,
And we know that her voice is rich and low,
Though we never have heard her speak;
So full are those gracious eyes of light,
That the blissful flood runs o'er,
And wherever her tranquil pathway tends
A glory flits on before!

O! very grand are the city belles,
Of a brilliant and stately mien,
As they walk the steps of the languid dance,
And flirt in the pauses between;
But beneath the boughs of the hoary oak,
When the minstrel fountains play,
I think that the artless village girl
Is sweeter by far than they.

O! very grand are the city belles,
But their hearts are worn away
By the keen-edged world, and their lives
have lost
The beauty and mirth of May;
They move where the sun and the starry
dews
Reign not; they are haughty and bold,
And they do not shrink from the cursed
mart,
Where faith is the slave of gold.

But the starry dews and the genial sun
Have gladdened *her* guileless youth;
And her brow is bright with the flush of
hope,
Her soul with the seal of truth;
Her steps are beautiful on the hills
As the steps of an Orient morn,
And Ruth was never more fair to see
In the midst of the autumn corn.

AFTER DEATH.

THE passionate sobs of the dear friends
that came
To look their last upon my living frame,
And catch the fainting accents of my
breath,
That fluttered in the atmosphere of
death,
Were hushed to silence, and the uncer-
tain light,
That flickered o'er the arras to my sight,
Grew paler and more tremulous, as life
Sunk 'neath the power of that unequal
strife,
Which pits humanity against the spell
Of one all flesh hath found invincible!

I could not see my foe: but the whole
space
Was redolent of pestilence, and grace
Of all things beautiful, and grand and
free,
Seemed lost in darkness evermore to
me:
I struggled with the invisible arm that
wound
So sternly round me, but could give no
sound
To the great agony that whelmed my
soul
In surges wilder than the eternal roll
Of a world's waters, thundering round
the Pole.

Downward, still downward, the relent-
less hand
Pressed on my being, and the iron wand
Of his malign enchantment struck my
heart
With a dull force that made the life-blood
start
Forever from its courses; then a sense
Of coming rest, more dreamless and in-
tense
Than ever wrapped mortality in still
And throbless freedom from all thoughts
of ill,
Stole o'er the vanquished form and glim-
mering sight,
Till silence ruled, with nothingness and
night!

SONNETS.

SONNETS.

OCTOBER.

THE passionate summer's dead! the sky's aglow
With roseate flushes of matured desire,
The winds at eve are musical and low,
As sweeping chords of a lamenting lyre,
Far up among the pillared clouds of fire,
Whose pomp of strange procession upward rolls,
With gorgeous blazonry of pictured scrolls,
To celebrate the summer's past renown;
Ah, me! how regally the heavens look down,
O'ershadowing beautiful autumnal woods
And harvest fields with hoarded increase brown,
And deep-toned majesty of golden floods,
That raise their solemn dirges to the sky,
To swell the purple pomp that floateth by.

LIFE AND DEATH.

I. — LIFE.

SUFFERING! and yet majestical in pain;
Mysterious! yet, like spring-showers in the sun,
Veiling the light with their melodious rain,
Life is a warp of gloom and glory spun;
Its darkling phases are as clouds that mourn
Beneath the loftier splendors of an arch
Where deathless orbs in golden daylight burn,
And God's great pulses beat their music march.
The heaven we worship dimly girt with tears,
The spirit-heaven, what is it but a life,
Lifting its soul beyond our mortal years
That oft begin, and ever end with strife:
Strife we must pass to win a happier height,
Nature but travails to reveal us — light.

II. — DEATH.

THEN whence, O Death! thy dreariness? We know
That every flower the breeze's flattering breath
Wooes to a blush, and love-like murmuring low,
Dies but to multiply its bloom in death:
The rill's glad, prattling infancy, that fills
The woodlands with its song of innocent glee,
Is passing through the heart of shadowy hills,
To swell the eternal manhood of the sea;
And the great stars, Creation's minstrel-fires
Are rolling toward the central source of light,
Where all their separate glory but expires
To merge into one world's unbroken might;
There is no death but change, soul claspeth soul,
And all are portion of the immortal whole.

SHELLEY.

Because they thought his doctrines were not just,
Mankind assumed for him the chastening rod,
And tyrants reared in pride, and strong in lust,
Wounded the noblest of the sons of God;
The heart's most cherished benefactions riven,
Basely they strove to humble and malign
A soul whose charities were wide as heaven,
Whose *deeds*, if not his *doctrines*, were divine;
And in the name of Him, whose sunshine warms
The evil as the righteous, deemed it good
To wreak their bigotry's relentless storms
On one whose nature was not understood.
Ah, well! God's ways are wondrous; it may be
His seal hath not been set to man's decree.

POETS OF THE OLDEN TIME.

The brave old poets sing of nobler themes
Than those weak griefs which harass craven souls;
The torrent of their lusty music rolls
Not through dark valleys of distempered dreams,
But murmurous pastures lit by sunny streams;
Or, rushing from some mountain height of thought,
Swells to strange meaning that our minds have sought
Vainly to gather from the doubtful gleams
Of our more gross perceptions. Oh, their strains
Nerve and ennoble manhood! no shrill cry,
Set to a treble, tells of querulous woe;
Yet numbers deep-voiced as the mighty main's
Merge in the ringdove's plaining, or the sigh
Of lovers whispering where sweet rivulets flow.

"NOW, WHILE THE REAR-GUARD."

Now, while the rear-guard of the flying year,
Rugged December on the season's verge
Marshals his pale days to the mournful dirge
Of muffled winds in far-off forests drear,
Good friend! turn with me to our in-door cheer;
Draw nigh; the huge flames roar upon the hearth,
And this sly sparkler is of subtlest birth,
And a rich vintage, poet souls hold dear;
Mark how the sweet rogue wooes us! Sit thee down,
And we will quaff, and quaff, and drink our fill,
Topping the spirits with a Bacchanal crown,
Till the funereal blast shall wail no more,
But silver-throated clarions seem to thrill,
And shouts of triumph peal along the shore.

"PENT IN THIS COMMON SPHERE."

Pent in this common sphere of sensual shows,
I pine for beauty; beauty of fresh mien,
And gentle utterance, and the charm serene,
Wherewith the hue of mystic dream-land glows;

I pine for lulling music, the repose
Of low-voiced waters, in some realm between
The perfect Adenne, and this clouded scene
Of love's sad loss, and passion's mournful throes;
A pleasant country, girt with twilight calm,
In whose fair heaven a moon of shadowy round
Wades through a fading fall of sunset rain;
Where drooping lotos-flowers, distilling balm,
Gleam by the drowsy streamlets sleep hath crown'd,
While Care forgets to sigh, and Peace hath balsamed Pain.

"BETWEEN THE SUNKEN SUN AND THE NEW MOON."

BETWEEN the sunken sun and the new moon,
I stood in fields through which a rivulet ran
With scarce perceptible motion, not a span
Of its smooth surface trembling to the tune
Of sunset breezes: "O delicious boon,"
I cried, "of quiet! wise is Nature's plan,
Who, in her realm, as in the soul of man,
Alternates storm with calm, and the loud noon
With dewy evening's soft and sacred lull:
Happy the heart that keeps *its* twilight hour,
And, in the depths of heavenly peace reclined,
Loves to commune with thoughts of tender power;
Thoughts that ascend, like angels beautiful,
A shining Jacob's ladder of the mind."

ANCIENT MYTHS.

Ye pleasant myths of Eld, why have ye fled?
The earth has fallen from her blissful prime
Of summer years, the dews of that sweet time
Are withered on its garlands sere and dead.
No longer in the blue fields overhead
We list the rustling of immortal wings,
Or hail at eve the kindly visitings
Of gentle Genii to fair fortunes wed:
The seas have lost their Nereids, the sad streams
Their gold-haired habitants, the mountains lone
Those happy Oreads, and the blithesome tone
Of Pan's soft pipe melts only in our dreams;
Fitfully fall the old faith's broken gleams
On our dull hearts, cold as sepulchral stone.

O GOD! WHAT GLORIOUS SEASONS BLESS THY WORLD!

O God! what glorious seasons bless thy world!
See! the tranced winds are nestling on the deep,
The guardian heavens unclouded vigil keep
O'er the mute earth; the beach birds' wings are furled
Ghost-like and gray, where the dim billows curled
Lazily up the sea-strand, sink in sleep,
Save when the random fish with lightning leap
Flashes above them, the far sky's impearled
Inland, with lines of silvery smoke that gleam
Upward from quiet homesteads, thin and slow:
The sunset girds me like a gorgeous dream
Pregnant with splendors, by whose marvellous spell,
Senses and soul are flushed to one deep glow,
The golden mood of thoughts ineffable!

"ALONG THE PATH THY BLEEDING FEET."

Along the path thy bleeding feet have trod,
O Christian Mother! do the martyr-years,
Crownèd with suffering through the mist of tears
Uplift their brows, thorn-circled, unto God;
Most bitterly our Father's chastening rod
Hath ruled within thy term of mortal days,
Yet in thy soul spring up the tones of praise,
Freely as flowers from out a burial-sod:
Nor hath a tireless faith essayed in vain
To win from sorrow that diviner rest,
Which, like a sunset, purpling through the rain
Of dying storms, maketh the darkness blest;
Grief is transfigured, and dethronèd Fears,
Pale in the glory beckoning from the West.

"TOO OFT THE POET IN ELABORATE VERSE."

Too oft the poet in elaborate verse,
Flushed with quaint images and gorgeous tropes,
Casteth a doubtful light, which is not hope's,
On the dark spot where Death hath sealed his curse
In monumental silence. Nature starts
Indignant from the sacrilege of words
That ring so hollow, and forlornly girds
Her great woe round her; there's no trick of Art's,

But shows most ghastly by a new-made tomb.
I see no balm in Gilead; he is lost,
The beautiful soul that loved thee, thy life's bloom,
Is withered by the sudden blighting frost;
O Grief! how mighty; Creeds! how vain ye are:
Earth presses closely, — Heaven is cold and far.

MOUNTAIN SONNETS.

[Written on one of the Blue Ridge range of Mountains.]

Here let me pause by the lone eagle's nest,
And breathe the golden sunlight and sweet air,
Which gird and gladden all this region fair
With a perpetual benison of rest;
Like a grand purpose that some god hath blest,
The immemorial mountain seems to rise,
Yearning to overtop diviner skies,
Though monarch of the pomps of East and West;
And pondering here, the genius of the height
Quickens my soul as if an angel spake,
And I can feel old chains of custom break,
And old ambitions start to win the light;
A calm resolve born with them, in whose might
I thank thee, Heaven! that noble thoughts awake.

Here, friend! upon this lofty ledge sit down,
And view the beauteous prospect spread below,
Around, above us; in the noonday glow
How calm the landscape rests! yon distant town,
Enwreathed with clouds of foliage like a crown
Of rustic honor; the soft, silvery flow
Of the clear stream beyond it, and the show
Of endless wooded heights, circling the brown
Autumnal fields, alive with billowy grain;
Say! hast thou ever gazed on aught more fair
In Europe, or the Orient? What domain
(From India to the sunny slopes of Spain)
Hath beauty, wed to grandeur in the air,
Blessed with an ampler charm, a more benignant reign?

The rainbows of the heaven are not more rare,
More various and more beautiful to view,
Than these rich forest rainbows, dipped in dew
Of morn and evening, glimmering everywhere
From wooded dell to dark-blue mountain mere;
O Autumn! wondrous painter! every hue
Of thy immortal pencil is steeped through
With essence of divinity; how bare
Beside thy coloring the poor shows of Art,
Though Art were thrice inspired; in dreams alone
(The loftiest dreams wherein the soul takes part)
Of jasper pavements, and the sapphire throne
Of Heaven, hath such unearthly brightness shone
To flush and thrill the visionary heart!

COMPOSED IN AUTUMN.

With these dead leaves stripped from a withered tree,
And slowly fluttering round us, gentle friend,

Some faithless soul a sad presage might blend;
To me they bring a happier augury;
Lives that shall bloom in genial sunshine free,
Nursed by the spell Love's dews and breezes send,
And when a kindly Fate shall speak the end,
Down dropping in Time's autumn silently;
All hopes fulfilled, all passions duly blessed,
Life's cup of gladness drained, except the lees,
No more to fear or long for, but the rest
Which crowns existence with its dreamless ease;
Thus when our days are ripe, oh! let us fall
Into that perfect Peace which waits for all!

GREAT POETS AND SMALL.

SHALL I not falter on melodious wing,
In that my notes are weak and may not rise
To those world-wide entrancing harmonies,
Which the great poets to the ages sing?
Shall my thought's humble heaven no longer ring
With pleasant lays, because the empyreal height
Stretches beyond it, lifting to the light
The anointed pinion of song's radiant king?
Ah! a false thought! the thrush her fitful flight
Ventures in vernal dawns; a happy note
Trills from the russet linnet's gentle throat,
Though far above the eagle soars in might,
And the glad skylark — an ethereal mote —
Sings in high realms that mock our straining sight.

MY STUDY.

THIS is my world! within these narrow walls,
I own a princely service; the hot care
And tumult of our frenzied life are here
But as a ghost, and echo; what befalls
In the far mart to me is less than naught;
I walk the fields of quiet Arcadies,
And wander by the brink of hoary seas,
Calmed to the tendance of untroubled thought:
Or if a livelier humor should enhance
The slow-timed pulse, 'tis not for present strife,
The sordid zeal with which our age is rife,
Its mammon conflicts crowned by fraud or chance,
But gleamings of the lost, heroic life,
Flashed through the gorgeous vistas of romance.

TO ——.

BELOVÈD! in this holy hush of night,
I know that thou art looking to the South,
Fair face and cordial brow bathed in the light
Of tender Heavens, and o'er thy delicate mouth
A dewy gladness from thy dark eyes shed;
O eloquent eyes! that on the evening spread
The glory of a radiant world of dreams
(The inner moonlight of the soul that dims
This moonlight of the sense), and o'er thy head,
Thrown back, as listening to a voice of hymns,
Perchance in thine own spirit, violet gleams

"This is my world! within these narrow walls,
I own a princely service."

From modest flowers that deck the window-bars,
While the winds sigh, and sing the far-off streams,
And a faint bliss seems dropping from the stars.
O! pour thine inmost soul upon the air
And trust to heaven the secrets that recline
In the sweet nunnery of thy virgin breast;
Speak to the winds that wander every-where,—
And sure must wander hither—the divine
Contentment, and the infinite, deep rest
That sway thy passionate being, and lift high
To the calm realm of Love's eternity,
The passive ocean of thy charmèd thought;
And tell the aerial element to bear
The burden of thy whispered heart to me,
By fairy alchemy of distance wrought
To something sacred as a saintly prayer,
A spell to set my nobler nature free.

TO W. H. H.

How like a mighty picture, tint by tint,
This marvellous world is opening to thy view!
Wonders of earth and heaven; shapes bright and new,
Strength, radiance, beauty, and all things that hint
Most of the primal glory, and the print
Of angel footsteps; from the globe of dew
Tiny, but luminous, to the encircling blue,
Unbounded, thou drink'st knowledge without stint;
Like a pure blossom nursed by genial winds,
Thy innocent life, expanding day by day,
Upsprings, spontaneous, to the perfect flower;
Lost Eden-splendors round thy pathway play,
While o'er it rise and burn the starry signs
Which herald hope and joy to souls of power.

I pray the angel in whose hands the sum
Of mortal fates in mystic darkness lies,
That to the soul which fills these deepening eyes,
Sun-crowned and clear, the spirit of Song may come;
That strong-winged fancies, with melodious hum
Of plumèd vans, may touch to sweet surprise
His poet nature, born to glow and rise,
And thrill to worship though the world be dumb;
That love, and will, and genius, all may blend
To make his soul a guiding star of time,
True to the purest thought, the noblest end,
Full of all richness, gentle, wise, complete,
In whose still heights and most ethereal clime,
Beauty, and faith, and plastic passion meet.

LINES.

Ye cannot add by any pile ye raise,
One jot or tittle to the statesman's fame;
That the world knows; to the far future days
Belongs his glory, and its radiant flame
Will burn, when ye are dead, decayed, forgot;
Therefore, your opposition matters not;
The thin-masked jealousies of present time,
Unburied in his grave, survive to keep

Rampant the hate he deemed his highest praise,
And the rude clash of discord o'er his sleep;
But for his great, wise acts, his faith sublime,
All that the soul of genius sanctifies,
These mount where viler passions cannot climb,
These live where palsied malice faints and dies.

Still must the common voice denounce the deed,
The common heart swell with an outraged pride,
That the poor purchase of that paltry meed
His country owed him should be thus denied;
Shame on the Senate! shame on every hand
Which did not falter when recording there,
The basest act achieved for many a year,
To fire the scorn of the whole Southern land;
Nor the South only, for our foes will cry
Out on your petty pasteboard chivalry!
The people who refuse to crown the great
And good with honor, do themselves eclipse,
And doubly shameless is the recreant State,
Whose condemnation comes from her own lips.

"AN IDLE POET DREAMING."

An idle poet, dreaming in the sun,
One given to much unhallowed vagrancy
Of thought and step; who, when he comes to die,
In the broad world can point to nothing done;
No chartered corporations, no streets paved
With very princely stone-work, no vast file
Of warehouses, no slowly-hoarded pile
Of priceless treasure, no proud sceptre waved
O'er potent realms of stock, no magic art
Lavished on curious gins, or works of steam;
Only a few wild songs that melt the heart,
Only the glow of some unearthly dream,
Embodied and immortal; what are these?
Sneers the sage world; chaff, smoke, vain phantasies!

Yet stock depreciates, even banks decay,
Merchant and architect are lowly laid
In purple palls, and the shrewd lords of trade
Lament, for they were wiser in their day
Than the clear sons of light; but prithee, how
Doth stand the matter, when the years have fled;
What means yon concourse thronging where the dead
Old singer sleeps; say! do they seek him now?
Now that his dust is scattered on the breath
Of every wind that blows; what meaneth this?
It means, thou sapient citizen, that death
Heralds the bard's true life, as with a kiss,
Wakens two immortalities; then bow
To the world's scorn, O poet, with calm brow.

DRAMATIC SKETCHES.

DRAMATIC SKETCHES.

ANTONIO MELIDORI.

[Among the heroes of the modern Greek revolution, none, perhaps, were so distinguished for acts of individual daring, and a spirit of romantic and chivalrous adventure, as Captain Antonio Melidori, a native of Candia. He waged against the Turks a partisan conflict, which was often eminently successful. His own deeds of strength, and reckless hardihood, made him terrible to the foe, who were persuaded finally to look upon him as one whose life was "charmed."

It did not prove so, however, as he fell a victim to the rage and jealousy of some of his own company. Having been invited by the malcontents to a feast, Rousso (the chief of the conspirators, whom Antonio appears to have rivalled successfully both in love and war), whilst in the very act of embracing the patriot, plunged a dagger into his bosom.

There is a tradition that Antonio loved a beautiful maiden, Philota, whom in the stirring and anxious scenes of the revolution he was ultimately led to neglect, if not to forsake. A writer in "Chambers' Journal" has from this episode in the private career of the Greek partisan taken the material for a touching and graphic narrative, which has been closely, often literally followed in the composition of the ensuing "sketch."]

SCENE I.

[A place not far from the summit of Mount Psiloriti, in the Isle of Candia. Philota discovered with a basket of grapes upon her head; she looks eagerly upward. Time, a littlé before sunset.]

PHILOTA.

Why comes he not? Here on this emerald sward,
Close to the cool shade of these ancient rocks,
We have met, and fondly lingered in the sunset,
Eve after eve, since first he said, "I love thee!"
Never, Antonio, hast thou been ere now
A loiterer! wherefore should my heart beat fast,
And my breath thicken, and the dew of fear
Stand chill upon my forehead? Is't an omen?

[*At this moment Antonio is seen bounding quickly down the mountain; he reaches Philota and embraces her.*]

ANTONIO.

Thou hast waited long, Philota, hast thou not?

PHILOTA.

'Tis true, Antonio! but thou know'st an hour,
Nay, a bare minute, drags the weariest length
When thou art from me!

ANTONIO.

Thanks, dearest, and, forgive me,
I did but dream upon the hill-top yonder
And, dreaming thus, forgot thee.

PHILOTA.

Forgot me!

ANTONIO.

Nay, nay, I mean not that! thy face, thy smiles,
Thy deep devotion, in my heart of hearts,
I keep them shrined forever, but my thoughts
Turned truant; who can hold his thoughts, Philota,
In a leash always? prithee reascend

The mountain with me, I would show the place
Which tempted my weak thoughts to wander thus.

[They reach the most elevated portion of the mountain, whence a wide circuit of land and sea becomes visible.]

PHILOTA.

How beautiful! how glorious! see, my love,
There's not a cloud, or shadow of cloud in heaven;
Even here, the winds breathe faintly, and afar
O'er the broad circuit of the watery calm,
Peace broods upon the ocean, rules the air,
And up the sunset's dazzling pathway walks
Like a saint entering Paradise.
'Twere sweet,
How sweet, Antonio, amid scenes like these,
To live and love forever!

ANTONIO *[absently]*.

Dost thou think so?
Ay! — well — perhaps ——

PHILOTA.

He heeds me not, his eye
Is cold and stern; what troubles thee, Antonio?

ANTONIO.

Trouble! I am not troubled.

PHILOTA.

But thou art,
I know thou art; would'st thou deceive Philota?

ANTONIO.

Now by the saints, not so; dismiss the fear
Which, like a tremulous shadow, breaks the calm
Of those soft eyes! *[after a pause]*
The matter, in brief, is this:
Tracking our mountain paths at early dawn,
Rousso — thou knowest him — hailed me from the rocks,
With words that sounded like the battle trumpets;
"It comes!" he cried; "the war-cloud rolls this way;
We too shall hear its thunders" ——

PHILOTA.

Ay! and feel
Its bolts perchance, — there's lightning in such clouds!

ANTONIO.

What if there be! who would not brave them all, —
All, for a cause like ours? Believe me, Love,
We stand upon the brink of troublous times:
All shall be changed here: men, — brave Grecian men, —
The blood of heroes in them, — cannot pause,
Storing the honey, harvesting the olive,
Or humbly following the tame herdsman's trade,
Whilst Freedom calls to conflict.
Look, Philota!
Dost mark yon lurid flash across the bay?
Our soldiers test their cannon! hark, below,
The drums of Affendouli — how they ring!
Already thousands of bold mountaineers
Have formed beneath his banners; dost thou hear me?

PHILOTA.

And wouldst thou wish to join them? Ah! I see,
I see it all! — a trouble on thy brow,
Borne upward from the restless gloom within,
Hath clouded o'er thy peace. I, — a frail girl,
And gifted only with the wealth of love,
How can I satisfy the burning need
Of a strong man's ambition? Yes, tis so,
'Tis even so! — love is the woman's heaven,
Her hope, her god, her life-blood! yet to man,
What is it but a pastime?

ANTONIO.

Speak not thus
Oh, speak not thus, Philota! I have loved
Thee, only thee, — so help me, Virgin Mother!
But comrades from whose lips a taunt is bitter,
Have dared to hint ——

PHILOTA.

What!

ANTONIO.

That I chose to stay,
Delving, like some base slave, our barren soil,
When not a Sphakiote that can carry arms
Has failed to seize them. Liars! pestilent liars,
I would have proved the falsehood were it not ——

PHILOTA.

For me — Philota! — well! I love thee dearly,
Deeply, — God knows, — but I would have this love
To crown thee as a garland, — not as a chain
To bind and fetter — thou art free, Antonio! —

ANTONIO.

But hast thou thought of all which follows this?
Thou shalt be left alone, no bridal feast
Can cheer the olive harvest!

PHILOTA.

I have thought,
And am determined; — thou art free, Antonio!

ANTONIO.

Oh, thanks, thanks, thanks! — lift up thy hopes, Philota,
Up to the height of mine! our cause is just,
And a just Fate shall guard it; wheresoe'er
Free thought finds utterance, and the patriot-soul
Thrills at the deeds of heroes, — we may look
For a "God speed!" The prayers of noble men,
The tears of women, — the whole world's applause
Do wait upon us!
Methinks I see the end,
A free, grand Commonwealth of Grecian States,
Built upon chartered rights, — each sealed with blood!

PHILOTA.

Enough! enough! Antonio, thou shalt go!
Greece is thy mistress, now.

SCENE II.

[The cottage of Philota, at the foot of Mount Psiloriti. Philota discovered at the window, looking out upon the night, which is bleak and stormy.]

PHILOTA.

Hark! how those lusty trumpeters, the winds,
Urge on the black battalions of the clouds;
And see! the swollen rivulets rushing down
The sides of Psiloriti! Yesterday,
'Neath the clear calm of the serenest morn
Earth ever stole from Paradise, they swept,
Bright curves of laughing silver in the sunshine;
But now, an overmastering rush of floods,
They thunder to the heavens, that answer back
From the wild depths of gloom, — an awful tempest!

[*Enter* ANTONIO *hastily.*]

ANTONIO.

Where is the priest, Philota? where is Andreas?
Was he not here to-night?

PHILOTA.

Ay! but left some half hour since!

ANTONIO.

What say you?
Oh, the poor father! — then 'twas him I saw
Pent 'twixt the mountain torrents; he is lost!
The good old man! — and yet, not so, not so!
Give me yon oaken staff, — and, hold; a flask
Of the best vintage; I'll be back anon,
And the dear father with me: —

[*Exit Antonio. Philota kneels before an image of the Virgin, and prays for the safety of her lover. After the lapse of some minutes, enter Rousso stealthily, wrapped in a cloak, which partly conceals his features.*]

ROUSSO [*aside*].

Faith! a pretty picture!
Now, were I what fools call poetical,
I'd worship her, whilst she adores the saint, —
A lovelier saint herself, and nearer truly
To the just standard of divinity
Than yonder painted image; there's the curve,
The old Greek curve, in the voluptuous swell
Of those full lips; the passion in her eyes
Is shadowed off to melancholy meaning,
Only to waken to meridian life,
When a like passion touches it to flame.

PHILOTA [*praying*].

Oh, merciful Mother! save him, — save Antonio!

ROUSSO [*aside*].

Oh, potent Devil! claim him, — claim Antonio!
What! shall this malapert boy dispute my love?

[*Philota, rising, discovers Rousso, towards whom (mistaking him for Antonio), she rushes, as if about to cast herself into his arms, but discovering her error, she shrinks back.*]

PHILOTA.

You here!

ROUSSO [*advancing*].

I crave protection, shelter, — may I stay?

PHILOTA.

At a safe distance, Sir!

ROUSSO.

Why, what means this?
I looked for kindlier welcome!

PHILOTA.

Wherefore, Rousso?
What thou hast asked, I grant, — protection, shelter;
Durst thou claim more than these?

ROUSSO.

I' faith thy temper is most strange and wayward!
Because, some months agone, not quite myself,
I ventured at the harvest of the olive,
Upon one innocent liberty ——

PHILOTA.

No liberty,
With me, at least, bold man! is rated thus!

ROUSSO.

I do repeat, that I was not myself;
Blame the hot wine of Cyprus; spare your slave! [*Kneeling.*]

PHILOTA.

A slave, indeed! —

ROUSSO.

But one who stoops to conquer, fair Philota;
If I have knelt, 'tis only that I may
Rise thus, and clasp thee! Hold, no foolish cries,
No weak, vain strugglings! Think'st thou that the storm
Pealing adown the mountain's rugged steeps
Can bear these feeble wailings to thy friends?
Come, come, Philota! — if thou could'st believe it,
I am the very worthiest of thy vassals:
List for an instant, while I paint the beauty
Of a far Eden waiting for the light,
The sundawn of thine eyes: —
Amid the waves
Of the Ægean, bosomed in the calm
Of ever-during summer, sleeps an isle
Whereon the ocean ripples into music;
Through whose luxuriant wilderness of blooms,

The soft winds sigh their breath away in dreams,
Where — (the deuce take me! I forget my part) —
Where — where — where — i' sooth, a place
To live, to love, to die in, and revisit
From the sad vale of shadows, with a touch
Of mortal fondness, overmastering death:
Wilt thou go thither with me? Nay, thou must!

[*As Rousso attempts to carry Philota from the apartment, she recovers, and, by a sudden effort, releases herself from his arms.*]

ROUSSO.

Pardon, Philota! 'tis my eager love
Which thus hath urged me on; thou tremblest! what?
I would not make thee fear me.

PHILOTA.

Fear! fear!
If my cheek pales, it is not cowardice
That plays the tyrant to the exiled blood;
If my frame trembles, there are other moods
Than that thou speak'st of, to unstring its firmness;
Thy presence brings no terrors; dost thou talk
Of fear to a Greek woman?

ROUSSO.

No! no! not fear, but love!

PHILOTA.

Man, man! I pray thee
Blaspheme not thus! what canst thou know of love?
'Tis true thou speak'st it boldly; from thy lips
The word falls with a rounded fullness off,
And yet, believe me, thou hast used a phrase,
(A sacred phrase, and wretchedly profaned),
Which, were thy years thrice lengthened out beyond
The general limit of our mortal lives,
And thou be made to pass through all extremes
Of multiform experience, it could never
Enter thy sordid soul to comprehend!

ROUSSO.

Bravely delivered! by my soul, I think
We both make good declaimers! Where did'st learn
That pretty speech, Philota?

PHILOTA.

Wilt thou leave me?

ROUSSO.

Pshaw! thou art less than courteous. Leave thee? no!
I will not leave thee! Hark ye, my proud damsel,
I am not one with whom 'tis safe to trifle,
Thou knowest, or shalt know this; so, mark my words,
Long have I wooed thee fairly, would have won thee,
Yea, and endowed thee with both wealth and station;
Twice hast thou heard my proffer, twice with loathing
Spurned it, and me; I shall not woo thee thrice
With honeyed words; no, 'tis the strong arm now.
I am prepared for all; come on!

[*He seizes Philota a second time, but enter on the instant Antonio, with the Monk Andreas leaning upon him.*]

PHILOTA [*faintly*].

Saved! saved!

ANTONIO.

Ha, Rousso, I have heard it whispered oft
Amongst thy watchful brethren in this isle,
That underneath that smooth and flattering front
There lurked a mine of blackest villany!
Faith! I denied it once; what shall I say
When next the public voice decries you, sir?

ROUSSO.

A jest! I do assure you but a jest!
This cloak, which in your self-devoted flight
To rescue the dear father, Andreas
(How glad I am to see his saintship safe),
You dropped some furlongs from the mountain's base,
I cast, in sportive fashion, on my person,
And deeming that Philota would rejoice
To hear that thou had'st so far braved the force
O' th' treacherous elements, I called upon her;
She did me the vast honor to confound
Your humble servant with Antonio,
And 'ere I was aware, sprang to my arms,
With such a blinded ecstasy of rapture,
That I had wellnigh sunk into the earth,
From the mere stress of native modesty!
A jest, a jest, and nothing but a jest.

ANTONIO.

Such jesting may be dangerous, — beware!

SCENE III.

[A year is supposed to have elapsed. The town of Sphakia after nightfall. Enter confusedly a band of Sphakiote soldiers, with Rousso amongst them. The streets are crowded with women, many of whom are heard lamenting the death of Antonio Melidori.]

ROUSSO [*in a disguised voice*].

Why will ye clamor thus, ye foolish jades?
Your handsome favorite, your renowned commander,
Is no more dead than I am!

A WOMAN.

Say'st thou so?
Where then is Melidori?

ROUSSO [*still disguising his voice*].

Would'st thou learn?
Women of Sphakia, your immaculate captain,
He for whose welfare, upon bended knees,
Ye nightly pray to heaven, whose name your infants
Lisp in their very slumbers, hath betrayed us!
Hold! hear me out! I am no dubious witness;
Thrice, whilst the battle raged along our front,
I saw the traitor creeping like a dog
Between the Turkish outposts!

[*Antonio appears in the rear, with a child in his arms.*]

ANTONIO.

It is false!
Here is your leader, Sphakiotes; what base slanderer
Dares to pronounce me traitor? I but paused
To save this weeping innocent, whose mother
Fell by some coward's sword!

ROUSSO.

Ha, Sphakiotes, see,
The noble Melidori waxes tender,
Soft as a woman! he must love the Moslem,
Who fosters thus their offspring! by the saints
A lusty brat! He'll thrive, good friends, believe me,
And grow betimes, to cut our infants' throats!

ANTONIO.

Let him who speaks stand forth; I would confront
My bold accuser. What! he clings to the dark!
Fit place for lies and liars!
Friends, I scorn
To parley with this viper; there's a way,
One only way, to deal with reptiles, crush them,
Thus, thus, and thus,
When they have crawled too near us;

[*Stamping violently upon the earth.*]

Till then, why let the ugly beasts hiss on,
And spit their harmless venom.

BIRTHPLACE OF PAUL HAMILTON HAYNE.

Charleston, S.C.

[*Turning to the women.*]

Mothers, wives,
Maidens of Sphakia, are there none amongst ye
Ready to take this poor unfortunate?
Just for my sake, fair countrywomen, list,
List to the blessèd word: — "The merciful
Shall obtain mercy!"

ROUSSO.

Heed him not, I say,
But seize the infidel whelp, and let him rock
On a steel bayonet! What! have we repelled
The invading foe, exterminated wholly
His forces and his empire, that we dare
Cherish his cubs among us? — and for what?
"Just for his sake, fair countrywomen, — his,
And mercy's!" Who showed mercy to our children,
When the Turk ravaged Scio? The young devil. —
Hear how he shrieks! ho! send him down to hell!
Down to his father! he's a grateful spirit,
And thankful for small favors!

[*The crowd begin to murmur, and move threateningly towards* ANTONIO.]

ANTONIO.

Shame upon you!
Though the poor boy were fifty times a Moslem,
I'll rear him as my own; he shall not perish;
Perchance, who knows, when I have died for you,
For you, and Grecian liberty, this babe,
Reared as a Greek, may yet avenge my death,
As none of you, false brethren, dare avenge it!
Once more I say, — Mothers, wives, maids of Sphakia,
Is there not one amongst ye to whose tendance
I may commit this trembling castaway?

PHILOTA [*veiled*].

Give me the child, — I'll nurture him with love,
And gentlest usage.

ANTONIO [*starting*].

Heavens! what voice is that?
You here, Philota? I had hoped you dwelt
Safely within the close heart of the mountains!

PHILOTA.

The mountains are not safe.

ANTONIO.

Why then did'st thou
Keep such strict silence? Answer me, Philota,
How hast thou lived. This peasant's dress ——

PHILOTA.

Is fittest
For me, Antonio, — by my handiwork,
And daily labor, I now earn my bread, —
For was it meet an unknown peasant girl
Should claim, as her betrothed, great Melidori,
Captain of Sphakia?

ANTONIO.

O, thou generous heart!
But stay, — the rabble must not catch our words;
Take thou the babe, — under the city-walls
I'll meet thee in the gloaming.

SCENE IV.

[A place under the city walls, — time, an hour after sunset.]

ANTONIO, [*embracing* PHILOTA *constrainedly*].

How kind thou art!

PHILOTA.

I but obeyed your mandate!

ANTONIO.

Nay, why so cold? my troth is thine,
Philota, —
Dost thou remember?

PHILOTA.

Would'st thou have me do so?
Methought that dream was over, — by
thy wish.

ANTONIO.

By heaven! I never said so!

PHILOTA.

Yet thy heart,
Thy heart, Antonio, spake the keen desire,
Although thy lips kept silence; — I have
learned
To read thy spirit like an open book,
And cannot be deceived; — all's changed
with us:
Never again, as in the time that's past,
Shall we, hand linked in hand, explore
the vales,
Or walk the shining hill-tops; thou hast
risen
Far, far above my level; a great man,
Among the greatest, — thou wert mad
t' espouse
A humble girl like me; I ask it not;
My love but burdens thy aspiring hopes,
So, I beseech thee, dwell no more upon
it:
Antonio, for thy welfare I would give
My soul's life; shall I then refuse to
yield
A personal joy, that thou may'st win
and wed
The immortal virgin — Glory? Dream
it not!
Oh! dream it not!

ANTONIO.

Now, gracious God, forgive me!
It were presumption, should I kiss thy
feet,
Thou pure, unselfish woman! yet thy
words
Are true, too true, and I dare not gainsay them.
One thing believe, Philota, I am
wretched,
Yes, far more so than thou art:

[*After a pause.*]

— Did'st thou know
The terrible life I lead in this dread warfare,
Through what an atmosphere of blood
and carnage
It is my doom to move, as through the
air
Of some plague-stricken city, thick with
curses;
Did'st know the numberless dangers,
that like demons
(Many unseen, — and therefore doubly
fearful),
Which hover 'round the soldier, hour by
hour
O'ershadowing life with the black gloom
of death;
Did'st know the coarse companions, the
rude manners
Of vile extortioners, bent alone on prey,
And personal profit, and the thousand
evils
Gendered of strife, and strife's unhallowed passions,
O, thou would'st shrink from following
such base courses,
Even as an angel from the brink of hell!

PHILOTA.

Thou wrong'st my love, and hast deceived thyself;
Where'er thou art, to me that place is
heaven;
Antonio, God alone, God and my soul
Know what I might, and would have
been to thee!
I would have shared thy fortunes, joined
my fate
For weal or woe, for honor or disgrace,
For life or death to thine; have tracked
thy steps,
(If need it were,) through seas of blood
and carnage,
Strengthened thy weakness, buoyed thy
sinking hopes,
Nor, at the worst, have shed one woman's tear

To shake thy manhood. Had heaven blessed thy cause,
I would have striven to make my spirit worthy
To mount with thee; so, when the orbèd glory
Shone like the fire of sunrise round thy brow,
No man dare say that with that lustre mingled
One blush of shame for Melidori's wife!
This might have been, and this shall never be. [*Wildly.*]
I' th' name of mercy, by thy mother's soul,
And the dear past, I pray thee leave me now,
While still thou lov'st me (dost thou not ?) a little.

ANTONIO.

And thou — and thou, Philota ? ———

PHILOTA.

I shall dwell
In peace; [*aside*] ay! broken hearts are peaceful!

ANTONIO.

But where ? ———

PHILOTA.

What matter where, so that I live in peace ?
Grieve not, Antonio. In my humble station
One thought shall bring content; — "he was not false,"
No mortal maiden stole Antonio's heart!

ANTONIO.

Blessèd words!
'Tis true I love but thee!

PHILOTA.

Then do not sorrow.
Love, I forgive thee; thou hast wronged me not.
And for the child — ah, I shall dream it thine;
Tend it as thine, and when the years have ripened
That infant soul, 'tis mine to lead to virtue,
I'll teach the boy how noble was the act
Whereby Antonio saved him; I'll be happy,
Oh, trust me, Love! so very, very happy!

ANTONIO.

Then be it so, Philota. I would bless thee,
But am not worthy; still, thou shalt be blessed.

PHILOTA.

And thou, too, if the Virgin hear my prayers;
And now that we are friends, *but* friends, though firm ones,
Beseech thee, list my tidings. There's a foe,
A deadly, treacherous foe in thine own camp,
And one who vows thy ruin; it is Rousso;
Thou knowest how first his envious, bitter temper
Was stung to hatred; since that time, thy will
Hath often clashed with his; besides, thy fame
In these fierce wars hath far o'ertopped his credit;
So he has sworn thy death; the voice was his,
That goaded on thy soldiers to rebellion;
And, as I threaded my uncertain pathway,
A short hour since, through the dark streets of Sphakia,
I heard thy name in whispers; two dim forms
(Men, as I knew by their hoarse tones,) conferred
With hurried, stealthy gestures, and one sentence
Startled me like a knell: — "His tomb is open,"
A deep voice said; "Antonio's tomb is open!"
Oh, then, beware. As lowly as thou deem'st me,
I'll watch above thy safety; the soft dove
May warn the eagle of the midnight spoiler!

ANTONIO.

And thy own life and safety ——

PHILOTA.

I am here
To spend them both for thee. But hark! thy name
Is shouted by thy comrades in the valley.
The hour has come that parts us. Fare thee well!

[*She gives him her hand.*]

ANTONIO.

'Twas not our wont to part in this cold fashion;
Come, one more kiss, Philota! let me feel
We were indeed betrothed; one last, last kiss! [*They embrace and part.*]

SCENE V.

[An apartment in the house of Affendouli, the Governor-General of Candia. Enter Antonio, and Affendouli, conversing.]

AFFENDOULI.

These private bickerings are the fruitful cause
Of all disgrace and failure; let us end them!

ANTONIO.

Most willingly! I have no feud with any,
Saving one quarrel, forced upon me, chief!

AFFENDOULI.

True, true! but even now a courier waits,
Charged with a special message of good will,
From Rousso, and his brother, Anagnosti:
They say, "We plead for peace! all personal hate
Henceforth be quelled between us; we would join
Our troop to Melidori's, and our banners
Wave side by side with his." Accept their proffer!

ANTONIO.

I will!

AFFENDOULI.

To show thou art sincere, fail not to test
Their hospitality.

ANTONIO.

As how?

AFFENDOULI.

They give
A solemn feast of unity and friendship,
To which thou art invited. Go, I charge thee.

ANTONIO.

Trust me, I shall be there, what day's appointed
Whereon to hold this festival of love?

AFFENDOULI.

This very day; thou knowest the camp of Rousso?

ANTONIO.

Ay! I'll be there anon!

[*Exit Antonio. Enter, after a brief interval, Philota, with a hurried and anxious mien.*]

PHILOTA.

Oh, pardon, pardon!
Most gracious Governor! but I come to seek
Ant—— Ant——, that is, the Captain Melidori,
With tidings of grave import.

AFFENDOULI.

Ha!
Thou luckless messenger! he has departed.
Gone——

PHILOTA [*wildly*].

Where, where?

AFFENDOULI.

To feast with Rousso.

PHILOTA [*rushing out*].

Then is he lost! O merciful God, protect us!

SCENE VI.

[An open space in a wood, — tables arranged for a banquet, — Rousso, Anagnosti, Antonio Melidori, and their followers, discovered feasting.]

ANAGNOSTI.

A soldier's life forever! free to pass
In feast or fray! how glorious this wild banquet
Compared to those dull, formal feasts of old,

Held at the olive harvest! Speak, Antonio.
Give us thy thought upon it: what! art silent?

ROUSSO.

Urge him no more; perchance Antonio pines
For the sweet quiet of that mountain life,
Which thou hast called so dull; its days of dream,
Its nights of warm voluptuous dalliance!

ANTONIO.

No, no, by heaven! those times are dead to me;
They had their pleasures, but not one to match
The keen delights of glory, the true honor
Which follows patriot service.

ROUSSO.

Gallant words,
Brave, and high-sounding; but for me and mine,
We do not fight for shadows!

ANTONIO [*coldly*].

I'm at fault,
Not clearly comprehending, sir, your meaning.

ROUSSO.

Oh! thou dost well to speak of glory, honors,
We know what rich rewards await thee, chief,
When the war's ended; spoils, and wealth and beauty.
But yestermorn, I saw thy winsome lady,
The bride to be, old Affendouli's daughter.
Nay, shrink not, man, she is a lovely maid,
Fair as her father's generous; what an eye!
Half arch, half languishing; and what a breast!
That heaves as 'twould burst outward to the day,
And strike men mad with its white panting passion!
No lovelier woman lives, unless, unless—
It be that poor young thing who doted on thee,
Before the war, — what was her name? Philota?

ANTONIO.

Thy thoughts run on fair damsels; let us talk
Like soldiers, not like brain-sick boys in love.

ROUSSO.

With all my heart; only, one pledge to thee,
And Affendouli's daughter!

ANTONIO.

I have borne
This jesting with the patience of a saint,
But now 'tis stretched to license. Prithee, cease!

ROUSSO.

God, how he winces! if Philota —

ANTONIO.

Villain!
Utter that sacred name again ——

ROUSSO [*rising suddenly and drawing his dagger*].

Oh, ho!
Wilt fight, wilt fight! I'm ready for thee; come.

ANTONIO [*aside*].

(He shall not trap me thus.) Thou art my host;
'Twere shame, yea, bitter shame, this brawl should end
In blows and bloodshed! when the time befits,

[*To* ROUSSO].

Doubt not that I shall call thee to account
For this day's work; meanwhile I leave a board
Where clownish insult poisons all your cups!

[*As he is about to depart, Anagnosti approaches, with an air of conciliation.*]

ANAGNOSTI.
Well spoken, noble captain, thou wert wronged;
But Rousso is so hasty! He repents;
Let not this solemn feast of unity
Break up in discord.

ROUSSO.
No, no, no, Antonio!
I do repent! Prithee embrace me, friend,
In sign of reconcilement.

[Rousso approaches Melidori with an unsteady step: while in the act of embracing, he stabs him in the side. Philota rushes upon the scene, with a cry of agony, and throws herself beside Antonio, whose head she supports.]

PHILOTA.
Too late! O God, too late! He faints, he dies!
Why stare ye thus upon us, cruel men?
Wine, wine, another cup, how slow ye move!
My scarf is drenched with blood, — ye pitiless fools!
Will not a creature loan me wherewithal
To bind his wretched wound up? There, 'tis stanched,
And he revives! Antonio, speak to me,
I am Philota!

ANTONIO [*his mind wandering*].
Where hast thou been, my love, this weary time?
Am I not true? I charge thee, heed them not!
The girl is nothing to me; Rousso's tongue,
His sharp false tongue first joined our names together;
She loves another, and I love but thee;
Draw nearer, let me whisper. I have dreamed,
Oh, such a dream! the valleys flowed with blood,
And ruin compassed all our island round,
And every town was sacked, and, hark ye, nearer!
I saw a mother murdered by a knave,
A coward knave, because she would not yield
Her body to him; but I saved her child,
And here he is, a pretty, pretty boy!
Take him, Philota. Ah, my heart, my heart!
It pains me sorely; 'twas a terrible dream,
But now, thank Heaven, 'tis over! Thou art pale;
What makes thee pale? Bear up, my dearest love!
This morn we shall be wedded, and I think
We will not part again. I had a foe,
His name is Rousso; but we are so happy,
Let us forgive all foes; invite him thither,

PHILOTA [*weeping*].
He breaks my heart —

ANTONIO.
How keen the wind is!
Keen, keen, and chill; it was not wont to blow
So coldly at this season: I am sick,
Yea, sick of very joy; but joy kills not;
My lids are heavy; I would sleep, Philota.
Wake me at early dawn; I told my mother,
That I would bring thee home, to-morrow morn.

[He dies.]

ALLAN HERBERT.

SCENE I.

[The hall of a country house in Westmoreland, surrounded with portraits of the M. . . . family. Allan Herbert, and Jocelyn, an old domestic, are seen standing before the likeness of a lady, young, and wonderfully fair.]

HERBERT.
The canvas speaks!

JOCELYN.
Ay, sir, 'tis very like;
Was she not beautiful?

HERBERT.
Was; yes, and is;
She had not lost one bloom when late I saw her.

"The canvas speaks."

JOCELYN.

Sir, she is dead!

HERBERT.

Ay, so they say, old man;
And yet I see her nightly, — in my dreams;
I tell you that her cheek is round and fair
As summer's fulness, that her eyes are lustrous,
And she, a perfect presence clasped in light!
Thus will she look, on resurrection morning.

JOCELYN [*aside*].

Alas, poor gentleman! how many loved her,
And loved her vainly! Pardon, sir, your name?

HERBERT.

My name is Allan Herbert.

JOCELYN.

Herbert, Herbert!
Where have I heard that dainty name before? (*musing*)
Oh, now I have it; my young mistress, sir,
She who is dead, was wont to read a book
A delicate gold-edged volume, that I'm sure
Bore some such name within it; she would sit
Beneath yon grape vine trellis toward the south
(This window, sir, commands it), and for hours,
Nay, days, bend o'er her favorite pages; once
She left the book behind her, and I saw
its leaves were touched with tears.

HERBERT.

Where is it now?
That book your mistress loved? Let me behold it!

JOCELYN.

In sooth, sir, I have never seen it since,
Or, if I have [*hesitating*], it lies beyond our reach.

HERBERT.

What meanest thou?

JOCELYN.

I mean that while she lay
Decked for her burial, whilst I stood beside her,
Looking my last upon her tranquil features,
The robe of death was fluttered by the wind,
A low sad wailing wind, that swept aside
The drapery for a moment, and I marked
The glimmer of the gold-edged pages placed
Right on her bosom! Master, you are pale,
You tremble; I have rudely touched the spring
Of some deep-seated sorrow!

HERBERT.

Yes, old man;
A sorrow most unlike to common griefs,
That pass like clouds or shadows; mine is mingled
With the dark hues of treachery and remorse;
A rayless, blank eclipse, through which I wander,
Accursed and hopeless; sometimes in a vision
Comes the sweet face of her I foully wronged,
And stabs me with a smile!

JOCELYN.

Did'st wrong her, Sir?
Did'st wrong my lady?

HERBERT.

Lead me to the grave;
I know 'tis near at hand.

JOCELYN.

The grave! what grave?
Moreover, — if you wronged her ——

HERBERT.

If I wronged her!
Why dost thou taunt me with it? thou on earth
With Mercy still beside thee, — I — in Hell?

JOCELYN.

Madman!

HERBERT.

I am not mad, my friend, but only wretched;
Once more, I pray thee, show me where she sleeps.

JOCELYN.

I must obey him; this way, — follow me.

SCENE II.

[A forest. — Deep in the shade a single monument appears, covered with wild-flowers and roses.]

HERBERT [*alone*].

'Tis fit she should be buried in this place
So fragrant and so peaceful: O, my love!
Thou hast grown dull of hearing! I may call
'Till the lone echoes shiver with thy name,
Thou wilt not heed me; dust, dust, dust indeed!
And thou — more glorious than the morning star;
More tender than the love-light of the eve!
They tell me thou shalt rise again, Christ's bride,
Not mine, most beautiful, yet changed;
Perchance I shall not know thee, or perchance,
The human love which made thine eyes like heaven —
My heaven of hope and worship — shall be lost
In some diviner splendor! all is hushed,
No smallest whisper trembles gently up
From the deep grave to soothe me; 'tis in vain
I agonize in thought. Eternal Nature!
She whom I once called "mother," wears an aspect
Callous and pitiless. I fain would solve
This terrible mystery that weighs down my soul
With nightmare fancies. Let me die in peace,
O God! and if I may not see her more
Through all the long eternities, nor hear
Her voice of tender pardon, let me rest
Next to some stream of Lethe, and repose
In everlasting slumbers! ———

[*Enter* JOCELYN.]

JOCELYN.

Come, let us hence! the darkness creeps upon us;
See, Sir! there's not a spark of sunset left
In all the waning West.

HERBERT.

Well, what of that!
I live in darkness, — the light burns my spirit,
It mocks and tortures me! Begone, I say,
And leave me to the dismal shade thou fearest!

JOCELYN.

Good Sir, be counselled — stay not in the wood;
Thine eye is troubled, and thy visage weary; —
'Tis a rash venture!

HERBERT.

Sooth to say, I thank thee;
Thou could'st not serve long in the household blessed
By her most merciful presence, and not catch
Some tenderness of temper; — take my thanks!
Yet will I stay in this same dreary wood,
And watch until the night is overpast.

JOCELYN.

Thou'lt find it lonely.

HERBERT.

Oh, I have my thoughts,
A stirring company, that never slumber.

JOCELYN.

Why, worse and worse! I've heard, such restless thoughts
Engender a sore sickness ———

HERBERT.

Of the mind;
Yet is my case already desperate,
Past healing, and past comfort. Go thy way.
Thou kind old man, thou canst not shake my purpose,
But when the last star wanes before the dawn,
Come back; my night will then be over-past,
And my watch ended; till that hour, farewell!

FROM THE CONSPIRATOR,

AN UNPUBLISHED TRAGEDY.

SCENE.

[A garden: Arnold De Malpas and Catharine discovered walking slowly towards a summer-house in the distance].

CATHARINE.

Art thou prepared to risk all this, De Malpas?

DE MALPAS.

Ay! this, and more, if I but thought— [*Hesitating*].

CATHARINE.

What, Arnold?

DE MALPAS.

If I but thought that when the strife was over,
The feeble prince hurled down, the throne secured,
She, for whose love I braved the people's hate,
Malice of rulers, and the headsman's axe,
Would deign to share with me that perilous height.

CATHARINE.

She! Oh, thou hast a lady-love!

DE MALPAS.

Cruel! Wouldst thou put by my passion thus,
With a feigned jest? Catharine, I stake my all,
Manhood's strong hopes and purpose, the heart's wealth,
And the mind's store of hard-bought lore, my peace
Of conscience, and my soul's immortal life,
To lift thee to the summit of thy wish;
(Oh! I have proved thee, and I know thy thoughts),
And yet, thou feignest ignorance!

CATHARINE.

Dear De Malpas,
Forgive me! let us both throw by the mask!
I hate the queen; even in our girlish days,
She was my rival; her mild-mannered arts
Stole suitors from me; the old priest, our teacher,
Though I eclipsed her ever in the school,
And shamed her dullness with keen-witted words
And quicker apprehension, shone on her
With sunny aspect, sleeked her golden hair,
Fondled and soothed and petted, whilst for me,
The apter scholar, he reserved harsh looks,
And harsher tones; (well, the old fool is dead!
In after time, some friend of holy church,
Some zealous friend, proved that his saintship taught
Schism and heresy, and so—he perished)!
But for this queen, this Eleanor! our souls
Nursed yearly a more fixed hostility;
We sat together at the knightly jousts,
And watched the conflict with high beating hearts,

Flushed cheeks, and fluttering pulses; she from fear,
I with the mounting heat of martial blood,
Thrilled with the music of the battle's roar,
The ring of mighty lances on steel helms,
Clangor of shields, and neighing of wild steeds:
One morn my knight was victor; as he placed
The crown of gems and laurel on my brow,
Methought that I was born to be a queen,
Not the brief ruler of a festal throng,
But 'stablished kingdoms, and a host of men
Bound to my sway forever!

DE MALPAS.

A true thought!
O, noble Catharine! thy aspiring spirit
Fires my purpose, and gives wings to action;
Thy rival hath sped past thee in the race,
But she shall fall midway; the blinded monarch
Walks on the brink of an abysmal deep,
And soon shall topple over; then, a victor,
(Not from the conflict with half-blunted spears,
In friendly tournament), but the tumult fierce
Of revolution, and the crash of states,
Shall set a weightier crown about thy brows,
And hail thee ruler, — not of festal throngs,
But 'stablished kingdoms, and a host of men
Bound to thy sway forever!

. . . .

DE MALPAS.

Speak. Bolton! what say these, my faithful friends,
Touching my present life?

BOLTON.

Why, Master Arnold,
I' sooth they're much divided; some assert,
That thou art moonstruck; that some morbid fancy,
Whether of love or pride, hath seized upon thee;
Others, that thou hast simply lost thy trust
In man and in thyself; and others still,
That thou hast sunk to base, inglorious ease,
Urging the languid currents of the blood
With fiery spurs of sense; a few there are,
Few, but most faithful, who at dead of night
In secret conclave, with low-whispered words
And pallid faces glancing back aghast,
Speak of a monstrous wrong, which thou ——

DE MALPAS.

[*Starting up, and seizing Bolton.*]

Unhappy wretch! therein thou speak'st thy doom!
That prying, curious spirit is thy fate.

[*Stabs him suddenly.*]

Did I not warn thee of it?

BOLTON.

Oh! I die!
Yet my soul swells and lightens; all the future
Flashes before me like a revelation.
Arnold De Malpas! thou shalt gain thine end!
The aged king shall fall, the throne be thine!
But, as thou goest to claim it, as thy foot
Presses the royal dais (mark my words)!
A bolt shall fall from heaven, sudden, swift,
Even as thy blow on me, thou'lt writhe i' the dust,
Down-trodden by the hostile heel of thousands.

Whilst she, for whom thou'st turned conspirator,
Smiling, shall gaze from out her palace doors,
And wave her broidered scarf, and join the music
Of her low witching laughter to the sneers
Of courtly parasites; "De Malpas bore
His honors bravely, did he not, my lords?
Now, by our lady, 'tis a grievous fall!"
"Yet pride, thou know'st, sweet Catharine,"—
"Ay, ay, ay!
"Prithee, Francisco, wilt thou dance to-night?"

DE MALPAS.

What, fool! wilt prate forever? Hence, I say,
And entertain the devil with thy dreamings!
[*Stabs him again.*]

. . . . .

DE MALPAS.

Thou hast been to court, Bernaldi, hast thou not?

BERNALDI.

Ay! all the forenoon!

DE MALPAS.

Didst thou see the lady,
Catharine of Savoy, whose miraculous beauty
Hath set all Spain aflame?

BERNALDI.

I did, my cousin,
But, I am bold to speak it, liked her not;
Her beauty is the beauty of the serpent,
Masking a poisonous spirit; there's no depth
Of womanly nature in her gleaming eyes,
Falsest when most they flatter; men have said
She owns the Borgia's blood; I know not that,
But, by St. Mark! she owns their temper, cousin!

EXPERIENCE IN POVERTY.

A. How bitterly you speak!
B. I have good warrant.
A. Well, for my part, I hold your creed is false,
Uncharitable, monstrous! I have seen
The world, sir; studied men and manners in it;
And though no doubt some selfishness and craft
May evermore be found by those who seek them,
Peering too closely underneath the mask
Of multiform conventions, yet, by heaven,
The world's a fair, good, reasonable world
To all who follow reason! Your high fancies,
Whose goal is vague impossibility,
Of course must miss their mark! We live not, sir,
In Eden, or the golden age.
B. Right! right!
You talk as is most natural in one
To whom all life hath been a gay parade,
A frolic pastime!—to whom subtle fortune
Hath never turned her dark and lowering front,
But round whose footsteps sowed with golden showers
Obsequious knaves and sweet-tongued servitors
Have fawned and lied and flattered, till your days
Borne bravely onward over perfumed tides
Passed like a steady bark 'twixt shores of flowers,
You know the world! its men and modes forsooth!
Wait, sir, until your purse grows lean as mine,
And fate within the compass of one evil
(A gaunt and loathsome poverty), includes
All ills that flesh is heir to! disrespect

From insolent curs that now you'd hardly stoop
To soil your lordly boot with! studied coldness
Of ancient friends whose easy faith declines
With your decreasing wine-butts! covert sneers,
Or open insult from the gaudy throng
Of parasites, who breathe alone in sunshine!
Grief without balm, and pain that knows not pity;
Dark days, and maddening midnights, and the pang
Of outraged feeling, and the soul's despair:
Ay! wait, I say, until from depths like these,
The lonely thunder growling overhead,
And misery like a cataract raging round
Your path of ruin, wild and desperate eyes
Are lifted to the summits of past hope,
Receding ever with their shows of joy,
Less real than the mirage, or the domes
Which sunset builds on clouds of phantasy!
Wait till the fiend that's born of famished hours
Shall grasp your hand in bony fellowship,
And lead you through the mist of ghastly dreams,
Helpless and tottering, to the brink of death!
Ha! ha! you shrink! the picture does not please
Your dainty fancy! Well, soft optimist,
Confess there's somewhat you have still to learn
Of this same fair, good, reasonable world!

THE TRUE PHILOSOPHY.

I'D have you use a wise philosophy,
In this, as in all matters, whereupon
Judgment may freely act; truth ever lies
Between extremes; avoid the spendthrift's folly
As you'd avoid the road of utter ruin;
For wealth, or at the least, fair competence,
Is honor, comfort, hope, and self-respect;
All, in a word, that makes our human life
Endurable, if not happy: scorn the cant
Of sentimental Dives, wrapped in purple,
Who over jewelled wine-cups and rich fare,
Affects to flout his gold, and prattles loosely
Of sweet content that's found in poverty:
As for the miser, he's a madman simply,
One who the means of all enjoyment holds,
Yet never dares enjoy: no, no, Anselmo,
Use with a prudent, but still liberal hand
That store the gods have given you; thus, my friend,
'Twixt the Charybdis of a churlish meanness,
And the swift Scylla of improvident waste,
You'll steer your bark o'er smooth, innocuous seas,
And reach at last a peaceful anchorage.

LOVE'S CAPRICES.

COME, sweetheart, hear me! I have loved thee well,
God knoweth. Through all these years my holiest thoughts,
Like those pure doves nurtured in antique temples,
Have fluttered ever round thine image fair,
And found in thee their shrine. No tenderest hope
Of mine, which hath not warmed its radiant wings
Within that heaven, thy presence, and drank strength
And sunshine from it.

How hast thou responded?
Sometimes thine eyes, like Eden gates unclosed,
Would pour such beams of sacred passion down,
That all my soul was flooded with its joy,
And I, methought, breathed as immortals breathe,
A deathless light and ether. Then, when most

"Come, sweetheart, hear me!"

I dreamed me happy, a strange change would come,
Sudden as strange; some wind of cold caprice,
Blowing, I knew not whence, an icy cloud
Upbore, and o'er the splendor of thy brow,
Of late so frankly beautiful, there hung
Ominous shadows, crossed by gleams of scorn;
Trifles as slight as eider-down have power
To move or sting thee, and a swarm of humors,
Gendered of morbid fancy, buzz and hiss

About some vacant chambers of thy mind,
By idle thoughts left open, making harsh,
Rude discord, where, if healthful will had sway,
Angels, perchance, might lift celestial voices!

Love, love, thou wrong'st thyself, and that sweet nature,
Sweet at the core, for all such small despites,
Wherewith kind heaven endowed thee; yet, beware!
Caprice, though frail its shafts, a poisoned barb
Hath bound on each; their points are sharp to wound,
And the wounds rankle! Giants great as Love
Have perished merely of an insect's venom,
And who through all God's universe can touch
Love's pulseless heart to warmth and life again?

CREEDS.

Friend, 'mid the complex and unnumbered creeds
Which meet and jostle on this mortal scene,
And sometimes fight *à l'outrance*, I perceive
Some precious seed of truth ennobling all:
Encased, it may be, like the mummy's wheat,
Locked in dead forms, yet waiting but a breath
Of honest air, an inch of wholesome soil,
To bloom and flourish heavenward; therefore, friend,
Walk hand in hand with clear-eyed Charity,
And Faith sublime, though simple, like a child's,
Who feels through densest midnight, next his own,
The loving throb of a kind father's heart.

THE UNIVERSALITY OF GRIEF.

I grant you that our fate is terrible,
Bitter as gall. What then? Will lamentation,
Childish complaint, everlasting wailings,
Grief, groans, despair, help to amend our doom?
Glance o'er the world — the world is full of pain
Akin to ours. If some dark spirit touched
Our vision to miraculous clearness, sights
Would meet our eyes, at which the coldest heart
Might weep blood-tears; there's not a moment passes
Which doth not bear its load of agonies
Out to the dim Eternity beyond;
The primal curse of earth, with heavier weight,
Descends on special victims; yet, bethink you,
All sorrow hath its bounds, o'er which there stands
That friend of misery, gentle-hearted Death.
Balms of oblivion holds he, and the realm
Wherein he rules hath murmurous caves of sleep.

THE PENITENT.

Thou see'st yon woman with the grave pelisse
Lined with dark sables? Is she not devout?
Her soul is in the service, and her eyes
Are dim with weeping, — weeping for the follies

Of a misguided youth; thus saith the world,
But I, who know her ladyship, know this:
She weeps that youth itself, and the lost triumphs
Which followed in its train; the scores of lovers
Dead now, or married off; the rout, the joust,
The sweet flirtations, merry carnivals,
And — (oh! supremest memory of all!) —
The banded serenaders 'neath the lattice,
Lifting the voice of passion in the night:
And one among the minstrels loved her well,
But him she laughed to scorn, his heart was riven;
She trampled on the purest pearl of love,
And cast it to the dogs; well, God is just!
She scorned his sacred gift, and so must walk,
Henceforth a lonely woman on the earth!

DRAMATIC FRAGMENT.

We might have been! ah, yes! we might have been
Among the laurelled noblemen of thought,
Who lift their species with them as they climb
To deathless empire in the realm of gods;
But some dark power — we will not call it Fate —
We dare not call it Providence — hath seized
The helm of our strange destinies, and steered
Right onward to the breakers. All is lost!
Hope's siren song of promise faints in sighs,
And joy — (but she ne'er charmed us, save in days
Of dim-remembered childhood);— let it pass!
Our lot's the lot of millions; for on life
A blight is preying, and a mystic wrong
Hath set our heartstrings to the tune of grief!

REWARD OF FICKLENESS.

ALTON.

You see that man with the quick eyes and brow,
Too ponderous almost for his slender frame,
His dark locks tinged with gray; you'd hardly think it,
But he's a moral dandy, *dilettante*
(As your Italians say), whose fickle taste
Leads him, like some fastidious bee, from flower
To flower of social pastime! A fair girl,
Pretty and piquante, fills his heart to-day;
On airy wings of sentiment he hovers
Lovingly round her, feeds the beauteous creature
On honeyed nothings in a tone so sweet,
They seem the genuine fruit of a strong soul
Nurtured by passion, and true adoration;
Then on the morrow when he meets once more
"That Cynthia of the minute," a cold crust
Of iciest form and etiquette o'erspreads
His words, look, bearing; the whole man is changed —
As if a Tropic landscape, bright with sunlight,
Had grown to frozen hardness in an hour: —
A demon, fickle, trifling, and capricious
O'errules his spirit always! with men likewise,
It is his pride to play the same vile game!
Why, sir, your patience would be taxed to count

His dupes within the year! he'll take a youth,
Bright-minded, trusting, whom perchance he meets
In casual fashion on the public square,
Caress, solicit, flatter him — at length
Bear the poor fool, elate and jubilant,
To banquet at his own well-ordered board,
Ply him with curious questions, draw him out
To make display of all his raciest wit,
And when, like a squeezed orange, all his sap's
Exhausted, — faith! Sir Dainty down the wind
Whistles his victim with a cool assurance,
Which is the calm sublime of impudence!
In fine, the man's a worn-out Epicurean,
A ceaseless hunter after new sensations,
To whom the world's a storehouse crammed with hearts
And minds for his amusement! as for hearts,
He'll toss 'em up, as jugglers toss their balls,
Proud of his sleight of hand, his impish cunning,
His matchless turns of quick dexterity!
And if the baubles break, he's sore amazed
That aught should be so brittle! yet thanks God
The earth is full of these same delicate toys;
And so he hurls the shattered plaything by,
To re-assume his honest, juggling tricks,
And charm his weary leisure-time with lies;
A silken, soft, fair-spoken, dangerous knave.

MARCUS.

Some day he'll find his match!

ALTON.

Ay! you may swear to that;
Some woman versed in every social art,
Some rare, majestic creature, whose rich beauty
Will set his amorous senses in a blaze;
Slowly around him she will draw the net
Of fascinations, multiform and strange;
Enchant his fancy with her regal wit,
His taste with every charm of female guile,
Inflame him with voluptuous blandishments,
By turns, sooth, flatter, madden, vow she loves
At one delicious moment, then the next
As warmly swear she loathes him! by a spell
Invisible, but potent as the sun,
She'll lead him, fawning, quivering to her feet,
And at the last, O! consummation just!
When on the very brink of blest fruition,
He hovers, arms outstretched, and soul aglow,
She'll freeze to sudden marble, wave him off
With such calm haughtiness of queenly scorn,
Imperious, crushing, fatal, that, by heaven,
I should not wonder if the terrible sting
Of disappointment and deceived desires,
Of baffled passion, wounded self-conceit,
And hope so swiftly murdered by despair,
Struck to the core of being, and this man
Falser than hell to others, perished wholly,
By his own pestilent trickery done to death!

A CHARACTER.

A. He is a man whose complex character
Few can decipher rightly; but for me
I have found the key at last!

B. What make you of it?
A. As mournful and as blurred a page, perchance,
As ever pained the seeker after truth:
Listen! this man, when like a factory slave
I toiled for some bald pittance in the city,
Came to me (unsolicited, remember),
With words of cheer, and honeyed courtesies;
His tone was soft as dulcet airs of May;
His heart the very fount of sympathy!
"What," said he, "shall you grind your genius here,
Down to the last faint edge; waste your rich thoughts"
(Mark you the subtle flattery of this language),
"Upon a thankless, ignorant, brutal fool,
Who plays the patron with the grace of Bottom,
His ass's head from out your flowering fancies
Grinning in dull and idiot self-applauses;
By every gentle muse this shall not be!"
Straightway, with hand caressing as a woman's,
He led me from hard desk and stifling air,
Forth to his bowery home amid the hills,
There fed me, sir, on kindness, day by day,
Until this starved and tortured spirit grew
Healthy and hale again! No wish had I,
He did not hasten blithely to forestall!
He called me "brother," drew from shy reserves
Of knowledge, feeling, poesy, full stores
Of all my wealth — by heart or brain amassed —
Ha! by Apollo! what rare times were those
We spent in 'rapt communion with the bards
Each worshipped, and what jovial laughter shook
The flying night-winds, when our graver books
Were cast aside, and he an artful mimic,
A famed *raconteur*, many a humorous scene
Enacted with such raciness of wit
Despair itself had checked its tears — to smile;
In brief, by every wile a man could use
To knit his fellow's heart-strings to his own,
He made me love him! other friends were gone
Forlornly mouldering in far churchyard shades
And therefore — undivided, ardent, sure,
Affection centred all its warmths on him!

And now, when wholly his, I would have dared
For him all danger (you will scarce believe it),
But suddenly, as sometimes on calm seas,
The watcher from some lonely headland views
A gallant bark sink swiftly in the deep,
Dissolving like a vision — thus his friendship,
Its glittering flags of promise flaunting still
The tranquil sunlight, sunk before mine eyes
And left me gazing like a man distraught
Across the mocking solitude!
B. What more?
A. What more? Why, truly, sir, the tale is done.
'Twas a sharp close, I grant you, to a dream
Which rose so fairly; yet there's comfort in't!
B. Comfort!
A. Ay, ay! rare comfort in the thought
That tho' my years should reach the utmost verge
Of mortal life, I shall not dream again!

But pshaw! push on the bottle, 'tis the last
Of a full bin that constant friend of mine,
That loyal, noble, pure Samaritan,
Gave me, with vows of everduring love,
Three months ago at Christmas! Stay, a toast:
"Fair health, long life, immortal honor crown
The man who's constant only to — himself!"

MORALS OF DESPERATION.

THE man who's wholly ruined, sir, fears nothing;
How can he when all's lost to him already?
There is a desperate gayety which comes
To buoy one up in such a strait as this;
Under whose spell, it is a sort of witchcraft,
Men lose all sense of wrong, or rather take
Wrong for their right, rejoicing even in crime.
Faith, now, I'd hardly answer for myself,
If in some garden solitude, like this, sir,
At the hour of midnight (hark! the deep church tower
Is tolling twelve), haply I chanced to meet
A pompous millionaire, a man who staggers
Under his golden burden, like a ship
Reeling 'neath too much canvass; I should ease
My laboring comrade, thus and thus, of all
His glittering superfluities; this ring
Is a brave diamond, and will serve me bravely:
And ha! by Pluto! what a massive chain
Meanders like a miniature Pactolus
Across your worship's vest; my lord, no wonder
You grow asthmatic with a weight like that
Pressed on your gasping lungs; I'll free you from it;
And blessed saints! but here's a fair-knit purse,
And fairly filled, too! Shame it were in sooth
To keep this gift of your sweet paramour,
Therefore, behold me! I pour out this coin;
O Jesu! what rich music! but the purse
Duly return you! haste, your worship, haste,
Or else these itching palms will find fresh work
About your silken doublet, and bright hose,
Or those trussed points you needs must clasp with jewels;
Ay, haste, and take you comfort in the text
Which the wise Messer Salvatore Duomo
Dins in our ears each sacred Sabbath morning,
That "blessed, three times blessed, are the poor!"

THE CONDEMNED.

As in those lands of mighty mountain heights,
The streams, by sudden tempests overcharged,
Sweep down the slopes, bearing swift ruin with them,
So I and all my fortunes were engulf'd
In sudden, swift, complete destruction;
The morning found me happy, rich, contented,
But ere the sunset that black ruin came,
And stared me in the face.

Sir, I had reach'd
A stage of middle life, when chains of habit

Cannot be broken, save by giant wrenches,
When to be rudely hurled from life-long grooves
Of thought and progress, leaves the staunchest mind
Broken, amazed, despondent. What had I,
A scholar, recluse, dreamer, thou may'st say,
In common with the work-day world of men?

"Almighty Nature, the first law of God,
Perforce I followed."

Yet, goaded on by fierce necessity,
I sought work in the crowded haunts of cities,
Thinking to draw on knowledge as a bank,
Exhaustless, opulent, whereby all needs,
Not born of random, loose extravagance,
Would be assuredly answered. Ah! poor fool:
Too soon experience clove the shining mist
Of hopeful fantasy, and like a wind,
Sullen at first and slow, but raised ere long
To tempest-madness, rent the veil away

O'er which a steel-blue melancholy heaven
Glared on me, like a mocking eye in death:
Then came by turn mistrust, despondence, dread,
And last, despair, with frenzy; the brute instincts,
That sleep like tigers, jungled, in the blood,
With hale or pampered bodies, at the sting
Of loathsome famine, woke, and raged and tore,
Till Conscience, whose fair seat is in the soul,
Till Reason, whose deep life is in the brain,
Lay silent, murdered. A mere animal thing —
Hyena, tiger, wolf — whate'er thou wilt —
I seized my prey and rent it. What to me
The complex figments of your juggling laws ?
Nature with countless clamorous tongues cried out,
" Thou hungerest, diest; snatch thy food from fate,
Though 'twixt thee and the life-sustaining bread
A hundred sleek, smooth, sneering tyrants stand
Laughing to scorn thine untold agonies!"
Almighty Nature, the first law of God,
Perforce I followed; the false codes of man
Perforce I broke. And so, for this, for *this*,
Man's law that fain would run a tilt at God,
Its puny weapon shivering like a reed,
'Gainst the great bosses of Jehovah's buckler,
Appoints me death. Well, well, I fear not death,
Trusting that death, perchance, is but a night
Shorn of all morrow, a long, dreamless slumber,
O'er which the ages, hoar and solemn nurses,
Chant their majestic lullabies, that hold
Spells of oblivion; either thus, or I,
Whose life-sun rose in shadow, sets in blood,
Shall find a nobler being in some star
Beyond the silvery Pleiads.

Friend, thy hand;
Alone of all earth's creatures do I love thee:
Thee, and the little soft-eyed, pensive child,
Thy fairy daughter. Strange! but when I drink
Light from the founts of her large, serious eyes,
I seem to near a trembling, spiritual joy,
To thrill upon the utmost verge and brink
Of mystic revelations. Prithee, therefore,
Bring the fair child once more; I yearn to carry
The dream of her sweet, pitiful, angel's face,
To cheer the realm of shadows. Will she come ?

ANTIPATHIES.

Love is no product of the obedient will,
It hath its root in those deep sympathies,
Mere ties of blood are powerless to control;
I love thee not because around thy heart
An Arctic nature hath built up the ice
Of thawless winter: vain it is to strive
Against the law of just antipathies:
The Tropic sunlight burns not at the Poles,
Nor blooms the lustrous foliage of the East

Among the rocky, storm-bound Hebrides;
To all my gods thou art antipodal,
Therefore, again, good sir! I love thee not.

MISCONSTRUCTION.

How man misjudges man! the outward seeming,
Gesture, or glance, or utterance that may jar
Against some petty, pampered, poor conceit,
Unworthy, undefined, is straightway made
To prove a vast obliquity of soul,
And shallow disputants, with ponderous show
Of judgment that provokes the wise to scorn,
Exhort the virtuous by the foul abuse
Which damns them to the level of their speech.

POEMS OF THE WAR.

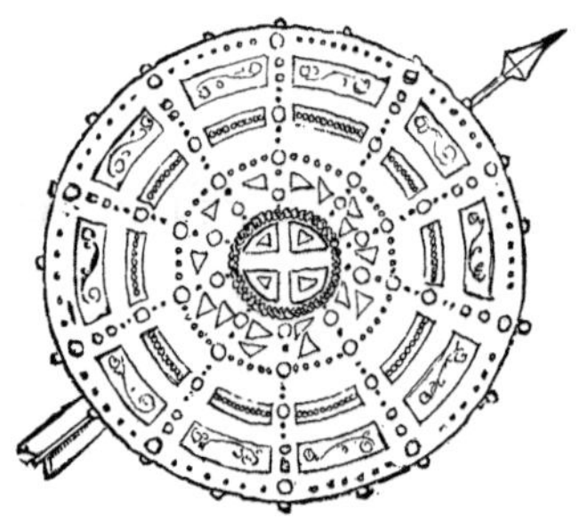

POEMS OF THE WAR.

1861–1865.

These poems are republished with no ill-feeling, nor with the desire to revive old issues; but only as a record and a sacred duty: —

"Fidelis ad urnam!"

MY MOTHER-LAND.

"Animis Opibusque Parati."

My Mother-land! thou wert the first to fling
Thy virgin flag of freedom to the breeze,
The first to front along thy neighboring seas,
The imperious foeman's power;
But long before that hour,
While yet, in false and vain imagining,
Thy sister nations would not own their foe,
And turned to jest thy warnings, though the low,
Portentous mutterings, that precede the throe
Of earthquakes, burdened all the ominous air;
While yet they paused in scorn,
Of fatal madness born,
Thou, oh, my mother! like a priestess bless'd
With wondrous vision of the things to come,
Thou couldst not calmly rest
Secure and dumb —
But from thy borders, with the sounds of drum
And trumpet rose the warrior-call,—
(A voice to thrill, to startle, to appall!)—
"Prepare! the time grows ripe to meet our doom!"
Thy careless sisters frowned, or mocking said:
"We see no threatening tempest overhead,
Only a few pale clouds, the west wind's breath
Will sweep away, or melt in watery death."

"Prepare! the time grows ripe to meet our doom!"
Alas! it was not till the thunder-boom
Of shell and cannon shocked the vernal day,
Which shone o'er Charleston Bay,*
That startled, roused, the last scale fallen away
From blinded eyes, our South, erect and proud,
Fronted the issue, and, though lulled too long,
Felt her great spirit nerved, her patriot valor strong.

. . . . .

Death! What of death? —
Can he who once drew honorable breath
In liberty's pure sphere,
Foster a sensual fear,
When death and slavery meet him face to face,

---

* Fort Sumter, March, 1861.

Saying: "Choose thou between us; here, the grace
Which follows patriot martyrdom, and there,
Black degradation, haunted by despair."

The very thought brings blushes to the cheek!
I hear all 'round about me murmurs run,
Hot murmurs, but soon merging into one
Soul-stirring utterance — hark! the people speak:

"Our course is righteous, and our aims are just!
Behold, we seek
Not merely to preserve for noble wives
The virtuous pride of unpolluted lives,
To shield our daughters from the servile hand,
And leave our sons their heirloom of command,
In generous perpetuity of trust;
Not only to defend those ancient laws,
Which Saxon sturdiness and Norman fire
Welded forevermore with freedom's cause,
And handed scathless down from sire to sire —
Nor yet our grand religion, and our Christ,
Unsoiled by secular hates, or sordid harms,
(Though these had sure sufficed
To urge the feeblest Sybarite to arms) —
But more than all, because embracing all,
Ensuring all, self-government, the boon
Our patriot statesmen strove to win and keep,
From prescient Pinckney and the wise Calhoun
To him, that gallant knight,
The youngest champion in the Senate hall,
Who, led and guarded by a luminous fate,
His armor, Courage, and his war-horse, Right,
Dared through the lists of eloquence to sweep
Against the proud Bois Guilbert of debate!*

"There's not a tone from out the teeming past,
Uplifted once in such a cause as ours,
Which does not smite our souls
In long reverberating thunder-rolls,
From the far mountain-steeps of ancient story,
Above the shouting, furious Persian mass,
Millions arrayed in pomp of Orient powers,
Rings the wild war-cry of Leonidas
Pent in his rugged fortress of the rock;
And o'er the murmurous seas,
Compact of hero-faith and patriot bliss
(For conquest crowns the Athenian's hope at last),
Come the clear accents of Miltiades,
Mingled with cheers that drown the battle-shock
Beside the wave-washed strand of Salamis.

"Where'er on earth the self-devoted heart
Hath been by worthy deeds exalted thus,
We look for proud exemplars; yet for us
It is enough to know
Our fathers left us freemen; let us show
The will to hold our lofty heritage,
The patient strength to act our father's part.

"Yea! though our children's blood
Rain 'round us in a crimson-swelling flood,

* *Vide* the Senatorial debate on "Foote's Resolution," in 1832.

Why pause or falter? — that red tide shall bear
The ark that holds our shrinèd liberty,
Nearer, and yet more near
Some height of promise o'er the ensanguined sea.

"At last, the conflict done,
The fadeless meed of final victory won,
Behold! emerging from the rifted dark
Athwart a shining summit high in heaven,
That delegated Ark!
No more to be by vengeful tempests driven,
But poised upon the sacred mount, whereat
The congregated nations gladly gaze,
Struck by the quiet splendor of the rays
That circle freedom's blood-bought Ararat!"

Thus spake the people's wisdom; unto me
Its voice hath come, a passionate augury!
Methinks the very aspect of the world
Changed to the mystic music of its hope.
For, lo! about the deepening heavenly cope
The stormy cloudland banners all are furled,
And softly borne above
Are brooding pinions of invisible love,
Distilling balm of rest and tender thought
From fairy realms, by fairy witchery wrought:
O'er the hushed ocean steal ethereal gleams
Divine as light that haunts an angel's dreams:
And universal nature, wheresoever
My vision strays — o'er sky, and sea, and river —
Sleeps, like a happy child,
In slumber undefiled,
A premonition of sublimer days,
When war and warlike lays
At length shall cease,
Before a grand Apocalypse of Peace,
Vouchsafed in mercy to all human kind —
A prelude and a prophecy combined!

ODE.

[In honor of the bravery and sacrifices of the soldiers of the South.]

WITH bayonets slanted in the glittering light,
With solemn roll of drums,
With star-lit banners rustling wings of might,
The knightly concourse comes!
The flower and fruit of all the tropic lands,
The unsheathed brightness of their stainless brands
Blazing in courtly hands,
One glorious soul within those thousand eyes,
One aim, one hope, one impulse from the skies,
While silent, awed and dumb,
A nation waits the end in dread surmise,
They come! they come!

The summer flaunts her vivid leaves above
The unwonted scene,
The summer heavens embrace with smiles of love
The hill-slopes green;
Far in the uppermost realms of silent air
Peace sits enthroned and happy, but on earth
The cymbals clash, and the shrill trumpets blare,
And Death, like some grim mower on the plain,
Topped by the ripened grain,
Whets his keen scythe, and shakes it fearfully!

Our serried lines march sternly to the front,
Where decked as if they rose to celebrate
A joyous festal morn,
In glistening pomp and splendid blazonry,
Slow moving as in scorn
Of those weak bands that guard the pass below,
Come gorgeous, flushed and proud, the cohorts of the foe!

They wheel! deploy, are stationed, down the cleft
Of the long gorge their signal thunders run!
A sullen answer echoes from our left
And the great fight's begun!
O! who shall picture the immortal fray?
Our Southern host that day
Breasted the onset of the invading sea
With wills of adamant; but stern-weighted strength,
Like waves by some infernal alchemy
Hardened, transformed to solid metal, burning
At white heat as they struck, and aye returning
Hotter and more resistless than before
(All flecked atop with foam of human gore),
Pierced here and there our crumbling ranks at length,
Which as a mountain shore,
Rock-ribbed and iron founded, still had stood,
And outward hurled
In bloody sprayings, that tremendous flood
Which, with wild charge and furious brunt on brunt,
Had dashed against us like a fiery world!

Unceasing still poured on the fateful tide,
And plumèd victory ever seemed to ride
On the red billows of the northland war!
Our glory and pride
Had fallen,—fallen in the terrible van,—
Like wine the life-streams ran;
"Back! back!" cried one (it was the voice of Bee,
Lifted in wrath and bitter agony),
"We're driven backward!" unto whom there came
An answer, like the rush of steady flame,
'Twixt ribs of iron, "We will give them yet
The bayonet!
The sharp edge of the Southern bayonet!"
At which the other's face flushed up, and caught
Light like a warrior-angel's, and he sprang
To the front rank, while swift as passionate thought
Leaped forth his sword, and this high summons rang:
"See! see! where fixed and grand,
Like a stone wall the braves of Jackson stand!
Forward!" and on he rushed with quivering breath,
On to his Spartan death!

Unceasing still poured down the fateful tide,
And plumèd victory ever seemed to ride
O'er the red billows of the northland war!
When faint and far,
Far on our left there rose a sound that thrilled
All souls, and even the battle's thunderous pulse
(Or so we deemed) for briefest space was stilled;
A sound, low hissing as a meteor-star,
But gathering depth of volume, till it burst
In one great flamelike cheer,
That seemed to rend and lift the cloud accurst,
The poisonous-clinging cloud
That wrapped us in its shroud,

While wounded men leaped on their feet to hear,
And dying men upraised their eyes to see
How on the conflict's lowering canopy,
Dawned the first rainbow hues of victory!

Have you watched the condor leap
From his proud Andean rock,
And with hurtling pinions sweep
On the valley-pasturing flock?
Have you watched an eygre vast
On the rude September blast
Roll adown with curvèd crest
O'er the low sands of the West?
O! thus and thus they came
(Four thousand men and more),
Hearts, faces, — all aflame,
And the grandeur of their wrath
Whirled the tyrant from their path
As the frightened rack is driven
By the unleashed winds in heaven;
Then, maddened, tossed about
In a reckless, hopeless rout,
The Northern army fled
O'er their dying and their dead,
And the Southern steel flashed out,
And their vengeful points were red
With the hot heart's tide that flowed
Where they sabred as they rode!
And the news sped on apace
(Where the Rulers, in their place,
Sat jubilant, one and all),
Till a shadow seemed to fall
Round their joyance like a pall,
And the inmost senate-hall
Pealed an echo of disgrace!
At the set of July's sun
They stood quivering and undone,
For the eagle standards waned and the Southern "stars" had won!

Thus loomed serene and large
Upon that desperate contest's lurid marge
Our orb of destiny; millions of hearts
Throb with bold exultation,
Till there starts
From mountain fastness, and from waving plain,
From wooded swamp and mist-encircled main,
From hamlet, city, field,
And the rich midland weald,
The spirit of the antique hero time!
O! 'twas a sight sublime
To watch the upheaval of the popular soul,
The stormy gathering, — the majestic roll
Upward of its wild forces, by the awe
Of Right and Justice steadied into law!
Faith lent our cause its heavenly consecration!
Hope its omnipotent might!
And Fame stood ready, with her flowers of light,
To crown alike the living and the dead,
While in the broadening firmament o'erhead
We seemed to read the fiat of our fate,
"Ye are baptized, — a Nation!
Amongst the freest, free, — amongst the mightiest, great!"
An ominous hush! and then the scattered clouds
In the dark northern heaven
(Clouds of a deadlier strife),
Urged by the poison wind
Of rage and rapine, sullenly combined,
Charged with the bolts of ruin! what were shrouds,
Crimsoned with gore? the widowed spirit riven?
The desecration of God's gift of life,
To that one thought (three fiery strands uniting,
Hot from a Hadéan loom),
"Conquest!" "Revenge!" Supremacy?" The blighting
Of untold promises, the grief, the gloom,
The desolate madness and the anguish blind,
All spreading on and on
From murdered sire to subjugated son,
Were less than nothing to the arrogant pride

Which treaties, compacts, honor, laws defied,
And aimed above the wrecks of temple and tower
To rear the symbols of its merciless power!

Four deadly years we fought,
Ringed by a girdle of unfaltering fire,
That coiled and hissed in lessening circles nigher.
Blood dyed the Southern wave;
From ocean border to calm inland river,
There was no pause, no peace, no respite ever.
Blood of our bravest brave
Drenched in a scarlet rain the western lea,
Swelled the hoarse waters of the Tennessee,
Incarnadined the gulfs, the lakes, the rills,
And from a hundred hills
Steamed in a mist of slaughter to the skies,
Shutting all hope of heaven from mortal eyes.
The Beaufort blooms were withered on the stem;
The fair gulf city in a single night
Lost her imperial diadem;
And wheresoe'er men's troubled vision sought,
They viewed MIGHT towering o'er the humbled crest of RIGHT!

But for a time, but for a time, O God!
The innate forces of our knightly blood
Rallied, and by the mount, the fen, the flood,
Upraised the tottering standards of our race.
O grand Virginia! though thy glittering glaive
Lies sullied, shattered in a ruthless grave,
How it flashed once! They dug their trenches deep
(The implacable foe), they ranged their lines of wrath;
But watchful ever on the imminent path
Thy steel-clad genius stood;
North, South, East, West, — they strove to pierce thy shield;
Thou would'st not yield!
Until, — unconquered, yea, unconquered still,
Nature's weakened forces answered not thy will,
And gored with wound on wound,
Thy fainting limbs and forehead sought the ground;
And with thee the young nation fell, a pall
Solemn and rayless, covering one and all!
God's ways are marvellous; here we stand to-day
Discrowned, and shorn, in wildest disarray,
The mock of earth! yet never shone the sun
On sterner deeds, or nobler victories won.
Not in the field alone; ah, come with me
To the dim bivouac by the winter's sea;
Mark the fair sons of courtly mothers crouch
O'er flickering fires; but gallant still, and gay
As on some bright parade; or mark the couch
In reeking hospitals, whereon is laid
The latest scion of a line perchance,
Whose veins were royal; close your blurred romance,
Blurred by the dropping of a maudlin tear,
And watch the manhood here;
That firm but delicate countenance,
Distorted sometimes by an awful pang,
Born in meek patience; when the trumpets rang
"To horse!" but yester-morn, that ardent boy

Sprung to his charger, thrilled with hope and joy
To the very finger-tips, and now he lies,
The shadows deepening in those falcon eyes,
But calm and undismayed,
As if the death that chills him, brow and breast,
Were some fond bride who whispered, "Let us rest!"

Enough! 'tis over! the last gleam of hope
Hath melted from our mournful horoscope,
Of all, of all bereft,
Only to us are left
Our buried heroes and their matchless deeds;
These cannot pass; they hold the vital seeds
Which in some far, untracked, unvisioned hour
May burst to vivid bud and glorious flower.
Meanwhile, upon the nation's broken heart
Her martyrs sleep. O! dearer far to her,
Than if each son, a wreathèd conqueror,
Rode in triumphant state
The loftiest crest of fate;
O! dearer far, because outcast and low,
She yearns above them in her awful woe.
One spring its tender blooms
Hath lavished richly by those hallowed tombs;
One summer its imperial largess spread
Along our heroes' bed;
One autumn wailing with funereal blast,
The withered leaves and pallid dust amassed
All round about them, till bleak winter now
Hangs hoar-frost on the grasses, and the bough
In dreary woodlands seems to thrill and start,
Thrill to the anguish of the wind that raves
Across those lonely desolated graves!

CHARLESTON.

Calmly beside her tropic strand,
An empress, brave and loyal,
I see the watchful city stand,
With aspect sternly royal;
She knows her mortal foe draws near,
Armored by subtlest science,
Yet deep, majestical, and clear,
Rings out her grand defiance.
Oh, glorious is thy noble face,
Lit up by proud emotion,
And unsurpassed thy stately grace,
Our warrior Queen of Ocean!

First from thy lips the summons came,
Which roused our South to action,
And, with the quenchless force of flame,
Consumed the demon, Faction;
First, like a rush of sovereign wind,
That rends dull waves asunder,
Thy prescient warning struck the blind,
And woke the deaf with thunder;
They saw, with swiftly kindling eyes,
The shameful doom before them,
And heard, borne wild from Northern skies,
The death-gale hurtling o'er them:

Wilt thou, whose virgin banner rose,
A morning star of splendor,
Quail when the war-tornado blows,
And crouch in base surrender?
Wilt thou, upon whose loving breast
Our noblest chiefs are sleeping,
Yield thy dead patriots' place of rest
To scornful alien keeping?
No! while a life-pulse throbs for fame,
Thy sons will gather round thee,
Welcome the shot, the steel, the flame,
If honor's hand hath crowned thee.

Then fold about thy beauteous form
The imperial robe thou wearest,
And front with regal port the storm
Thy foe would dream thou fearest;
If strength, and will, and courage fail
To cope with ruthless numbers,

And thou must bend, despairing, pale,
Where thy last hero slumbers,
Lift the red torch, and light the fire
Amid those corpses gory,
And on thy self-made funeral pyre,
Pass from the world to glory.

STUART.

A CUP of your potent "mountain dew,"
By the camp-fire's ruddy light;
Let us drink to a spirit as leal and true
As ever drew blade in fight,
And dashed on the foeman's lines of steel,
For God and his people's right.

By heaven! it seems that his very name
Embodies a thought of fire;
It strikes on the ear with a sense of flame,
And the life-blood boundeth higher,
While the pulses leap and the brain expands,
In the glow of a grand desire.

Hark! in the day-dawn's misty gray,
Our bugles are ringing loud,
And hot for the joy of a coming fray,
Our souls wax fierce and proud,
As we list for the word that shall launch us forth,
Like bolts from the mountain-cloud.

We list for the word, and it comes at length,
In a strain so mighty and clear,
That we rise to the sound with an added strength,
And our hearts are glad to hear,
And a stir, like the breath of the boding storm
Thrills through us, from van to rear.

Then, with the rush of the whirlwind freed,
We rush, by a secret way,
And merry on sabre, and helmet, and steed,
Do the autumn sunbeams play,
And the devil must sharpen his keenest wits,
To rescue "his own" to-day.

Ho, ye who dwell in the fertile vales
Of the pleasant land of Penn,
Who feast on the fat of her fruitful dales,
How little ye dream or ken
That the southern Murat has bared his brand,
That the Stuart rides again.

"Close up, close up! we have travelled long,
But a jovial night's in store,
A night of wassail, and wit, and song,
In yon cosy town before.
Quick, sergeant! spur to the front in haste,
And knock at the mayor's door."

Behold, he comes with a ghost-like grace,
And his knee-joints out of tune;
And the cold, cold sweat runs down his face,
I' the light of the autumn moon,
While his husky voice, like an ancient crone's,
Dies in a hollow croon.

He cannot speak; but his buxom dame,
With her trembling daughters nigh,
Shrieks out, "Oh, honor their virgin fame,
Pass the poor maidens by."
(Whereon, with a grievous heave and sob,
She paused in her speech — to cry.)

"Rise up! we leave to the churlish brood
Our vengeance hath sought ere now,
The fame which springs from the ruthless mood
That crimsons a woman's brow;
For sons are we of a kindly race,
And bound by a knightly vow.

"Rise up! we war with the strong alone;
For where was the caitiff found,
To sport with an outraged woman's moan,
Where the southern trumpets sound?

. . . . . .

"Enough! while I speak of the past, my lad,
There's coming — (hush! lean thee near!) —
There's coming a raid that shall drive them mad,
And cover their land with fear;
And you and I, by the blessing of God,
Ay, you and I shall be there."

"They arose with the sun, and caught life from his light."

BEYOND THE POTOMAC.

THEY slept on the field which their valor had won,
But arose with the first early blush of the sun,
For they knew that a great deed remained to be done,
When they passed o'er the river.

They arose with the sun, and caught life from his light,
Those giants of courage, those Anaks in fight,
And they laughed out aloud in the joy of their might,
Marching swift for the river.

On, on! like the rushing of storms through the hills;
On, on! with a tramp that is firm as their wills;
And the one heart of thousands grows buoyant, and thrills,
At the thought of the river.

Oh, the sheen of their swords! the fierce gleam of their eyes!
It seemed as on earth a new sunlight would rise,
And, king-like, flash up to the sun in the skies,
O'er their path to the river.

But their banners, shot-scarred, and all darkened with gore,
On a strong wind of morning streamed wildly before,
Like wings of death-angels swept fast to the shore,
The green shore of the river.

As they march, from the hillside, the hamlet, the stream,
Gaunt throngs whom the foemen had manacled, teem,
Like men just aroused from some terrible dream,
To cross sternly the river.

They behold the broad banners, blood-darkened, yet fair,
And a moment dissolves the last spell of despair,
While a peal, as of victory, swells on the air,
Rolling out to the river.

And that cry, with a thousand strange echoings, spread,
Till the ashes of heroes were thrilled in their bed,
And the deep voice of passion surged up from the dead,
"*Ay, press on to the river!*"

On, on! like the rushing of storms through the hills,
On, on! with a tramp that is firm as their wills;
And the one heart of thousands grows buoyant and thrills,
As they pause by the river.

Then the wan face of Maryland, haggard and worn,
At this sight lost the touch of its aspect forlorn,
And she turned on the foemen, full-statured in scorn,
Pointing stern to the river.

And Potomac flowed calmly, scarce heaving her breast,
With her low-lying billows all bright in the west,
For a charm as from God lulled the waters to rest
Of the fair rolling river.

Passed! passed! the glad thousands march safe through the tide;
Hark, foeman, and hear the deep knell of your pride,
Ringing weird-like and wild, pealing up from the side
Of the calm-flowing river.

'Neath a blow swift and mighty the tyrant may fall;
Vain, vain! to his gods swells a desolate call;
Hath his grave not been hollowed, and woven his pall,
Since they passed o'er the river?

BEAUREGARD'S APPEAL.

YEA! since the need is bitter,
Take down those sacred bells,
Whose music speaks of hallowed joys,
And passionate farewells!

But ere ye fall dismantled,
  Ring out, deep bells! once more:
And pour on the waves of the passing
      wind
  The symphonies of yore.

Let the latest born be welcomed
  By pealings glad and long,
Let the latest dead in the churchyard
      bed
  Be laid with solemn song.

And the bells above them throbbing,
  Should sound in mournful tone,
As if, in grief for a human death,
  They prophesied their own.

Who says 'tis a desecration
  To strip the temple towers,
And invest the metal of peaceful notes
  With death-compelling powers?

A truce to cant and folly!
  Our people's ALL at stake,
Shall we heed the cry of the shallow
      fool,
  Or pause for the bigot's sake?

Then crush the struggling sorrow!
  Feed high your furnace fires,
And mould into deep-mouthed guns of
      bronze,
  The bells from a hundred spires.

Methinks no common vengeance,
  No transient war eclipse,
Will follow the awful thunder-burst
  From their adamantine lips.

A cause like ours is holy,
  And it useth holy things;
While over the storm of a righteous
      strife,
  May shine the angel's wings.

Where'er our duty leads us,
  The grace of God is there,
And the lurid shrine of war may hold
  The Eucharist of prayer.

THE SUBSTITUTE.

[THE crime of McNeil, perpetrated in one of our Western States, has now met with the reprobation of Christendom. But at the time the following verses — cast, as the reader will perceive, in a partly dramatic mould — were composed, *ten* Confederates had been hastily executed by order of a Federal commander, on a charge afterwards proven to be false; and *one* of the unfortunate victims (a mere youth) voluntarily sacrificed his life to rescue his friend, a man advanced in years and with a large family.

In the poem this latter individual is represented as unaware of the youth's resolve until it has been executed.

Between the first and second parts of the piece, about *twenty-four hours* are supposed to have elapsed.]

PART I.

[PLACE — *A Federal Prison — A Confederate chained, and a Visitor, his Friend.*]

"How say'st thou? die to-morrow?
      Oh! my friend!
  The bitter, bitter doom!
What hast thou done to tempt this
      ghastly end —
  This death of shame and gloom?"

"What done? Do tyrants wait for
      guilty deeds,
  To find or prove a crime —
They, who have cherished hatred's fiery
      seeds:
  Hot for the harvest-time?

"A sneer! a smile! vague trifles light as
      air —
  Some foolish, false surmise —
Lead to the harrowing drama of despair
  Wherein — the victim dies!

"And I shall perish! Comrade, heed
      me not!
  For thus my tears must start —
Not for the misery of my blasted lot,
  But hers who holds my heart!

"And theirs, the flowers that wreathe
      my humble hearth
  With roseate blush and bloom.

To-morrow eve, they stand alone on earth,
Beside their father's tomb!

"There's Blanche, my serious beauty, lithe and tall,
With pensive eyes and brow —
There's Kate, the tenderest darling of them all,
Whose kisses thrill me now!

"There's little Rose, the sunshine of our days —
A tricky, gladsome sprite —
How vividly come back her winsome ways,
Her laughters, and delight!

"And my brave boy — my Arthur! Did his arm
Second his will and brain,
I should not groan beneath this iron charm,
Clasping my chains in vain!

"Oh, Christ! and hath it come to this? Will none
Ward off the ghastly end?
And yet methinks I heard the voice of one
Who called the old man — Friend!

"May all the curses caught from deepest hell
Light on the blood-stained knave
Who laughs to hear the patriot's funeral knell,
Blaspheming o'er his grave!

"Away! Such dreams are madness! My pale lips
Had best besiege Heaven's ear,
But in the turmoil of my mind's eclipse,
No thought, no wish is clear.

"Dear friend, forgive me! Sorrow, frenzy, ire —
My bosom's raging guests —
By turn have whelmed me in their floods of fire,
Fierce passions, swift unrests.

"And now, farewell! The sentry's warning hand,
Taps at my prison bars.
We part, but not forever! There's a land,
Comrade, beyond the stars!"

"Yea!" said the youth, and o'er his kindling face
A saint-like glory came,
As if some prescient Angel, breathing grace,
Had touched it into flame.

PART II.

[PLACE — *The same Prison.* PERSONS — *Confederate Prisoner, together with McNeil and the Jailer.*]

The hours sink slow to sunset! Suddenly
Rose a deep, gathering hum;
And o'er the measured stride of soldiery
Rolled out the muffled drum!

The prisoner started! crushed a stifling sigh,
Then rose erect and proud!
Scorn's lightning quivering in his stormy eye,
'Neath the brow's thunder-cloud!

And girding round his limbs and stalwart breast
Each iron chain and ring,
He stood sublime, imperial, self-possessed —
And haughty as a king!

The "dead march" wails without the prison gate
Up the calm evening sky;
And ruffian jestings, born of ruffian hate,
Make loud, unmeet reply!

The hired bravoes, whose pitiless features pale
In front of armed men,
But whose *magnanimous* courage will not quail
Where none can strike again!

"The flowers that wreathe my humble hearth
With roseate blush and bloom."

The "dead march" wails without the prison wall,
Up the calm evening sky:
And timed to the dread dirge's rise and fail,
Move the fierce murderers by!

They passed; and wondering at his doom deferred,
The captive's lofty fire
Sank in his heart, by torturing memories stirred
Of husband, and of sire!

But hark! the clash of bolt and opening door!
The tramp of hostile heel!
When lo! upon the darkening prison floor,
Glared the false hound — McNeil.

And next him, like a bandog scenting blood,
Roused from his drunken ease,
The grimy, low-browed jailer glowering stood,
Clanking his iron keys.

"Quick! jailer! strike yon rebel's fetters off,
And let the old fool see
What ransom [with a low and bitter scoff],
What ransom sets him free."

As the night traveller in a land of foes
The warning instinct feels,
That through the treacherous dimness and repose
A shrouded horror steals.

So, at these veilèd words, the captive's soul
Shook with a solemn dread,
And ghostly voices, prophesying dole,
Moaned faintly overhead.

His limbs are freed! his swarthy, scowling guide
Leads through the silent town,
Where from dim casements, black with wrathful pride,
Stern eyes gleam darkly down.

They halted where the woodland showered around
Dank leaflets on the sod,
And all the air seemed vocal with the sound
Of wild appeals to God.

Heaped, as if common carrion, in the gloom,
Nine mangled corpses lay —
All speechless now — but with what tongues of doom
Reserved for judgment day.

And near them, but apart, one youthful form
Pressed a fair upland slope,
O'er whose white brow a sunbeam flickering warm,
Played like a heavenly hope.

There, with the same grand look which yester-night
That face at parting wore,
The self-made martyr in the sunset light
Slept on his couch of gore.

The sunset waned; the wakening forest waved,
Struck by the north wind's moan,
While he, whose life this matchless death has saved
Knelt by the corse — alone.

BATTLE OF CHARLESTON HARBOR,

April 7, 1863.

Two hours, or more, beyond the prime of a blithe April day,
The Northmen's mailed "Invincibles" steamed up fair Charleston Bay;
They came in sullen file, and slow, low-breasted on the wave,
Black as a midnight front of storm, and silent as the grave.

A thousand warrior-hearts beat high as these dread monsters drew
More closely to the game of death across the breezeless blue,
And twice ten thousand hearts of those who watch the scene afar,
Thrill in the awful hush that bides the battle's broadening star.

Each gunner, moveless by his gun, with rigid aspect stands,
The reedy linstocks firmly grasped in bold, untrembling hands,
So moveless in their marble calm, their stern, heroic guise,
They look like forms of statued stone with burning human eyes!

Our banners on the outmost walls, with stately rustling fold,
Flash back from arch and parapet the sunlight's ruddy gold—
They mount to the deep roll of drums, and widely echoing cheers,
And then, once more, dark, breathless, hushed, wait the grim cannoneers.

Onward, in sullen file, and slow, low-glooming on the wave,
Near, nearer still, the haughty fleet glides silent as the grave,
When shivering the portentous calm o'er startled flood and shore,
Broke from the sacred Island Fort the thunder wrath of yore! *

The storm has burst! and while we speak, more furious, wilder, higher,
Dart from the circling batteries a hundred tongues of fire;
The waves gleam red, the lurid vault of heaven seems rent above—
Fight on, oh, knightly gentlemen! for faith, and home, and love!

* Fort Moultrie.

There's not, in all that line of flame, one soul that would not rise,
To seize the victor's wreath of blood, though death must give the prize;
There's not, in all this anxious crowd that throngs the ancient town,
A maid who does not yearn for power to strike one foeman down!

The conflict deepens! ship by ship the proud Armada sweeps,
Where fierce from Sumter's raging breast the volleyed lightning leaps,
And ship by ship, raked, overborne, 'ere burned the sunset light,
Crawls in the gloom of baffled hate beyond the field of fight!

CHARLESTON AT THE CLOSE OF 1863.

WHAT! still does the mother of treason uprear
Her crest 'gainst the furies that darken her sea,
Unquelled by mistrust, and unblanched by a fear,
Unbowed her proud head, and unbending her knee,
Calm, steadfast and free!

Ay! launch your red lightnings! blaspheme in your wrath!
Shock earth, wave, and heaven with the blasts of your ire;
But she seizes your death-bolts yet hot from their path,
And hurls back your lightnings and mocks at the fire
Of your fruitless desire!

Ringed round by her brave, a fierce circlet of flame
Flashes up from the sword-points that cover her breast;
She is guarded by love, and enhaloed by fame,

And never, we swear, shall your foot-
steps be pressed,
Where her dead heroes rest.

Her voice shook the tyrant, sublime from
her tongue
Fell the accents of warning! a prophet-
ess grand —
On her soil the first life notes of liberty
rung,
And the first stalwart blow of her
gauntleted hand
Broke the sleep of her land.

What more? she hath grasped in her
iron-bound will
The fate that would trample her honors
to earth;
The light in those deep eyes is luminous
still
With the warmth of her valor, the
glow of her worth,
Which illumine the earth.

And beside her a knight the great Bayard
had loved,
"Without fear or reproach," lifts her
banner on high;
He stands in the vanguard majestic, un-
moved,
And a thousand firm souls when that
chieftain is nigh,
Vow "'tis easy to die!"

Their words have gone forth on the fet-
terless air,
The world's breath is hushed at the
conflict! Before
Gleams the bright form of Freedom, with
wreaths in her hair —
And what though the chaplet be crim-
soned with gore —
We shall prize her the more!

And while Freedom lures on with her
passionate eyes
To the height of her promise, the
voices of yore
From the storied profound of past ages
arise,
And the pomps of their magical music
outpour
O'er the war-beaten shore!

Then gird your brave empress, O heroes!
with flame
Flashed up from the sword-points that
cover her breast!
She is guarded by Love and enhaloed by
Fame,
And never, stern foe! shall your foot-
steps be pressed
Where her dead martyrs rest!

SCENE IN A COUNTRY HOSPITAL.

HERE, lonely, wounded and apart,
From out my casement's glimmering
round,
I watch the wayward bluebirds dart
Across yon flowery ground;
How sweet the prospect! and how fair
The balmy peace of earth and air.

But, lowering over fields afar,
A red cloud breaks with sulphurous
breath,
And well I know what gory star,
Is regnant in his house of death;
Yet faint the conflict's gathering roll,
To the fierce tempest in my soul.

I, who the foremost ranks had led,
To strike for cherished home and land,
Groan idly on this torturing bed,
With broken frame and palsied hand,
So nerveless, 'tis a task to scare,
The insects fluttering round my hair.

O God! for one brief hour again,
Of that grim joy my spirit knew,
When foemen's life-blood poured like
rain,
And sabres flashed and trumpets blew:
One hour to smite, or smitten die
On the wild breast of victory!

It may not be; my pulses beat
  Too feebly, and my heart is chill.
Death, like a thief with stealthy feet
  Draws nigh to work his ruthless will;
Hope, Honor, Glory, pass me by,
But *he* stands near with mocking eye!

Ay, smooth the couch! — pour out the draught,
  That, haply, for a season's space,
Hath power to charm his fatal shaft,
  And warn the death-damps off my face,
A blest reprieve! — a wondrous boon,
Thank Heaven! this — all — ends with me soon.

VICKSBURG. — A BALLAD.

For sixty days and upwards,
  A storm of shell and shot
Rained round us in a flaming shower,
  But still we faltered not.
"If the noble city perish,"
  Our grand young leader said,
"Let the only walls the foe shall scale
  "Be ramparts of the dead!"

For sixty days and upwards,
  The eye of heaven waxed dim;
And e'en throughout God's holy morn,
  O'er Christian prayer and hymn,
Arose a hissing tumult,
  As if the fiends in air
Strove to engulf the voice of faith
  In the shrieks of their despair.

There was wailing in the houses,
  There was trembling on the marts,
While the tempest raged and thundered,
  'Mid the silent thrill of hearts;
But the Lord, our shield, was with us,
  And ere a month had sped,
Our very women walked the streets
  With scarce one throb of dread.

And the little children gambolled,
  Their faces purely raised,
Just for a wondering moment,
  As the huge bombs whirled and blazed,
Then turned with silvery laughter
  To the sports which children love,
Thrice-mailed in the sweet, instinctive thought
  That the good God watched above.

Yet the hailing bolts fell faster,
  From scores of flame-clad ships,
And about us, denser, darker,
  Grew the conflict's wild eclipse,
Till a solid cloud closed o'er us,
  Like a type of doom and ire,
Whence shot a thousand quivering tongues
  Of forked and vengeful fire.

But the unseen hands of angels
  Those death-shafts warned aside,
And the dove of heavenly mercy
  Ruled o'er the battle tide;
In the houses ceased the wailing,
  And through the war-scarred marts
The people strode, with step of hope,
  To the music in their hearts.

THE LITTLE WHITE GLOVE.

The early springtime faintly flushed the earth,
And in the woods, and by their favorite stream
The fair, wild roses blossomed modestly,
Above the wave that wooed them: there at eve,
Philip had brought the woman that he loved,
And told his love, and bared his burning heart.
She, Constance, — the shy sunbeams trembling oft,
Through dewy leaves upon her golden hair, —
Made him no answer, tapped her pretty foot,
And seemed to muse: "To-morrow I depart,"
Said Philip, sadly, "for wild fields of war;

Shall I go girt with love's invisible mail,
Stronger than mortal armor, or, all stripped
Of love and hope, march reckless unto death?'

A soft mist filled her eyes, and overflowed
In sudden rain of passion, as she stretched
Her delicate hand to his, and plighted troth,

"And by their favorite stream,
The fair, wild roses blossomed modestly
Above the wave that wooed them."

With lips more rosy than the sun-bathed flowers;
And Philip pressed the dear hand fervently,
Wherefrom in happy mood, he gently drew
A small white glove, and ere she guessed his will,
Clipped lightly from her head one golden curl,
And bound the glove, and placed it next his heart.

"Now I am safe," cried Philip; "this pure charm
Is proof against all hazard or mischance.
Here, yea, unto this self-same spot I vow
To bring it stainless back; and you shall wear
This little glove upon our marriage eve."
And Constance heard him, smiling through her tears.

Another springtime faintly flushed the earth,
And in the woods, and by their favorite stream,
The fair, wild roses blossomed modestly
Above the wave that wooed them: there at eve
Came a pale woman with wild, wandering eyes,
And tangled, golden ringlets, and weak steps
Tottering towards the streamlet's rippling marge,
She seemed phantasmal, shadowy, like the forms

By moonlight conjured up from a place of graves;
There, crouching o'er the stream, she laved and laved
Some object in it, with a strained regard.
And muttered fragments of distempered words,
Whereof were these: "He vowed to bring it back,
The love-charm that I gave him — my white glove —
Stainless and whole. He has not kept his oath!
Oh, Philip, Philip! have you cast me off,
Off, like this worthless thing you send me home,
Tattered and mildewed? Look you! what a rent,
Right through the palm! It cannot be my glove;
And look again; what horrid stain is here?
My glove; you placed it next your heart, and swore
To keep it safe, and on this self-same spot,
Return it to me on our marriage eve;
And now — and now — I *know* 'tis not my glove, —
Yet Philip, sweet! it was a cruel jest,
You surely did not mean to fright me thus?
For hark you! as I laved the loathsome thing,
To see what stain defiled it — (do not smile,
I feel that I am foolish, foolish, Philip) —
But, God of Heaven! I dreamed that stain was *blood!*"

STONEWALL JACKSON.

The fashions and the forms of men decay,
The seasons perish, the calm sunsets die,
Ne'er with the *same* bright pomp of cloud or ray
To flush the golden pathways of the sky;
All things are lost in dread eternity, —
States, empires, creeds, the lay
Of master poets, even the shapes of love,
Bear ever with them an invisible shade,
Whose name is Death; we cannot breathe nor move,
But that we touch the darkness, till dismayed,
We feel the imperious shadow freeze our hearts,
And mortal hope grows pale and fluttering life departs.
All things are lost in dread eternity,
Save that majestic virtue which is given
Once, twice, perchance beneath our earthly heaven,
To some great soul in ages: O! the lie,
The base, incarnate lie we call the world,
Shakes at his coming, as the forest shakes,
When mountain storms, with bannered clouds unfurled,
Rush down and rend it; sleek convention drops
Its glittering mass, and hoary, cobwebbed rules
Of petty charlatans or insolent fools
Shrink to annihilation, — Truth awakes,
A morning splendor in her fearless eyes,
Touching the delicate stops
Of some rare lute which breathes of promise fair,
Or pouring on the covenanted air
A trumpet blast which startles, but makes strong,
While ancient Wrong,
Driven like a beast from his deep-caverned lair,
Grows gaunt, and inly quakes,
Knowing that retribution draws so near!

Whether with blade or pen
Toil these immortal men,
Theirs is the light supreme, which genius wed
To a clear spiritual dower.

Hath ever o'er the arousèd nations shed
Joy, faith, and power;
Whether from wrestling with the god-like thought,
They launch a noiseless blessing on mankind,
Or through wild streams of terrible carnage brought,
No longer crushed and blind,
Trampled, dishevelled, gored,
They proudly lift, where kindling soul and eye
May feast upon her beauty as she stands
(Girt by the strength of her invincible bands),
And freed through keen redemption of the sword,
Thy worn, but radiant form, victorious Liberty!

We bow before this grandeur of the spirit;
We worship, and adore
God's image burning through it evermore;
And thus, in awed humility to-night,*
As those who at some vast cathedral door
Pause with hushed faces, purified desires,
We contemplate his merit,
Who lifted failure to the heights of fame,
And by the side of fainting, dying right,
Stood, as Sir Galahad pure, Sir Lancelot brave,
The quick, indignant fires
Flushing his pale brow from the passionate mind
No strength could quell, no sophistry could bind,
Until that moment, big with mystic doom
(Whose issue sent
O'er the long wastes of half a continent
Electric shudders through the deepening gloom),
When in his knightly glory "Stonewall" fell,
And all our hearts sank with him; for we knew
Our staff, our bulwark broken, the fine clew
To freedom snapped, his hands had held alone,
Through all the storms of battle overblown, —
Lost, buried, mouldering in our hero's grave.

O soul! so simple, yet sublime!
With faith as large, and mild
As that of some benignant, trustful child,
Who mounts to heaven on bright, ethereal stairs
Of tender-worded prayers, —
Yet strong as if a Titan's force were there
To rise, to act, to suffer, and to dare, —
O soul! that on our time
Wrought, in the calm magnificence of power
To ends *so* noble, that an antique light
Of grace and virtue streamed along thy way,
Until the direst hour
Of carnage caught from that immaculate ray
A consecration, and a sanctity!
Thou art not dead, thou nevermore canst die,
But wide and far,
Where'er on Christian realms the morning star
Flames round the spires that tower towards the sky, —
Thy name, a household word,
In cottage homes, by palace walls, is heard,
Breathed with low murmurs, reverentially!

Even as I raise this faltering song to one,
Who now beyond the empires of the sun,

* This Ode was originally written to be delivered before a Southern patriotic association.

Looks down perchance upon our mournful sphere,
With the deep pity of seraphic eyes,
Fancy unveils the future, and I see
Millions on millions, as year follows year,
Gather around our warrior's place of rest
In the green shadows of Virginian hills;
Not with the glow of martial blazonry,
With trump and muffled drum,
Those pilgrim millions come,
But with bowed heads, and measured footsteps slow,
As those who near the presence of a shrine,
And feel an air divine,
All round about them blandly, sweetly blow,
While like dream-music the faint fall of rills,
Lapsing from steep to steep,
The wood-dove 'plaining in her covert deep,
And the long whisperings of the ghostly pine
(Like ocean-breathings borne from tides of sleep),
With every varied melody expressed
In Nature's score of solemn harmonies,
Blends with a feeling in the reverent breast
Which cannot find a voice in mortal speech,
So deep, so deep it lies beyond the reach
Of stammering words, — the pilgrims only know
That slumbering, O! so calmly there, below
The dewy grass, the melancholy trees,
Moulders the dust of him,
By whose crystalline fame, earth's scarlet pomps grow dim,
The crownèd heir
Of two majestic immortalities,
That which is earthly, and yet scarce of earth,
Whose fruitful seeds
Were his own grand, self-sacrificing deeds,
And that whose awful birth
Flowered into instant perfectness sublime,
When done with toil and time,
He shook from off the raiments of his soul,
The weary conflict's desecrating dust,
For stern *reveillés*, heard the angels sing,
For battle turmoils found eternal calm,
Laid down his sinless sword to clasp the palm,
And where vast heavenly organ-notes outroll
Melodious thunders, 'mid the rush of wing,
And flash of plume celestial, paused in peace,
A rapture of ineffable release
To know the long fruition of the just!

SONNETS.

I.

ON THE CHIVALRY OF THE PRESENT TIME.

Ah! foolish souls and false! who loudly cried
"True chivalry no longer breathes in time."
Look round us now; how wondrous, how sublime
The heroic lives we witness; far and wide,
Stern vows by sterner deeds are justified;
Self abnegation, calmness, courage, power,
Sway with a rule august, our stormy hour,
Wherein the loftiest hearts have wrought and died —
Wrought grandly, and died smiling. Thus, oh God,
From tears, and blood, and anguish, thou hast brought
The ennobling act, the faith-sustaining thought —
'Till in the marvellous present, one may see

A mighty stage, by knight and patriots trod,
Who had not shunned earth's haughtiest chivalry.

II.

ELLIOTT IN FORT SUMTER.

AND high amongst these chiefs of iron grain,
Large-statured natures, souls of Spartan mien,
Superbly brave, inflexibly serene,
Man of the stalwart hope, the sleepless brain.
Well dost thou guard our fortress by the main!
And what, though inch by inch old Sumter falls,
There's not a stone that forms those sacred walls,
But holds a tongue, which shall not speak in vain!
A tongue that tells of such heroic mood,
Such nerved endurance, such immaculate will,
That after times shall hearken and grow still,
With breathless admiration, and on thee
(Whose stern resolve our glorious cause made good).
Confer an antique immortality!

OUR MARTYRS.

I AM sitting alone and weary,
  By the hearth of my darkened room,
And the low wind's *miserere*,
  Makes sadder the midnight gloom.
"There's a nameless terror nigh me—
  There's a phantom spell on the air,
And methinks, that the dead glide by me,
  And the breath of the grave's in my hair!"

'Tis a vision of ghastly faces,
  All pallid and worn with pain,
Where the splendor of manful graces
  Shines dim thro' a scarlet rain:—
In a wild and weird procession
  They sweep by my startled eyes,
And stern with their Fate's fruition,
  Seem melting in blood-red skies.

Have they come from the shores supernal;
  Have they passed from the spirit's goal,
'Neath the veil of the life eternal
  To dawn on my shrinking soul?
Have they turned from the choiring angels,
  Aghast at the woe and dearth,
That war with his dark evangels
  Hath wrought in the loved of earth?

Vain dream! amid far-off mountains
  They lie where the dew mists weep,
And the murmur of mournful fountains
  Breathes over their painless sleep;
On the breast of the lonely meadows
  Safe, safe, from the despot's will,
They rest in the starlit shadows,
  And their brows are white and still,

Alas! for our heroes perished!
  Cut down at their golden prime,
With the luminous hopes they cherished,
  On the height of their faith sublime!
For them is the voice of wailing
  And the sweet blush-rose departs.
From the cheeks of the maidens paling
  O'er the wreck of their broken hearts.

And alas! for the vanished glory
  Of a thousand household spells!
And alas! for the tearful story
  Of the spirit's fond farewells!
By the flood, on the field, in the forest,
  Our bravest have yielded breath,
Yet the shafts that have smitten the sorest,
  Were launched by a viewless death.

Oh, Thou! that hast charms of healing,
  Descend on a widowed land,
And bind o'er the wounds of feeling,
  The balms of thy mystic hand;

Till the lives that lament and languish,
Renewed by a touch divine,
From the depths of their mortal anguish,
May rise to the calm of Thine.

FORGOTTEN.

Forgotten! Can it be a few swift rounds
Of Time's great chariot wheels have crushed to naught
The memory of those fearful sights and sounds,
With speechless misery fraught —
Wherethro' we hope to gain the Hesperian height,
Where Freedom smiles in light?

Forgotten! scarce have two dim autumns veiled
With merciful mist those dreary burial sods,
Whose coldness (when the high-strung pulses failed,
Of men who strove like gods)
Wrapped in a sanguine fold of senseless dust
Dead hearts and perished trust!

Forgotten! While in far-off woodland dell,
By lonely mountain tarn and murmuring stream,
Bereavèd hearts with sorrowful passion swell —
Their lives one ghastly dream
Of hope outwearied and betrayed desire,
And anguish crowned with fire!

Forgotten! while our manhood cursed with chains,
And pilloried high for all the world to view,
Writhes in its fierce, intolerable pains,
Decked with dull wreaths of rue,
And shedding blood for tears, hands waled with scars,
Lifts to the dumb, cold stars!

Forgotten! Can the dancer's jocund feet
Flash o'er a charnel-vault, and maidens fair
Bend the white lustre of their eyelids sweet,
Love-weighed, so nigh despair,
Its ice-cold breath must freeze their blushing brows,
And hush love's tremulous vows?

Forgotten! Nay: but all the songs we sing
Hold under-burdens, wailing chords of woe;
Our lightest laughters sound with hollow ring,
Our bright wit's freest flow,
Quavers to sudden silence of affright,
Touched by an untold blight!

Forgotten! No! we cannot all forget,
Or, when we do, farewell to Honor's face,
To Hope's sweet tendance, Valor's unpaid debt,
And every noblest Grace,
Which, nursed in Love, might still benignly bloom
Above a nation's tomb!

Forgotten! Tho' a thousand years should pass,
Methinks our air will throb with memory's thrills,
A conscious grief weigh down the faltering grass,
A pathos shroud the hills,
Waves roll lamenting, autumn sunsets yearn
For the old time's return!

LEGENDS AND LYRICS.

LEGENDS AND LYRICS.

1865–1872.

DAPHLES.

AN ARGIVE STORY.

ONCE on the throne of Argos sat a maid,
Daphles the fair; serene and unafraid
She ruled her realm, for the rough folk were brought
To worship one they deemed divinely wrought
In beauty and mild graciousness of heart:
Nobles and courtiers, too, espoused her part,
So that the sweet young face all thronged to see,
Glanced from her throne-room's silken canopy
(Broidered with leaves, and many a snow-white dove),
Rosily conscious of her people's love.
Only the chief of a far frontier clan,
A haughty, bold, ambitious nobleman,
By law her vassal, but self-sworn to be
From subject-tithe and tribute boldly free,
And scorning most this weak girl-sovereign's reign,
Now from the mountain fastness to the plain
Summoned his savage legions to the fight, —
Wherein he hoped to wrench the imperial might
From Daphles, and confirm his claim thereto.
But Doracles, the insurgent chief, could know
Naught of the secret charm, the subtle stress
Of beauty wed to warm unselfishness,
Which, in her hour of trial, wrapped the Queen
Safely apart in golden air serene
Of deep devotion, and fond faith of those
The steadfast hearts betwixt her and her foes.
The oldest courtier, schooled in state-craft guile,
Some loyal fire at her entrancing smile
Felt strangely kindled in his outworn soul;
Far more the warrior youths her soft control
Moulded to noble deeds, till all the land,
Aroused at Love's and Honor's joint command,
Bristled with steel and rang with sounds of war.

Still rashly trusting in his fortunate star,
This arrogant thrall who fain would grasp a crown,
Backed by half-barbarous hordes, marched swiftly down
'Twixt the hill ramparts and the Western Sea.
First, blazing homesteads greet him, whence did flee
The frightened hinds through fires themselves had lit
'Mid the ripe grain, lest foes should reap of it;
Or here and there, some groups of aged folk,

Women and men bent down beneath the yoke
Of cruel years and babbling idiot speech.
"Methinks," cried Doracles, "our arms will reach
The realm's unshielded heart; for lo! the breath,
The mere hot fume of rapine and of death
Which flames before our legions like a blight
Withers this people's valor and their might."

The fifes played shriller; the wild trumpet's blast
Smote the great host and thrilled them as it passed;
While clashing shields, and spears which caught the morn,
And splendid banners in strong hands upborne,
And plumèd helms, and steeds of matchless race,
And in the van that clear, keen eagle face
Of Doracles, firm set on shoulders tall,
Squared like a rock, and towering o'er them all,
With all the pomp and swell of martial strife,
Woke the burnt plains and bleak defiles to life.
So phalanx after phalanx glittering filed
Firm to the front: their haughty leader smiled
To see with what a bold and buoyant air
The lowliest footman marched before him there,
Till his proud head he lifted to the sun,
And his heart leaped as at a victory won
That self-same hour, o'er which bright-hovering shone
The steadfast image of an ivory throne.

But the Queen's host by skilful champions led,
Its powers meanwhile concentred to a head,
Lay, an embattled force with wary eye,
Ready to ward or strike whene'er the cry
Of coming foemen on their ears should fall,
Nigh the huge towers which guard the capital.

Not long their watch: one bluff October day,
There rose a blare of trumpets far away,
And sound of thronging hoofs which muffled came,
Borne on the wind, like the dull noise of flame
Half stifled in dense woodlands; then the wings
Of the Queen's host, as each swift section flings
The imperial banner proudly fluttering out,
Spread from the royal centre. Hark! a shout,
As from those thousand hearts in one great soul
Sublimely fused, rose thunder-deep, to roll,
In wild acclaim, far down the quivering van;
And wilder still the heroic tumult ran
From front to rear, when through her palace gate,
Daphles, in unaccustomed martial state,
A keen spear shimmering in its silver hold,
And on her brow the Argive crown of gold,
Flashed like a sunbeam on her warriors' sight.
Girt by her generals, on a neighboring height
She reined her Lybian courser, while the air
Played with the bright waves of her meteor hair,
And on her lovely April face the tide
Of varied feeling — now a jubilant pride

In those strong arms and stronger hearts below,
And now a prescient fear did ebb and flow,
Its sensitive heaven transforming momently.
But soon the foeman's cohorts, like a sea,
With waves of steel, and foam of snow-white plumes,
Slowly emerged from out the forest glooms,
In splendid pomp and antique pageantry.
An ominous pause! And then the trumpets high
Sounded the terrible onset, and the field
Rocked as with earthquake, and the thick air reeled
With clangors fierce from echoing hill to hill.

Bloody but brief the contest! All the skill
Of Doracles against the steadfast will
Planted by love in faithful hearts that day
Frothed like an idle tide that slips away
From granite walls! His knights their furious blows
Discharged on what seemed statues whose repose
Was iron, or their fated coursers hurled
On spears unbent as bases of a world!
Meanwhile the whole dread scene did Daphles view
With anguished, tearless eyes. But when she knew
The victory hers, down the hill-slopes she urged
Her restless steed, where still but faintly surged
The last worn waves of tumult; there her bands
Of conquering captains she with fervent hands
And o'erfraught swelling breast did proudly greet;
Yet her pale face was touched with pity sweet
While the chained rebels passed her worn and sore
With ghastly wounds, and shivering in their gore.
But when, untamed, uncowed, in 'midst of these,
The grand, defiant form of Doracles
Rose like a god discrowned, her wan cheeks flushed,
And through her heart a quick, hot torrent rushed
Of undefined, mysterious sympathy.
Viewing that haughty brow, that unbent knee,
"O kingly head!" she thought, "too well I know
How bitter-keen to him the signal blow
This day hath dealt! O kingly resolute eyes,
Shrining the sov'ran soul! 'twere surely wise
To change their glance of cold vindictive gloom
To grateful light, and make what seemed a doom
Heavy as death, the clouded path to fame,
Lordship, and honor!" Ah, but pity came
To crown admiring kindness with a flame
Of subtler life; for he, the vanquished one,
On whom that day his fate's malignant sun
Had set in storms, that night would slumber, kissed
By a fair phantom girt with golden mist,
A new-born delicate love, but dimly guessed
Even in the pure depths of the maiden breast,
Whence the sweet sylph had 'scaped her unaware.
But when the evening silence drew anear,
And round about the borders of the world

The second night since that great contest furled
Its brooding shades, the young Queen, all alone,
Paused by the dungeon floor whereon were thrown,
At listless length, the limbs of Doracles.
"How, how," she murmured, "may I best appease
His stricken pride, or touch to tender calm
His fevered honor? with what healing balm
Allay the smart wherewith his spirit groans?"
Perplexed, and yearning, on the dismal stones
Without the prison door she walked apart,
Love, doubt, and shame, all struggling in her heart,
Till the large flood of mingled love and woe
Rose to her snowy eyelids and did flow
In soft refreshing tears like spring-tide showers;
Then, bright and blushing as the moss-rose bowers
Of dewy May, she pushed the huge grate back,
And through the dusky glooms, the shadows black
Dawned glowingly! Next for a moment she
Stood in a timid, strange uncertainty,
Changing from rosy red to deathly white;
When, as a Queen sustained by true love's right,
She spake in mild, pure, steadfastness of soul:
"I come, O Doracles, with no mean dole
Of transient pity, but to show thee how
Thy mistress would exalt the abasèd brow
Of one who knows her not!" Therewith she freed
His fettered limbs, or yet his brain could heed
Or comprehend her mercy's cordial scope:
His soul had shrunk too low for dreams of hope,
Such swift misfortunes smote him: still, when all
The Queen's fair meaning on his mind did fall,
The locked and frozen sternness of his look
Broke up, as breaks the death-cold wintry brook
Its icy spell at noonday; yet his face
Was lighted not by thankful, reverent grace,
But flashed an evil triumph where he stood
Spurning his unloosed chains. In such base mood,
One eager foot pressed on the dungeon stair,
"What terms," he asked, "O Queen, demand'st thou here?
I pledge thee faith!" Silent were Daphles' lips,
And all her gentle hopes by swift eclipse
Were darkened. With a deathly smile she signed
The chief farewell, as one who scorned to bind
Her mercy with set terms. He turned to go,
Self-centred, callous, dreaming not how low
Her heart had sunk at each cold, shallow word
With which his barren nature, faintly stirred
By ruth, or love, or pardon, dared repay
Her matchless mercy. On his unchecked way
He turned to go, when, with one shuddering sob,
And deep-drawn, plaintive breath, which seemed to rob
Life of its last dear hope, the Queen sank down,
Wrapped in a death-like trance. With sullen frown,

And many a muttered oath, he raised her form,
Frail now as some pale lily by the storm
Wind-blown and beaten; for at woman's love
He could but vaguely guess, and no poor dove
Pierced by the woodman's shaft was less to him
Than this fair spirit struggling in the dim
And tortured twilight of unshared desire;
Nor could he part the pure romantic fire
Of such high passion from the lukewarm flame
That feebly burns in sordid hearts and tame,
Not of love's heat, but vacant flattery's born,
To feed his pride, yet stir the latent scorn
Of that rough manhood such hard natures know.
Waked from her trance, with wandering eyes and slow
The Queen looked round, but dimly conscious yet,
Until at last her faltering glance was set
On Doracles, to whom — that he might see
How a soft ruth to love's intensity
Had strangely grown — she laid her deep heart bare:
Then, with a sweet but nobly queen-like air,
She said, "O Doracles, in just return
For all this love and pity, which did yearn
To lift thee fallen, and to find thee, lost,
And slowly sickening underneath the frost
Of bleak despair, I well might ask of thee
Thy heart, with all its rarest freight in fee,
Save that I feel my virgin fame and life
Must count as pure, when thou hast made me wife,
Though but a wife in state and name alone.
Behold, O chief! I proffer, too, my throne,
Not as thy freedom's sole condition given,
But that men's eyes and scornful thoughts be driven
Away from what in me may seem as ill,
If — if — perchance, thou shouldst reject me still."
At which hard word she droops her head, and sighs,
While patient tears bedew her downcast eyes.

Now, with sly semblance of a soul at ease,
Her liberal proffer crafty Doracles
Freely embraced. They passed the prison-bound,
And that same day with silver-ringing sound
Of trump and cymbal, the state heralds cried
Abroad through all the city, far and wide,
The Queen's vast pardon; whereupon her court, —
Nobles and dames, — each quaintly gorgeous sport,
Known in the old time, bold or debonair,
With feasts, and mimic strifes, and pageants rare,
Did hold in honor of their sovereign's choice;
A choice none there would question! Not a voice,
Gentle or simple, but was raised to bless,
And pray the kindly gods for happiness
And peace on both! Meanwhile the thrall made king,
Albeit a secret anger still would wring
His thankless soul, in princely fashion took
The general homage, nor by word or look

Betrayed the festering consciousness within:
So gracious seemed he, Daphles' hopes begin
To wake, and whisper fond, sweet, foolish words
Close to her heart, that flutters like a bird's
Wooed in the spring-dawn: yet, alas! alas!
For joy that dies, and dreamy hopes that pass
To nothingness! In 'midst of this, her trust,
Came a swift blow which smote her to the dust;
News that her ingrate love had basely fled,
Whither none knew. Scarce had this shaft been sped
From fate's unerring bow, than swift again
Hurtled a second steeped in poisoned pain;
For now the whole dark truth came sternly out:
Leagued with her bitterest foes, a savage rout
Of mountain-robbers o'er the frontier land,
He unto whom she proffered heart and hand,
Kingdom and crown, had bared his treacherous blade,
And of the great and just gods unafraid,
Upreared his standard 'neath the blood-red star,
And raised once more the incarnate curse of war!
So from that day all gladness left the heart
Of broken Daphles; she would muse apart
From court and friends, her once blithe footsteps slow,
Her once proud head bowed down, and such wild woe
Couched in the clouded depths of mournful eyes
That few could mark her misery but with sighs
Deep almost as her own. At last, she wrote
(For still her soul hailed, watery and remote,
One beam of hope) a missive tender-sweet,
Charmed with such pathos, to her delicate feet
It might have lured a spirit, nigh to death,
And straight imbued with warm compassionate breath
A heart as cold as spires of Arctic ice!

Ah, futile hope! Ah, fond and vain device!
Not all the pleading eloquence of wrong,
Veiling its wounds, and golden-soft as song
Trilled by the brown Sicilian nightingales,
In dusky nooks of melancholy vales,
Could melt the granite will of Doracles.
Each tender line she sent him did but tease
And sting his obdurate temper into hate,
As if the deep harmonious terms that wait
On truest love, were wasp-like, poisoned things:
Her timorous hints, her sweet imaginings,
Far thoughts, and dreams evanishing, but high,
Filled with the maiden dews of sanctity,
He crushed, as one might crush in maddened hours
The fairest of the sisterhood of flowers;
No further answer made he than could be
Couched in brief terms of cold discourtesy,
Holding *all* love — the noblest love on earth —
Of lesser moment than an insect's birth,

Buzzing its life out 'twixt the dawn and dark.
That letter stifled the last healthful spark
Of the Queen's flickering reason, turned her wit
To wild and errant courses, sadly lit
By wandering stars, and orbs of fantasy.
Deeming that she full soon must sink and die,
Daphles, still true to that one dominant thought
And firm affection which such ill had brought,
Summoned her learned scribes and bade them draw
After strict form and precedents of law,
Her solemn testament; whereby she gave
Her throne to Doracles, whene'er the grave
Closed o'er her broken heart and humbled head.
But now her chiefs and nobles, hard bestead
By circumstance, and dreading much lest he,
The renegade, and rebel, who did flee
From love to league with license, yet should sway
The honored Argive sceptre, on a day
Called forth to solemn council and debate
Lords, liegemen, ministers, to save the state
From threatened tyranny and upstart rule:
Thereto the wan Queen, powerless now to school
Features or mind to subjugation meet,
Came weakly tottering; in her lofty seat
She sank bewildered, listless; all could mark
Beneath her languid eyes the hollows dark.
And — save that sometimes as she slowly turned
Her wasted form, the fires of fever burned.
Death's prescient blazon, on each sunken cheek —
Her face was pallid as a cold white streak
Of wintry moonlight on Siberian snows;
Her quivering mouth and chill contracted brows
Bespoke an inward torture, while from all
The shrewd debate within that council hall
Her dim thoughts wandered vaguely, lost and dumb.
But when her pitying maidens round her come,
And gently strive on her drooped head to place
The self-same laurel garland which did grace
Her warm, white temples on that morn of strife
And woeful victory, her sick brain seemed rife
Once more with memories; in her hand she pressed
The half-dead wreath, and o'er her flowing vest
Strewed the plucked leaves those aimless fingers tore
Unwittingly; which on the marble floor,
Down fluttering, one by one, lay blurred and dead,
Like the sere hopes her withered heart had shed,
Smitten of love; for now she touched the close
Of the soul's dreamy autumn, and the snows
Of winter soon would clasp her eyelids cold.
Yea, soon, too soon! for while her fingers fold
The garland loosely, and in fitful grief
She still would strip the circlet, leaf by leaf,
Till now one-half the wreath is plucked and bare,
She lifts her dim eyes, hearkening, as though 'ware
Of mystic voices calling on her name;
Therewith her cheek, whence the quick, fevered flame

Had quite pulsed out, with one last quiver, she
Drops on the cushioned dais, passively;
For death, more kind than love, hath brought her peace.

Long was it ere her stricken realm could cease
To mourn for Daphles; yet her burial rites,
With all their mournful pomp, their sombre sights
Funereal, scarce were passed, when her last will,
Despite its humbling terms, which rankled still
In all men's minds, her faithful courtiers sent,
With news of that móst sudden, sad event
Which made him king, to restless Doracles.
What recked he then that to its bitterest lees
A pure young soul had quaffed of misery's cup,
And after, death's? "My star," he thought, "flames up,
Fronting the heights of empire! All is well!"
Thereon, impelled by keen desire to dwell
In his new realm, with reckless haste he rode
From town to town, till now the grand abode,
The palace of the royal Argive race,
Did rise before him in its lofty place,
O'erlooking leagues of golden fields and streams,
Fair hills and shadowy vineyards, by great teams
Of laboring oxen rifled morn by morn,
Till the bared, tremulous branches swung forlorn
'Gainst the red flush of autumn's sunset sky.
Housed with rich state therein, full regally
The king his sovereign life and course began,
Striving at one swift bound to reach the van
Of princely fame; his rare magnificence
Of feasts, shows, pageants, and high splendors, whence
The wondering guests all dazzled went their way,
Grew to a world-wide proverb for display
And costly lavishness. Yet one there was
O'er whose gray head these days of pomp did pass
Like purpling shadows o'er the faded grass:
Wit touched him not to smiles, gay music's flow
Fell powerless on his closed heart's secret woe,
While at their feasts silent he sat, and grim.
Ofttimes the king a cold glance cast on him,
As one who marred their mirthful revelry,
And in the boisterous spring-tide of their glee
Rose like a boding phantom! More and more
He felt a vague, dim trouble at the core
Of his rude nature stirred, whene'er he saw
Phorbas draw near; something akin to awe,
If not to dread, for this old man did stand
Chiefest of Daphles' mourners in her land,
As chief of her life's friends, ere that black doom
Stole from her heart its joy, her cheek its bloom.

Just where the mellowed rays of noonday light
Streamed through the curtained gloom, obscurely bright,

"Leagues of golden fields and streams,
Fair hills and shadowy vineyards, by great teams
Of laboring oxen rifled morn by morn."

Which wrapped the great art-galleries richly round,
There hung, 'mid many a stately portrait, bound
In frames of costly ivory, carved and wrought,
A picture, which the king's eyes oft had sought
With anxious wonder; for day following day
Would Phorbas, mutely sorrowing, make delay
Going or coming from the council-hall
To view that muffled mystery on the wall.
Over it flowed a veil of silvery hue,
With here and there fine threads of gold shot through
The delicate woof; and whoso chanced to turn
A glance thereon, would feel his spirit burn
To pierce the jealous veil whose folds might hide
Some priceless marvel. Now, at high noontide
Of one calm autumn day, the king again
Met Phorbas — his worn features drawn with pain,
And in his eyes the sharp salt-rheum of age —
Still poring on the picture! "Thou a sage!"
Sneered Doracles, "yet idly bent, forsooth,
On vaporing fancies?" Then, more harsh, "The truth!
The *truth*, old man! What strong spell drags thee here?
(Some charm, methinks, 'twixt passion and despair:)
Morn after morn, forcing thine eyes to stray
O'er yon blank mystery? Prythee, Phorbas, say
What image lurks beneath that glimmering shroud?
Perchance the last king's? Well! am I less proud
And princely wise than he? Or art thou bold
To deem *me* all unworthy to behold
My brave forerunner?" Thereupon he knit
His rugged brows, the while his soul was lit
To keen, impatient wrath. With trembling hands —
But not for fear — Phorbas unloosed the bands,
Studded with diamond points, which clasped the veil
Close to its place. The startled prince grew pale,
As there, in all her fresh young grace, did shine
The face of Daphles, with a smile divine,
Into arch dimples rippling joyfully!
Some faintly-pensive memory seemed to vie
With deeper feelings, in the low, quick tone
Wherewith the king spake, whispering to his own
Half-wakened heart, — "Certes, it could not be,
That she, who owned the glorious face I see,
Bright with all brightness of a young delight,
Yet pined and withered 'neath the fatal night
Of starless grief!" To which, "Thy pardon, sire,"
The old man said, "but ere my life's low fire
Hath quite gone out, I fain would free my soul
Of that which long hath borne me care and dole;
So, sovereign lord, list to the tale I tell!"
And therewithal did Phorbas deem it well
To show how Daphles' darkened life did wane;
How love, first touched by doubt, soon changed to pain,

And, last, blank desolation, whose wild stress
Wrecked and made bare her perfect loveliness,
O'erwhelming wit with beauty. "Still," said he,
"O sire! to her last hour most tenderly
She spake of thee, her twilight reason set
On the sole thought, '*My love may love me yet:*
For man's love comes with knowledge, so I deem,
Slow-hearted man's!' Ah, heaven! she could not dream,
But *thy* name filled her dreams. When madness stole
Like a dread mist about her, and her soul,
Wound in its viewless cerement-folds accursed ——"
"Madness!" the king cried in a sharp outburst
Of wild amazement: "madness! *I* have known
The mad impatience of a will o'ergrown,
When sternly thwarted in its fiery zeal,
But dreamed not how these fairy creatures feel,
These soft, frail-natured women, if, perchance,
Love turn on them a cold or lukewarm glance
Of brief denial!" Then the impatient red,
In a swift flood, — but not of anger, — spread
O'er the king's face; convulsed it seemed, and stern.
But when from garrulous Phorbas he did learn
How the queen's laurel wreath half bare became,
The hot blood ebbed, and o'er its waning flame
Coursed the first tear his warrior-soul had shed.
Nor could he rouse again the lustihead
Of ruder thoughts, but, thickly muttering, laid
On the fair portrait of the sovereign maid
A reverent hand; from 'midst the painted dome
Of the great gallery forth he bore it home
Unto the secret chamber of his rest;
There next his couch he placed the beauteous guest;
There feasted on its sweetness; and since naught
Of public import now did claim his thought,
No fierce war threatened, no shrewd treaties pressed,
Strangely the picture mastered him; it grew,
As days, then weeks, and seasons, o'er him flew,
A part, an inmost essence of all life,
Which touched to joy or thrilled to shuddering strife
The soul's deep-seated issues: yet, at last,
Stronger the fierce strife waxed; the bliss was passed;
And, wheresoe'er the king went, night or day,
One haunting phantom barred his doomèd way!

But ere he reached the worst wild stage of woe,
Through many a change of passion, swift or slow,
The king passed downward, nearing treacherous death;
And thus it happed, our old-world legend saith:

The more he gazed on Daphles' blooming face,
All flushed with happy youth and Hebe grace,
The more her marvellous image seemed alive;
He saw, or dreamed he saw, the warm blood strive,

In ruddier tide, with conscious hues to dye
Her lovely brow and swanlike neck, or vie
With Syrian roses on her cheeks of flame;
The more he gazed, the more her lips became
Instinct with timorous motion, till a sigh,
New-born of honeyed love unwittingly,
Seemed hovering like a murmurous fairy-bee
About their rich, half-parted comeliness:
What slight breath softly stirs the truant tress,
Which like a waif of sunset light did rest
In wandering golden lustre on her breast?
And what dear thought her bosom graciously
Heaves into gentle billows, like a sea
Moon-kissed, and whispering? Thus the king would task
Long hours with doting questions, when the mask
Of dull state forms and ceremonial play
With wearied brain and hand was cast away,
And he a dead maid's crafty image turned
To breathing life, and blissful love that burned
From her wild pulses and fond heart to his,
And on her mouth he pressed a bridegroom's kiss.

Then the sweet spell was broken; conscience spoke;
And in her burning depths pale memory woke.
Even in that gentle shape his cold self-will
Had strangely turned, and wrought him direful ill;
Distempered, moody, sometimes nigh distraught
With ceaseless pressure of one harrowing thought,
He grew, and hapless thrills of lonely pain;
Her picture, imaged on his heart and brain,
Ruled all his tides of being, as the moon
Draws changeful seas; now in a clear high noon
Of memories bitter-sweet his soul would swim,
Anon to sink in turbulent gulfs and dim
Of wild regret, or as the dead to lie
Locked in a mute, life-withering lethargy.
Creator sweet of all his fortunes high,
Oh, that in Hades she could hear his cry
Remorseful, and come back in pitying guise
To ease his grief and calm his tortured sighs!
A thousand, thousand times this wild desire
Would wake, and surge through all his veins like fire:
Followed, alas, too soon, by such deep sense
Of powerless will, and mortal impotence,
As in red hurry up from soul to cheeks
Runs rioting, and ever harshly seeks
To drag them into gaunt, gray lines of care!
Months sped eventless, with his dark despair
Grown darker; till, one sad November morn,
Set to the rhythmic wail of winds forlorn,
They found, just where the morning's shadowy gloom
Had gathered deepest in the prince's room,
His prostrate body, cold and turned in part
Upwards, — the blade's hilt glittering o'er his heart,

Where his own mad right arm had sent
it home.
Beneath him, in soft-tinted, fadeless
bloom,
Beneath him smiled the portrait he had
torn
Madly from off the wall, his wan face
borne
Next the clear brightness of that life-
like one
For whose fair sake he lay, at last un-
done;
But whose glad smile, could *she* have
lived that hour,
Had waned and withered inward, like a
flower
The storm-wind blights, at stern re-
venge, like this,
Of love's cold scorn and passion's unpaid
kiss.

AËTHRA.

It is a sweet tradition, with a soul
Of tenderest pathos! Hearken, love!—
for all
The sacred undercurrents of the heart
Thrill to its cordial music:
Once, a chief,
Philantus, king of Sparta, left the stern
And bleak defiles of his unfruitful
land—
Girt by a band of eager colonists—
To seek new homes on fair Italian
plains.
Apollo's oracle had darkly spoken:
"*Where'er from cloudless skies a
plenteous shower
Outpours, the Fates decree that ye should
pause
And rear your household deities!*"
Racked by doubt
Philantus traversed with his faithful
band
Full many a bounteous realm; but still
defeat
Darkened his banners, and the strong-
walled towns
His desperate sieges grimly laughed to
scorn!
Weighed down by anxious thoughts, one
sultry eve
The warrior—his rude helmet cast
aside—
Rested his weary head upon the lap
Of his fair wife, who loved him ten-
derly;
And there he drank a generous draught
of sleep.
She, gazing on his brow all worn with
toil
And his dark locks, which pain had
silvered over
With glistening touches of a frosty
rime,
Wept on the sudden bitterly; her
tears
Fell on his face, and, wondering, he
woke.
"O blest art thou, my Aëthra, *my clear
sky*,"
He cried exultant, "from whose pitying
blue
A heart-rain falls to fertilize my fate:
Lo! the deep riddle's solved—the gods
spake truth!"

So the next night he stormed Tarentum,
took
The enemy's host at vantage, and o'er-
threw
His mightiest captains. Thence with
kindly sway
He ruled those pleasant regions he had
won,—
But dearer even than his rich demesnes
The love of her whose gentle tears un-
locked
The close-shut mystery of the Oracle!

RENEWED.

Welcome, rippling sunshine!
Welcome, joyous air!
Like a demon shadow
Flies the gaunt despair!

Heaven, through heights of happy calm,
Its heart of hearts uncloses,
To win earth's answering love in balm,
Her blushing thanks — in roses!

Voices from the pine-grove,
Where the pheasant's drumming,
Voices from the ferny hills
Alive with insect humming;

Voices low and sweet
From the far-off stream,
Where two rivulets meet
With the murmur of a dream;
Voices loud and free
From every bush and tree,
Of sportive forest bards outpouring songs of gladness;
But over them still
With its passionate trill,
The mock-bird's jocund madness!

"Voices low and sweet
From the far-off stream."

Deep down the swampy brake
Even the poison-snake,
Uncoiled and basking in the noontide splendor,
May feel, perchance on this auspicious day
(All dark clouds rolled away),
Through his stagnant blood,
Warmed by the sunlight flood
A faint, far sense,
Coming he knows not whence,
Of dim intelligence,—
The thinnest conscious thrill that human is, and tender!

Look! where on luminous wing
The ether's stately king,
The lone sea-eagle, circling proud and slow,
Towers in the sapphire glow;
From out whose dazzling beam,
His resonant scream;
Heard even here, — a note of fierce desire, —
Hushes to silent awe the sylvan choir,
Till bird and note in airy deeps up-drawn
Are melting toward the dawn!

And hear! O! hear!
No longer wildly terrible and drear,
But as if merry pulses timed their beating,
The frolic sea-waves near,

Dancing along like happy maidens playing
When blithe love goes "a-Maying,"
And wreaking on the shore their panting blisses
In coy impulsive kisses;
Whilst he — poor dullard — cannot catch nor hold them,
Nor in his massive, earthen arms enfold them,
The laughing virgin waves, so archly, swiftly fleeting!
This subtle atmosphere,
So magically clear,
Melts, as it were upon my eager lip;
From some invisible goblet of delight
Idly I sip and sip
A wine so warm and golden
(From some enchanted bin the wine was stolen),
A wine so sweet and rare,
Methinks a nobler birth
Illuminates the earth,
And in my heart I hear a fairy singing;
Yet well I know 'tis but my soul renewed,
Reborn and bright,
From grief and grief's malignant solitude!
Yet well I know, Joy is the Ganymede,
Who in my yearning need,
Turns to a cordial rich the balmy air;
And 'tis but Hope's, divinest Hope's return,
Which makes my inmost spirit throb and burn,
And Hope's triumphant song,
So sweet and strong,
That all creation seems with that weird music ringing!

KRISHNA AND HIS THREE HANDMAIDENS.

And where he sat beneath the mystic stars,
Nigh the twin founts of Immortality,
That feed fair channels of the Stream of Trance, —
To Krishna once his three handmaidens came,
Asking a boon: "O king! O lord!" they said,
"Test thou thy servants' wisdom; long in dreams,
Born of the waters of thy Stream of Trance,
Have we, thy fond handmaidens wandered free,
And lapped in airiest wreaths of fantasy;
Now would we, viewless, bearing each some gift
From thee, our father, seek the world of man,
The world of man and pain, which whoso leaves
Better or brighter, for thy gift bestowed
Most worthily, shall claim thy just reward,
The Crown of Wisdom!" Krishna heard, and gave
To each one tiny drop of diamond dew,
Drawn from the founts that feed the Stream of Trance,
Wherewith, on waftage of miraculous winds,
Breathing full south, they sought the world of man,
The world of man and pain, that shrank in drought,
Palsied and withered, like an old man's face
Death-smitten.

And the first handmaiden saw
A monarch's fountain, sparkling in the waste,
Glowing and fresh, though all the land was sick,
Gasping for rain, and famished thousands died:
"O brave," she said, "O beautiful bright waves!
Like calls to like;" and so her dewdrop glanced,
And glittered downward as a fairy star
Loosed from a tress of Cassiopeia's hair,
Down to the glorious fountain of the king.

Over the passionless bosom of the sea,
The Indian Sea, cerulean, crystal-clear,
And calm, the second handmaid, hovering, viewed —
Far through the tangled sea-weed and cool tides
Pulsing 'twixt coral branches — the wide lips
Of purpling shells that yearned to clasp a pearl:
So where the oyster, blindly reared, awaits
Its priceless soul — she lets the dewdrop fall,
Thenceforth to grow a jewel fit for courts,
And shine on swanlike necks of haughty queens!

But Krishna's third handmaiden scarce had felt
The fume from parchèd plains that made the air
As one vast caldron of invisible fire,
Than casting downward pitiful eyes, she saw,
Crouched in the brazen cere of that red heat,
A tiny bird — a poor, weak, suffering thing
(Its bright eyes glazed, its limbs convulsed and prone), —
Dying of thirst in torture: "Ah, kind Lord
Krishna," his handmaid murmured, "speed thy gift,
Best yielded here, to soothe, perchance to save
The lowliest mortal creature cursed with pain!"
Gently she shook the dewdrop from her palm
Into the silent throat that thirst had sealed,
Soon silent, sealed no more, — for, lo! the bird
Fluttered, arose, was strengthened, and through calms
Of happy ether, echoing fair and far,
Rang the charmed music of the nightingale.

And so, where crowned beneath the mystic stars,
Nigh the twin founts of immortality,
Krishna, the father, saw what ruth was hers,
And, smiling, to his wise handmaiden's rule
Gave the great storm-clouds and the mists of heaven,
Till at her voice the mighty vapors rolled
Up from the mountain-gorges, and the seas,
And cloudland darkened, and the grateful rain,
Burdened with benedictions, rushed and foamed
Down the hot channels, and the foliaged hills,
And the frayed lips and languid limbs of flowers;
And all the woodlands laughed, and earth was glad!

UNDER THE PINE.

TO THE MEMORY OF HENRY TIMROD.

THE same majestic pine is lifted high
  Against the twilight sky,
The same low, melancholy music grieves
  Amid the topmost leaves,
As when I watched, and mused, and dreamed with him,
  Beneath these shadows dim.

O Tree! hast thou no memory at thy core
  Of one who comes no more?
No yearning memory of those scenes that were
  So richly calm and fair,
When the last rays of sunset, shimmering down,
  Flashed like a royal crown?

And he, with hand outstretched and eyes ablaze,
Looked forth with burning gaze,
And seemed to drink the sunset like strong wine,
Or, hushed in trance divine,
Hailed the first shy and timorous glance from far
Of evening's virgin star?

O Tree! against thy mighty trunk he laid
His weary head; thy shade
Stole o'er him like the first cool spell of sleep:
It brought a peace *so* deep
The unquiet passion died from out his eyes,
As lightning from stilled skies.

And in that calm he loved to rest, and hear
The soft wind-angels, clear
And sweet, among the uppermost branches sighing:
Voices he heard replying
(Or so he dreamed) far up the mystic height,
And pinions rustling light.

O Tree! have not his poet-touch, his dreams
So full of heavenly gleams,
Wrought through the folded dullness of thy bark,
And all thy nature dark
Stirred to slow throbbings, and the fluttering fire
Of faint, unknown desire?

At least to me there sweeps no rugged ring
That girds the forest-king
No immemorial stain, or awful rent
(The mark of tempest spent),
No delicate leaf, no lithe bough, vine-o'ergrown,
No distant, flickering cone,
But speaks of him, and seems to bring once more
The joy, the love of yore;
But most when breathed from out the sunset-land
The sunset airs are bland,
That blow between the twilight and the night,
Ere yet the stars are bright;

For then that quiet eve comes back to me,
When, deeply, thrillingly,
He spake of lofty hopes which vanquish Death;
And on his mortal breath
A language of immortal meanings hung,
That fired his heart and tongue.

For then unearthly breezes stir and sigh,
Murmuring, "Look up! 'tis I:
Thy friend is near thee! Ah, thou canst not see!"
And through the sacred tree
Passes what seems a wild and sentient thrill—
Passes, and all is still!—

Still as the grave which holds his tranquil form,
Hushed after many a storm,—
Still as the calm that crowns his marble brow,
No pain can wrinkle now.—
Still as the peace—pathetic peace of God—
That wraps the holy sod,

Where every flower from our dead minstrel's dust
Should bloom, a type of trust,—
That faith which waxed to wings of heavenward might
To bear his soul from night,—
That faith, dear Christ! whereby we pray to meet
His spirit at God's feet!

A DREAM OF THE SOUTH WINDS.

O FRESH, how fresh and fair
Through the crystal gulfs of air,
The fairy South Wind floateth on her subtle wings of balm!
And the green earth lapped in bliss,
To the magic of her kiss
Seems yearning upward fondly through the golden-crested calm!

From the distant Tropic strand,
Where the billows, bright and bland,
Go creeping, curling round the palms with sweet, faint undertune
From its fields of purpling flowers
Still wet with fragrant showers,
The happy South Wind lingering sweeps the royal blooms of June.

All heavenly fancies rise
On the perfume of her sighs,
Which steep the inmost spirit in a languor rare and fine,
And a peace more pure than sleep's
Unto dim, half-conscious deeps,
Transports me, lulled and dreaming, on its twilight tides divine.

Those dreams! ah me! the splendor,
So mystical and tender,
Wherewith like soft heat-lightnings they gird their meaning round,
And those waters, calling, calling,
With a nameless charm enthralling,
Like the ghost of music melting on a rainbow spray of sound!

Touch, touch me not, nor wake me,
Lest grosser thoughts o'ertake me,
From earth receding faintly with her dreary din and jars, —
What viewless arms caress me?
What whispered voices bless me,
With welcomes dropping dewlike from the weird and wondrous stars?

Alas! dim, dim, and dimmer
Grows the preternatural glimmer
Of that trance the South Wind brought me on her subtle wings of balm,
For behold! its spirit flieth,
And its fairy murmur dieth,
And the silence closing round me is a dull and soulless calm!

IN THE MIST.

MORE fearful grows the hillside way,
The gloom no softening breeze hath kissed!
I glance far upward to the day,
But scarce can catch one faltering ray
From out the mist!

Ah, heaven! to think youth's morning prime,
All flushed with rose and amethyst,
Its tender loves, its hopes sublime,
Should shrink to this dull twilight-time
Of cold and mist!

No tranquil evening hour descends,
When peace with memory holds her tryst,
But doubt with prescient terror blends,
And grief her mournful curfew sends
Along the mist!

Weird shapes and wild, stalk strangely by,
And say, what bodeful voices hissed
Where yonder blasted pine-trunks lie?
What mystic phantoms shuddering fly
Far down the mist?

Dark omens all! they bid me stay,
Unsheathe resolve, pause, strive, resist
That poisonous charm which haunts my way;
Alas! the fiend, more bold than they,
Still rules the mist!

And now from gulfs of turbulent gloom
A torrent's threatening thunder; — list!
That ravening roar! that hungry boom!
Down, down I pass to meet my doom
Within the mist!

A SUMMER MOOD.

"Now, by my faith a gruesome mood, for summer!" — THOMAS HEYWARD (1597).

AH, me! for evermore, for evermore
These human hearts of ours must yearn and sigh,
While down the dells and up the murmurous shore
Nature renews her immortality.

The heavens of June stretch calm and bland above,
June roses blush with tints of Orient skies,
But we, by graves of joy, desire, and love,
Mourn in a world which breathes of Paradise!

The sunshine mocks the tears it may not dry,
The breezes — tricksy couriers of the air —
Child-roisterers winged, and lightly fluttering by —
Blow their gay trumpets in the face of care;

And bolder winds, the deep sky's passionate speech,
Woven into rhythmic raptures of desire,
Or fugues of mystic victory, sadly reach
Our humbled souls, to rack, not raise them higher!

The field-birds seem to twit us as they pass
With their small blisses, piped so clear and loud;
The cricket triumphs o'er us in the grass,
And the lark, glancing beamlike up the cloud,

Sings us to scorn with his keen rhapsodies;
Small things and great unconscious tauntings bring
To edge our cares, whilst we, the proud and wise,
Envy the insect's joy, the birdling's wing!

And thus for evermore, till time shall cease,
Man's soul and Nature's — each a separate sphere —
Revolve, the one in discord, one in peace,
And who shall make the solemn mystery clear?

MIDNIGHT.

The Moon, a ghost of her sweet self,
And wading through a watery cloud,
Which wraps her lustre like a shroud,
Creeps up the gray, funereal sky,
Wearily! how wearily!

The Wind, with low, bewildered wail
A homeless spirit, sadly lost,
Sweeps shuddering o'er the pallid frost,
And faints afar, with heart-sick sigh,
Drearily! how drearily!

And now a deathly stillness falls
On earth and heaven, save when the shrill,
Malignant owl o'er heath and hill
Smites the wan silence with a cry,
Eerily! how eerily!

THE BONNY BROWN HAND.

OH, drearily, how drearily, the sombre eve comes down!
And wearily, how wearily, the seaward breezes blow!
But place your little hand in mine — so dainty, yet so brown!
For household toil hath worn away its rosy-tinted snow;

"The Moon, a ghost of her sweet self, . .
Creeps up the gray, funereal sky,
Wearily! how wearily."

But I fold it, wife, the nearer,
And I feel, my love, 'tis dearer
Than all dear things of earth,
As I watch the pensive gloaming,
And my wild thoughts cease from roaming,
And birdlike furl their pinions close beside our peaceful hearth:
Then rest your little hand in mine, while twilight shimmers down, —
That little hand, that fervent hand, that hand of bonny brown, —
The hand that holds an honest heart, and rules a happy hearth.

Oh, merrily, how merrily, our children's voices rise!
And cheerily, how cheerily, their tiny footsteps fall!
But, hand, you must not stir awhile, for there our nestling lies,
Snug in the cradle at your side, the loveliest far of all;
And she looks so arch and airy,
So softly pure a fairy, —
She scarce seems bound to earth;
And her dimpled mouth keeps smiling,
As at some child fay's beguiling,
Who flies from Ariel realms to light her slumbers on the hearth.
Ha, little hand, you yearn to move, and smooth the bright locks down!
But, little hand, — but, trembling hand, — but, hand of bonny brown,
Stay, stay with me! — she will not flee, our birdling on the hearth.

Oh, flittingly, how flittingly, the parlor shadows thrill,
As wittingly, half wittingly, they seem to pulse and pass!
And solemn sounds are on the wind that sweeps the haunted hill,
And murmurs of a ghostly breath from out the graveyard grass.
Let me feel your glowing fingers
In a clasp that warms and lingers
With the full, fond love of earth,
Till the joy of love's completeness
In this flush of fireside sweetness,
Shall brim our hearts with spirit-wine, outpoured beside the hearth.
So steal your little hand in mine, while twilight falters down, —
That little hand, that fervent hand, that hand of bonny brown, —
The hand which points the path to heaven, yet makes a heaven of earth.

SONNETS.

THE COTTAGE ON THE HILL.

On a steep hillside, to all airs that blow,
Open, and open to the varying sky,
Our cottage homestead, smiling tranquilly,
Catches morn's earliest and eve's latest glow;
Here, far from worldly strife, and pompous show,
The peaceful seasons glide serenely by,
Fulfil their missions, and as calmly die,
As waves on quiet shores when winds are low.
Fields, lonely paths, the one small glimmering rill
That twinkles like a wood-fay's mirthful eye,
Under moist bay-leaves, clouds fantastical
That float and change at the light breeze's will, —
To me, thus lapped in sylvan luxury,
Are more than death of kings, or empires' fall.

NOVEMBER.

Within the deep-blue eyes of Heaven a haze
Of saddened passion dims their tender light,
For that her fair queen-child, the Summer bright,

Lies a wan corse amidst her mouldering bays:
The sullen Autumn lifts no voice of praise
To herald Winter's cold and cruel might,
But winds foreboding fill the desolate night,
And die at dawning down wild woodland ways:
The sovereign sun at noonday smileth cold,
As through a shroud he hath no power to part,
While huddled flocks crouch listless round their fold;
The mock-bird's dumb, no more with cheerful dart
Upsoars the lark through morning's quivering gold,
And dumb or dead, methinks, great Nature's heart!

SYLVAN MUSINGS. — IN MAY.

Couched in cool shadow, girt by billowy swells
Of foliage, rippling into buds and flowers,
Here I repose o'erfanned by breezy bowers, —
Lulled by a delicate stream whose music wells
Tender and low through those luxuriant dells,
Wherefrom a single broad-leaved chestnut towers; —
Still musing in the long, lush, languid hours, —
As in a dream I heard the tinkling bells
Of far-off kine, glimpsed through the verdurous sheen,
Blent with faint bleatings from the distant croft, —
The bee-throngs murmurous in the golden fern,
The wood-doves veiled by depths of flickering green, —
And near me, where the wild "queen fairies" * burn,
The thrush's bridal passion, warm and soft!

POETS.

Some thunder on the heights of song, their race
Godlike in power, while others at their feet
Are breathing measures scarce less strong and sweet
Than those which peal from out that loftiest place;
Meantime, just midway on the mount, his face
Fairer than April heavens, when storms retreat,
And on their edges rain and sunshine meet,
Pipes the soft lyrist lays cf tender grace;
But where the slopes of bright Parnassus sweep
Near to the common ground, a various throng
Chant lowlier measures, — yet each tuneful strain
(The silvery minor of earth's perfect song)
Blends with that music of the topmost steep,
O'er whose vast realm the master minstrels reign!

SONNET.

Behold! how weirdly, wonderfully grand
The shades and colors of yon sunset sky!
Rare isles of light in crimson oceans lie,
Whose airy waves seem rippling, bright and bland,
Up the soft slopes of many a mystic strand, —

* "Queen fairy," the name given popularly to an exquisite Southern wild flower.

While luminous capes, and mountains towering high
In golden pomp and proud regality,
O'erlook the frontier of that fairy land,
But now, in transformations swift and strange
The vision changes! Castles glittering fair,
And sapphire battlements of loftiest range
Commingle with vast spire and gorgeous dome,
Round which the sunset rolls its purpling foam,
Girding this transient Venice of the air.

"Upveiled in yonder dim ethereal sea,
Its airy towers the work of phantom spells,
A viewless belfry tolls its wizard bells."

THE PHANTOM BELLS.

UPVEILED in yonder dim ethereal sea,
Its airy towers the work of phantom spells,
A viewless belfry tolls its wizard bells,
Pealed o'er this populous earth perpetually.
Some hear, some hear them not; but aye they be
Laden with one strange note that sinks or swells,
Now dread as doom, now gentle as farewells,
Time's dirge borne ever toward eternity.
Each hour its measured breath sobs out and dies,
While the bell tolls its requiem,—"*Passing, past,*"—
The sole sad burden of their long refrain.

Still, with those hours each pang, each pleasure flies,
Brief sweet, brief bitter, — all our days are vain,
Knolled into drear forgetfulness at last.

THE LIFE-FOREST.

In springtime of our youth, life's purpling shade,
Foliage and fruit, do hang so thickly round,
We seem glad tenants of enchanted ground,
O'er which for aye dream-whispering winds have played.
Then summer comes, her full-blown charm is laid
On all the forest aisles; from bound to bound
Floats woodland music, and the silvery sound
Of fountains babbling to the golden glade.
Next, a chill breath, the breath of Autumn's doom
Strips the fair sylvan branches, one by one,
Till the bare landscape broadens to our view;
Behind, black tree boles blot the twilight blue,
Before, unfoliaged, bald of light and bloom,
Our pathway darkens towards the darkening sun!

CLOUD FANTASIES.

Wild, rapid, dark, like dreams of threatening doom,
Low cloud-racks scud before the level wind;
Beneath them, the bare moorlands, blank and blind,
Stretch, mournful, through pale lengths of glimmering gloom;
Afar, grand mimic of the sea waves' boom,
Hollow, yet sweet as if a Titan pined
O'er deathless woes, yon mighty wood, consigned
To autumn's blight, bemoans its perished bloom;
The dim air creeps with a vague shuddering thrill
Down from those monstrous mists the sea-gale brings,
Half formless, inland, poisoning earth and sky;
Most from yon black cloud, shaped like vampire wings
O'er a lost angel's visage, deathly-still,
Uplifted toward some dread eternity.

SONNET.

I fear thee not, O Death! nay, oft I pine
To clasp thy passionless bosom to mine own,
And on thy heart sob out my latest moan,
Ere lapped and lost in thy strange sleep divine;
But much I fear lest that chill breath of thine
Should freeze all tender memories into stone, —
Lest ruthless and malign Oblivion
Quench the last spark that lingers on love's shrine:
O God! to moulder through dark, dateless years,
The while all loving ministries shall cease,
And time assuage the fondest mourner's tears!
Here lies the sting! — this, *this* it is to die!
And yet great nature rounds all strife with peace,
And life or death, each rests in mystery!

SONNET.

Of all the woodland flowers of earlier spring,
These golden jasmines, each an air-hung bower,

Meet for the Queen of Fairies' tiring
hour,
Seem loveliest and most fair in blossoming;
How yonder mock-bird thrills his fervid wing
And long, lithe throat, where twinkling
flower on flower
Rains the globed dewdrops down, a diamond shower,
O'er his brown head poised as in act to
sing;
Lo! the swift sunshine floods the flowery
urns,
Girding their delicate gold with matchless light,
Till the blent life of bough, leaf, blossom,
burns;
Then, then outbursts the mock-bird clear
and loud,
Half-drunk with perfume, veiled by radiance bright,
A star of music in a fiery cloud!

FIRE-PICTURES.

O! THE rolling, rushing fire!
O! the fire!
How it rages, wilder, higher,
Like a hot heart's fierce desire,
Thrilled with passion that appalls us,
Half appalls, and yet enthralls us,
O! the madly mounting fire!

Up it sweepeth,— wave and quiver, —
Roaring like an angry river, —
O! the fire!
Which an earthquake backward turneth,
Backward o'er its riven courses,
Backward to its mountain sources,
While the blood-red sunset burneth,
Like a God's face grand with ire,
O! the bursting, billowy fire!

Now the sombre smoke-clouds thicken
To a dim Plutonian night; —
O! the fire!
How its flickering glories sicken,
Sicken at the blight!
Pales the flame, and spreads the vapor,
Till scarce larger than a taper,
Flares the waning, struggling light:
O! thou wan, faint-hearted fire,
Sadly darkling,
Weakly sparkling,
Rise! assert thy might!
Aspire! aspire!

At the word, a vivid lightning,
Threatening, swaying, darting, brightening,
Where the loftiest yule-log towers, —
Bursts once more,
Sudden bursts the awakened fire;
Hear it roar!
Roar, and mount high, high, and higher,
Till beneath,
Only here and there a wreath
Of the passing smoke-cloud lowers, —
Ha! the glad, victorious fire!

O! the fire!
How it changes,
Changes, ranges
Through all phases fancy-wrought,
Changes like a wizard thought;
See Vesuvian lavas rushing
'Twixt the rocks! the ground asunder
Shivers at the earthquake's thunder;
And the glare of Hell is flushing
Startled hill-top, quaking town;
Temples, statues, towers go down,
While beyond that lava flood,
Dark-red like blood,
I behold the children fleeting
Clasped by many a frenzied hand;
What a flight, and what a meeting,
On the ruined strand!

O! the fire!
Eddying higher, higher, higher
From the vast volcanic cones;
O! the agony, the groans
Of those thousands stifling there!
"Fancy," say you? but how near
Seem the anguish and the fear!
Swelling, turbulent, pitiless fire:

'Tis a mad northeastern breeze
Raving o'er the prairie seas;
How, like living things, the grasses
Tremble as the storm-breath passes,
Ere the flames' devouring magic
Coils about their golden splendor,
And the tender
Glory of the mellowing fields
To the wild destroyer yields;
Dreadful waste for flowering blooms,
Desolate darkness, like the tomb's,
Over which there broods the while,
Instead of daylight's happy smile,
A pall malign and tragic!

Marvellous fire!
Changing, ranging
Through all phases fancy-wrought,
Changing like a charmèd thought;
A stir, a murmur deep,
Like airs that rustle over jungle-reeds,
Where the gaunt tiger breathes but half asleep;
A bodeful stir, —
And then the victim of his own pure deeds,
I mark the mighty fire
Clasps in its cruel palms a martyr-saint,
Christ's faithful worshipper;
One mortal cry affronts the pitying day,
One ghastly arm uplifts itself to heaven —
When the swart smoke is riven, —
Ere the last sob of anguish dies away,
The worn limbs droop and faint,
And o'er those reverend hairs, silvery and hoary,
Settles the semblance of a crown of glory.

Tireless fire!
Changing, ranging
Through all phases fancy-wrought,
Changing like a Prótean thought;
Here's a glowing, warm interior,
A Dutch tavern, rich and rosy
With deep color, — sill and floor
Dazzling as the white seashore,
Where within his armchair cozy
Sits a toper, stout and yellow,
Blinking o'er his steamy bowl;
Hugely drinking,
Slyly winking,
As the pot-house Hebe passes,
With a clink and clang of glasses;
Ha! 'tis plain, the stout old fellow —
As his wont is — waxes mellow,
Nodding 'twixt each dreamy leer,
Swaying in his elbow chair,
Next to one, — a portly peasant, —
Pipe in hand, whose swelling cheek,
Jolly, rubicund, and sleek,
Puffs above the blazing coal;
While his heavy, half-shut, eyes
Watch the smoke-wreaths evanescent,
Eddying lightly as they rise,
Eddying lightly and aloof
Toward the great, black, oaken roof!

Dreaming still, from out the fire
Faces grinning and grotesque,
Flash an eery glance upon me;
Or, once more, methinks I sun me
On the breadths of happy plain
Sloping towards the southern main,
Where the inmost soul of shadow
Wins a golden heat,
And the hill-side and the meadow
(Where the vines and clover meet,
Twining round the virgins' feet,
While the natural arabesque
Of the foliage grouped above them
Droops, as if the leaves did love them,
Over brow, and lips, and eyes)
Gleam with hints of Paradise!

Ah! the fire!
Gently glowing,
Fairly flowing,
Like a rivulet rippling deep
Through the meadow-lands of sleep,
Bordered where its music swells,
By the languid lotos-bells,
And the twilight asphodels;
Mingled with a richer boon
Of queen-lilies, each a moon,
Orbèd into white completeness;
O! the perfume! the rare sweetness

"Countless coruscations glimmer,
Glow and darken, wane and shimmer, . . .
By mysterious currents stirred
Of great winds."

Of those grouped and fairy flowers,
Over which the love-lorn hours
Linger, — not alone for them,
Though the lotos swings its stem
With a lulling stir of leaves,—
Though the lady-lily waves,
And a silvery undertune
From some mystic wind-song grieves
Dainty sweet amid the bells
Of the twilight asphodels;
But because a charm more rare
Glorifies the mellow air,
In the gleam of lifted eyes,
In the tranquil ecstasies
Of two lovers, leaf-embowered,
Lingering there,
Each of whose fair lives hath flowered,
Like the lily-petals finely,
Like the asphodel divinely.

Titan arches!
Titan spires!
Pillars whose vast capitals
Tower toward Cyclopean halls,
And whose unknown bases pierce
Down the nether universe;
Countless coruscations glimmer,
Glow and darken, wane and shimmer,
'Twixt majestic standards, swooping, —
Like the wings of some strange bird
By mysterious currents stirred
Of great winds, — or darkly drooping,
In a hush sublime as death,
When the conflict's quivering breath
Sobs its gory life away,
At the close of fateful marches,
On an empire's natal day:
Countless coruscations glimmer,
Glow and darken, wane and shimmer,
Round the shafts, and round the walls,
Whence an ebon splendor falls
On the scar-seamed, angel bands, —
(Desolate bands!)
Grasping in their ghostly hands
Weapons of an antique rage,
From some lost, celestial age,
When the serried throngs were hurled
Blasted to the under world:
Shattered spear-heads, broken brands,
And the mammoth, moonlike shields,
Blazoned on their lurid fields,
With uncouth, malignant forms,
Glowering, wild,
Like the huge cloud-masses piled
Up a Heaven of storms!

. . . . .

Ah, the faint and flickering fire!
Ah, the fire!
Like a young man's transient ire,
Like an old man's last desire,
Lo! it falters, dies!
Still, through weary, half-closed lashes,
Still I see,
But brokenly, but mistily,
Fall and rise,
Rise and fall,
Ghosts of shifting fantasy;
Now the embers, smouldered all,
Sink to ruin; sadder dreams
Follow on their vanished gleams;
Wailingly the spirits call,
Spirits on the night-winds solemn,
Wraiths of happy Hopes that left me;
(Cruel! why did ye depart?)
Hopes that sleep, their youthful riot
Mergèd in an awful quiet,
With the heavy grief-moulds pressed
On each pallid, pulseless breast,
In that graveyard called THE HEART,
Stern and lone.
Needing no memorial stone,
And no blazoned column:
Let them rest!
Let them rest!
Yes, 't is useless to remember
May-morn in the mirk December;
Still, O Hopes! because ye were
Beautiful, and strong, and fair,
Nobly brave, and sweetly bright,
Who shall dare
Scorn me, if through moistened lashes,
Musing by my hearthstone blighted,
Weary, desolate, benighted, —
I, because those sweet Hopes left me,
I, because my fate bereft me,
Mourn my dead,
Mourn, — and shed
Hot tears in the ashes?

AN ANNIVERSARY.

O LOVE, it is our wedding day!
This morn,—how swift the seasons flee!—
A virgin morn of cloudless May,
You gave your loyal hand to me,
Your dainty hand, clasped sweet and sure
As Love's sweet self, for evermore!

O Love, it is our wedding-day,
And memory flies from now to then;
I mark the soft heat-lightning play
Of blushes o'er your cheek again,
And shy but fond foreshadowings rise
Of tranquil joy in tender eyes.

O Love, it is our wedding-day;
The very rustling of your dress,
The trembling of your arm that lay
On mine, with timorous happiness,
Your fluttered breath and faint foot-fall,—
Ah, sweet, I hear, I see them all!

O Love, it is our wedding-day,
And backward Time's strange current rolls,
Till life's and love's auspicious May
Once more is blooming in our souls,
And larklike, swell the songs of hope,
Your blissful bridal horoscope.

O Love, it is our wedding-day,—
Yet say, did those fair hopes but sing,
Lapped in the tuneful morn of May,
To die or droop on faltering wing,
When noontide heats and evening chills
Made pale the flowers and veiled the hills?

O Love, it is our wedding-day,
And none of those glad hopes of youth,
Thrilled to its height, outpoured a lay
To match our future's simple truth:
Though deep the joy of vow and shrine,
Our wedded calm is more divine!

O Love, it is our wedding-day!
Life's summer, with slow-waning beam,
Tints the near autumn's cloud-land gray
To softness of a fairy dream,
Whence peace by musing pathos kissed,
Smiles through a veil of golden mist.

O Love, it is our wedding-day;
The conscious winds are whispering low
Those passionate secrets of the May
Fraught with your kisses long ago;
Warm memories of our years remote
Are trembling in the mock-bird's throat.

O Love, it is our wedding-day,—
And not a thrush in woodland bowers,
And not a rivulet's silvery lay,
Nor tiny bee-song 'mid the flowers,
Nor any voice of land or sea,
But deepens love to ecstasy!

Our wedding-day! The soul's noontide!
In these rare words at watchful rest
What sweet, melodious meanings hide
Like birds within one balmy nest,
Each quivering with an impulse strong
To flood all heaven and earth with song!

FROM THE WOODS.

WHY should I, with a mournful, morbid spleen,
Lament that here, in this half-desert scene,
My lot is placed?
At least the poet-winds are bold and loud,—
At least the sunset glorifies the cloud,
And forests old and proud
Rustle their verdurous banners o'er the waste.

Perchance 'tis best that I, whose Fate's eclipse
Seems final,—I, whose sluggish life-wave slips
Languid away,—

Should here, within these lowly walks, apart
From the fierce throbbings of the populous mart,
Commune with mine own heart,
While Wisdom blooms from buried Hope's decay.

Nature, though wild her forms, sustains me still;
The founts are musical, — the barren hill
Glows with strange lights;
Through solemn pine-groves the small rivulets fleet
Sparkling, as if a Naiad's silvery feet
In quick and coy retreat,
Glanced through the star-gleams on calm summer nights;

And the great sky, the royal heaven above,
Darkens with storms or melts with hues of love;
While far remote,
Just where the sunlight smites the woods with fire,
Wakens the multitudinous sylvan choir;
Their innocent love's desire
Poured in a rill of song from each harmonious throat.

My walls are crumbling, but immortal looks
Smile on me here from faces of rare books:
Shakspeare consoles
My heart with true philosophies; a balm
Of spiritual dews from humbler song or psalm
Fills me with tender calm,
Or through hushed heavens of soul Milton's deep thunder rolls!

And more than all, o'er shattered wrecks of Fate,
The relics of a happier time and state,
My nobler life
Shines on unquenched! O deathless love that lies
In the clear midnight of those passionate eyes!
Joy waneth! Fortune flies!
What then? Thou still art here, soul of my soul, my Wife!

DOLCE FAR NIENTE.

LET the world roll blindly on!
Give me shadow, give me sun,
And a perfumed eve as this is:
Let me lie,
Dreamfully,
When the last quick sunbeams shiver
Spears of light athwart the river,
And a breeze, which seems the sigh
Of a fairy floating by,
Coyly kisses
Tender leaf and feathered grasses;
Yet so soft its breathing passes,
These tall ferns, just glimmering o'er me,
Blending goldenly before me,
Hardly quiver!

I have done with worldly scheming,
Mocking show and hollow seeming!
Let me lie
Idly here,
Lapped in lulling waves of air,
Facing full the shadowy sky.
Fame! — the very sound is dreary, —
Shut, O soul! thine eyelids weary,
For all nature's voices say,
"'Tis the close — the close of day,
Thought and grief have had their sway:"
Now Sleep bares her balmy breast, —
Whispering low
(Low as moon-set tides that flow
Up still beaches far away;
While, from out the lucid West,
Flutelike winds of murmurous breath
Sink to tender-panting death),
"On my bosom take thy rest;
(Care and grief have had their day!)
'Tis the hour for dreaming,
Fragrant rest, elysian dreaming!"

CAMBYSES AND THE MACROBIAN BOW.

One morn, hard by a slumberous streamlet's wave,
The plane-trees stirless in the unbreathing calm,
And all the lush-red roses drooped in dream,
Lay King Cambyses, idle as a cloud
That waits the wind,— aimless of thought and will, —
But with vague evil, like the lightning's bolt
Ere yet the electric death be forged to smite,
Seething at heart. His courtiers ringed him round,
Whereof was one who to his comrades' ears,
With bated breath and wonder-archèd brows,
Extolled a certain Bactrian's matchless skill
Displayed in bowcraft: at whose marvellous feats,
Eagerly vaunted, the King's soul grew hot
With envy, for himself erewhile had been
Rated the mightiest archer in his realm.
Slowly he rose, and pointing southward, said,
"Seest thou, Prexaspes, yonder slender palm,
A mere wan shadow, quivering in the light,
Topped by a ghastly leaf-crown? Prithee, now,
Can this, thy famous Bactrian, standing here,
Cleave with his shaft a hand's breadth marked thereon?"
To which Prexaspes answered, "Nay, my lord;
I spake of feats compassed by mortal skill,
Not of gods' prowess." Unto whom, the King: —
"And if myself, Prexaspes, made essay,
Think'st thou, wise counsellor, I too should fail?"
"Needs must I, sire," — albeit the courtier's voice
Trembled, and some dark prescience bade him pause, —
"Needs must I hold such cunning more than man's;
And for the rest, I pray thy pardon, King,
But yester-eve, amid the feast and dance,
Thou tarried'st with the beakers overlong."

The thick, wild, treacherous eyebrows of the King,
That looked a sheltering ambush for ill thoughts
Waxing to manhood of malignant acts,
These treacherous eyebrows, pent-house fashion, closed
O'er the black orbits of his fiery eyes, —
Which, clouded thus, but flashed a deadlier gleam
On all before him: suddenly as fire,
Half choked and smouldering in its own dense smoke,
Bursts into roaring radiance and swift flame,
Touched by keen breaths of liberating wind, —
So now Cambyses' eyes a stormy joy
Stormily filled; for on Prexaspes' son,
His first-born son, they lingered, — a fair boy
('Midmost his fellow-pages flushed with sport),
Who, in his office of King's cupbearer,
So gracious and so sweet were all his ways,
Had even the captious sovereign seemed to please;
While for the court, the reckless, revelling court,
They loved him one and all:
"Go," said Cambyses now, his voice a hiss,
Poisonous and low, "go, bind my dainty page

To yonder palm-tree; bind him fast and sure,
So that no finger stirreth; which being done,
Fetch me, Prexaspes, the Macrobian bow."

Thus ordered, thus accomplished, fast they bound
The innocent child, the while that mammoth bow,
Brought by the spies from Ethiopian camps,
Lay in the King's hand; slowly, sternly up,
He reared it to the level of his sight,
Reared, and bent back its oaken massiveness
Till the vast muscles, tough as grapevines, bulged
From naked arm and shoulder, and the horns
Of the fierce weapon groaning, almost met,
When, with one lowering glance askance at him, —
His doubting satrap, — the King coolly said,
"Prexaspes, look, my aim is at the heart!"

Then came the sharp twang and the deadly whirr
Of the loosed arrow, followed by the dull,
Drear echo of a bolt that smites its mark;
And those of keenest vision shook to see
The fair child fallen forward across his bonds,
With all his limbs a-quivering. Quoth the King,
Clapping Prexaspes' shoulder, as in glee,
"Go thou, and tell me how that shaft hath sped!"
Forward the wretched father, step by step,
Crept, as one creeps whom black Hadèan dreams,
Visions of fate and fear unutterable,
Draw, tranced and rigid, towards some definite goal
Of horror; thus he went, and thus he saw
What never in the noontide or the night,
Awake or sleeping, idle or in toil,
'Neath the wild forest or the perfumed lamps
Of palaces, shall leave his stricken sight
Unblasted, or his spirit purged of woe.

Prexaspes saw, yet lived; saw, and returned
Where still environed by his dissolute court,
Cambyses leaned, half scornful, on his bow:
The old man's face was riven and white as death;
But making meek obeisance to his King,
He smiled (ah, *such* a smile!) and feebly said,
"What *am* I, mighty master, what am *I*,
That I durst question my lord's strength and skill?
His arrows are like arrows of the god,
Egyptian Horus, — and for proof, — but now,
I felt a child's heart (once a child was *mine*,
'Tis my Lord's now and Death's), all mute and still,
Pierced by his shaft, and cloven, ye gods! in twain!"

Then laughed the great King loudly, till his beard
Quivered, and all his stalwart body shook
With merriment; but when his mirth was calmed,
"Thou art forgiven," said he, "forgiven, old man;
Only when next these Persian dogs shall call
Cambyses drunkard, rise, Prexaspes, rise!
And tell them how, and to what purpose, once,

Once, on a morn which followed hot and wan
A night of monstrous revel and debauch,
Cambyses bent this huge Macrobian bow."

BY THE AUTUMN SEA.

FAIR as the dawn of the fairest day,
Sad as the evening's tender gray,
By the latest lustre of sunset kissed,
That wavers and wanes through an amber mist,
There cometh a dream of the past to me,
On the desert sands, by the autumn sea.

All heaven is wrapped in a mystic veil,
And the face of the ocean is dim and pale,
And there rises a wind from the chill northwest,
That seemeth the wail of a soul's unrest,
As the twilight falls, and the vapors flee
Far over the wastes of the autumn sea.

A single ship through the gloaming glides
Upborne on the swell of the seaward tides;
And above the gleam of her topmost spar
Are the virgin eyes of the vesper-star
That shine with an angel's ruth on me,
A hopeless waif, by the autumn sea.

The wings of the ghostly beach-birds gleam
Through the shimmering surf, and the curlew's scream
Falls faintly shrill from the darkening height;
The first weird sigh on the lips of Night
Breathes low through the sedge and the blasted tree,
With a murmur of doom, by the autumn sea.

Oh, sky-enshadowed and yearning main,
Your gloom but deepens this *human* pain;
Those waves seem big with a nameless care,
That sky is a type of the heart's despair,
As I linger and muse by the sombre lea,
And the night shades close on the autumn sea.

THE WIFE OF BRITTANY.

[Suggested by the Frankeleine's Tale of Chaucer.]

PROEM.

TRUTH wed to beauty in an antique tale,
Sweet-voiced like some immortal nightingale,
Trills the clear burden of her passsionate lay,
As fresh, as fair as wonderful to-day
As when the music of her balmy tongue
Ravished the first warm hearts for whom she sung.

Thus, when the early spring-dawn buds are green,
Glistening beneath the sudden silvery sheen
Of glancing showers; while heaven with bridegroom-kiss
Wakens the virgin earth to bloom and bliss,
Enamored breathing and soft raptures born
About the roseate footsteps of the morn,
An old-world song, whose breezy music pours
Through limpid channels 'twixt enchanted shores,
Steals on me wooingly from that far time
When tuneful Chaucer wrought his lusty rhyme
Into rare shapes and fancies and delight,
For May winds blithely blew, and hawthorn flowers were bright.

"There cometh a dream of the past to me,
On the desert sands by the autumn sea."

O brave old poet! genius frank and bold!
Sustain me, cherish and around me fold
Thine own hale, sun-warm atmosphere of song,
Lest I, who touch thy numbers, do thee wrong:
Speed the deep measure, make the meaning shine
Ruddy and high with healthful spirit wine,
Till to attempered sense and quickening ears
My strain some faint harmonious echo bears
From that rich realm wherein thy cordial art
Throbbed with its pulse of fire 'gainst youthful England's heart.

THE STORY.

WHERE the hoarse billows of the northland Sea
Sweep the rude coast of rockbound Brittany,
Dwelt, ages since, a knight whose warrior-fame
Might well have struck all carpet-knights with shame;
Vowed to great deeds and princely manhood, he
Burgeoned the topmost-flower of chivalry:
Yet gentle-hearted, nursed one delicate thought
Fixed firm in love: with anxious pain he sought
To serve his lady in the noblest wise,
And many a labor, many a grand emprise
He wrought ere that sweet lady could be won.
She was a maiden bright-aired as the sun,
And graceful as the tall lake-lilies are
Flushed 'twixt the twilight and the vesper-star;
But born to such rare state and sovereignty,
He hardly durst before her bend the knee
In passion's ardor and keen heart distress;
Still, at the last, his loyal worthiness
And mild obeisance, his observance high
Of manly faith, firm will, and constancy
Aroused an answering pity to his sighs,
Till pity, grown to love, beamed forth from genial eyes.

Thus with pure trust, and cheerful calm accord,
She made this gentle suitor her soul's lord;
And he, that thence their happy fates should stray
Through pastures beauteous as the fields of May,
Swore of his own free mind to use the right
Her mercy gave him, with no churlish might,
Nor e'er in wanton freaks of mastery,
Ire-bred perverseness, or sharp jealousy,
Vex the clear-flowing current of her days.
She thanked him in a hundred winning ways:
"And I," she said, "will be thy loyal wife;
Take here my vows, my solemn troth for life."

On a June morning, when the verdurous woods
Flushed to the core of dew-lit solitudes,
Murmured almost as with a human feeling,
Tenderly, low, to frolic breezes stealing
Through dappled shades and depths of dainty fern,
Crushed here and there by some low-whimpering burn,

These twain were wedded at a forest shrine.
O saffron-vested Hymen the divine!
Did aught of gloom or boding shadow weigh
Upon thy blushing consciousness that day?
No! thy frank face breathed only hope and love;
Earth laughed in wave and leaf, all heaven was fair above.

Home to the land wherein the knight was born
Blithely they rode upon the morrow-morn,
Not far from Penmark; there they lived in ease
And solace of matured felicities,
Until Arviragus whose soul of fire
Not even fruition of his love's desire
Could fill with languorous idlesse, cut the tie,
Which bound to silken dalliance suddenly,
Sailing the straits for England's war-torn strand,
There ampler bays to pluck from victory's "red right hand."

But Iolene, fond Iolene, whose heart
Can beat no longer, lonely and apart
From him she loves, save with a sickening stress
Of fear o'erwrought and brooding tenderness,
Mourns for his absence with soul-wearying plaint,
Slow, pitiful tears and midnight murmurings faint,
And thus the whole world sadly sets at naught.
Meanwhile her friends, who guess what canker-thought
Preys on her quiet, with a mild essay
Strive to subdue her passion's torturing sway:
"Beware! beware, sweet lady, thou wilt slay
Thy reason! nay thy very life's at stake!
By love, and love's dear pleadings, for his sake
Who yearns to clasp thee scathless to his breast,
We pray thee, soothe these maddening cares to rest!"

Even as the patient graver on a stone,
Laboring with tireless fingers, sees anon
The shape embodying his rare fancies grow
And lighten, thus upon her stubborn woe
Their tireless comforts wrought, until a trust,
Clear-eyed and constant, raised her from the dust
And ashy shroud of sorrow; her despair
Gave place to twilight gladness and soft cheer
Confirmed ere long by letters from her love:
"Dear Iolene!" he wrote, "thou tender dove
That tremblest in thy chilly nest at home,
Prithee embrace meek patience till I come.
Lo, the swift winds blow freshening o'er the sea,
From out the sunset isles I speed to rest with thee!"

The knight's ancestral home stood grim and tall
Beyond its shadowy moat and frowning wall;
It topped a gradual summit crowned with fir,
Green murmurous myrtle, and wild juniper,
Fronting a long, rude, solitary strand,
Whereon the earliest sunbeam, like a hand
Of tremulous benediction, rested bland,
And warmly quivering; o'er the wave-worn lea
Gleamed the broad spaces of the open sea.

Now often, with her pitying friends beside,
She walked the desolate beach and watched the tide,
Forth looking through unconscious tears to view
Sail after sail pass shimmering o'er the blue;
And to herself, ofttimes, "Alas!" said she,
"Is there no ship, of all these ships I see,
Will bring me home my lord? Woe, woe is me!
Though winds blow fresh, and sea-birds skim the main,
Thou still delay'st, my liege! Ah, *wilt* thou come again?"

Sometimes would she, half-dreaming, sit and think,
Casting her dark eyes downward from the brink;
And when she saw those grisly rocks beneath,
Round which the pallid foam, in many a wreath
White as the lips of passion, faintly curled,
Her thoughts would pierce to the drear under-world,
'Mid shipwrecks wandering, and bleached bones of those
O'er whom the unresting ocean ebbs and flows;
And though the shining waters hushed and deep,
Might slumber like an innocent child asleep,
From out the North her prescient fancy raised
Huge ghostlike clouds, and spectral lightnings blazed
I' th' van of phantom thunder, and the roar
Of multitudinous waters on the shore,
Heard as in dreadful trance its billowy swells
Blent with the mournful tone of far funereal bells!

Her friends perceiving that this seaside walk,
Though gay and jovial their unstudied talk,
But dashed her dubious spirits, kindly took
And led her where the blossom-bordered brook
Babbled through woodlands, and the limpid pool
Lay crouched like some shy Naiad in the cool
Of mossy glades; or when a tedious hour
Pressed on her with its dim, lethargic power,
They wooed her with glad games or jocund song,
Till the dull demon ceased to do her wrong.

So, on a pleasant May morn, while the dew
Sparkled on tiny hedgerow-flowers of blue,
Passing through many a sun-brown orchard-field,
They reach a fairy pleasaunce, which revealed
Such prospects into breezy inland vales,
The natural haunt of plaining nightingales,
Such verdant, grassy plots, through which there rolled
A gleeful rivulet glimpsing sands of gold,
And winding slow by clumps of plumèd pines,
Rich realms of bay, and gorgeous jasmine-vines,
That none who strayed to that fair flowery place
Had paused in wonder if its sylvan grace,
Embodied, beauteous, with an arch embrace
Had stopped, and smiling, kissed them face to face.

A buoyant, blithesome company were they,
Grouped round the pleasaunce on that morn of May;
Wit, song, and rippling laughter, and arch looks
That might have lured the wood-gods from their nooks,
Echoed and flashed like dazzling arrows tipped
With amorous heat; and now and then there slipped
From out the whirling ring of jocund girls,
Wreathing white arms and tossing wanton curls,
Some maiden who with momentary mien
Of coy demureness bent o'er Iolene,
And whispered sunniest nothings in her ear.

First 'mid the brave gallants assembling there
Aurelian came, a squire of fair degree,
Tall, vigorous, handsome, his whole air so free,
Yet courteous, and such princely sweetness blent
With every well-timed, graceful compliment,
That sooth to speak, where'er Aurelian went,
To turbulent tilt-yard and baronial hall,
Sporting afield or at high festival,
Favor, like sunshine, filled his heart and eyes.

Thus nobly gifted, high-born, opulent, wise,
One hidden curse was his: for troublous years,*
Secretly, swayed in turn by hopes and fears,
And all unknown to her, his heart's desire,
This youth had loved with wild, delirious fire,
The lonely, sad, unconscious Iolene.
He durst not show how love had brought him teen,
Nor prove how deep his passion's inward might;
Thinking, half maddened, on her absent knight;
Save that the burden of a love-lorn lay
Would somewhat of his stifled flame betray,
But in those vague complainings poets use,
When charging Love with outrage and abuse
Of his all-potent witchery. "Ah," said he,
"I love, but ever love despondently;
For though one vision haunts me, and I burn
To hold that dream incarnated, I yearn
In vain, in vain; love breathes no bland return!"

Thus only did Aurelian strive to show
What pangs of hidden passion worked below
The surface calmness of his front serene;
Unless perhaps he met his beauteous Queen,
Scarce brightening at the banquet or the dance;
When, with a piercing yet half-piteous glance,
His eyes would search, then strangely shun her face,
As one condemned, who fears to sue for grace.

But on this self-same day, when homeward bound,
Her footsteps sought the loneliest path that wound
Through tangled copses to the upland ground

* We are to suppose that Aurelian had seen Iolene previous to her marriage, and that circumstances had prevented his becoming intimate with her, or in any way prosecuting his suit honestly and frankly.

And orchard close, — her fair companions kissed
With tearful thanks, and all kind friends dismissed, —
Aurelian, who the secret pathway knew,
Through the dense growth and shrouded foliage drew
Near the pale Queen, the lady of his dreams:
The evening's soft, pathetic splendor streams
O'er her clear forehead and her chestnut hair,
All glorified as in celestial air;
But the dark eyes a wistful light confessed,
And some soft murmuring fancies heaved her breast
Benignly, like enamored tides that rise
And sink melodious to the west wind's sighs.

He gazed, and the long passion he had nursed,
Impetuous, sudden, unrestrained, o'erburst
All bounds of custom and enforced restraint:
"O lady, hear me: I am deadly faint,
Yet wild with love! such love as forces man
To beard conventions, trample on the ban
Of partial laws, spurn with contemptuous hate
Whate'er would bar or blight his blissful fate,
And in the feverous frenzy of his zeal,
Even from the shrinking flower he dotes on, steal
Blush, fragrance, and heart-dew! Forgive! forgive!
What! have I dared to tell thee this, to live
For aye hereafter in thy cold regard?
Yet veil thy scorn; nor make more cold and hard
The anguished life now cowering at thy feet."

As o'er a billowy field of ripened wheat
One sees perchance the spectral shadows meet,
Cast by a darkened heaven whose lowering hush
Broods, thunder-charged, above its golden flush, —
So, a dark wonder, a sublime suspense,
Of gathering wrath at this wild insolence,
Dimmed the mild glory of her brow and lips;
Her beauty, more majestic in eclipse,
Shone with that awful lustre which of old,
In the gods' temples and the fanes of gold,
Blazed in the Pythia's face, and shook her form
With throes of baleful prophecy; a storm
She stood incarnate, in whose ominous gloom
Throbbed the red lightning on the verge of doom.

But as a current of soft air, unfelt
On the lower earth, is seen ere long to melt
The up-piled surge of tempests slowly driven
In scattered vapors through the deeps of heaven,
Thus a serener thought tenderly played
Across her spirit; its portentous shade,
Big with unuttered wrath and meanings dire,
Began with slow, wan pulsings to expire;
A far ethereal voice she seemed to hear
Luting its merciful accents in her ear,
Subtly harmonious: "Yea," she thought, "in truth,
A rage, a madness holds him, the poor youth
Is drunk with passion! Shall I, deeply blessed
By all love's sweets, its balm and trustful rest,

Crush the less fortunate spirit! utterly
Blight and destroy him, *all for love of me?*
His hopes, if hopes he hath, must surely die;
Still would I nip their blossoms tenderly,
With a slight, airy frost-bite of contempt.
God's mercy, good Sir Squire, art thou exempt
Of courtesy as of reason? What weird spell
Doth work this madness in thee and compel
Thy nobler nature to such base despites?
Forsooth, thou'lt blush some day the flower of knights,
Should this thy budding virtue wax and grow
To natural consummation! Come! thy flow
Of weak self-ruth might shame the veriest child,
A six years' peevish urchin; whimpering wild,
And scattering his torn locks, because afar
He sees and yearns to clasp, but cannot clasp, a star!"

She ceased, with shame and pity weighing down
Her dovelike lids demurely, and a frown
Just struggling faintly with as faint a smile
(For the mute trembling squire still knelt the while)
Round the arch dimples of her rosy mouth:
Whereon, in fitful fashion, like the South
Which sweeps with petulant wing a field of blooms,
Then dies a heedless death 'mong golden brooms
And lavish shrubbery, briefly she resumes,
With quick-drawn breath, the courses of her speech:
"Aurelian, rise! Behold'st thou yonder beach,
And the blue waves beyond? those bristling rocks,
O'er which the chafed sea, in quick thunder-shocks,
Leaps passionate, panting through the showery spray,
Roaring defiance to the calm-eyed day?
Ah, well, fantastic boy! I blithely swear
When yon rude coast beneath us rises clear
(Down to the farthest bounds of wild Bretaigne),
Of that black rampart darkening sky and main,
I'll pay thy vows with answering vows again,
And be—God save the mark!—thy paramour."

Her words struck keen and deep, even to the core
Of the rash listener's soul; they seemed to be
More fatal in their careless irony
Than if the levin bolt, hurled from above,
Had slain at once his manhood and his love.
What more he felt in sooth 'twere vain to tell;
He only heard her whispering, "Fare-thee-well,
And Heaven assoil thee of all sinful sorrow!"
Then with a grace and majesty which borrow
Fresh lustrous sweetness from an inward stress
And hidden motion of chaste gentleness,
She glideth like some beauteous cloud apart;
Aurelian saw her pass with yearning pangs at heart.

PART II.

Soul-epochs are there, when grief's pitiless storm
O'erwhelms the amazèd spirit; when the warm
Exultant heart whose hopes were brave and high,
Shrinks in the darkness withering all its sky:
Then, like a wounded bird by the rude wind
Clutched and borne onward, tortured, reckless, blind,
Too frail to struggle with that passionate blast,
We take wild, wavering courses, and at last
Are dashed, it may be, on the rocky verge,

"Those bristling rocks,
O'er which the chafed sea, in quick thunder-shocks,
Leaps passionate, panting through the showery spray."

Or hurled o'er the unknown and perilous surge
Of some dark doom, when, bruised and tempest-tost,
We sink in turbulent eddies, and are lost.

Urged by a mood thus desperate, careless what
Thenceforth befell him, from that hateful spot,
The scene of such stern anguish and despair,
Aurelian rushed, he knew not, recked not, where.
All night he wandered in the forest drear,
Till on the pale phantasmal front of morn
The first thin flickering day-gleam glanced forlorn,
Wan as the wraith of perished hopes, the ghost
Of wishes long sustained and fostered most,
Now gone for evermore. "O Christ! that I,"
He muttered hoarsely, "might unsought for lie
Here, in the dismal shadows and dank grass,
And close my heavy eyelids, and so pass

With one brief struggle from the world of men,
Never to grieve or languish, — never again!
Never to sow live seeds of expectation
And joyous promise, to reap desolation;
But as the seasons fly, snow-wreathed, or crowned
With odorous garlands, rest in the mute ground,
Peaceful, oblivious, — a Lethéan cloud
Wrapped round my faded senses like a shroud,
And all earth's turmoil and its juggling show
Dead as a dream dissolved ten thousand years ago!"

Long, long revolving his sad thoughts he stood,
When gleefully from out the lightening wood
Came the sharp ring of horn and echoing steed;
A score of huntsmen, scouring at full speed,
Flashed like a brilliant meteor o'er the scene,
In royal pomp of glimmering gold and green;
Whereat, with wrathful gestures, 'neath the dome
Of the old wood he hastened towards his home,
Where day by day he grew more woeful-pale,
Calling on Heaven unheard to ease his bale.

Among his kinsfolk, many in hot haste,
To salve an unknown wound with balms misplaced,
Came the squire's brother, Curio, — a wise scribe,
Modest withal, and nobler than his tribe;
With heart as loving as his brain was wise:
He could not see with cold, indifferent eyes
Aurelian pass to madness or the grave,
While care and wit of man perchance might save;
So, pondering o'er what seemed a desperate case,
At length there leapt into his kindling face
The flush of a bright thought. "By Heaven!" cried he,
"O brother, there may still be hope for thee;
Therefore, take heart of grace, for what I tell
Doubtless preludes a health-inspiring spell;
And thou, released from this long, sorrowful blight,
Shalt feel the stir of joy, and bless the morning light.

"Ten years — ten centuries sometimes they would seem —
Passed idly o'er me like a mystic's dream;
Ten years agone, when these dull locks of mine
Flowed round broad shoulders with a perfumed shine,
And life's clear glass o'erbrimmed with purpling wine,
I met in Orleans a shrewd clerk-at-law,
One all his comrades loved, yet viewed with awe,
To whom the deepest lore of antique ages,
The storèd secrets of old seers and sages
In Greece, or Ind, or Araby, lay bare;
From out the vacant kingdoms of the air,
He could at will call forth a hundred forms,
Hideous or lovely; the wild wrath of storms;
The zephyr's sweetness; bird, beast, wave, obeyed
The luminous signs his slender wand conveyed,

At whose weird touch men sick in flesh or brain
Became their old, bright, hopeful selves again.
Aurelian, rise! shake off this vile disease,
And ride with me to Orleans; an' it please
God and our Lady, we may chance to meet
Mine ancient comrade, who with deftest feat
Of magic skill may cut the Gordian knot
That long hath bound, and darkly binds thy lot."

"But," said Aurelian, with a listless turn
Of his drooped head, and wandering eyes that burn
With a quick feverish brilliance, "dost thou speak
Of thine own knowledge, when thou bid'st me seek
This rare magician? Hast *thou* looked on aught
Of all the mighty marvels he hath wrought?"

"Yea! I bethink me how, one summer's day,
He led me through the city gates, away
To the dark hollows 'neath a lonely hill:
So hushed the noontide, and so breathless-still
The drowsy air, the voice of one far stream
Came like thin whispers murmuring in a dream;
The blithesome grasshopper, his sense half closed
To all his verdurous luxury, reposed
Pendent upon the quivering, spearlike grain;
Steeped in the mellow sunshine's noiseless rain,
All Nature slept; alone the matron wren,
From the thick coverts of her thorny den,
Teased the hot silence with her twittering low:
My inmost soul accordant, seemed to grow
Languid and dumb within that mystic place.
At length the Wizard's hand across my face
Was waved with gentle motion; a vague mist
Flickered before me, on a sudden kissed
To warmth and glory by an influence bright;
The strangest glamour hovered o'er my sight,
Wherethrough I saw, methought, a palace proud,
Crowned by a lightning-veinèd thunder-cloud,
Whose wreaths of vapory darkness gleamed with eyes
Of multitudinous shifting fantasies;
Its pinnacles like diamond spars outshone
The starry splendors of an orient zone;
And, leading towards its lordly entrance, rose
Through slow gradations to its marbled close,
White terraces where golden sunflowers bloomed;
Above a ponderous portal archway loomed,
High-columned, quaint, majestical: we passed
Within that palace, gorgeous, wild, and vast.
Ah! blessed saints! what wonders weirdly blent
Did smite me with a hushed astonishment!
A troop of monsters couchant lined our path,
Their tawny manes and eyes of fiery wrath
Erect and blazing; an unearthly roar
Of fury, shaking vaulted roof and floor,

Burst from each savage, inarticulate
throat,
In sullen echoings lost through halls and
courts remote.

"At the far end of glimmering colon-
nades
That gleamed gigantic through the dusky
shades,
Two mighty doors swept backward noise-
lessly;
There heaved beyond us a vast laboring
sea;
Not vacant, for a stately vessel bore
Swift down the threatening tides that
flashed before,
Thronged with black-bearded Titans,
such as moved
In far-off times heroic, well-beloved
Of the old gods; there at his stalwart
ease,
Shouldering his knotted club, great Her-
cules
Towered, his fierce eyes touched to dewy
light,
And rapt on Hylas, who, serenely bright,
With intense gaze uplifted, tranced and
mute,
Heard, in ecstatic reverie, the lute
Of Orpheus plaining to the waves that
bow
And dance subsiding round the blazoned
prow;
Till the rude winds blew meekly, and
caressed
The mimic golden fleeces o'er the crest
Of bard and warrior, on their secret quest
Bound to the groves of Colchis; and the
bark,
Round which had frowned a threatening
shape and dark,
Now seemed to thrill, like some proud,
sentient thing
That glories in the prowess of its wing.
The gusty billows of that turbulent sea
Their wild crests smoothed, and slowly,
pantingly,
Sunk to the quiet of a charmèd calm;
What odors Hesperéan, what rich balm
Freight the fair zephyrs, as they shyly
run
O'er the lulled waters dimpling in the
sun!
And murmurings, hark! soft as the long-
drawn kiss
Pressed by a young god-lover in his
bliss
On lips immortal, when the world was
new;
And, lo! across the pure, pellucid
blue,
A barge, with silken sails, whose beaute-
ous crew,
Winged fays and Cupids, curl their
sportive arms
O'er one, more lovely in her noontide
charms
Than youngest nymphs of Paphos; fra-
grant showers
Of freshening roses, all luxuriant flowers
That feed on eastern dews, their fairy
bands
Scatter about her from white liberal
hands;
While o'er the surface of the dazzling
water,
Dark-eyed, mysterious, many an ocean
daughter
Flashes a vanishing brightness on her
way,
Half seen through tiny tinklings of the
spray;
And music its full heart in airy falls
Outpours, like silvery cascades down the
walls
Of haunted rocks, and golden cymbals
ring,
And lutelike measures on voluptuous
wing
Rise gently to the trancèd heavens, re-
plying
From azure-tinted deeps in a low pas-
sionate sighing.

"Then were all climes, all ages, wildly
blended
On blood-red fields, wherefrom shrill
shouts ascended

Of naked warriors, huge and swart of limb,
Mixed with the mailèd Grecians' ominous hymn,
Where mighty banners starlike waved and shone
'Mid cloven bucklers grandly; and anon
Marched the stern Roman phalanx, with a ring
And clash of spears, and lusty trumpeting,
And steeds that neighed defiance unto death,
And all war's dreadful pomp and hot, devouring breath.
Last, on a sudden, the whole tumult died,
The vision disappeared; pale, leaden-eyed,
Bewildered, on the enchanted floor I sank;
When next my wakening spirit faintly drank
Life's consciousness, within my lonely room
I sat, and round me drooped the dreary twilight gloom."

Enough, good brother! By the Holy Rood
Thy tale is medicínal! the black mood,
Which like a spiritual vulture seized and tore
My heart-strings, and imbued its beak in gore
Hot from the soul, beneath the golden spell
Of sovereign hope hath sought its native hell.
Then, ho! for Orleans!" At the word he sprung
Light to his feet; it seemed there scarcely hung
One trace of his long madness round him now,
So blithe his smile, so bright his kindling brow.
All day they rode till waning afternoon,
Through breezy copses, and the shadowy boon
Of mightier woods, when, as the latest glance
Of sunset, like a level burnished lance,
Smote their steel morions, sauntering near the town,
With thoughtful mien, robed in his scholar's gown,
They met a keen-eyed man, ruddy and tall;
O'er his grave vest a beard of wavy fall
Flowed like a rushing streamlet, rippling down:
"Welcome!" he cried in mellow accents deep;
"The stars have warned me, and my visioned sleep
Foretold your mission, gentles. Curio, what!
Thine ancient, loving comrade quite forgot?
Spur thy dull memory, gossip!"

"By St. Paul!
The learned clerk, the gracious Artevall,
Or glamour's in it," shouted Curio; "yet
Thou look'st as hale, as young, as firmly set
In face and form, as if for thee old Time
Had stopped his flight." A lofty glance, sublime
And swift as lightning, from the Magian's eye
Darted some latent meaning grave and high.
He spake not, but the twain he gently led
Where grassy pathways and fair meads were spread,
Skirting the city walls, till near them stood,
Fronting the gloomy boskage of a wood,
The wizard's lonely home, I need not pause
To tell how magic and the occult laws

Of sciences long dead that sage's lore
Did in the spectral midnight hours explore.
Enough, that his strange spells a marvel wrought
Beyond the utmost reach of credulous thought.
At last he said, "Sir Squire, my task is o'er;
Go when thou wilt, and view the Breton shore,
And thou shalt see a wide unwrinkled strand,
Smooth as thy lovely lady's delicate hand,
Washed by a sea o'er which the halcyon West
Broods like a happy heart whose dreams are dreams of rest."

PART III.

Meanwhile Arviragus, a year before
Returned in honor from the English shore,
Led with his faithful Iolene that life
Harmonious, justly balanced, free from strife,
Which crowns our hopes with a true-hearted wife.

Ne'er dreamed he, as she laid her happy head
Close to his heart, what cloud of shame and dread
Gloomed o'er his placid roof-tree; but content
To think how nobly his late toils had spent
Their force beneath Death's gory dripping brow
Through shocks of battle, a fresh laurel bough
Plucking therefrom to flourish green and high
About his war-worn temples' majesty,
Gladly from bloodshed, conflicts, and alarms
Here rested in those white, encircling arms,
And oft his strong heart thrilled, his eyes grew dim,
To know, kind heaven! how deep her love for him.

Thus month on month the cheerful days went by,
Like carolling birds across an April sky,
A fairy sky undimmed by clouds or showers.
But on a morning, while her favorite flowers
Iolene tended, in the garden-walks
Pausing to clip dead leaves and prop the stalks
Of drooping plants, herself more sweet and fair
Than any flower, the brightest that blushed there,
Her lord stole gently on her unaware;
His haughty grace all softened, he bowed down
To kiss the stray curls of her locks of brown,
Thick sown with threads of tangled, glimmering gold:
"At need," he said, "thou canst be calm and bold;
Therefore, thou wilt not yield to foolish woe
If duty parts us briefly. Wife, I go
To scourge some banded ruffians who of late
Assailed our peaceful serfs, and our estate —
Thou knowest it well — northwest of Penmark town,
Ravished with sword and fire. Thy lord's renown,
Yea, and thy lord, were soon the scoff of all,
If in his own fair fief such crimes befall
Unscourged of justice; so, dear love, adieu!
Nor fear the end of that I have to do."

Thus spake the knight, who forthwith raised a shout,
And bade them bring his stalwart war-horse out;
When, on the sudden, a steed, tall, jet-black,
Led by a groom came whinnying down the track,
'Twixt the green myrtle hedges; at a bound
He vaulted in the selle; smilingly round
He turned to wave "farewell" with mailèd hand,
And then rode blithely down the sunlit land.

That evening, at the close of vesper prayer,
Wandering along through the still twi-light air,
Iolene, somewhat sad and sick in mind,
Met in her homeward pathway, low-re-clined
Beneath the blasted branches of an oak,
Aurelian, her wild lover of old days:
She started backward in a wan amaze.
But he, uprising calmly, bowed and spoke;
"Ha! thou recall'st me, lady? I had deemed
These bitter years which have so scarred and seamed
Whate'er of grace I owned in youthful prime,
Had razed me from thy memory. See a rime
Like that of age hath touched my locks to white;
Yet never once, — so help me heaven! — by night
Or day, in storm or brightness, hath my soul
Veered but a point from thee, its starry goal.
A mighty purpose doth itself fulfil,
Wise men have said. Lady! I love thee still,
And Love works marvels. Prithee come with me,
Ay, quickly come, and thou thyself shalt see
I am no falsehood-monger. Yea, come, come!"
His words, his sudden passion, smote her dumb,
And from her cheeks, those delicate gar-dens, wane
The rare twin roses, as when autumn rain,
Fatally sharp, sweeps o'er some doomed domain
Of matron blooms, and their rich colors fade
Like rainbows slowly dying, shade by shade,
Unto wan spectres of the flowers that were.
With languid head and thoughts of pre-scient fear,
Passively following where Aurelian guides,
She hears anon the surge and rush of tides
On the seashore, and feels the freshen-ing spray
Bedew her brow. "Lady, look forth, and say
If, to a love unquenched, unquenchable,
Eternal Nature yields not; its strong spell
Hath toiled for me, till the rocks rooted under
Those heaving waters have been rent asunder,
And the wide spaces of the ocean plain,
Down to the farthest bounds of wild Bretaigne,
Rise calmly glorious in the day-god's beam.
Look, look thy fill! it is no vanishing dream:
Lo! now I claim thy promise!"

A keen gleam
Shot its victorious radiance o'er his brow.
But she, bewildered, tremulous, shrink-ing low,

Her clinched hands pale even to the finger-tips,
Pressed on her blinded eyes and faltering lips,
Sued in a voice like wailing wind that breaks
From aspen coverts over lonely lakes,
In the shut heart of immemorial dells, —
A fitful, sobbing voice, whose anguish swells,
Burdened with deep upyearning supplication,
Coldly across his evil exultation.
She pleads for brief delay, with frenzied pain
Grasping at some dim phantom of the brain,
Shadowing a vague deliverance. "As thou wilt,"
He answered slowly. "Well I know the guilt
Of broken vows can never rest on thee!
Pass by unhurt!" Mutely she turned to flee,
Nor paused until her chambered privacy
She reached with panting sides, pallid as death,
And gasping with short, anguished sobs for breath.
"Caught am I, trapped like a poor fluttering bird,
Or dappled youngling from the innocent herd
Lured to a pitfall! Yet such oath as *this*
Were surely void? If not, he still shall miss —
Whate'er betide — his long-expected bliss!
Better pure-folded arms, and stainless sleep
Where the gray-drooping willow-branches weep,
Than meet a fate so hideous! Let me think!
Others, — pure wives, brave virgins, on the brink
Of shame and ruin, have struck home and fled,
To find unending quiet with the dead."

Borne down as by a demon's hand which pressed
Invisible, but stifling on her breast,
With brain benumbed, yet burning, and a sense
Of utter, wearied, desperate impotence,
Her forlorn glance around the darkening room
Roving in helpless search, from out the gloom
Caught the blue glitter of a half-sheathed blade,
A small but trenchant steel, whose lustre played
Balefully bright, and like a serpent's eye
Fixed on her with malign expectancy,
Drew her perforce towards Death, — that death which seemed
The sole, stern means through which her fame redeemed,
Should soar in spiritual beauty o'er the tomb
Wherein might rest her body's mouldering bloom.

Ah, me! the looks distraught, the passionate care,
The whole wild scene, its misery and despair,
Come back like scenes of yesterday. Half bowed
Her queenly form, and the pent grief allowed
A moment's freedom shakes her to the core,
The inmost seat of reason. "All is o'er,"
She murmurs, as her slender fingers feel
The deadly edge of the cold shimmering steel.
At once her swift arm flashes to its height,
While the poised death hangs quivering, and her sight
Grows dazed and giddy: when from far, so far
It sounded like the weird voice of a star,

"He turned to wave 'farewell' with mailèd hand,
And then rode blithely down the sunlit land."

Muffled by distance, yet distinct and deep,
About her in the terrible silence creep
Accents that seize as with a bodily force
On her white arm suspended, and its course
To fatal issues, with arresting will
Hold rigid, till supine it drops and still,
Back to its drooping level, and a clang
Of the freed steel through all the chamber rang
Sharply, and something shuddered down the air
Like wings of baffled fiends passing in fierce despair.

A warning blent of prescient wrath and prayer
Those accents seemed, where through a palpable dread
Ran coldly shivering. "Pause, pause, pause!" they said;
"Bar not thy hopes 'gainst chance of happier fate!
The circuit vast which rounds life's dial-plate
Hath many lights and shades; its hand which lowers
So threatening *now*, may move to golden hours,
And thou on this sad time may'st look like one
Smiling on mortal woes from some unsetting sun."

Motionless, overcome by hushing awe,
She heard the mystic voice, and dreamed she saw,
Just o'er the dubious borders of the light,
A wavering apparition, scarce more bright
Than one faint moon-ray, through the misty tears
Of clouded evenings seen on breezeless mountain meres.
Mistlike it waned; but in her heart of hearts
The solemn counsel sank: with guilty starts,
She thought how near, through grief's bewildering blight,
How near to death, to death and shame, this night
Her reckless soul had strayed. Yet short-lived hope
Moved hour by hour through paths of narrowing scope,
As, day by day, her term of grace passed by,
Like phantom birds across a phantom sky;
Her lord still absent, and Aurelian bound
(For thus he wrote her) to one weary round,
Morn after morn, of pacings to and fro,
Within the wooded garden-walls below
The city's southward portals. "There," said he,
"Each day, and all day long, impatiently
I wait thy will."

As when in dewy spring,
'Mid the moist herbage closely nestling,
Ofttimes we see the hunted partridge cling,
Panting and scared, to the thick-covering grass,
The while above her couch doth darkly pass
What seemeth the shadow of a giant wing,
And she, more lowly, with a cowering stoop,
Shivers, expecting the fell, fiery swoop
Of the gaunt hawk, that corsair of the breeze,
And feels beforehand his sharp talons seize
And rend her tender vitals; so at home,
Iolene, trembling at the stroke to come,
Touched by the lurid shadow of her doom,
Lingered; until, upon a sunny dawn,
Her lord returning, gayly up the lawn

Urged his blithe courser, and, dismounting, came
Upon her, warmly glowing, all aflame
With hope and love. But as her dreary eyes
Were turned on his, a quick, disturbed surprise
And then a terror, smote him, and the voice
All jubilant, full-breathed to say, "Rejoice,
Our foes are slain!" clave stammering in his throat.
But she, her loose, dishevelled locks afloat
Round the fair-sloping shoulders, her hands clasped
About his mailèd knees, brokenly gasped
Her anguish forth, and told her sorrowful tale.
Dizzy and mute, and as the marble pale
Whereon he leaned, unto the desperate close
The knight heard all, locked in a cold repose
More dread than storniest passion; life and strength
Seemed slowly ebbing from him, till at length
His soul, like one that walks the fatal sand
(Whose treacherous smoothness looks a solid strand,
But tempts to ruin), felt all earth grow dim,
And round him saw, as in a chaos, swim
Joy's fair horizon melting in the cloud.
But soon his stalwart will, rugged and proud,
Woke lionlike to action; a swift flush
Rushed like a sunset river's reddening glow
O'er the tempestuous blackness of his brow,
Pregnant with thunder; through the dismal hush,
His pitiless voice, sharp-echoing round about
The clanging court, leaped like a falchion out.

"Thou hast played with honor as a juggler's ball;
God strikes thee from thy balance, and the thrall
Art thou, henceforth, of one vainglorious deed.
What! shall we plant with rash caprice the seed
Of bitterness, nor look for some harsh fruit
To spring untimely from its poisonous root?
What! a lewd spark, a perfumed popinjay,
Dares in the broad-browed, honest gaze of day,
To dash a foul thought, like the hideous spray
Of Hell, right in thy forehead, — and thy hand,
Which should have towered as if the levin-brand
Of scorn and judgment armed it, but a bland
Dismissal signs him! not one hint which tells
Thy lord, meantime, what loathsome secret dwells
Here, by his hearthstone, muffled up, concealed,
And like a corse corrupting, till, revealed
By vengeful doom, its pestilent odor steals
Outward, while all the wholesome blood congeals
To a chill horror, and the air grows vile,
And even the blessed sun a death's-head smile
Assumes in our distempered fantasy?
By Heaven! this withering curse which hangs o'er thee,
O Iolene!" — but here his angry voice
Broke short, — "There is no choice," he moaned, "no choice.

Yea, wife! may Christ adjudge me if I lie,
To endless, as now keen calamity,
But through this troublous gloom my mind discerns
One lonely light to guide us; lo, it burns
Lurid, yet clear, by whose fierce flame I see —
Ah, grief malign! ah, bitter destiny! —
As if God's own right hand the blazing pain
And fiery bale did stamp on soul and brain,
These terms of doom:
Shame and despair for both,
Sorrow and heartbreak! Through all, keep thine oath,
Thou woman, self-involved, self-lost; and so
Face the black front of this tremendous woe!"

She bowed as if a blast of sudden wind,
Breathing full winter, smote her cold and blind;
Then as one wandering in a soul-eclipse,
Feebly she rose, and with her quivering lips
Kissed her pale lord, stifling one desolate cry.
Anon she moved around him noiselessly
Bent on the small, sweet offices of love;
And sometimes pausing, she would glance above
With tearless eyes, for solemn griefs like this,
Blighting at once both root and flowers of bliss,
Are arid as the desert, and in vain
Thirst for the cooling freshness of the rain,
Fitfully led from treasured nook to nook
Of her dear home, she walked with far-off look,
And absent fingers, plying household tasks:
Bravely her sunless wretchedness she masks
Through moments deemed unending while they passed —
When passed, a flickering point! Hark! The doomed hour at last!

. . . . . .

An afternoon it was, stirless and calm:
From field and garden-close rare breaths of balm
Made the air moist and odorous. Nature lay
Divinely peaceful; only far away
In the broad zenith, a strange cloud unfurled
Its boding banner weirdly o'er the world;
Whilst Iolene, her veiled head sadly bowed,
Passed through the gay thorpe and its motley crowd,
To where a great wall towered this side a wood.
All things her mazed, chaotic fancy viewed
Looked dreamlike; even Aurelian lingering there,
To meet her in the shadiest forest-lair,
Gleamed ghostly dim, a dreadful ghost in sooth, —
For still a hideous trance appeared to press
Upon her and a nightmare helplessness,—
To whom she knelt in sad mechanic guise,
Pleading for mercy with such piteous eyes,
And such soft flow of self-bewailing ruth,
Aurelian felt his passion's quivering chords
Stilled at the touch of those pathetic words,
That glance of wild appealing agonies.
Stirred by his nobler nature's grave command
(That fair, indwelling angel sweet and grand,
Born to transmute the worn and blasted soil
Of sinful hearts by his celestial toil

To Eden places and the haunts of God),
He stooped, and, courteous, raised her from the sod,
And whispered closely in her eager ear
Words which his guardian genius smiled to hear;
Words of release, and balmy breathing cheer.
And while his softening gaze a grateful mist
Feelingly dimmed, with knightly grace he kissed
Her drooping forehead, and loose tresses thrown
In rippling waves adown the heaving zone;
Once, twice, he kissed her thus, with reverence meek;
But when her brimming eyes uplifted, seek
Aurelian now, with eloquent looks to tell
What tenderest words could not convey so well,
She only hears the tree-stems, tall and brown,
The golden leaves come faintly fluttering down,
And only hears the wind of sunset moan:
Midmost the twilight wood the lady stands alone.

Stung by his misery into frenzied motion,
Her lord meantime beside the restless ocean
Roamed, hearkening to the mournful undertone
Of the sea's mighty heart, which touched his own,
O God, how sadly! when abruptly lifting
His furrowed brow, long fixed upon the shifting
And mimic whirlwinds of loose sand that flew
Hither and thither, as the brief winds blew
At fitful whiles from o'er the watery waste,
He saw, as if she spurned the earth in haste,
His gentle wife returning, with a face
Whereon there dwelt no shadow of disgrace;
A face that seemed transfigured in the light
Of Paradise, it shone so softly bright.
Beautiful ever, round her now there hovered
A subtle, new-born glory, which discovered
A shape so dazzling, you had thought the plume
Of some archangel's pinion cast its bloom
About her, and the veil of heaven withdrawn,
She viewed the mystic streams, the sapphire dawn,
And heard the choirs celestial, tier on tier
Uptowering to the uttermost golden sphere,
Sing of a vanquished dread, a blest release,
The effluence and the solemn charm of peace.

Evening closed round them; o'er the placid reach
Stretching far northward of the sea-girt beach,
They passed, while night's first planet in the sky
Faltered from out the stillness timidly,
And perfumed breezes rustled murmuring by,
'Twixt the grim headlands up the glens to die,
And white-winged sea-birds, with a long-drawn cry,
Which spake of homeward flight and billowy nest,
Glanced through the sunset down the wavering West.

Evening closed o'er them, mellowing
into dark;
Along the horizon's edge, a tiny spark,
Dull-red at first, but broadening to a
white
And tranquil orb of silver-streaming
light,
Slowly the Night Queen fair her heaven
ascends:
The outlines of those loving forms she
blends
Into one luminous shade, which seems
to float,
Mingle and melt in shining mists remote;
Type of two perfect lives, whose single
soul
Outbreathes a cordial music, sweet and
whole,
One will, one mind, one joy-encircled
fate,
And one winged faith that soars beyond
the heavenly gate.

My song, which now hath long flowed
unperplexed
Through scenes so various, calm as
heaven, or vexed
By gusty passion, reaches the lone shore,
Ghostlike and strange, of silence and old
dreams;
Far-off its weird and wandering whisper
seems
Like airs that faint o'er untracked oceans
hoar
On haunted midnights, when the moon
is low.
And now 'tis ended: long, yea, long
ago,
Lost on the wings of all the winds that
blow,
The dust of these dead loves hath passed
away;
Still, still, methinks, a soft, ethereal
ray
Illumes the tender record, and makes
bright
Its heart-deep pathos with a marvellous
light,
So that whate'er of frenzied grief and
pain
Marred the pure currents of the crystal
strain,
Transfigured shines through fancy's mel-
lowing trance,
Touching with golden haze the quaint
old-world romance.

NOTE. — Of "The Frankleines Tale," the plot of which has been followed in "The Wife of Brittany," Richard Henry Horne, the author of "Orion," says: "It is a noble story, perfect in its moral purpose, and chivalrous self-devotion to a feeling of truth and honor; but it would have been more satisfactory in an intellectual sense had a distinction been made between a sincere pledge of faith and a 'merry bond!'"

THE RIVER.

["Man's life is like a river, which likewise hath its seasons or phases of progress: first, its spring rise, gentle and beautiful; next, its summer, of eventful maturity, mixed calm, and storm, followed by autumnal decadence, and mists of winter, after which cometh the all-embracing sea, type of that mystery we call eternity!"]

UP among the dew-lit fallows
  Slight but fair it took its rise,
And through rounds of golden shallows
  Brightened under broadening skies;
While the delicate wind of morning
  Touched the waves to happier grace,
Like a breath of love's forewarning,
  Dimpling o'er a virgin face, —
Till the tides of that rare river
  Merged and mellowed into one,
Flashed the shafts from sundawn's quiver
  Backward to the sun.

Royal breadths of sky-born blushes
  Burned athwart its billowy breast, —
But beyond those roseate flushes
  Shone the snow-white swans at rest;
Round in graceful flights the swallows
  Dipped and soared, and soaring sang,
And in bays and reed-bound hollows,
  How earth's wild, sweet voices rang!

Till the strong, swift, glorious river
Seemed with mightier pulse to run,
Thus to roll and rush forever,
Laughing in the sun.

Nay; a something born of shadow
Slowly crept the landscape o'er, —
Something weird o'er wave and meadow,
Something cold o'er stream and shore;
While on birds that gleamed or chanted,
Stole gray gloom and silence grim,
And the troubled wave-heart panted,
And the smiling heavens waxed dim,
And from far strange spaces seaward,
Out of dreamy cloud-lands dun,
Came a low gust moaning leeward,
Chilling leaf and sun.

Then, from gloom to gloom intenser,
On the laboring streamlet rolled,
Where from cloud-racks gathered denser,
Hark! the ominous thunder knolled!
While like ghosts that flit and shiver,
Down the mists, from out the blast,
Spectral pinions crossed the river, —
Spectral voices wailing passed!
Till the fierce tides, rising starkly,
Blended, towering into one
Mighty wall of blackness, darkly
Quenching sky and sun!

Thence, to softer scenes it wandered,
Scents of flowers and airs of balm,
And methought the streamlet pondered,
Conscious of the blissful calm;
Slow it wound now, slow and slower
By still beach and ripply bight,
And the voice of waves sank lower,
Laden, languid with delight;
In and out the cordial river
Strayed in peaceful curves that won
Glory from the great Life-Giver,
Beauty from the sun!

Thence again with quaintest ranges,
On the fateful streamlet rolled
Through unnumbered, nameless changes,
Shade and sunshine, gloom and gold,
Till the tides, grown sad and weary,
Longed to meet the mightier main,
And their low-toned *miserere*
Mingled with his grand refrain;
Oh, the languid, lapsing river,
Weak of pulse and soft of tune, —
Lo! the sun hath set forever,
Lo! the ghostly moon!

But thenceforth through moon and star-light
Sudden-swift the streamlet's sweep;
Yearning for the mystic far-light,
Pining for the solemn deep;
While the old strength gathers o'er it,
While the old voice rings sublime,
And in pallid mist before it,
Fade the phantom shows of time, —
Till with one last eddying quiver,
All its checkered journey done,
Seaward breaks the ransomed river,
Goal and grave are won!

THE STORY OF GLAUCUS THE THESSALIAN.*

TO ——

List to this legend, which an antique poet
Hath left among the musty tomes of eld,
Like a flushed rosebud pressed between the leaves
Of some worn, dark-hued volume. What a light
Of healthful bloom about it! What an air
Seems breathing round its delicate petals still!
Wilt thou not take it, lady, — thou, whose face
Is lovely as a lost Arcadian dream, —
And place it next thy heart, and keep it fresh
With balmy dews thy gentle spirit sends

* The elements of this story are to be found in Apollonius Rhodius, and Leigh Hunt has embodied them in a graceful prose legend.

"On the fateful streamlet rolled
Through unnumbered, nameless changes,
Shade and sunshine, gloom and gold."

Up to the deep founts of the tenderest eyes
That e'er have shone, I think, since in some dell
Of Argos and enchanted Thessaly,
The poet, from whose heart-lit brain it came,
Murmured this record unto her he loved?

THE STORY.

Glaucus, a young Thessalian, while the dawn
Of a fresh spring-tide brightened copse and lawn,
Sauntered, with lingering steps and dreamy mood,
Adown the fragrant pathway of a wood
Which skirted his small homestead pleasantly, —
And there he saw a tall, majestic tree,
An oak of untold summers, whose broad crown,
Quivering as if in some slow agony,
And trembling inch by inch forlornly down,
Threatened, for want of a kind propping care,
To leave its breezy realm of golden air,
And from its leafy heights, with shriek and groan,
Like some proud forest empire overthrown,
Measure its vast bulk on the greensward lone.

Glaucus beheld and pitied it. He saw
The approaching ruin with a touch of awe,
No less than genial sympathy,— for men,
In those old times, pierced with a wiser ken
To the deep soul of Nature, and from thence
Drew a serene and mystic influence,
Which thrilled all life to music. Therefore he
Called on his slaves, and bade them prop the tree.

Musing he passed to a still lonelier place
In the dim forest, by this act of grace
Lightened and cheered, when, from the copse-wood nigh,
There dawned upon his vision suddenly
A shape more fair and lustrous than the star
Which rides o'er Cloudland on her sapphire car
When vesper winds are fluting solemnly.
"Glaucus," she said, in tones whose liquid flow,
Mellow, harmonious, passionately low,
Stole o'er his spirit with a strange, wild thrill,
"I am the Nymph of that fair tree thy will
Hath saved from ruin; but for thee my breath
Had vanished mistlike, — my glad eyes in death
Been sealed for evermore. Yes! but for thee
I must have lost that half-divinity
Whose secret essence, spiritually fine,
Hath warmed my veins like Hebe's heavenly wine.
No more, no more amid my rippling hair
Could I have felt soft fingers of the air
Dallying at dawn or twilight, — on my cheek
Have felt the sun rest with a rosy streak,
Pulsing in languor; nor with pleasant pain
Drooped in the cool arms of the loving Rain,
That wept its soul out on my bosom fair.
But now, in long, calm, blissful days to be,
This life of mine shall lapse deliciously
Through all the seasons of the bounteous year;
Beneath my shade mortals shall sit, and hear
Benignant whispers in the shimmering leaves;
And sometimes, upon warm and odorous eves,

Lovers shall bring me offerings of sweet things, —
Honey and fruit, — and dream they mark the wings
Of Cupids fluttering through the oak-boughs hoar.
All this I owe thee, Glaucus, — all, and more!
Ask what thou wilt! — thou shalt not ask in vain!"

Then Glaucus, gazing in her glorious eyes,
And rallying from his first unmanned surprise,
Emboldened, too, by her soft looks, which drew
A spell about his heart like fire and dew
Mingled and melting in a love-charm bland, —
And by the twinkling of her moon-white hand,
That seemed to beckon coyly to her side,
And by her maiden sweetness deified,
And something that he deemed a dear unrest
Heaving the unveiled billows of her breast —
(As if her preternatural part, as free
And wild as any nursling of the lea,
Yearned wholly downward to humanity) —
Emboldened thus, I say, Glaucus replied:
"O fairest vision! be my love, — my bride!"

Over her face there passed an airy flush,
The roseate shade, the twilight of a blush,
Ere the low-whispering answer pensively
Stirred the dim silence in its trancèd hush.
"Thy suit is granted, Glaucus! though, perchance
A peril broods o'er this, thy bright romance,
Like a lone cloudlet o'er a lake that's fair.
When the high noon, flaunting so hotly now
Fades into evening, thou may'st meet me here,
Just in the cool of this rill-shadowing bough;
My favorite bee, my fairy of the flowers,
Shall bid thee come to that pure tryst of ours."

Who now so proud as Glaucus? "I have won,"
Lightly he said, "the marvellous benison
Of love from her in whose soft-folding arms
Gods might forget Elysium! O! her charms
Are perfect, — perfect heaven and perfect earth,
Blest and commingled in one exquisite birth
Of beauty, — and for me! I know not why,
But rosy Eros ever seems to fly
Gayly before me, armed for victory,
In every pleasant love-strife!" On this theme
Deeply he dwelt, till a vain self-esteem
Obscured his worthier spirit. Thus he went
Out from the haunted wood, his nature toned
Down to the common daylight, disenzoned
Of all its rare, ethereal ravishment.

Still in this mood, he sought the neighboring town,
Met with some gay young comrades, and sat down
To dice and wassail. All that morn he played,
And quaffed, and sang, and feasted, till the shade
Of evening o'er earth's forehead cast a gloom;
And still he played, when on his ear the boom

Of a swift, shining, yellow-breasted bee
Rung out its small alarum. Teasingly
The insect hummed about him, went and came,
And like a tiny hell of circling flame
And discord seemed to Glaucus, who at last
Struck at the wingèd torment testily.
The bee — poor go-between! — in either thigh
Cruelly maimed, with feeble flutterings, passed
Back to its home amid the foliaged bloom.

At length, in two most fortunate throws, the game
Was won by Glaucus! With triumphant smile
He seized and pocketed a glittering pile
Of new sestertii. "Ay! 'tis e'er the same,"
He muttered; "dice or women, I *must* win!
But hold! — by Venus! 'twere a burning sin,
And false to my fond wild flower of the wood
Longer to dally here. O Fortune! good,
Kind mistress, speed me still! Would that each heel
Were plumed like happy Hermes'!" His late zeal
Spurred the youth onward to the place of tryst, —
One final burst of sunset — amethyst,
Ruby, and topaz — blazed among the boughs,
Whence a sad voice, — "*Breaker of solemn vows,*
What dost thou here? Thine hour has past for aye!"
Glaucus, with startled eyes, peered through the sway
Of moistened fern and thicket, but his view
Rested alone on vacancy, or caught,
Swift as the shifting glamour of a thought,
Only the golden and evanishing ray,
Which, softened by cool sparkles of the dew,
Flashed through the half-closed lids of weary Day.

"Here am I," said the voice, so sadly sweet,
The listener thrilled even to his pausing feet, —
"Here, right before thee, Glaucus!" Yet again
The youth with straining eyeballs and hot brain,
Searched the dense thickets, — it was all in vain.
"Alas! alas!" (and now a tremulous moan
Sobbed through the voice, like a faint minor tone
In mournful human music) — "thou canst see
My face no more, for sternly, drearily,
A wildering cloud of sense, that shall not rise,
Hath come between me and thy darkening eyes.
O shallow-hearted! nevermore on thee
Shall visions of that finer world above
Dawn from the chaste auroras of their love;
But common things, seen in a funeral haze
Of earthiness, and sorrow, and mistrust,
Weigh the soul down, and soil its hopes with dust;
A hand like Fate's with cruel force shall press
Thy spirit backward into heaviness,
And the base realm of that forlorn abyss
Wherein the serpent Passions writhe and hiss
In savage desolation! Blind, blind, blind
Art thou henceforth in heart, and hope, and mind!
For he to whom my messenger of joy
And soothing promise only brought annoy

And sharp disquiet in his low-born lust, —
What, what to him *Ideal Beauty's* kiss,
The charm of lofty converse in the dells,
Of divine meetings, musical farewells,
And glimpses through the flickering leaves at night
Of such fair mysteries in awe-hushing light
That even I, who in these forests dwell
Purely with innocent creatures, unto whom
All Nature opes her innermost heart of bloom
And blessedness, by some majestic spell
Uplifted unto realms ineffable,
Faint almost in the splendor large and clear?
The winds have ceased their murmurings, — on my ear
The rill-songs melt to threads of delicate tune,
And every small mote dancing in the moon
Expands, and brightens to a spiritual eye,
Luring me up to Immortality.
O! then my earthly nature, loosening slips
Down like a garment, and invisible lips
Whisper the secrets of their happier sphere!
This bliss, O youth! my soul had shared with one
Worthy the gift! Alas! *thou* art not he!"

The voice died off toward the waning sun!
Glaucus looked up, — the gaunt, gray forest trees
Seemed to close o'er him like a vault of stone.
"*Just Gods!*" he sighed, "*I am indeed alone!*"

THE NEST.

At the poet's life-core lying
Is a sheltered and sacred nest,
Where, as yet, unfledged for flying,
His callow fancies rest:

Fancies, and thoughts, and feelings,
Which the mother Psyche breeds,
And passions whose dim revealings
But torture their hungry needs.

Yet, — there cometh a summer splendor
When the golden brood wax strong,
And, with voices grand or tender,
They rise to the heaven of song.

NOT DEAD.

TO J. A. D.

Here, at the sweetest hour of this sweet day,
Here in the calmest woodland haunt I know,
Benignant thoughts around my memory play,
And in my heart do pleasant fancies blow,
Like flowers turned to thee, radiant and aglow,
Flushed by the light of times forever fled,
Whose tender glory pales, but is not dead.

The warm south wind is like thy generous breath,
Laden with kindly words of gentle cheer,
And every whispering leaf above me saith,
She whom thou dream'st so distant hovers near;
Her love it is that thrills the sunset air
With mystic motions from a time that's fled,
Long past and gone, in sooth, — but, oh! not dead!

The drowsy murmur of cool brooks below;
  The soft, slow clouds that seem to *muse* on high;
Love-notes of hidden birds, that come and go,
  Making a sentient rapture of the sky;
  All the rare season's peaceful sorcery,
These hints of cordial joys forever fled,
Joys past, indeed, and yet they are not dead:

Far from the motley throng of sordid men,
  From fashion far, mean strife and frenzied gain,
In those dear days through many a mountain glen,
  By mountain streams, and fields of rippling grain,
  We roamed untouched by Passion's feverish pain,
But quaffing Friendship's tranquil draughts instead,
Its waters clear whose sweetness is not dead!

Above that nook of fair remembrance stands
  A dove-eyed Faith, that falters not, nor sleeps;
No flowers of Lethe droop in her white hands,
  And if the watch that steadfast angel keeps
  Be pensive and some transient tears she weeps,
They are but tears a fond regret may shed
O'er twilight joys which fade, but are not dead!

Not dead! not dead! but glorified and fair,
  Like yonder marvellous cloudland floating far
Between the mellowing sunset's amber air
  And the mild lustre of eve's earliest star,
  Oh, such, so pure, so bright, these memories are!
Earth's warmth and Heaven's serene around them spread,
They pass, they wane, but, sweet! they are not dead!

SONNET.

HAST thou beheld a landscape dull and bare,
  On which, at times, a flying gleam was shed
  From some shy sunbeam shifting overhead,
That made the scene for one brief moment fair?
Such is the light, so transient, flickering, rare,
  Which, from fate's sullen heavens above me spread,
  Hath flushed the path my weary footsteps tread,
And lent to darkness glimpses of sweet cheer.
Alas! alas! that I, whose soul doth burn
  With such deep passion for a steadfast bliss,
Must bend forever o'er hope's burial urn,
  And greet even love with a half-mournful kiss!
  In sooth, what stern, malignant doom is this?
Joy! delicate Ariel! ah! return! return!

MARGUERITE.

SHE was a child of gentlest air,
Of deep-dark eyes, but golden hair,
And, ah! I loved her unaware,
          Marguerite!

She spelled me with those midnight eyes,
The sweetness of her naïve replies,
And all her innocent sorceries,
          Marguerite!

The fever of my soul grew calm
Beneath her smile that healed like balm,
Her words were holier than a psalm,
Marguerite!

But 'twixt us yawned a gulf of fate,
Whose blackness I beheld, — too late.
O Christ! that love should smite like hate,
Marguerite!

She did not wither to the tomb,
But round her crept a tender gloom
More touching than her earliest bloom,
Marguerite!

The sun of one fair hope had set,
A hope she dared not all forget,
Its twilight glory kissed her yet, —
Marguerite!

And ever in the twilight fair
Moves with deep eyes and golden hair
The child who loved me unaware!
Marguerite!

—◇—

APART.

Come not with empty words that say,
"Your strength of manhood wastes away
In long, ignoble, fruitless years!"
I live apart from pain and tears,
Wherewith the ways of men are sown,
Nor dwell I loveless and alone;
One tender spirit shares my days,
One voice is swift to yield me praise,
One true heart beats against my own!
What more, what more could man desire
Than love that burns a steadfast fire
And faith that ever leads him higher
Along the path which points to peace?

Oh, far and faint I hear the din
Of battle-blows, and mortal sin
From out the stir and press of life;
Those hollow muffled sounds of strife
Seem rolled from thunder-clouds upcurled
About a dim and distant world;
Below me, in the sunless gloom;
But round my brow the amaranths bloom
Of sober joy with heart's-ease furled;
For more, what more can man desire
Than love that burns a steadfast fire,
And faith that ever leads him higher,
Where all the jars of earth shall cease?

A present glory haunts my way,
A promise of diviner day
Illumes the flushed horizon's verge;
And fainter, farther still, the surge
Of buffeting waves that beat and roar
Up the dim world's tempestuous shore
Beneath me in the moonless airs;
Alas, its passions, sorrows, cares!
Alas, its fathomless despairs!
Yet dreams, vague dreams, they seem to me,
On these clear heights of liberty,
These summits of serene desire, —
Whence love ascends, a quenchless fire,
And sweet faith ever leads me higher
To pearly paths of perfect peace!

—◇—

THE LOTOS AND THE LILY.

The little poems which follow were suggested by an oriental idea developed in Alger's "Specimens of Eastern Poetry." The moon is strangely spoken of as masculine.

THE LOTOS.

Drooping in the sunlit streams,
We are wrapped all day in dreams;

Morn and noon and evening light
Robed for us in garbs of night.

Only when the moon appears
Through a silvery mist of tears,

From the waters dark and still,
We arise to drink our fill

Of the tender love he sheds
On our fair enamored heads.

Ah! no longer wrapped in dreams,
How we pant beneath his beams!

How, with breath of softest sighs,
We unclose our yearning eyes,

And our snowy necks in pride
Curve about the glittering tide!

Warmth for warmth and kiss for kiss,
All our pulses burn with bliss,

Till revealed our inmost charms
Glowing in the night-god's arms.

"View us, white robed lilies,
We, whose beauty's rareness
Sleeps until the bridegroom sun
Woos our virgin fairness."

THE LILY.

View us, white-robed lilies,
We whose beauty's rareness
Sleeps until the bridegroom Sun
Woos our virgin fairness.

Then, our bosoms baring,
'Neath his ardent kisses,
Stem, and leaf, and delicate heart
Trembling into blisses,

The full, fervid godhead
Thrills our being tender,
And our happy souls expand
In ecstatic splendor.

Thus all, *all* we yield him
Of our shrinèd sweetness, —
All that maiden warmth may grant
To true love's completeness,

WINDLESS RAIN.

The rain, the desolate rain!
  Ceaseless, and solemn, and chill!
How it drips on the misty pane,
  How it drenches the darkened sill!
O scene of sorrow and dearth!
  I would that the wind awaking
To a fierce and gusty birth,
    Might vary this dull refrain
    Of the rain, the desolate rain:
  For the heart of heaven seems breaking
In tears o'er the fallen earth,
    And again, again, again
    We list to the sombre strain,
The faint, cold monotone—
Whose soul is a mystic moan—
Of the rain, the mournful rain,
The soft, despairing rain!

The rain, the murmurous rain!
  Weary, passionless, slow,
'Tis the rhythm of settled sorrow,
  'Tis the sobbing of cureless woe!
And all the tragic of life,
  The pathos of Long-Ago,
    Comes back on the sad refrain
    Of the rain, the dreary rain,
Till the graves in my heart unclose,
  And the dead that its depths enfold,
From a solemn and weird repose
  Awake,—but with eyelids cold,
And voices that melt in pain
On the tide of the plaintive rain,
The yearning, hopeless rain,
The long, low, whispering rain!

"IN UTROQUE FIDELIS."

Along the woods the whispering night-airs swoon,
  A single bird-note dies adown the trees,
Clear, pallid, mournful, droops the summer moon,
  Dipped in the foam of cloudland's phantom seas;—
    Soundless they heave above
The dim, ancestral home that holds my love.

How breathless still! A mystic glamour keeps
  Calm watch and ward o'er this weird, drowsy hour:
Yon heaven's at peace, the earth benignly sleeps;
  And thou, thou slumberest too, my woodland flower,—
    Fair lily steeped in light
And happy visions of the marvellous night!

I waft a sigh from this fond soul to thine,—
  A little sigh, yet honey-laden, dear,
With fairy freightage of such hopes divine
  As fain would flutter gently at thine ear,
    And, entering, find their way
Down to the heart so veiled from me by day.

In dreams, in dreams, perchance, thou art not coy;
  And one keen hope more bold than all the rest
May touch thy spirit with a tremulous joy,
  And stir an answering softness in thy breast:
    O sleep! O blest eclipse!
What murmured word is faltering at her lips?

Awake for one brief moment, genial South:
  Breathe o'er her slumbers,—waft that word to me,
Warm with the fragrance of her rosebud mouth,
  Enwreathed in smiles of dreamful fantasy:
    Come, whisper, low and light,
The name which haunts her maiden trance to-night.

Still, breathless-still! No voice in earth or air:
  I only know my delicate darling lies,

A twilight lustre glimmering in her hair,
And dews of peace within her languid eyes:
Yea, only know that I
Am called from love and dreams, perhaps to die, —

Die when the heavens are thick with scarlet rain,
And every time-throb's fated: even there
Her face would shine through mists of mortal pain,
And sweeten death, like some incarnate prayer:
Hark! 'tis the trumpet's swell!
O love! O dreams! farewell, farewell, farewell!

NATURE, BETROTHED AND WEDDED.

HAVE you not noted how in early spring,
From out the forests, past the murmuring brooks,
O'er the hillsides, Nature, with airy grace,
Like some fair virgin, touched by lights and shades,
Glides timidly, a veil of golden mist
About her brows, and budding bosom draped
In maiden coyness? She's a bride betrothed
Unto that mystic god, who comes from far,
Rich Orient lands upon the winds of June,
That bear him like swift ardors, winged with fire;
And when, on some calm, lustrous morn, her lord
Uplifts the golden veil, and weds to hers
The quickening warmth of ripe, immortal lips,
How the broad earth leaps into raptured life,
And thrills with music! Then a queenly spouse
Raised unto fruitful empire, through all hours
Of bounteous summer, she walks proudly on,
Shining with blissful eyes of matronhood,
Till, at the last, autumn, with reverent hand,
Doth crown her with such full, completed joy,
Such wealth of sovereign beauty, she once more
About her brows and sumptuous bosom folds
That golden veil, — not in the tremulous fear
Of maiden coyness now, but lest rash men,
Drawn by her awful loveliness, should dare
To gaze too closely on it, and thus fall,
Smitten and blind, at her imperial feet!

CHLORIS.

WHAT time the rosy-flushing West
Sleeps soft on copse and dingle,
Wherein the sunset shadows rest,
Or richly float and mingle;

When down the vale the wood-dove's tone
Thrills in a cadence tender,
And every rare, ethereal mote
Turns to a wingèd splendor.

Just as the mystic cloudlands ope,
Far up their sapphire portal,
Fair as the fairest dream of Hope,
Half goddess and half mortal,

I see that lovely genius rise,
That child of Orient trances,
On whose sweet face the glory lies
Of weird Hellenic fancies, —

Chloris! beneath whose procreant tread
All earth yields up her sweetness, —
The violet's scent, the rose's red,
The dahlia's orbed completeness,

And verdures on the myriad hills,
  The breath of her pure duty
Hath nursed to life by sparkling rills
  And foliaged nooks of beauty;

Till bloom and odor, blush and song,
  So fill earth's radiant spaces,
The fading touch of sin, or wrong,
  Leaves glad the weariest faces;

And so, through happy spring-tide dells,
  O'er mount, and field, and river,
Her zephyr's fairy clarion swells,
  Her footsteps glance forever!

FORTUNIO.

A PARABLE FOR THE TIMES.

WHO at the court of Astolf, the great King,
King of a realm of firs, and icy floes,
Cold bright fiords, and mountains capped with clouds.
Who there so loved and honored as the knight,
The youthful knight Fortunio? Whence he came,
None knew, nor whom his kindred: at a bound
He passed all rivals moving towards the throne,
And stood firm-poised above them; yet with mien
So sweet it honeyed envy, and surprised
The bitterest railers into complaisance!
Low-voiced and delicate-featured, with a cheek
As soft as peach down, or the golden dust
Shrined in a maiden lily's heart of hearts,
Yet a stern will bent bowlike, with the shaft
Of some keen purpose swiftly drawn to head,
Or launched unerring at its lofty mark,
Rose thrilled with action, or high strung at aim,
Beneath his jewelled doublet! While the hand
So warm, so white, and wont to press the palm
In palpitating clasp of fair sixteen,
Could wield the ponderous battle-axe, or flash
The lightning rapier in the foeman's eyes.
Prince of the tourney and the dance alike,
War's fiercer lists had seen his furrowless brow
Flushed red with heat of battle, heard his voice
Shrilled clear beyond the clarions, mount and break
In larklike song far o'er the mists of blood,
Through victory's calmer heaven. Mixed love and fear,
With love ofttimes preponderant, girded him
Closely as with an atmosphere disturbed
Only by hints of thunder, ghosts of cloud.
But love, all love, love in her passionate eyes,
Love 'twixt the pure twin rosebuds of her mouth,
Love in the arch of brooding, beauteous brows,
And every wavering dimple wherein smiles
At hide-and-seek with sly, mock frownings played,—
All love was Freyla, though a princess she,
For this unknown Fortunio! Wildly beat
And burned her heart at each soft glance he gave,
Or softer word, albeit as yet unthrilled
By answering passion! Swiftly flew her dreams
Birdlike on balmy winds of fancy borne,

To bridal realms empurpled and divine,—
Alas! but Scorn, that long had lurked and spied
In ambush, shot its sudden bolts, and brought
Those wingèd dreams transfixed to earth and dead!
While Rage, Scorn's ally, in her father's breast,
Clutched the sweet dreamer rudely, dragged her soul
Into the garish glare of commonplace
(Soon to be lit by horror's lurid star!)
And so convulsed her tenderness with threats,

"King of a realm of firs, and icy floes,
Cold bright fiords, and mountains capped with clouds."

That all her being seemed collapsed to fall
Crushed, as in moral earthquake: "Doting fool,"
Outshrieked the King, "dost dream great Odin's blood
Could mix with veins plebeian? Purge thy thoughts,
Unvirgined, vile, of sacrilegious sin!
But for this boy, our twelvemonth's grace hath raised
So high, a moment's justice shall cast down
To fathomless depths of ruin!"
Wherewithal
(Harping on justice still, though justice slept)
The King decreed, "This youth Fortunio dies!"
So, on a bright spring morn, the knight stood up,
Fronting the royal doomsmen, with a face
Sublimely calm; they tore his bravery off,
His jewelled vest and knighthood's golden spurs,

And bared his heart to catch the arrowy hail,—
When lo! beneath those rough, disrobing hands,
The dangerous, lewd seducer, coyly bowed,
Outbeamed a virgin beauty chaste and fair!

The King, beholding, started, and then smiled:
"Thou wanton madcap," said he, "go in peace!"

O cordial eyes, the brown eyes and the blue,
Or ye dark eyes, with deeps like midnight heavens,
Where unimagined worlds of thought and love
Shine starlike, would ye quench your glorious rays
In the low levels of the lives of men?
O gracious souls of women tender-sweet,
And luminous with goodness, would ye soil
Your nascent angel-plumage in the stye
Of sordid worldliness? Be warned, be warned!
Set not the frail spears of your rash caprice
In rest against great Nature's pierceless shield;
Strive not to grasp monopolies impure,
Man's fated heritage. Be warned, be warned!
For surely as yon bright sun dawns and dies,
And sure as Nature, all immutable,
Year after year completes her mystic round
Through law's vast orbit,—so ye desperate Fair,
Arrayed against the eternal force of God,
Must fall discomfited, and like that knight,
The false Fortunio, rest your claims at last,
Not on deft spells of simulated power,
But on the soft white bosom which enspheres
The sacred charms of perfect womanhood!

A FEUDAL PICTURE.

[SCENE—The Corridor of a Palace. PERSONS—A young Knight and his Mentor. TIME—The Fourteenth Century.]

MENTOR.

WITH what a grace she passed us by just now!
Her delicate chin half raised, her cordial brow
A cloudless heaven of bland benignities!
What tempered lustre too in her dove's eyes,
Just touched to archness by the eyebrow's curve,
And those quick dimples which the mouth's reserve
Stir and break up, as sunlit ripples break
The cool, clear calmness of a mountain lake!
A woman in whom majesty and sweetness
Blend to such issues of serene completeness,
That to gaze on her were a prince's boon!
The calm of evening, the large pomp of noon,
Are hers; soft May morns melting into June,
Hold not such tender languishments as those
Which steep her in that dew-light of repose,
That floats a dreamy balm around the full-blown rose:—
And yet, 'tis not her beauty, though so bright
(Clear moon-fire mixed with sun-flame), nor the light,
Transparent charm we feel so exquisite,

Whereby she's compassed as a wizard
star
By its own life-air! 'tis not one, nor all
Of these, whereby we're mastered, Sir,
and fall
Slavelike before her: doubtless such
things *are*
Potent as spells, — still there's a some-
thing fine,
Subtler than hoar-rime in the faint
moonshine,
More potent yet! — an undefinèd art,
'Twere vain to question: your whole
being, heart,
Brain, blood, seem lapsing from you,
fired and fused
In hers. — a terrible power, and if
abused ———
But by St. Peter! 'tis not safe to talk
Of yon weird woman! turn now! watch
her walk
'Twixt the tall tiger-lilies, — there's a
free,
Brave grace in every step, — but still to
me,
It hath — I know not what — of covert-
ness,
Cunning, and cruel purpose! can you
guess
The picture it brings up? — a lonely
rock
From which a young Bedouin guards his
flock,
In the swart desert: — there's a tawny
band,
A curved and tangled pathway of loose
sand,
Winding above him; — the tranced airs
make dim
His slumberous senses! — his great
brown eyes swim
In th' mist of dreams, when gliding
with mute tread
Forth from the thorn-trees, o'er his
nodding head,
Moves a lithe-bodied panther; — (God!
how fair
The beast is, with her moony-spotted
hair,
And her deft desert paces!) — one breath
more!
And you'll behold the spouting of fresh
gore,
Heart blood that's human! — can aught
save him now? —
Hist! the sharp crackle of a blasted
bough,
Whence flies a huge hill-eagle, rustling
O'er the boy's forehead his vast breadths
of wing,
And sweeping as a half-seen shade,
'twould seem,
Betwixt his startled spirit, and its
dream;
He's roused! espies his danger! at a
bound
Leaps into safety where the low-set
ground
Is buttressed 'neath two giant crags
thereby
(Now hark ye! 'tis no pictured phantasy,
This scene, my Anslem! but all's true
and clear
Before me, though full many a weary
year
Has waxed and waned since then):
My meaning prithee? foolish youth, be-
ware!
There's treachery lurking in the gay
parterre,
As in the hoary desert's silentness,
And dreams with danger, death per-
chance behind,
May lull young sleepers in the perfumed
wind,
Which hardly lifts the tiniest truant
tress
It toys with coyly, of a woman's
hair:
Our sternest fates have risen in forms as
fair,
As — let us say for lack of similes, —
As, hers, who bends now with such
gracious ease,
O'er her rich tulip-beds!
Were I the bird,
Wert thou the shepherd Anslem of my
tale,

(And that thou hast not hearkened, boy, unstirred
Is clear, albeit thou need'st not wax so pale).
What would true wisdom whisper, now 'tis done,
My warning, and thy day-dream in the sun?
What! why, her mandate's plain: I hear her say,
'Young Knight! to horse! leave the Queen's Court to-day!'"

THE WARNING.

Patience! I yet may pierce the rind
Wherewith are shrewdly girded round
The subtle secrets of his mind:
A dark, unwholesome core is bound
Perchance within it! Sir, you see,
Men are not what they *seem* to be!

A candid mien and plausible tongue!
A bearing calmly frank and fair,
The tear ('twould seem) by pity wrung,
All these are his, but still, beware!
A something strange, false, unbegot
Of virtue, whispers, trust him not:
But yesterday, his mask (I know
He wears one), for a moment's space,
By chance dropped off and swift below
The smile just waning on his face,
I caught a look, flashed sudden, keen
As lightning, which he deemed unseen.

I will not pause to tell thee what
That look betrayed! enough I think,
To smite the spirit cold and hot,
By turns, and make one inly shrink
From contact with a soul that keeps
Such wild-fire smouldering in its deeps:
So friend, be warned! he is not one
Thy youth should trust, for all his smiles,
Frank foreheads, genial as the sun,
May hide a thousand treacherous wiles,
And tones, like music's honeyed flow,
May work (God knows!) the bitterest woe!

DRIFTING.

I have settled at last in a sombre nook,
In the far-off heart of the Norland hills,
There's a dark pine forest before my gates,
And behind is the voice of rills
That murmur all day, and murmur all night,
Through the tangled copses green and lone,
Where, couched in the depths of the shadowy leaves,
The wood-dove makes her moan.

My home is a castle ancient and worn,
With hoary walls, and with crumbling floors,
And the burglar-winds their entrance force
Through the cobwebbed panes and doors.
I can hardly say that a roof is mine,
For whene'er the mountain tempests rise,
A deluge is poured through its countless rents,
Wide open to air and skies!

Ah! Nature alone keeps a wholesome mien,
In the midst of a squalor wildly bare,
And I draw sometimes from her bounteous breast
Brief balms for the heart's despair;
All *human* friends that were loyal have died,
And the false and treacherous only stay,
To poison the soul with their serpent tongues
In my fortune's dull decay!

Distant and dim in the perishing past
Grow the joys that made its springtime sweet,
And the last of the saving angels — Hope —

Hath spurned my lot with her shining feet;
Ambition is dead, and if love survives,
Her lip, it is pale, and her eyes forlorn
As beams of the waning stars that melt
In a clouded winter's morn.
I have met my fate as a man should meet
What cannot be vanquished, nor put aside,
I have striven with spirit and force to stem
Its rushing and mighty tide;
But the godlike nerve, and the iron will,
They were not granted to me, I say,
And therefore a waif on an angry sea,
I am drifting, drifting away!

Ay! drifting, and drifting, and drifting away,
Not a hand upraised, nor a cry for aid;
And hoarser the voice of the storm-wind swells,
And darker the wild night-shade;
There are breakers ahead that will crush me soon,
How much, O God! do thy creatures bear!
I marvel if somewhere, in heaven or hell,
This riddle of life grows clear!

SONNETS.

LEIGH HUNT.

"Leigh Hunt *loves everything;* he catches the sunny side of everything, and — except a few polemical antipathies — finds everything beautiful." — HENRY CRABB ROBINSON.

DESPITE misfortune, poverty, the dearth
Of simplest justice to his heart and brain,
This gracious optimist lived not in vain;
Rather, he made a partial Heaven of Earth;
For whatsoe'er of pure and cordial birth
In body or soul dawned on him, he was fain
To bless and love, as an immortal gain
A thing divine, of fair immaculate worth: —
The clearest, cleanest nature given to man
In these, our latter days, methinks was his,
With instincts which alone did bring him bliss;
All life he viewed as one long, luminous plan
Wherein God's love and wisdom meet and kiss, —
His sole brave creed, the creed Samaritan!

SOUL-ADVANCES.

HE, who with fervent toil and will austere,
His innate forces and high faculties
Develops ever, with firm aim, and wise,
He *only* keeps his spiritual vision clear;
To him earth's treacherous shadows shift and veer
Like idle mists o'ercrowding windless skies,
Where through ofttimes to purged and prayerful eyes,
The steadfast heavens seem beckoning calm and near:
Still o'er life's rugged heights, with many a slip,
And painful pause he journeys, and sad fall,
Toward death's dark strand, washed by a mystic sea;
There her worn cable straining to be free,
He sees, and enters Faith's majestic ship,
To sail — *where'er the voice of God may call!*

CAROLINA.

THAT fair young land which gave me birth is dead!
Lost as a fallen star that quivering dies
Down the pale pathway of autumnal skies,

A vague faint radiance flickering where
it fled;
All she hath wrought, all she hath
planned or said,
Her golden eloquence, her high emprise
Wrecked, on the languid shore of Lethe
lies,
While cold Oblivion veils her piteous
head:*
O mother! loved and loveliest! debonair
As some brave queen of antique chiv-
alries.
Thy beauty's blasted like thy desolate
coasts:—
Where now thy lustrous form, thy shin-
ing hair?
Where thy bright presence, thine impe-
rial eyes?
Lost in dim shadows of the realm of
Ghosts!

SONNET.

In yonder grim, funereal forest lies
A foul lagoon, o'erfilmed by dust and
slime,
Hidden and ghastly, like a thought of
crime
In some stern soul kept secret from
men's eyes:
But if perchance a healthful breeze
should rise,
And part those stifling boughs, sweet
morning's prime,
And the fair flush of evening's cordial
clime,
Reflect therein the calmly glorious skies:
Is't so with man? holds not the dark-
ened breast,
Turbid, corrupt, o'ergrown by worldli-
ness,
One little spot whereon love's smile may
rest?
Lo! a pure impulse breathes, the sin-
clouds part,
The grief-defilements melt in hopes that
bless,
And pour God's quickening sunshine on
the heart!

ODE TO SLEEP.

Beyond the sunset, and the amber sea
To the lone depths of Ether, cold and
bare,
Thy influence, soul of all tranquillity,
Hallows the earth and awes the reverent
air;
Yon laughing rivulet quells its silvery
tune,
The pines, like priestly watchers tall and
grim,
Stand mute, against the pensive twi-
light dim,
Breathless to hail the advent of the
moon;
From the white beach the ocean falls
away
Coyly, and with a thrill; the sea-birds
dart
Ghostlike from out the distance, and
depart

* This may be esteemed an *exaggeration*: but really it is the sober and melancholy truth. The fame of the great statesmen and orators, for example, who once flourished in South Carolina, and made her name illustrious from one end of the Union to the other, is fast becoming a mere shadowy tradition. With a single exception, their works have never been collected for publication, nor have their lives been written, unless in the most fragmentary and imperfect fashion. The period during which these things might have been rightly done has forever passed.

Thus, over their genius and performances, as over their native State,—the Carolina of old,—oblivion, day by day, is more darkly gathering. If elements of a new political birth exist in that unfortunate section, they are *now* hopelessly confused and chaotic!

While the Past recedes, becoming momently more ghostly and phantasmal, the Future is wrapped in thick clouds and darkness! Where, indeed, is the prophet or son of a prophet who can predict the nature of that new polity destined to rise from the old institutions and the defunct civilization?

With a gray fleetness, moaning the dead day:
The wings of Silence overfolding space,
Droop with dusk grandeur from the heavenly steep,
And through the stillness gleams thy starry face,
Serenest Angel—Sleep!

Come! woo me here, amid these flowery charms,
Breathe on my eyelids; press thy odorous lips
Close to mine own, enwreathe me in thine arms,
And cloud my spirit with thy sweet eclipse;
No dreams! no dreams! keep back the motley throng,—
For such are girded round with ghastly might,
And sing low burdens of despondent song,
Decked in the mockery of a lost delight;
I ask oblivion's balsam! the mute peace
Toned to still breathings, and the gentlest sighs,
Not music woven of rarest harmonies
Could yield me such elysium of release:
The tones of earth are weariness,—not only
'Mid the loud mart, and in the walks of trade,
But where the mountain Genius broodeth lonely,
In the cool pulsing of the sylvan shade;
Then, bear me far into thy noiseless land,
Surround me with thy silence, deep on deep,
Until serene I stand
Close by a duskier country, and more grand,
Mysterious solitude, than thine, O Sleep!

As he whose veins a feverous frenzy burns,
Whose life-blood withers in the fiery drought,
Feebly, and with a languid longing, turns
To the spring breezes gathering from the South,
So, feebly, and with languid longing, I
Turn to thy wished Nepenthe, and implore
The golden dimness, the purpureal gloom
Which haunt thy poppied realm, and make the shore
Of thy dominion balmy with all bloom:
In the clear gulfs of thy serene profound,
Worn passions sink to quiet, sorrows pause,
Suddenly fainting to still-breathèd rest;
Thou own'st a magical atmosphere, which awes
The memories seething in the turbulent breast;
Which muffling up the sharpness of all sound
Of mortal lamentation,—solely bears
The silvery minor toning of our woe,
All mellowed to harmonious underflow,
Soft as the sad farewells of dying years,—
Lulling as sunset showers that veil the west,
And sweet as Love's last tears
When overwelling hearts do mutely weep:
O griefs! O wailings! your tempestuous madness,
Merged in a regal quietude of sadness,
Wins a strange glory by the streams of sleep!

Then woo me here amid those flowery charms,
Breathe on my eyelids, press thy odorous lips,
Close to mine own,—enfold me in thine arms,
And cloud my spirit with thy sweet eclipse;
And while from waning depth to depth I fall,

Down lapsing to the utmost depths of all,
Till wan forgetfulness obscurely stealing,
Creeps like an incantation on the soul,
And o'er the slow ebb of my conscious life
Dies the thin flush of the last conscious feeling,
And like abortive thunder, the dull roll
Of sullen passions ebbs far, far away, —
O Angel! loose the chords which cling to strife,
Sever the gossamer bondage of my breath,
And let me pass gently as winds in May,
From the dim realm which owns thy shadowy sway,
To thy diviner sleep, O sacred death!

SONG.

O! to be
By the sea, the sea!
While a brave nor'wester's blowing,
With a swirl on the lee,
Of cloud-foam free,
And a spring-tide deeply flowing!
With the low moon red and large,
O'er the flushed horizon's marge,
And a little pink hand in mine,
On the sands in the long moonshine!

O! to be
By the sea, the sea!
With the wind full west and dying,
With a single star
O'er the misty bar,
And the dim waves dreamily sighing!
O! to be there, but there!
With my sweet love nestling near!
Near, near, till her heart-throbs blend with mine,
Through the balmy hush of the night's decline,
On the glimmering beach, in the soft star-shine!

HOPES AND MEMORIES.

OUR hopes in youth are like those roseate shadows
Cast by the sunlight on the dewy grass
When first the fair morn opes her sapphire eyes;
They seem gigantic and yet graceful shades,
Touched with bright color. As our sun of life
Rises towards meridian, less and less
Grow the bright tremulous shadows, till at last,
In the hot dust and noontide of our day,
They glimmer to blank nothingness. Again,
That grand climacteric passed, the shadows gleam
Bright still, perchance (if our past deeds be pure), —
Bright still, but all reversed! Eastward they point,
Lengthening and lengthening ever toward the dawn;
For hopes have then grown memories, whose strange life
Deepens and deepens as the sunset dies.

WIDDERIN'S RACE.

AUSTRALIAN.

[The incidents of the following sketch will be found in "The Recollections of Geoffrey Hamlyn," by Henry Kingsley.]

"A HORSE amongst ten thousand! on the verge,
The extremest verge of equine life he stands;
Yet mark his action, as those wild young colts
Freed from the stock-yard gallop whinnying up;
See how he trots towards them, — nose in air,
Tail arched, and his still sinewy legs out-thrown

"Our hopes in youth are like those roseate shadows
Cast by the sunlight on the dewy grass."

In gallant grace before him! A brave beast
As ever spurned the moorland, ay, and more,
He bore me once,—such words but smite the truth,
I' the outer ring, while vivid memory wakes,
Recalling now, the passion and the pain.—
He bore me once from earthly hell to heaven!

"The sight of fine old Widderin (that's his name,
Caught from a peak, the topmost rugged peak
Of tall Mount Widderin, towering to the North
Most like a steed's head, with full nostrils blown,
And ears pricked up),—the sight of Widderin brings
That day of days before me, whose strange hours
Of fear and anguish, ere the sunset, changed
To hours of such content and full-veined joy,
As Heaven can give our mortal lives but once.

"Well, here's the story: While yon bush-fires sweep
The distant ranges, and the river's voice
Pipes a thin treble through the heart of drought,
While the red heaven like some huge caldron's top
Seems with the heat a-simmering, better far
In place of riding tilt 'gainst such a sun,
Here in the safe veranda's flowery gloom,
To play the dwarfish Homer to a song,
Whereof myself am hero:

"Two decades
Have passed since that wild autumn-time when last
The convict hordes from near Van Diemen, freed
By force or fraud, swept, like a blood-red fire,
Inland from beach to mountain, bent on raid
And rapine; fiends o' th' lowest pit, they spared
Nor sex, nor age, nor infancy; the vulture
Followed their track, and a black smoke like hell's
Hung its foul reek above each home accursed,
Sacked by their greed, or ravished by their lust.
Their crimes were monstrous, weird, unutterable,
Not to be hinted, save in awe-struck whispers
Dropped by dark hearthstones, far from maidens' ears,
In the blank silent midnight! all the land
Uprose to seek, confront and decimate
These devils spawned of Tophet; but their bands
At the first bruit of battle, the first clang
Of sabres girding honest loins, and champ
Of horse-bits held by manly hands that burned
To smite them, hip and thigh,—fled, disappeared,
And crouched in hiding, wheresoe'er the earth,
By wave and hill-side, forest, and bleak tarn,
Vouchsafed to shield them; as the time rolled on,
Our fears grew lighter, and all dread was quelled,
When on a morning, 'mid the outmost reefs
Of rough Cape Bolling, our chief herdsman found
The carcass of a huge boat overturned,
All stoven, and firmly wedged between the jaws

Of monster rocks, whereby three bodies lay,
Splashing and gurgling in the refluent tides,
Well known as corses of three desperate men,
The outlaws' leaders; thereupon 'twas deemed, —
And all must own with fairest likelihood,
That glutted by their vengeance, or spurred on
By hopes of rapine, beckoning otherwhere, —
The whole foul crew embarking, had been seized
By wind and wave, God's executioners,
The pitiless doomsmen of the wrath of Heaven, —
And so, crushed out of being, and made less
Than the vile seaweed dabbling in the surf.

"Thenceforth, our caution cooled; save here and there,
At critical mountain-passes, or lone caves,
And sheltered inlets of the wild south-west,
No sentinels watched; and wherefore should they watch?
The storm had threatened, broken and was passed!

"So, in late autumn, — 'twas a marvellous morn,
With breezes from the calm snow-river borne
That touched the air, and stirred it into thrills,
Mysterious and mesmeric, a bright mist
Lapping the landscape like a golden trance,
Swathing the hilltops with fantastic veils,
And o'er the moorland-ocean quivering light
As gossamer threads drawn down the forest aisles
At dewy dawning, — on this marvellous morn,
I, with four comrades, in this self-same spot,
Watched the fair scene, and drank the spicy airs,
That held a subtler spirit than our wine,
And talked and laughed, and mused in idleness,
Weaving vague fancies, as our pipe-wreaths curled
Fantastic, in the sunlight! I, with head
Thrown back, and cushioned snugly, and with eyes
Intent on one grotesque and curious cloud,
Puffed upward, that now seemed to take the shape
Of a Dutch tulip, now a Turk's face topped
By folds on folds of turban limitless, —
Heard suddenly, just as the clock chimed one,
To melt in musical echoes up the hills,
Quick footsteps on the gravelled path without, —
Steps of the couriers of calamity, —
So my heart told me, ere with blanched regards,
Two stalwart herdsmen on our threshold paused,
Panting, with lips that writhed, and awful eyes;
A breath's space in each other's eyes we glared,
Then, swift as interchange of lightning thrusts
In deadly combat, question and reply
Clashed sharply, 'What! the Rangers?' 'Ay, by Heaven!
And loosed in force, — the hell-hounds!' 'Whither bound?'
I stammered, hoarsely. 'Bound,' the elder said,
'Southward! — four stations had they sacked and burnt,
And now, drunk, furious ——' but I stopped to hear

No more; with booming thunder in mine ears,
And blood-flushed eyes, I rushed to Widderin's side,
Drew tight the girths, upgathered curb and rein,
And sprang to horse ere yet our laggard friends,
Now trooping from the green veranda's shade,
Could dream of action!

"Love had winged my will,
For to the southward, fair Garoopna held
My all of hope, life, passion; she whose hair
(Its tiniest strand of waving, witch-like gold)
Had caught my heart, entwined, and bound it fast,
As 'twere some sweet enchantment's heavenly net!

"I only gave a hand-wave in farewell,
Shot by, and o'er the endless moorland swept
(Endless it seemed, as those weird, measureless plains,
Which in some nightmare vision, stretch and stretch
Towards infinity!) like some lone ship
O'er wastes of sailless waters; now, a pine,
The beacon pine gigantic, whose grim crown
Signals the far land-mariner from out
Gaunt boulders of the gray-backed Organ hill,
Rose on my sight, a mistlike, wavering orb,
The while, still onward, onward, onward still,
With motion winged, elastic, equable,
Brave Widderin cleaved the air tides, tossed aside
The winds as waves their swift, invisible, breasts,
Hissing with foamlike noise when pressed and pierced
By that keen head and fiery-crested form!

"The lonely shepherd guardian on the plains,
Watching his sheep through languid half-shut eyes,
Looked up, and marvelled, as we passed him by,
Thinking perchance it was a glorious thing,
So dressed, so booted, so caparisoned,
To ride such bright blood-coursers unto death!
Two sun-blacked natives, slumbering in the grass,
Just rose betimes to 'scape the trampling hoofs,
And hurled hot curses at me as I sped;
While here and there, the timid kangaroo
Blundered athwart the mole-hills, and in puffs
Of steamy dust-cloud vanished like a mote!

"Onward, still onward, onward, onward still!
And lo! thank Heaven, the mighty Organ hill,
That seemed a dim blue cloudlet at the start,
Hangs in aërial, fluted cliffs aloft,
And still as through the long, low glacis borne,
Beneath the gorge borne ever at wild speed,
I saw the mateless mountain eagle wheel
Beyond the stark height's topmost pinnacle;
I heard his shriek of rage and ravin die
Deep down the desolate dells, as far behind
I left the gorge and far before me swept
Another plain, tree-bordered now, and bound
By the clear river gurgling o'er its bed.

"By this, my panting, but unconquered steed
Had thrown his small head backward, and his breath
Through the red nostrils burst in labored sighs;
I bent above his outstretched neck, I threw
My quivering arms about him, murmuring low,
'Good horse! brave heart! a little longer bear
The strain, the travail; and thenceforth for thee
Free pastures all thy days, till death shall come!
Ah, many and many a time, my noble bay,
Her lily hand hath wandered through thy mane,
Patted thy rainbow neck, and brought thee ears
Of daintiest corn from out the farmhouse loft,—
Help, help, to save her now!'

"I'll vow the brute
Heard me and comprehended what he heard!
He shook his proud crest madly, and his eye
Turned for a moment sideways, flashed in mine
A lightning gleam, whose fiery language said,
'I know my lineage, will not shame my sire.
My sire, who rushed triumphant 'twixt the flags,
And frenzied thousands, when on Epsom downs
Arcturus won the Derby! — no, nor shame
My granddam, whose clean body, half enwrought
Of air, half fire, through swirls of desert sand
Bore Shiëk Abdallah headlong on his prey!"

"At last came forest shadows, and the road
Winding through bush and bracken, and at last
The hoarse stream rumbling o'er its quartz-sown crags.

"No, no! stanch Widderin! pause not now to drink;
An hour hence, and thy dainty nose shall dip
In richest wine, poured jubilantly forth
To quench thy thirst, my beauty! but press on,
Nor heed these sparkling waters. God! my brain's
On fire once more! an instant tells me all:
All! — life or death, — salvation or despair! —
For yonder, o'er the wild grass-matted slope
The house stands, or it stood but yesterday.

"A Titan cry of inarticulate joy
I raised, as calm and peaceful in the sun,
Shone the fair cottage, and the garden-close,
Wherein, white-robed, unconscious, sat my Love
Lilting a low song to the birds and flowers.
She heard the hoof-strokes, saw me, started up,
And with her blue eyes wider than their wont,
And rosy lips half tremulous, rushed to meet
And greet me swiftly. 'Up, dear Love!' I cried,
'The Convicts, the Bush-Rangers! — let us fly!'
Ah, then and there you should have seen her, friend,
My noble beauteous Helen! not a tear,
Nor sob, and scarce a transient pulse-quiver,
As, clasping hand in hand, her fairy foot

Lit like a small bird on my horseman's boot,
And up into the saddle, lithe and light,
Vaulting she perched, her bright curls round my face!

"We crossed the river, and, dismounting, led
O'er the steep slope of blended rock and turf,
The wearied horse, and there behind a Tor
Of castellated bluestone, paused to sweep
With young keen eyes the broad plain stretched afar,
Serene and autumn-tinted at our feet:
'Either,' said I, 'these devils have gone East,
To meet with bloodhound Desborough in his rage
Between the granite passes of Luxorme,
Or else, — dear Christ! my Helen, low! stoop low!'
(These words were hissed in horror, for just then,
'Twixt the deep hollows of the river-vale,

"No, no! stanch Widderin! pause not now to drink."

The miscreants, with mixed shouts and curses, poured
Down through the flinty gorge tumultuously,
Seeming, we thought, in one fierce throng to charge
Our hiding-place.) I seized my Widderin's head,
Blindfolding him, for with a single neigh
Our fate were sealed o' th' instant! As they rode,
Those wild, foul-languaged demons, by our lair,
Scarce twelve yards off, my troubled steed shook wide
His streaming mane, stamped on the earth, and pawed
So loudly that the sweat of agony rolled
Down my cold forehead; at which point I felt
My arm clutched, and a voice I did not know,
Dropped the low murmur from pale, shuddering lips,
'O God! if in those brutal hands I fall,
Living, look not into your mother's face
Or *any* woman's more!'

"What time had passed
Above our bowed heads, we pent, pinioned there
By awe and nameless horror, who shall tell?

Minutes, perchance, by mortal measurement,
Eternity by heart-throbs! — when at length
We turned, and eyes of mutual wonder raised,
We gazed on alien faces, haggard, worn,
And strange of feature as the faces born
In fever and delirium! Were we saved?
We scarce could comprehend it, till, from out
The neighboring oak-wood, rode our friends at speed,
With clang of steel and eyebrows bent in wrath.
But warned betimes, the wily ruffians fled
Far up the forest-coverts, and beyond
The dazzling snow-line of the distant hills,
Their yells of fiendish laughter pealing faint,
And fainter from the cloudland, and the mist
That closed about them like an ash-gray shroud:
Yet were these wretches marked for imminent death:
The next keen sunrise pierced the savage gorge,
To which we tracked them, where, mere beasts at bay,
Grimly they fought, and brute by brute they fell."

OCTOBER.

Afar from the city, its cark and care, —
Thank God! I am cosily seated here,
On this night of hale October, —
While the flames leap high on the roaring hearth,
And voices, the dearest to me on earth,
Ring out in the music of household mirth,
For the time is blithe October!

There's something, — but *what* I can scarce divine, —
Perchance 'tis the breath like a potent wine,
Of the cordial, clear October,
Which makes, when the jovial month comes round,
The life-blood bloom, and the pulses bound,
And the soul spring forth like a monarch crown'd, —
God's grace on the brave October!

Come, sweetheart! open your choicest bin,
For who, I would marvel, could deem it sin,
On this night of keen October,
To quaff one health to his ruddy cheer,
On the golden edge of the waning year,
To his eyes so bright, and his cheeks so clear,
Our bluff "King Hal," — October?

Away with Rhenish and light champagne!
'Tis not in these we must pledge the reign
Of the stout old lord, — October;
But in mighty stoups of the "mountain dew,"
With "beads" like tears in an eye of blue,
But tears of a laughter, sound and true,
As thine honest heart, October!

He brought me love and he brought me health,
He brought me *all* but the curse of wealth,
This kindly and free October;
And forever and aye I will bless his name,
While his winds blow fresh, and his sunsets flame,
And the whole earth burns with his crimson fame,
This prince of the months, — October!

WILL.

YOUR face, my boy, when six months old,
We propped you laughing in a chair,
And the sun-artist caught the gold
Which rippled o'er your waving hair!
And deftly shadowed forth the while
That blooming cheek, that roguish smile,
Those dimples seldom still:
The tiny, wondering, wide-eyed elf!
Now, *can* you recognize yourself
In that small portrait, Will?

I glance at it, then turn to you,
Where in your healthful ease you stand,
No beauty, — but a youth as true,
And pure as any in the land!
For Nature, through fair sylvan ways,
Hath led and gladdened all your days,
Kept free from sordid ill;
Hath filled your veins with blissful fire,
And winged your instincts to aspire
Sunward, and Godward, Will!

Long-limbed and lusty, with a stride
That leaves me many a pace behind,
You roam the woodlands, far and wide,
You quaff great draughts of country wind:
While tree and wildflower, lake and stream,
Deep shadowy nook, and sunshot gleam,
Cool vale and far-off hill,
Each plays its mute mysterious part,
In that strange growth of mind and heart
I joy to witness, Will!

"Can this tall youth," I sometimes say,
"Be mine? *my son?*" it surely seems
Scarce further backward than a day,
Since watching o'er your feverish dreams
In that child-illness of the brain,
I thought (O Christ, with what keen pain!)
Your pulse would soon be still,
That all your boyish sports were o'er,
And I, heart-broken, nevermore
Should call, or clasp you, Will!

But Heaven was kind, death passed you by;
And now upon your arm I lean,
My second self, of clearer eye,
Of firmer nerve, and steadier mien;
Through you, methinks, my long-lost youth
Revives, from whose sweet founts of truth
And joy, I drink my fill:
I feel your every heart-throb, know
What inmost hopes within you glow,
One soul's between us, Will!

Pray Heaven that this be always so!
That ever on your soul and mine
Though my thin locks grow white as snow,
The self-same radiant trust may shine;
Pray that while this, my life, endures,
It aye may sympathize with yours
In thought, aim, action still;
That you, O son (till comes the end),
In me may find your comrade, friend,
And *more* than father, Will!

---

*HERE AND THERE.**

HERE the warm sunshine fills
Like wine of gods the deepening, cup-shaped dells,
Embossed with marvellous flowers; the happy rills
Roam through the autumnal fields whose rich increase
Of gathered grain smiles under heavens of peace;
While many a bird-song swells
From glades of neighboring woodlands, cool and fair. —
Content and peace are *here*.

---

* Written during the war between France and Germany.

There the wild battle's wrath
Thunders from castled height to storied plain,
Ploughs with red lightning-bolts its terrible path,
And sows the abhorrent seeds of blood and death,
Blown far on Desolation's tameless breath,
While for autumnal grain
Time reaps the harvest of a bleak despair, —
God's curse consumes them *there*.

Here jovial children play
Beneath the latest vine-leaves; innocent kings,
And blissful queens, — on them the matron Day,
Like a sweet mother drops her kisses light;
The very clouds some secret joy makes bright,
And round us clings and clings,
With Ariel arms, the season's influence rare, —
Heaven's heart beats near us *here*.

There love bemoans its lost,
Countless as seaside sands; all joys of life
Rest locked and stirless in the blood-red frost;
Ye drums, roll out, shrill clarions, peal your parts!
Ye cannot drown the wail of broken hearts,
Nor still that spiritual strife
Which thrills through Victory's voice its death-notes drear, —
Dear Christ, soothe, save them *there*.

WELCOME TO WINTER.

Now, with wild and windy roar,
Stalwart Winter comes once more, —
O'er our roof-tree thunders loud,
And from edges of black cloud
Shakes his beard of hoary gold,
Like a tangled torrent rolled
Down the sky-rifts, clear and cold!

Hark! his trumpet summons rings,
Potent as a warrior-king's;
Till the forces of our blood
Rise to lusty hardihood,
And our summer's languid dreams
Melt, like foam-wreaths, down the streams,
When the fierce northeasters roll,
Raving from the frozen pole.

Nobler hopes and keener life,
Quicken in his breath of strife;
Through the snow-storms and the sleet
On he stalks with armèd feet,
While the sounding clash of hail
Clanging on his icy mail,
Stirs whate'er of generous might
Time hath left us in his flight,
And our yearning pulses thrill
For some grand achievement still!

Lord of ice-bound sea and land,
Let me grasp thy kingly hand,
And from thy great heart and bold,
Hecla-warm, though all is cold
Round about thee, catch the fire
Of my lost youth's brave desire;
Let me, in the war with wrong,
Like thy storms, be swift and strong,
Gloomy griefs, and coward cares
Broods of 'wildering, dark despairs,
Making all life's glory dim,
Let me rend them, limb from limb,
As the forest-boughs are rent
When thou wak'st the firmament,
And with savage shriek and groan,
All the wildwood's overthrown!

TO MY MOTHER.

LIKE streamlets to a silent sea,
These songs with varied motion
Flow from bright fancy's uplands free,
To Lethe's clouded ocean;

They lapse in deepening music down
  The slopes of flower-lit meadows,
Nor dream, poor songs! how near them
      frown
  Oblivion's rayless shadows!

Yet though of brief and dubious life,
  All wed to incompleteness, —
The voices of these lays are rife
  With frail and fleeting sweetness;
One chord to make more full the strain,
  One note I may not smother,
Is echoed in the heart's refrain
  Which holds thy name, my mother!

To thee my earliest verse I brought,
  All wreathed in loves and roses,
Some glowing boyish fancy, fraught
  With tender May-wind closes;
Thou did'st not taunt my fledgling song,
  Nor view its flight with scorning:
"The bird," thou saidst, "grown fleet
      and strong,
  Might yet outsoar the morning!"

Ah me! between that hour and this,
  Eternities seem flowing;
O'er hapless graves of youth and bliss
  Dark cypress boughs are growing;
Our Fate hath dimmed with base alloy
  The rich, pure gold of pleasure,
And changed the choral chant of joy
  To care's heart-broken measure!

But through it all, — the blight, the pall,
  The stress of thunderous weather,
That God who keeps wild chance in
      thrall
  Hath linked our lots together;
So, hand in hand, we sail the gloom,
  Faith's mystic plummet casting
To sound the ways which end in bloom
  Of Edens everlasting!

I bless thee, Dear, with reverent
      thought!
  Pale face, and tresses hoary,
Whose every silvery thread hath caught
  Some hint of heavenly glory; —
To thee, with trust assured, sublime,
  Death's angel-call that waitest,
To thee, as once my earliest rhyme,
  Lo! now, I bring — my latest!

SONNETS.

ILLEGITIMATE.

The maiden Spring came laughing down
      the dales,
Her fair brows arched, and on her rose-
      bud mouth,
The balm and beauty of the lustrous
      South;
Through soft green fields, from hills to
      happy vales,
She tripped, her small feet twinkling in
      the sun,
Her delicate finger raised with girlish
      mirth,
Pointed at graybeard Winter, who, in
      dearth,
Toiled toward his couch, his long day
      labor done;
Ah no, not done! for hark! a sudden
      wind,
Death-laden, sweeps from realms of arc-
      tic sky,
And blurred with storm, the morn grows
      crazed and blind;
Then Winter, mocking, backward turns
      apace,
Where pallid Spring all vainly strives to
      fly,
And with brute buffet scars her shrink-
      ing face!

SONNET.

I cast this sorrow from me like a
      crown
Of bitter nettles, and unwholesome
      weeds,
Nursed by cold night-dews, from malig-
      nant seeds,
Ill Fortune sowed, when all the heaven
      did frown;
Its loathsome round I trample deeply
      down

In mire and dust, to burn my brain no more;
From off my brow I wipe the trickling gore,
While all about me, like keen clarions blown,
From breezy dells, and golden heights afar,
Their stern *reveillé* the wild March winds sound;
They wake an answering passion in my soul,
Whence, marshalled as brave warriors, taking ground
For noblest conflict, freed from doubt or dole,
Great thoughts uprising front Hope's morning star!

VERNAL PICTURES (WITHOUT AND WITHIN).

AMID fresh roses wandering, and the soft
And delicate wealth of apple-blossoms spread
In tender spirals of blent white and red,
Round the fair spaces of our blooming croft,
This morn I caught the gurgling note, so oft
Heard in the golden spring-tides that are dead, —
The swallow's note, murmuring of winter fled,
Dropped silverly from passionless calms aloft:
"O heart!" I said, "thy vernal depths unclose,
That mirror Nature's; warm airs, come and go
Of whispering ardors o'er thought's budded rose,
And half-hid flowers of sweet philosophy;
While now upglancing, now borne swift and low,
Song like the swallow darts through fancy's sky."

*THE MOUNTAIN OF THE LOVERS.**

I.

LOVE scorns degrees! the low he lifteth high,
The high he draweth down to that fair plain
Whereon, in his divine equality,
Two loving hearts may meet, nor meet in vain;
'Gainst such sweet levelling Custom cries amain,
But o'er its harshest utterance one bland sigh,
Breathed passion-wise, doth mount victorious still,
For Love, earth's lord, must have his lordly will.

II.

But ah! this sovereign will oft works at last
The deadliest bane, as happed erewhile to her,
Earl Godolf's daughter, many a century past:

* The most important feature in the landscape of this poem the old Chronicler persists in designating as a mountain of "steep" and "terrible" ascent; but that it could not have been a mountain, and, despite certain obstacles which made it dangerous for men on horseback, it might not even have been a *very* "terrible" hill, is shown by the fact, that among the crowd who reached the summit soon after the catastrophe, were "old men," whom the excitement of the time and scene would hardly have sufficed to bear safely up were the Chronicler's expressions to be *literally* accepted. To any man loaded as Oswald was, the ascent of a comparatively moderate height would prove a fearful trial; but in his case the atrocious cruelty of the experiment, and the life and death issues involved, became so closely associated in the spectators' minds with the *material* scene of the tragedy, that the latter was not unnaturally beheld through the magnifying medium of pity and terror. Thus the hill was elevated into a mountain! The old Chronicler celebrates it as such. We follow the old Chronicler — to the death!

She loved her father's low born forester,
About whose manful grace did breathe and stir
So clear a radiance, by soul-virtues cast,
He moved untouched of social blight or ban —
Nature's serene, true-hearted gentleman.

III.

Yet she alone of all the household saw
That softy soul beneath his serf's attire;
But of the ruthless Earl so great her awe,
Close, close she kept her spirit's veiled desire,
Nor outward shone one spark of hidden fire.
Too well she knew to what stern feudal law
She and her hapless Love perforce must yield,
If once this tender secret were revealed.

IV.

Yea! even by Oswald's self her covert flame
Undreamed of burned; proud stood she, coldly fair,
When, to report of woodcraft lore, he came
To the Earl's hall, and she was lingering there.
"Cold heart!" thought he; "who 'midst her liegemen, dare
Play as I played with death a desperate game
For her sweet sake? and yet, alas! and yet,
She scorns the service and disowns the debt."

V.

For sooth it was that one keen winter's night,
While slowly journeying homeward through a wood
Whose every deepest copse in moonshine bright
Glimmered from hoary trunk to frost-tipped bud,
On sire and child there burst a cry of blood,
Followed by hurrying feet, and the dread sight
Of scores of gray-skinned brutes — a direful pack
Of wolves half-starved that yelled along their track.

VI.

In vain his frantic team Earl Godolf smote,
With blended prayer and curse; nigh doom were they,
Riders and steeds, for now each ravening throat
Yawned like a foul tomb. On the bounding sleigh
The fierce horde gained, when from the silvery-gray,
Cold-branchèd glades outrang a bugle note,
With next a bowstring's twang, an arrowy whir,
As shaft on shaft the keen-eyed forester

VII.

Launched on the foe, each hurtling shaft a fate.
Then Oswald, 'twixt pursuers and pursued
Leapt, sword in hand, his eyes of fiery hate
Fixed on the baffled horde, whose doubtful mood
Changed to quick fear, they scoured adown the wood,
Their long gaunt lines, in fiend-like, vanquished state,
Fading with flash of blood-red orbs from far,
Till the last vanished like a baleful star!

VIII.

Now, by the mass! abrupt and brief, I ween,
The rude Earl's thanks for rescued limbs and life;
But not so graceless proved the fair Catrine,
As glancing backward to the field of strife
She flashed a smile with cordial meaning rife,
Which struck our sylvan hero (who did lean,
Pale, on his bow,) as 'twere the piercing gleam
Of some strange, sudden, half bewildering dream.

IX.

Alack! the dream waxed not, but seemed to wane,
As if a cloudless sun but late arisen,
Back journeying, passed across the ethereal plain,
And the fresh dawn it brought, died out in heaven;
For from that eve no subtlest signs were given,
As erst we said, that passion's blissful pain
Touched the maid's heart, or that her days were caught
In those fine meshes woven by love for thought.

X.

In Britain dwelt Earl Godolf, nigh the bounds
Of the Welsh marches; a wild rover he
In his hot youth, inured to strife and wounds
Through many a foray fierce by land and sea;
But, after years of bright tranquillity —
Years linked to love through pleasure's peaceful bounds —
So gently lapsed, the unmailed warrior's hand
Forgot almost the use of spear or brand.

XI.

A bride erewhile won by his dauntless blade
In a great sea fight — where his arm had slain
Some half score foemen — wan and half afraid,
Homeward he brought, whose every delicate vein
Pulsed the rich blood and tropic warmth of Spain;
But when pure wifehood crowned the noble maid,
Heart-fruits for him his beauteous lady bore,
Of whose strange sweets he had not dreamed before.

XII.

She strove his nature's ruggedness to smooth,
And in his bosom dropped a fruitful germ
Of those mild virtues given our lives to soothe,
And change their gusty solitude to warm
Beneficent calm, — divinest after storm.
Within him flowered a pallid grace of ruth,
Nor oft, as once, o'er bleeding breasts he trod
Straight to his purpose, blind to law and God.

XIII.

And in fair fulness of the ripened time,
Still gentler grew his dark, war-furrowed mien;
He quaffed the sunshine of a fairy clime,
Love charmed, hope gladdened, when, to crown the scene
Of transient bliss, there smiled a new Catrine —

"Every deepest copse in moonshine bright,
Glimmered from hoary trunk to frost-tipped bud. . . .
Scores of gray-skinned brutes — a direful pack
Of wolves half-starved that yelled along their track."

The loveliest babe e'er lulled by mother's rhyme—
Whose tiny fingers o'er her heart-strings played,
Making ineffable music where they strayed.

XIV.

Woe worth the end! for though the infant thrived
Slowly the hapless mother pined away;
Love to the last in pleading eyes survived—
Those fond, fond eyes doomed to the churchyard clay,
Coffined, and shut from all blithe sights of day;
But Christ! in thee her stainless spirit lived,
Whose memory—a white star—should evermore
O'er her lord's paths have beamed to keep them pure.

XV.

Nathless, some souls there are by cruel loss
Stung, as with scourge of scorpions, to despair;
These will not seek the Christ, nor clasp His cross,
But, groping vaguely through sulphureous air,
Strike hands with Satan, in the murky glare
Of furious hell, whose billows rage and toss
About their tortured being, urged to curse
That mystic will which rules the universe.

XVI.

Yea, such the Earl's; no cooling dew did fall
To heal his wound; 'gainst heaven and earth he turned,
Girt to his sense with one vast funeral pall;
And the sore heart within him writhed and burned
With baffled hope, and pain that madly yearned,
Vainly and madly, for dear love's recall.
No light o'ershone grief's ocean drear and black,
The while old passions thronged tumultuous back.

XVII.

So, his last state was worse than e'en his first;
Murder and rapine, pitiless greed, and ire
Raged wheresoe'er his raven banner burst,
'Mid shrieks and wails, and hollow roar of fire,
Which lapped the household porch and crackling byre;
He seemed demoniac in his aims accurst,
Wrath in his soul, and on his brow the sign
Of hell—a human scourge by power divine

XVIII.

For some mysterious end permitted still—
As many an evil thing our God allows
To range the world, and work its dreadful will,
Whether in form of chiefs, with laurelled brows,
Or spies and traitors in the good man's house;
Or, it may be, some slow, infectious ill,
Untraced, and rising like a mist defiled
With poisonous odors on a lonely wild,

XIX.

Albeit no marsh is near, or steamy fen.
More monstrous year by year Earl Godolf's deeds
Flared in hell's livery on the eyes of men;
All growths of transient goodness checked by weeds,

Sin-bred; and, ah! *one* angel's bosom bleeds
To know she may not meet her love again;
And even the vales immortal seemed less sweet,
Because too pure for his crime-cumbered feet.

XX.

But, weal or woe, the world rolls blindly on,
While nature's charm, in child, and bird, and flower,
Works its rare marvels 'neath the noon-day sun,
And the still stars in midnight's slumberous hour.
And so a human bud, through beam and shower,
Glad play, and easeful sleep—the orphaned one,
The beauteous babe—a sour old beldame's care,
Upflowered at length a matchless maid, and fair.

XXI.

Most fair to all but him to whom she owed
Her life and place in this bewildering world;
For he, a changed man since that hour which showed
His wife's worn form in earthly cerements furled,
Cold scorn had launched, or captious passion hurled
At this sole offspring of his lone abode,
Till grown, alas! too early grave and wise,
She viewed her sire, in turn, with loveless eyes.

XXII.

Still in benignant arms did nature fold
Her favored child, and on her richly showered
All gifts of beauty; with long hair of gold
And lucid, languid eyes the maid she dowered,
And her enticing loveliness empowered
With charms to melt the wintriest temper's cold
Charms wrought of sunrise warmth, and twilight balm,
Passion's deep glow, and pity's saint-like calm.

XXIII.

Tall, lithe, and yielding as a young bay tree
Her perfect form; but 'neath its lissom grace
There lurked a latent strength keen eyes could see,
Drawn from her father's undegenerate race;
The dazzling fairness of her Saxon face,
Contrasted with the dark eyes' witchery,
Shone with such light as northern noon-days wake
Through the clear shadows of a mountain lake.

XXIV.

Her full blown flower of beauty lured ere long
Unnumbered suitors round her; these declare
Boldest report hath done the virgin wrong,
And past all power of words they deem her fair;
The kingdom's princeliest youth besiege her ear
And heart with ardent vows and amorous song;
Love, rank and wealth their splendid beams combine,
She the rare orb about whose path they shine.

XXV.

Still would she wed with none till rudely pressed
To the last boundary of her patience sweet;

No more she struggled in a yearning breast
To hide her passion, howsoe'er unmeet
For one high placed as she; her fervent feet
Oft bore her now where woodland flowers caressed
The grand old oaks, beneath whose sheltering boughs
The lovers mused, or, whispering, breathed their vows.

XXVI.

But ere to such sweet pass their fates had led,
Or ere her thought unbosomed utterly,
To the rapt youth, in tremulous tones, she said,
"*I love thee*," through full many a fine degree
Of feeling, touched by sad uncertainty,
That truth they neared, which, like a bird o'erhead,
Still faltering flew, till borne through shade and sun,
It nestled warm in two hearts made as one!

XXVII.

The truth, the fond conviction that all earth
Was less than naught — a mote, a vanishing gleam,
Matched with the glow of that transcendent birth
Of love which wrapped them in his happiest dream;
Entrancèd thus, shut in by beam on beam
Of glory, is it strange but trivial worth
Their dazzled minds in transient doubts should see
Which some times crossed their keen felicity?

XXVIII.

Their love awhile, like some smooth rivulet borne
Through drooping umbrage of a lonely dell,
By clouds unvisited, by storms untorn,
Passed, rippling music; like a magic bell
Out rung by spirit hands invisible,
Each tender hour of meeting, eve or morn,
Above them, stole in rhythmic sweetness, blent
With rare fruition of supreme content.

XXIX.

But in the sunset tide of one calm day,
When, all unconscious at the place of tryst,
Beyond their wont they lingered; with dismay
They saw, begirt by gold and amethyst,
Of that rich time, gigantic in the midst
Of shimmering splendor, which did flash and play
About his form, and o'er his visage dire,
The wrathful Earl, midmost the sunset fire.

XXX.

No word he uttered, but his falchion drew,
Red with the slain boar's blood, and pointed grim
Where 'gainst the eastern heavens' slow-deepening blue
Uprose his castle turrets, tall and dim.
The maid's eyes close; she feels each nerveless limb
Sink nigh to swooning; but, heart-brave and true,
Clings to her Love, while from pale lips a sigh
Doth faintly fall, which means "*with him I die!*"

XXXI.

Gravely advancing, the Earl's stalwart hand
Rests on her shuddering shoulder; one quick glance,
Haughty and high, rife with severe command,
On the 'mazed woodsman doth he dart askance,

Who doubtful bides, as one half roused from trance,
Striving to know on what new ground his stand
Thenceforth shall be; or if life's priceless all,
Put to the test just then, must rise or fall.

XXXII.

Fate wrought the issue! for as Oswald waits
Biding his time to smite, or else retreat,
With the maid's hand his own Earl Godolf mates,
And from the wood they pass with footsteps fleet;
One tearful, backward look vouchsafed his sweet,
Just as the castle gates — those iron gates,
Heavy and stern, like Death's — were closed between
His burning vision and the lost Catrine.

XXXIII.

To heaven he raises wild despairing eyes,
But heaven responds not; then to earth returns
His baffled gaze from ranging the cold skies,
And earth but seems a place for burial urns;
In sooth, the whole creation mutely spurns
His prayer for aid; alas! what kind replies
Can woeful man from fair, dumb Nature draw
Locked in the grasp of adamantine Law?

XXXIV.

Three morns thereafter, in the market place
Of the small town, from Godolf's castle wall
Distant, it might be, some twelve furlongs' space,
Came, grandly robed, our Lord's high seneschal;
To all the lieges, with shrill trumpet call,
In name of his serene puissant grace
Godolf, the Earl; to all folk, bond or free,
With strident voice he read this foul decree:

XXXV.

"Whereas our virgin daughter, hight Catrine,
False to her noble race and lineage proud,
Hath owned her love for one of birth as mean
As any hind's who creeps among the crowd
Of common serfs, with cowering shoulders bowed —
Oswald by name — the whom ourselves have seen,
When least he deemed us nigh, his traitorous part
Press with hot wooing on the maiden's heart:

XXXVI.

"Let all men know hereby our will it is,
To-morrow morn their trial morn must be;
Either the serf shall win, and call her his,
Or both shall taste such bitter misery
As even in dreams the boldest soul would flee;
If lips unlicensed thus will meet and kiss,
Reason it seems that such unhallowed flame
Of love should end in agony and shame.

XXXVII.

"Therefore, the morrow morn shall view their doom
Accomplished; 'mid the ferns of Bolton Down,
Where Bolton Height doth catch the purpling bloom

Of early sunrise on his treeless crown,
We say to all — knight, burgher, squire and clown —
Just as the castle's morning bell shall boom
O'er the far hills, and brown moor's blossoming,
Come, and behold a yet undreamed-of thing.

XXXVIII.

"For then and there must Oswald bear aloft,
By his sole strength, unaided and alone,
The blameful maid, whose nature, grown too soft,
Durst thus betray our honor and her own;
Yet, if he gain the height, untamed, unthrown,
All hands applaud him, and all plumes be doffed;
While for ourselves, we vow they both shall fare
Unharmed beyond our realm — we reck not where."

XXXIX.

So, as decreed, the next morn, calm and clear,
Witnessed, in many a diverse mode conveyed,
A mixed and mighty concourse gathering near
The appointed height, some in rough frieze arrayed,
And some in gold; there blushed the downcast maid,
Urged to this cruel test, a passionate tear
Misting her view, as surged the living sea.
Behind her, his arms folded haughtily,

XL.

His comely head thrown back, his eyes on fire
With hot contempt, fixed on an armèd band
Which, stationed near him at the Earl's desire,
His every move o'erlooked, did Oswald stand,
Striving his rousèd anger to command,
And lift his clouded aspirations higher
Than thoughts revengeful. Hark! a deepening hum
On the crowd's verge — the trial hour has come!

XLI.

Divided, then, betwixt his ire and scorn,
Outspake the Earl, in tones of savage glee:
"Woodsman! essay thy task, for lo! the morn
Grows old, and I this wretched mummery
Would fain see ended."
— With mien gravely free,
Clad in light garb, o'erwrought by hound and horn,
Oswald stood forth, nor quelled by frail alarms,
About the maiden clasped his reverent arms;

XLII.

And she, like some pure flower by May tide rain
Gracefully laden, turns her eyes apart
From the great throng, and, pierced by modest pain,
Veiled her sweet face upon her lover's heart;
Whereat the youth is seen to thrill and start,
While o'er his own face, calm and pale but now,
Rush the deep crimson waves from chin to brow;

XLIII.

Then do they ebb away, and leave him white
As the vexed foam on ocean's stormy swell,

Yet cool and constant in his manful
might
As some stanch rock 'gainst which the
tides rebel
In useless rage, with hollow, billowy
knell;
Meanwhile advancing with sure steps
and light,
He moves in measured wise to dare his
fate
Beneath those looks of blended ruth and
hate.

XLIV.

Stirred by his generous bravery, and the
sight
Of such young lives — their love, hope,
joyance set
On the hard mastery of yon terrible
height,
Whose rugged slopes and sheer descent
are wet
And slippery with the dews of dawning
yet, —
Through the dense rout, which swayed
now left, now right,
Low, inarticulate murmurs faintly ran,
And one keen, quivering shock from
man to man.

XLV.

The watchful matrons sob, the virgins
weep
Full tears, but all unheeded, as with
slow,
Sure footfalls still he mounts the hostile
steep
On to a point where two great columns
show
Their rounded heads, crowned by the
morning glow.
His task half done, a sigh, long, grateful,
deep,
Breaks from his heaving heart; secure
he stands,
A sunbeam glimmering on his claspèd
hands,

XLVI.

And the glad lustre of his wind-swept
locks
More radiant made thereby; his tall
form towers
'Gainst the dark background, piled
with rocks on rocks
Precipitous, whose grim, gaunt visage
lowers,
As if in league they were — like Titan
powers
Victorious long o'er storms and earth-
quake shocks —
To cast mute scorn on him whose doubt-
ful path
Leads near the threatening shadows of
their wrath.

XLVII.

From the charmed crowd then rose an
easeful breath,
Lightening the dense air; but, 'midst
doubt and bale,
Raves the wild Earl, reckless of life or
death,
If so his tyrannous purpose could pre-
vail;
For, almost mad, he smites his gloves of
mail,
Goading with frenzied heel the steed
beneath
His barbarous rule; in reason's fierce
eclipse,
A blood-red foam burns on his writhing
lips.

XLVIII.

Meanwhile, brief space for needful
respite given,
With quickened pace, onward and
upward still,
And fanned by freshening gales, as
nearer heaven
He climbs o'er granite passways of the
hill,
Oswald ascends, untamed of strength or
will,

"The kingdom's princeliest youth besiege her ear.'

Striving, as ne'er before had mortal striven,
Boldly to win, and proudly wear as his,
The prize he bore of that bright, breathing bliss.

XLIX.

Two thirds, two thirds and more, of that last half
Of his fell journey had he stoutly won;
And now he pauses the cool breeze to quaff,
And feel the royal heartening of the sun
Nerving his soul for what must yet be done,
When with a gentle, quivering, flutelike laugh,
Holding a sob, the maiden rose and kissed
Her hero's lips, sought through a tremulous mist

L.

Of love and pride! The on-lookers, ranged afar,
Saw, and more boldly blessed them; all are moved
To trust that theirs may prove the fortunate star
Fate brightly kindles for young lives beloved:
"His truth and valor hath he nobly proved;
How brave, how constant both these lovers are;
Sooth! the sweet heavens seem with them." Thus, full voiced,
Yet with some lingering doubts, the folk rejoiced.

LI.

Alas! for false forecasting, and surmise!
Though small the space betwixt him and his goal,
Oswald doth stagger now in feeblest wise,
And like some drunken carl, with heave and roll,
Blindly he staggers in his lost control
Of sense, or power; and so, with anguished sighs,
Turned on his love — the goal in easy reach —
His yearning woe too deep for mortal speech.

LII.

Whereon the lady's arms are wildly raised,
Perchance in prayer, perchance with pitying aim
His strain to ease, when lo! (dear Christ be praised!)
It seemed new strength, fresh courage o'er him came,
And through his spirit rushed a glorious flame,
At which the crowd stood moveless, dumb, amazed,
For, like a god, with swift, resistless tread,
He strides to clasp the near goal o'er his head.

LIII.

A savage cliff of beetling brow it was,
Midmost the summit of the lowering height,
Rooted amongst low shrubs and sun-dried grass,
And reared in blackness, like a cloud of night,
On whose dull breast no beacon star is bright.
Thitherward, from cold terrors of the pass
Well nigh of death, the hero speeds amain,
Nor seems his matchless labor wrought in vain.

LIV.

Yea; for a single rood's length oversped
And victory crowns him! God! how still the crowd,
Once rife with voices! silent as the dead
Lodged in their earthly crypt and mouldering shroud ;

But suddenly a great cry mounted loud
And shrill above them, as in ruthful dread,
They saw the lovers, linked in close embrace,
Fall headlong down by that wild trysting place.

LV.

Then comes a quick revulsion, when, the pain
Of fear and choking sympathy gone by,
Hope reappears — aye, joy and triumph reign —
For though supine on yonder height they lie,
Still, brow to brow, turned from the deepening sky,
'Tis but the faintness of the mighty strain —
Or so they dream — on o'erworked nerve and will,
Which leaves them moveless on the conquered hill.

LVI.

Spurring his courser, in vexed doubt and haste,
The Earl charged on the dangerous height, as though
Firm-trenched, defiant, 'mid the rock-strewn waste
Glittered the spear-points of his mortal foe;
The horse's hoof struck fire, hurling below
Huge stones and turf his goaded limbs displaced,
Till checked midway, his reckless rider found
He needs must climb afoot the treacherous ground

LVII.

And next the throng had caught, and past him swept,
Clothed as he was in armor; a young knight
Headed the rout, whose feverish fingers crept
Oft to his sword hilt; on the topmost height,
Pausing with veilèd eyes, his gaze he kept
Fixed on the prostrate pair, o'er whom the light
Of broadening sunrise now was mixed with shade,
And still the knight's hand wandered round his blade.

LVIII.

Impatient, spleenful, struggling with the tide
Of common folk, who seemed to heed no more
His sullen passion and revengeful pride,
Than if just then he were the veriest boor, —
The Earl at length with bent brows strode before
The mongrel horde, and unto Oswald cried:
"Rise, traitor, rise! by some foul, juggling sleight,
Through the fiend's help, thou hast attained the height:

LIX.

Part them, I say!" To whom in measured tone,
Measured and strange, the young knight answering said:
"Earl, well I know thou wear'st for heart a stone,
Yet dar'st thou part these twain whom death has wed,
No longer twain, but one? Look! overhead
The burning sun mounts to his noonday throne;
But o'er the sun, as o'er this fateful sod,
Rules a great King, the King whose name is God!

LX.

"Deem'st thou for this day's work His wrath shall rest?"
Whereon, low murmuring like a hive of bees,
With stifled groans and tears, the people pressed
Round the fair corpses — women on their knees
Embraced them — and old men — but dusky lees
Of feeling left — did touch them, and caressed
The maid's soft hair, the woodsman's noble face,
Praying, under breath, that Christ would grant them grace.

. . . . .

LXI.

That mournful day had waned; by sunset rose
A wailing wind from out the dim northeast;
Which, as the shadows waxed at twilight's close
O'er moat and wood, to a shrill storm increased:
But in his castle hall, with song and feast,
Varied full oft by ribald gibes and blows
Twixt ruffian guests in rage or maudlin play,
The wild night raved its awful hours away.

LXII.

With not a pang at thought of her whose form
In pallid beauty lay unwatched and dead,
In a far turret chamber, where the storm,
Thundering each moment louder overhead,
Entered and shook the close-draped, sombre bed,
The barbarous sire with wine and wassail warm,
Lifting his cup 'mid brutal jest and jeer,
Banned his pale daughter, slumbering on her bier.

LXIII.

Just as those impious words had taken flight,
In the red dusk beyond the torch's glare,
Stole a vague shape that 'scaped the revellers' sight,
Slowly toward Earl Godolf, unaware
Even as the rest, what fateful foe drew near.
Muffled the shape was, masked and black as night,
And now for one dread instant with raised sword
Stood hovering o'er the heedless banquet board.

LXIV.

And next with flashing motion fierce and fast,
Vengeance descended on that glittering blade;
The amazed spectators started, dumb, aghast,
While at their feet the caitiff lord was laid,
His heart's blood trickling o'er the purple braid
(For through his heart the avenger's brand had passed),
And silver broidery of his gorgeous vest,
Drawn drop by drop from out his smitten breast.

LXV.

The muffled shape which as a cloud did rise
On the wild orgie, as a cloud departs;
Wan hands are swept across bewildered eyes,
And awe stilled now the throbbing at their hearts,
When suddenly one death-pale reveller starts

Up from the board and in shrill accent cries,
"Curst is this roof-tree, curst this meat and wine,
Fly, comrades; fly with me the wrath Divine!"

LXVI.

In haste, in horror, and great tumult, fled
The affrighted guests; then, on the vacant room
No maddening voice thenceforth disquieted,
Fell the stern presence of a ghastly gloom.
A place 'twas deemed of hopeless, baleful doom;
Barred from all mortal view in darkness dread,
Only the spectral forms of woe and sin
Thro' the long years cold harborage found therein.

---

*THE VENGEANCE OF THE GODDESS DIANA.**

WHAT time the Norman ruled in Sicily
At that mild season when the vernal sea,
O'erflitted by the zephyr's frolic wing,
Dances and dimples in the smile of spring
A goodly ship set sail upon her way
From Ceos unto Smyrna; through the play
Of wave and sunbeam touched with fragrant calm,
She passed by beauteous island shores of palm,
Until so sweet the tender wooing breeze,
So fraught the hours with balms of slumbrous ease,
That those who manned her, in the genial air
And dalliance of the time, forgot the care
Due to her courses; in the bland sunshine
They lay enchanted, dreaming dreams divine,
While idly drifting on the halcyon water,
The bark obeyed whatever currents caught her.

Borne onward thus for many a cloudless day,
They reach at length a wide and wooded bay,
The haunt of birds whose purpling wings in flight
Make even the blushful morning seem more bright,
Flushed as with darting rainbows; through the tide,
By overripe pomegranate juices dyed,
And laving boughs of the wild fig and grape,
Great shoals of dazzling fishes madly ape
The play of silver lightnings in the deep
Translucent pools; the crew awoke from sleep,
Or rather that strange trance that on them pressed
Gently as sleep; yet still they loved to rest,
Fanned by voluptuous gales, by morphean languors blessed.

---

* Sixteen years ago, in a volume of comparatively youthful verses, the above poem appeared under the title of "*Arolio; a legend of the island of Cos.*" The original narrative has now been carefully rewritten and amended and upwards of a hundred and fifty lines of entirely new matter have been added thereto. So far as we know, the only poet who has celebrated this significant and beautiful tradition, is William Morris, in the first section of whose "Earthly Paradise" there is a story (called "*The Lady of the Land*") founded upon some of its more obvious and popular incidents. Since Morris's wonderful tales were not published until 1868, we can, at least, assert the humble claim of precedence in the poetical treatment of *this* legend.

The shore sloped upward into foliaged hills,
Cleft by the channels of rock-fretted rills,
That flashed their wavelets, touched by iris lights,
O'er many a tiny cataract down the heights.

Green vales there were between, and pleasant lawns
Thick set with bloom, like sheen of tropic dawns,
Brightening the orient; further still the glades
Of whisperous forests, flecked with golden shades,
Stretched glimmering southward; on the wood's far rim,
Faintly discerned thro' veiling vapors, dim
As mists of Indian summer, the broad view
Was clasped by mountains flickering in the blue
And hazy distance; over all there hung
The morn's eternal beauty, calm and young.
Amid the throng, each with a marvelling face
Turned on that island Eden and its grace,
Was one — Avolio — a brave youth of Florence,
Self-exiled from his country, in abhorrence
Of the base, blood-stained tyrants dominant there.

A gentleman he was, of gracious air,
And liberal as the summer, skilled in lore
Of arms, and chivalry, and many more
Deep sciences which others left unlearned.
He loved adventure; how his spirit burned
Within him, when, as now, a chance arose
To search untravelled forests, and strange foes
Vanquish by púissance of knightly blows,
Or rescue maidens from malignant spells,
Enforced by hordes of wizard sentinels.
So in the ardor of his martial glee,
He clapped his hands and shouted suddenly:
"Ho! sirs, a challenge! let us pierce these woods
Down to the core: explore their solitudes,
And make the flowery empire all our own:
Who knows but we may conquer us a throne?
At least, bold feats await us, grand emprise
To win us favor in our ladies' eyes;
By heaven! he is a coward who delays."

So saying, all his countenance ablaze
With passionate zeal, the youth sprang lightly up,
And with right lusty motion, filled a cup —
They brought him straightway — to the glistening brim
With Cyprus wine: "Now glory unto him,
The ardent knight, no mortal danger daunts,
Whose constant soul a fiery impulse haunts,
Which spurs him onward, onward, to the end;
Pledge we the brave! and may St. Ermo send
Success to crown our valiantest!"
This said,
Avolio shoreward leaped, and with him led
The whole ship's company.

A motley band
Were they who mustered round him on the strand,

Mixed knights and traders; the first fired for toil
Which promised glory; the last keen for spoil!
Thro' breezy paths and beds of blossoming thyme
Kept fresh by secret springs, the showery chime
Of whose clear falling waters in the dells
Played like an airy peal of elfin bells —
With eager minds, but aimless, idle feet
(The scene about them was so lone and sweet
It spelled their steps), 'mid labyrinths of flowers,
By mossy streams and in deep shadowed bowers,
They strayed from charm to charm thro' lengths of languid hours.
In thickets of wild fern and rustling broom,
The humble bee buzzed past them with a boom
Of insect thunder; and in glens afar
The golden firefly — a small animate star —
Shone from the twilight of the darkling leaves.
High noon it was, but dusk like mellow eve's
Reigned in the wood's deep places, whence it seemed
That flashing locks and quick arch glances gleamed
From eyes scarce human. Thus the fancy deemed
Of those most given to marvels; the rest laughed
A merry jeering laugh; and many a shaft
Launched from the Norman cross bow, pierced the nooks,
Or cleft the shallow channels of the brooks,
Whence, as the credulous swore, an Oread shy,
Or a glad nymph, had peeped out cunningly.
Thus wandering, they reached a sombre mound
Rising abruptly from the level ground,
And planted thick with dim funereal trees,
Whose foliage waved and murmured, tho' the breeze
Had sunk to midnight quiet, and the sky
Just o'er the place seemed locked in apathy,
Like a fair face wan with the sudden stroke
Of death, or heart-break. Not a word they spoke,
But paused with wide, bewildered, gleaming eyes,
Standing at gaze; what spectral terrors rise
And coil about their hearts with serpent fold,
And oh! what loathly scene is this they hold,
Grasping with unwinking vision, as they creep,
Urged by their very horror, up the steep,
And the whole preternatural landscape dawns
Freezingly on them; a broad stretch of lawns,
Sown with rank poisonous grasses, where the dew
Of hovering exhalations flickered blue
And wavering on the dead-still atmosphere —
Dead-still it was, and yet the grasses sere
Stirred as with horrid life amidst the sickening glare.
The affrighted crew, all save Avolio, fled
In wild disorder from this place of dread;
In him, albeit his terror whispered "fly!"
The spell of some uncouth necessity
Baffled retreat, and ruthless, scourged him on;
Meanwhile, the sun thro' darkening vapors shone,

Nigh to his setting, and a sudden blast —
Sudden and chill — woke shrilly up, and passed
With ghostly din and tumult; airy sounds
Of sylvan horns, and sweep of circling hounds
Nearing the quarry. Now the wizard chase
Swept faintly, faintly up the fields of space,
And now with backward rushing whirl roared by
Louder and fiercer, till a maddening cry —
A bitter shriek of human agony —
Leaped up, and died amid the stifling yell
Of brutes athirst for blood; a crowning swell
Of savage triumph followed, mixed with wails
Sad as the dying songs of nightingales,
Murmuring the name Actæon!
Even as one,
A wrapt sleep-walker, through the shadows dun
Of half oblivious sense, with soulless gaze,
Goes idly journeying through uncertain ways,
Thus did Avolio, sore perplexed in mind
(Excess of mystery made his spirit blind),
Grope through the gloom. Anon he reached a fount
Whose watery columns had long ceased to mount
Above its prostrate Tritons. Near at hand,
Dammed up in part by heaps of tawny sand,
All dull and lustreless, a streamlet wound
By trickling banks, with dark, dank foliage crowned,
That gloomed 'twixt sullen tides and lowering sky;
The melancholy waters seemed to sigh
In wailful murmurs of articulate woe,
Till at the last arose this strange dirge from below:

SONG OF THE IMPRISONED NAIAD.

"Woe! woe is me! the centuries pass away,
The mortal seasons run their ceaseless rounds,
While here I wither for the sunbright day,
Its genial sights and sounds.
Woe! woe is me!

"One summer night, in ages long agone,
I saw my woodland lover leave the brake;
I heard him plaining on the peaceful lawn
A plaint 'for my sweet sake.'
Woe! woe is me!

"My heart upsprang to answer that fond lay,
But suddenly the star-girt planets paled,
And high into the welkin's glimmering gray
Majestic Dian sailed!
Woe! woe is me!

"She swept aloft, bold almost as the sun,
And wrathful red as fiery-crested Mars;
Ah! then I knew some fearful deed was done
On earth, or in the stars.
Woe! woe is me!

"With ghastly face upraised, and shuddering throat,
I watched the omen with a prescient pain;
When, lightning-barbed, a beamy arrow smote,
Or *seemed* to smite, my brain.
Woe! woe is me!

"Oblivion clasped me, till I woke forlorn,
Fettered and sorrowing on this lonely bed,
Shut from the mirthful kisses of the morn —
Earth's glories overhead.
Woe! woe is me!

"The south wind stirs the sedges into song,
The blossoming myrtles scent the enamored air;
But still, sore moaning for another's wrong,
I pine in sadness here.
Woe! woe is me!

"Alas! alas! the weary centuries flee,
The waning seasons perish, dark or bright;
My grief alone, like some charmed poison-tree,
Knows not an autumn blight.
Woe! woe is me!"

The mournful sounds swooned off, but Echo rose,
And bore them up divinely to a close
Of rare mysterious sweetness; nevermore
Shall mortal winds to listening wood and shore
Waft such heart-melting music. "Where, oh! where,"
Avolio murmured — "to what haunted sphere —
Has fate at length my errant footsteps brought?"

Launched on a baffling sea of mystic thought,
His reason in a whirling chaos, lost
Compass and chart and headway, vaguely tossed
'Mid shifting shapes of wingèd fantasies.
Just then, uplifting his bewildered eyes,
He saw, half hid in shade, on either hand,
Twin pillars of a massive gateway grand
With gold and carvings; close behind it stood
A sombre mansion in a beech tree wood.

Long wreaths of ghostly ivy on its walls
Quivered like goblin tapestry, or palls,
Tattered and rusty, mildewed in the chill
Of dreadful vaults; across each window sill
Curtains of weird device and fiery hue
Hung moveless, — only when the sun glanced through
The gathering gloom, the hieroglyphs took form
And life and action, and the whole grew warm
With meanings baffling to Avolio's sense;
He stood expectant, trembling, with intense
Dread in his eyes, and yet a struggling faith,
Vital at heart. A sudden passing breath —
Was it the wind? — thrilled by his tingling ear,
Waving the curtains inward, and his fear
Uprose victorious, for a serpent shape,
Tall, supple, writhing, with malignant gape,
Which showed its cruel fangs — hissed in the gleam
Its own fell eyeballs kindled! Oh! supreme
The horror of that vision! — as he gazed,
Irresolute, all wordless, and amazed,
The monster disappeared — a moment sped!
The next it fawned before him on a bed
Of scarlet poppies. "Speak," Avolio said;
"What art thou? Speak! I charge thee in God's name!"

A death-cold shudder seized the serpent's frame,
Its huge throat writhed, whence bubbling with a throe
Of hideous import, a voice thin and low
Broke like a muddied rill: "Bethink thee well,
This isle is Cos, of which old legends tell
Such marvels. Hast thou never heard of me,
The island's fated queen?" "Yea, verily,"
Avolio cried, "thou art that thing of dread ——"
Sharply the serpent raised its glittering head
And front tempestuous: "Hold! no tongue save mine
Must of these miseries tell thee! Then incline

"A monster meet for Tartarus, a thing
Whereon men gaze with awe and shuddering."

Thine ear to the dark story of my grief,
And with thine ear yield, yield me thy belief.
Foul as I am, there *was* a time, O youth,
When these fierce eyes were founts of love and truth;
There *was* a time when woman's blooming grace
Glowed through the flush of roses in my face;
When—but I sinned a deep and damning sin,
The fruit of lustful pride nurtured within
By weird, forbidden knowledge—I defied
The night's immaculate goddess, purest eyed,
And holiest of immortals; I denied
The eternal Power that looks so cold and calm;
Therefore, O stranger, am I what I am,
A monster meet for Tartarus, a thing
Whereon men gaze with awe and shuddering,

And stress of inward terror; through all time,
Down to the last age, my abhorrèd crime
Must hold me prisoner in this vile abode.
Unless some man, large-hearted as a God,
Bolder than Ajax, mercifully deign
To kiss me on the mouth!"

She towered amain,
With sparkling crest, and universal thrill
Of frenzied eagerness, that seemed to fill
Her cavernous eyes with jets of lurid fire,
Pulsed from the burning core of unappeased desire.

Back stepped Avolio with a loathing fear,
Sick to the inmost soul; then did he hear
The awful creature vent a tortured groan,
Her frantic neck and dragon's forehead thrown
Madly to earth, whereon awhile she lay,
Her glances veiled, her dark crest turned away.

As thus she grovelled, quivering on the ground,
Stole through the brooding silence a faint sound
As 'twere of hopeless grief — it seemed to be
A human voice weeping how piteously!
Yet its deep passion striving to subdue.
Just then the serpent writhed her folds anew,
And while from earth her horrent crest she rears,
The loathly creature's face is bathed in tears!

"Lady!" the knight said, "if in sooth thou art
A maid and human, wherefore thus depart
From truth's plain path to blind me? well I know
This Dian, famed and worshipped long ago
By heathen folk, was as the idle fume
Formed into shifting shapes of vaporous bloom
O'er her vain altars. Ah!" (he shuddered now,
Growing death-pale from tremulous chin to brow)
"*Ah, God! I cannot kiss thee!* Ne'ertheless,
Fain am I in the true God's name to bless,
And even to mark thee with His sacred cross!"

As one weighed down by anguish and the loss
Of one last hope, in faltering tones and sad
The serpent spake: "Deem'st thou that Dian had
No life but that wherewith her votaries vain
Invested a vague image of the brain?
Nay, she both *was* and *was not*, as on earth,
Even to this day, full many a thing from birth
To death lapses alike through bane and bliss;
Full many a thing, which is not and yet is,
Save to man's purblind vision; — in the end
Some clearer spirits may rise to comprehend
This strange enigma! but meanwhile, meanwhile
The sure heavens change not, star and sunbeam smile
Fair as of yore; eternal nature keeps
Her strength and beauty, though the mortal weeps

In desolation! Oh! wert *thou* but true
And brave enow this thing I ask to do,
Then human, happy, beauteous would I be.
Ye merciful Gods! once more!"

Then suddenly
She writhed her vast neck round, her glittering crest
Cast backward o'er the fierce, tumultuous breast,
Red as a stormy sunset — with a moan,
"Pass on, weak soul!" she said, "leave me alone:"
Then, wildly, "Go! I would not catch thine eye:
Go, and be safe! for swiftly, furiously,
Surges a cruel thought through all my blood,
And the brute instincts turn to hardihood
Of vengeful impulse all my gentler frame:
Go! for I would not harm thee; yet a flame
Of blasting torments have I power to raise
Through all thy being, and mine eyes *could* gaze,
Gloating on pain. Is this not horrible?"
And therewithal the wretched monster fell
To open weeping, with sad front, and bowed.

Something in such base cruelty avowed,
Blent with the softer will which disallowed
Its exercise, so on Avolio wrought,
That sore perplexed, revolving many a thought,
He lingered still, lost in a spiritual mist;
But when the mouth that waited to be kissed,
Fringed with a yellow foam, malignly rose
Before him, his first fear its terrible throes
Renewed. "And how, O baleful shape!" said he —
Striving to speak in passionless tones, and free —
"How can I tell, what certain gage have I,
That this strange kiss thine awful destiny
Hath not ordained — the least elaborate plan
Whereby to snare and slay me?" "O man! man!"
The serpent answered, with a loftier mien —
A voice grown clear, majestic and serene —
"Shall *matter* always triumph? the base mould
Mask the immortal essence, uncontrolled
Save by your grovelling fancies mean and cold?
O green and happy woods, breathing like sleep!
O quiet habitants of places deep
In leafy shades, that draw your peaceful breaths,
Passing fair lives to rest in tranquil deaths!
O earth! O sea! O heavens! forever dumb
To man, while ages go and ages come
Mysterious, have the dark Fates willed it so
That nevermore the sons of men shall know
The secret of your silence? the wide scope
Granted your basking pleasures, and sweet hope,
Revived in vernal warmth and springtide rains,
Your long, long pleasures, and your fleeting pains?
And must the lack of what is brave and true,
From other souls, callous or blind thereto,
From what themselves beauteous and truthful are,

Differ for aye as glow-worms from a star?
Is such our life's decretal? Shall the faith
Which even, perchance, the clearest spirit hath
In good within us, always prove less bold
Than keen suspicions, nursed by craven doubt,
Of treacherous ills, and evil from without?"
Then, after pause, with passion: "O etern
And bland benignities, that breathe and burn
Throughout creation, are we but the motes
In some vague dream that idly sways and floats
To nothingness? or are your glories pent
Within ourselves, to rise omnipotent
In bloom and music, when we bend above,
And wake them by the kisses of our love?
I yearn to be made beautiful. Alas!
Beauty itself looks on, prepared to pass,
In hardened disbelief! *one* action kind
Would free and save me — why art thou so blind,
Avolio?" While she spoke, a timorous hare,
Scared by a threatening falcon from its lair,
Rushed to the serpent's side. With fondling tongue
She soothed it as a mother soothes her young.

Avolio mused: "Can innocent things like this
Take refuge by her? then, perchance, some good,
Some tenderness, if rightly understood,
Lurks in her nature. *I will do the deed!*
Christ and the Virgin save me at my need."

He signed the monster nearer, closed his eyes,
And with some natural shuddering, some deep sighs!
Gave up his pallid lips to the foul kiss!
What followed then? a traitorous serpent hiss,
Sharper for triumph? Ah! not so — he felt
A warm, rich, yearning mouth approach and melt
In languid, loving sweetness on his own,
And two fond arms caressingly were thrown
About his neck, and on his bosom pressed
Twin lilies of a snow white virgin breast.

He raised his eyes, released from brief despair;
They rested on a maiden tall and fair —
Fair as the tropic morn, when morn is new —
And her sweet glances smote him through and through
With such keen thrilling rapture that he swore
His willing heart should evermore adore
Her loveliness, and woo her till he died.

"I am thine own," she whispered, "thy true bride,
If thou wilt take me!"
Hand in hand they strayed
Adown the shadows through the woodland glade,
Whence every evil influence shrank afraid,
And round them poured the golden eventide.
Swiftly the tidings of this strange event
Abroad on all the garrulous winds were sent,
Rousing an eager world to wonderment!

Now 'mid the knightly companies that came
To visit Cos, was that brave chief, by fame

Exalted for bold deeds and faith divine,
So nobly shown erewhile in Palestine —
Tancred, Salerno's Prince — he came in state,
With fourscore gorgeous barges, small and great,
With pomp and music, like an ocean Fate;
His blazoned prows along the glimmering sea
Spread like an eastern sunrise gloriously.

Him and his followers did Avolio feast
Right royally, but when the mirth increased,
And joyous-wingèd jests began to pass
Above the sparkling cups of Hippocras,
Tancred arose, and in his courtly phrase
Invoked delight and length of prosperous days
To crown that magic union; one vague doubt
The Prince did move, and this he dared speak out,
But with serene and tempered courtesy:
"It could not be that their sweet hostess still
Worshipped Diana and her heathen will?"

"Ah sir! not so!" Avolio flushing cried,
"But Christ the Lord!"
No single word replied
The beauteous lady, but with gentle pride
And a quick motion to Avolio's side
She drew more closely by a little space,
Gazing with modest passion in his face,
As one who yearned to whisper tenderly:
"O, brave kind heart! I worship only thee!"

THE SOLITARY LAKE.

From garish light and life apart,
Shrined in the woodland's secret heart,
With delicate mists of morning furled
Fantastic o'er its shadowy world,
The lake, a vaporous vision, gleams
So vaguely bright, my fancy deems
'Tis but an airy lake of dreams.

Dreamlike, in curves of palest gold,
The wavering mist-wreaths manifold
Part in long rifts, through which I view
Gray islets throned in tides as blue
As if a piece of heaven withdrawn —
Whence hints of sunrise touch the dawn —
Had brought to earth its sapphire glow,
And smiled, a second heaven, below.

Dreamlike, in fitful, murmurous sighs,
I hear the distant west wind rise,
And, down the hollows wandering, break
In gurgling ripples on the lake,
Round which the vapors, still outspread,
Mount wanly widening overhead,
Till flushed by morning's primrose-red.

Dreamlike, each slow, soft-pulsing surge
Hath lapped the calm lake's emerald verge,
Sending, where'er its tremors pass
Low whisperings through the dew-wet grass;
Faint thrills of fairy sound that creep
To fall in neighboring nooks asleep,
Or melt in rich, low warblings made
By some winged Ariel of the glade.

With brightening morn the mockbird's lay
Grows stronger, mellower; far away
'Mid dusky reeds, which even the noon
Lights not, the lonely-hearted loon
Makes answer, her shrill music shorn
Of half its sadness; day, full-born,
Doth rout all sounds and sights forlorn.

Ah! still a something strange and rare
O'errules this tranquil earth and air,
Casting o'er both a glamour known
To *their* enchanted realm alone;
Whence shines, as 'twere a spirit's face,
The sweet coy genius of the place,

Yon lake beheld as if in trance,
The beauty of whose shy romance
I feel — whatever shores and skies
May charm henceforth my wondering
eyes, —
Shall rest, undimmed by taint or stain,
'Mid lonely byways of the brain,
There, with its haunting grace, to seem
Set in the landscape of a dream.

THE VOICE IN THE PINES.

THE morn is softly beautiful and still,
Its light fair clouds in pencilled gold
and gray
Pause motionless above the pine-grown
hill,
Where the pines, tranced as by a wizard's will,
Uprise as mute and motionless as
they!

Yea! mute and moveless; not one flickering spray
Flashed into sunlight, nor a gaunt
bough stirred;
Yet, if wooed hence beneath those pines
to stray,
We catch a faint, thin murmur far away,
A bodiless voice, by grosser ears unheard.

What voice is this? what low and solemn tone,
Which, though all wings of all the
winds seem furled,
Nor even the zephyr's fairy flute is blown,
Makes thus forever its mysterious moan
From out the whispering pine-tops'
shadowy world?

Ah! can it be the antique tales are true?
Doth some lone Dryad haunt the
breezeless air,
Fronting yon bright immitigable blue,
And wildly breathing all her wild soul
through
That strange unearthly music of despair?

Or can it be that ages since, stormtossed,
And driven far inland from the roaring lea,
Some baffled ocean-spirit, worn and lost,
Here, through dry summer's dearth and
winter's frost,
Yearns for the sharp, sweet kisses of
the sea?

Whate'er the spell, I hearken and am
dumb,
Dream-touched, and musing in the
tranquil morn;
All woodland sounds — the pheasant's
gusty drum,
The mock-bird's fugue, the droning insect's hum —
Scarce heard fòr that strange, sorrowful voice forlorn!

Beneath the drowsèd sense, from deep to
deep
Of spiritual life its mournful minor
flows,
Streamlike, with pensive tide, whose
currents keep
Low murmuring 'twixt the bounds of
grief and sleep,
Yet locked for aye from sleep's divine
repose.

VISIT OF THE WRENS.

FLYING from out the gusty west,
To seek the place where last year's nest,
Ragged, and torn by many a rout
Of winter winds, still rocks about
The branches of the gnarled old tree
Which sweep my cottage library —
Here on the genial southern side,
In a late gleam of sunset's pride,
Came back my tiny, springtide friends,
The self-same pair of chattering wrens
That with arch eyes and restless bill
Used to frequent yon window sill,
Winged sprites, in April's showery
glow.

'Tis now twelve weary months ago
Since first I saw them; here again
They drop outside the glittering pane,
Each bearing a dried twig or leaf,
To build with labor hard, yet brief,
This season's nest, where, blue and round,
Their fairy eggs will soon be found.
But sky and breeze and blithesome sun,
Until that little home is done,
Shall — wondering, maybe — hear and see
Such chatter, bustle, industry,
As well may stir to emulous strife
Slow currents of a languid life,
Whether in bird or man they run!

But when, in sooth, the nest complete
Swings gently in its green retreat,
And soft the mother birdling's breast
Doth in the cozy circlet rest,
How, back from jovial journeying,
Merry of heart, though worn of wing,
Her brown mate, proudly perched above
The limb that holds his brooding love,
His head upturned, his aspect sly,
Regards her with a cunning eye,
As one who saith, "How well you bear
The dullness of these duties, dear;
To dwell so long on nest or tree
Would be, I know, slow death to me;
But, then, you women folk were made
For patient waiting, in — the shade!"

So tame one little guest becomes —
'Tis the male bird — my scattered crumbs
He takes from window sill and lawn
Each morning in the early dawn;
And yesterday he dared to stand
Serenely on my outstretched hand,
While his wee wife, with puzzled glance,
Looked from her breezy seat askance!

My pretty pensioners! ye have flown
Twice from your winter nook unknown,
To build your humble homestead here,
In the first flush of springtide cheer;
But ah! I wonder if again,
Flitting outside the window pane,
When next the shrewd March winds shall blow,
Or in mild April's showers glow,
New come from out the shimmering west,
You'll seek the place of this year's nest,
Ragged and torn by then, no doubt,
And swinging in worn shreds about
The branches of the ancient tree.

Nay, who may tell? Yet, verily,
Methinks when, spring and summer passed,
Adown the long, low autumn blast,
In some dim gloaming, chill and drear,
You, with your fledglings, disappear,
That ne'er by porch or tree or pane
Mine eyes shall greet your forms again!

What then? At least the good ye brought,
The delicate charms for eye and thought
Survives; though death should be your doom
Before another spring flower's bloom,
Or fairer clime should tempt your wings
To bide 'mid fragrant blossomings
On some far Southland's golden lea,
Still may fresh spring morns light for me
Your tiny nest, their breezes bear
Your chirping, household joyance near
And all your quirks and tricksome ways
Bring back through many smiling days
Or future Aprils; not the less
Your simple drama shall impress
Fancy and heart, thus acted o'er
Toward each small issue, as of yore,
With sun and wind and skies of blue
To witness, wondering, all you do,
Because your happy toil and mirth
May be of fine, ideal birth;
Because each quick, impulsive note
May thrill a visionary throat,
Each flash of glancing wing and eye
Be gleams of vivid fantasy;

Since whatsoe'er of form and tone
A past reality hath known,
Most charming unto soul and sense,
But wins that subtle effluence,
That spiritual air which softly clings
About all sweet and vanished things,
Causing a bygone joy to be
Vital as actuality,
Yet with each earthlier tint or trace
Lost in a pure, ethereal grace!

FOREST PICTURES.

MORNING.

O GRACIOUS breath of sunrise! divine air!
That brood'st serenely o'er the purpling hills;
O blissful valleys! nestling, cool and fair,
In the fond arms of yonder murmurous rills,
Breathing their grateful measures to the sun;
O dew-besprinkled paths, that circling run
Through sylvan shades and solemn silences,
Once more ye bring my fevered spirit peace!

The fitful breezes, fraught with forest balm,
Faint, in rare wafts of perfume, on my brow;
The woven lights and shadows, rife with calm,
Creep slantwise 'twixt the foliage, bough on bough
Uplifted heavenward, like a verdant cloud
Whose rain is music, soft as love, or loud
With jubilant hope — for there, entranced, apart,
The mock-bird sings, close, close to Nature's heart.

Shy forms about the greenery, out and in,
Flit 'neath the broadening glories of the morn;
The squirrel — that quaint sylvan harlequin —
Mounts the tall trunks; while swift as lightning, born
Of summer mists, from tangled vine and tree
Dart the dove's pinions, pulsing vividly
Down the dense glades, till glimmering far and gray
The dusky vision softly melts away!

In transient, pleased bewilderment I mark
The last dim shimmer of those lessening wings,
When from lone copse and shadowy covert, hark!
What mellow tongue through all the woodland rings!
The deer-hound's voice, sweet as the golden bell's,
Prolonged by flying echoes round the dells,
And up the loftiest summits wildly borne,
Blent with the blast of some keen huntsman's horn.

And now the checkered vale is left behind;
I climb the slope, and reach the hilltop bright;
Here, in bold freedom, swells a sovereign wind,
Whose gusty prowess sweeps the pineclad height;
While the pines — dreamy Titans roused from sleep —
Answer with mighty voices, deep on deep
Of wakened foliage surging like a sea;
And o'er them smiles Heaven's calm infinity!

"The woven lights and shadows, rife with calm,
Creep slantwise 'twixt the foliage, bough on bough."

GOLDEN DELL.

BEYOND our moss-grown pathway lies
A dell so fair, to genial eyes
It dawns an ever-fresh surprise!

To touch its charms with gentler grace,
The softened heavens a loving face
Bend o'er that sweet, secluded place.

There first, despite the March wind's cold,
Above the pale-hued emerald mould
The earliest spring-tide buds unfold;

There first the ardent mock-bird, long
Winter's dumb thrall, from winter's wrong
Breaks into gleeful floods of song;

Till, from coy thrush to garrulous wren,
The humbler bards of copse and glen
Outpour their vernal notes again;

While such harmonious rapture rings,
With stir and flash of eager wings
Glimpsed fleetly, where the jasmine clings

To bosk and briar, we blithely say,
"Farewell! bleak nights and mornings gray,
Earth opes her festal court to-day!"

There, first, from out some balmy nest,
By half-grown woodbine flowers caressed,
Steal zephyrs of the mild southwest;

O'er purpling rows of wild-wood peas,*
So blandly borne, the droning bees
Still suck their honeyed cores at ease;

Or, trembling through yon verdurous mass,
Dew-starred, and dimpling as they pass
The wavelets of the billowy grass!

But, fairest of fair things that dwell
'Mid sylvan nurslings of the dell,
Is that clear stream whose murmurs swell

To music's airiest issues wrought,
As if a Naiad's tongue were fraught
With secrets of its whispered thought.

Yes, fairest of fair things, it flows
'Twixt banks of violet and of rose,
Touched always by a quaint repose.

How golden bright its currents glide!
While goldenly from side to side
Bird shadows flit athwart the tide.

So Golden Dell we name the place,
And aye may Heaven's serenest face
Dream o'er it with a smile of grace;

For next the moss-grown path it lies,
So pure, so fresh to genial eyes
It glows with hints of Paradise!

* In the Southern woods, often among sterile tracts of pine barren, a species of *wild pea* is found, or a plant which in all externals resembles the pea plant.

ASPECTS OF THE PINES.

TALL, sombre, grim, against the morning sky
They rise, scarce touched by melancholy airs,
Which stir the fadeless foliage dreamfully,
As if from realms of mystical despairs.

Tall, sombre, grim, they stand with dusky gleams
Brightening to gold within the woodland's core,
Beneath the gracious noontide's tranquil beams—
But the weird winds of morning sigh no more.

A stillness, strange, divine, ineffable,
Broods round and o'er them in the wind's surcease,
And on each tinted copse and shimmering dell
Rests the mute rapture of deep hearted peace.

Last, sunset comes — the solemn joy and might
Borne from the West when cloudless day declines —
Low, flutelike breezes sweep the waves of light,
And lifting dark green tresses of the pines,

Till every lock is luminous — gently float,
Fraught with hale odors up the heavens afar
To faint when twilight on her virginal throat
Wears for a gem the tremulous vesper star.

MIDSUMMER IN THE SOUTH.

I LOVE Queen August's stately sway,
And all her fragrant south winds say,
With vague, mysterious meanings fraught,
Of unimaginable thought;
Those winds, 'mid change of gloom and gleam,
Seem wandering thro' a golden dream —
The rare midsummer dream that lies
In humid depths of nature's eyes,
Weighing her languid forehead down
Beneath a fair but fiery crown:
Its witchery broods o'er earth and skies,
Fills with divine amenities
The bland, blue spaces of the air,
And smiles with looks of drowsy cheer
'Mid hollows of the brown-hued hills;
And oft, in tongues of tinkling rills,
A softer, homelier utterance finds
Than that which haunts the lingering winds!

I love midsummer's azure deep,
Whereon the huge white clouds, asleep,
Scarce move through lengths of trancéd hours;
Some, raised in forms of giant towers —
Dumb Babels, with ethereal stairs
Scaling the vast height — unawares
What mocking spirit, æther-born,
Hath built those transient spires in scorn,
And reared towards the topmost sky
Their unsubstantial fantasy!
Some stretched in tenuous arcs of light
Athwart the airy infinite,
Far glittering up yon fervid dome,
And lapped by cloudland's misty foam,
Whose wreaths of fine sun-smitten spray
Melt in a burning haze away:
Some throned in heaven's serenest smiles,
Pure-hued, and calm as fairy isles,
Girt by the tides of soundless seas —
The heavens' benign Hesperides.

I love midsummer uplands, free
To the bold raids of breeze and bee,
Where, nested warm in yellowing grass,
I hear the swift-winged partridge pass,
With whirr and boom of gusty flight,
Across the broad heath's treeless height:
Or, just where, elbow-poised, I lift
Above the wild flower's careless drift
My half-closed eyes, I see and hear
The blithe field-sparrow twittering clear
Quick ditties to his tiny love;
While, from afar, the timid dove,
With faint, voluptuous murmur, wakes
The silence of the pastoral brakes.

I love midsummer sunsets, rolled
Down the rich west in waves of gold,
With blazing crests of billowy fire.
But when those crimson floods retire,
In noiseless ebb, slow-surging, grand,
By pensive twilight's flickering strand,
In gentler mood I love to mark
The slow gradations of the dark;
Till, lo! from Orient's mists withdrawn,
Hail! to the moon's resplendent dawn;
On dusky vale and haunted plain
Her effluence falls like balmy rain;
Gaunt gulfs of shadow own her might;
She bathes the rescued world in light,
So that, albeit my summer's day,
Erewhile did breathe its life away,

Methinks, whate'er its hours had won
Of beauty, born from shade and sun,
Hath not perchance so wholly died,
But o'er the moonlight's silvery tide
Comes back, sublimed and purified!

CLOUD-PICTURES.

Here in these mellow grasses, the whole morn,
I love to rest; yonder, the ripening corn
Rustles its greenery; and his blithesome horn

Windeth the frolic breeze o'er field and dell,
Now pealing a bold stave with lusty swell,
Now falling to low breaths ineffable

Of whispered joyance. At calm length I lie,
Fronting the broad blue spaces of the sky,
Covered with cloud-groups, softly journeying by:

An hundred shapes, fantastic, beauteous, strange,
Are theirs, as o'er yon airy waves they range
At the wind's will, from marvellous change to change;

Castles, with guarded roof, and turret tall,
Great sloping archway, and majestic wall,
Sapped by the breezes to their noiseless fall!

Pagodas vague! above whose towers outstream
Banners that wave with motions of a dream —
Rising, or drooping in the noontide gleam;

Gray lines of Orient pilgrims: a gaunt band
On famished camels, o'er the desert sand
Plodding towards their prophet's Holy Land;

'Mid-ocean, — and a shoal of whales at play,
Lifting their monstrous frontlets to the day,
Thro' rainbow arches of sun-smitten spray;

Followed by splintered icebergs, vast and lone,
Set in swift currents of some arctic zone,
Like fragments of a Titan's world o'erthrown;

Next, measureless breadths of barren, treeless moor,
Whose vaporous verge fades down a glimmering shore,
Round which the foam-capped billows toss and roar!

Calms of bright water — like a fairy's wiles,
Wooing with ripply cadence and soft smiles,
The golden shore-slopes of Hesperian Isles;

Their inland plains rife with a rare increase
Of plumèd grain! and many a snowy fleece
Shining athwart the dew-lit hills of peace;

Wrecks of gigantic cities — to the tune
Of some wise air-God built! — o'er which the noon
Seems shuddering; caverns, such as the wan Moon

Shows in her desolate bosom; then, a crowd
Of awed and reverent faces, palely bowed
O'er a dead queen, laid in her ashy shroud —

A queen of eld — her pallid brow impearled
By gems barbaric! her strange beauty furled
In mystic cerements of the antique world.

Weird pictures, fancy-gendered! — one by one,
'Twixt blended beams and shadows, gold and dun,
These transient visions vanish in the sun.

SONNET.

SUNSET, the god-like artist, paints on air
Pictures of loveliness and terror blent!
Lo! yonder clouds, like mountains tempest-rent,
Through whose abysmal depths the lightning's glare
Darts from wild gulfs and caverns of despair:
O'er these a calm, majestic firmament,
Flushed with rich hues, with rainbow isles besprent,
Like homes of peace in oceans heavenly fair:

But *still*, beyond, one lone mysterious cloud,
Steeped in the solemn sunset's fiery mist,
Strange semblance takes of Him whose visage bowed,
Divinely sweet, o'er all things, dark or bright,
Yet draws the darkness ever toward His light
The tender eyes and awful brow of Christ!

IN THE PINE BARRENS.

SUNSET.

HARK! to the mournful wind; its burden drear
Borne over leagues of desert wild and dun,
Sinks to a weary cadence of despair,
Beyond the closing gateways of the sun.

Yon clouds are big with flame, and not with rain,
Massed on the marvellous heaven in splendid pyres,
Whereon ethereal genii, half in pain
And half in triumph, light their fervid fires:

Kindled in funeral majesty to rise
Above the perished day, whose latest breath
Exhaled, a roseate effluence to the skies,
Still lingers o'er the pageantry of death.

. . . . .

One stalwart hill his stern defiant crest
Boldly against the horizon line uprears,
His blasted pines, smit by the fiery West,
Uptowering rank on rank, like Titan spears;

Fantastic, bodeful, o'er the rock-strewn ground
Casting grim shades beyond the hill slope riven,
Which mock the loftier shafts, keen, lustre-crowned
And raised as if to storm the courts of Heaven!

As sinks the wind, so wane those wondrous lights;
Slowly they wane from hill and sky and cloud,
While round the woodland waste and glimmering heights
The mist of gloaming trails its silvery shroud!

Through which, uncertain, vague as shifting ghosts,
The forms of all things touched by mystery seem,
I walk, methinks, on pale Plutonian coasts,
And grope 'mid spectral shadows of a dream.

SONNET.

In the deep hollow of this sheltered dell
I hear the rude winds chant their giant staves
Far, far beyond me, where in darkening waves
The airy seas of cloudland sink or swell.

No faint breeze stirs the wild-flower's soundless bell,
Here in the quiet vale, whose rivulet laves
Banks silent almost as those desert graves,
Whereof the worn Zaharan wanderers tell.

Oh! thus from out still depths of tranquil doom,
My soul beyond her views life's turmoil vast,
Hearkening the windy roar and rage of men,

Vain to *her* eyes as shades from cloudland cast,
And to *her* ears like far-off winds that boom,
Heard, but scarce heard, in this Arcadian glen!

THE WOODLAND PHASES.

Yon woodland, like a human mind,
Hath many a phase of dark and bright;
Now dim with shadows, wandering blind,
Now radiant with fair shapes of light.

They softly come, they softly go,
Capricious as the vagrant wind,
Nature's vague thoughts in gloom or glow,
That leave no airiest trace behind.

No trace, no trace! yet wherefore thus
Do shade and beam our spirit's stir?
Ah! Nature may be cold to us,
But we are strangely moved by her.

The wild bird's strain, the breezy spray,
Each hour with sure earth-changes rife
Hint more than all the sages say,
Or poets sing of death and life.

For truths half drawn from Nature's breast,
Through subtlest types of form and tone,
Outweigh what man, at most, hath guessed
While heeding his own heart alone.

And midway, betwixt heaven and us,
Stands Nature in her fadeless grace,
Still pointing to our Father's house,
His glory on her mystic face.

AFTER THE TORNADO.

Last eve the earth was calm, the heavens were clear;
A peaceful glory crowned the waning west,
And yonder distant mountain's hoary crest
The semblance of a silvery robe did wear,
Shot through with moon-wrought tissues; far and near
Wood, rivulet, field — all Nature's face — expressed
The haunting presence of enchanted rest.
One twilight star shone like a blissful tear,
Unshed. But now, what ravage in a night!

Yon mountain height fades in its cloud-
girt pall;
The prostrate wood lies smirched with
rain and mire;
Through the shorn fields the brook
whirls, wild and white;
While o'er the turbulent waste and
woodland fall,
Glares the red sunrise, blurred with
mists of fire!

IN THE BOWER.

The gusty and passionate March hath
died;
And now in the golden April-tide
There sits in the shade of her jasmine
bower
A maid more fair than an April flower.

The delicate curve of her perfect mouth,
Whose tints grow warm in the fervid
South,
She stoops to press, as she murmurs
low,
On a note upraised in her hand of snow.

What words are writ on the tiny scroll?
What thoughts lie deep in the maiden's
soul?
Oh, is it with bliss of her love she sighs?
Is the light but love's in those shy
brown eyes?

So thinks the mock-bird trilling his lay
On the tremulous top of the lilac spray;
He views the maid, on his perch apart,
And his song is meant for her secret
heart.

So thinks the breeze, for its frolic free
With the rose's stem, and the wing o'
the bee
It leaves, to sigh in the maiden's ear,
"He is coming, sweet! he is almost
here!"

So thinks the sun, for his ardent beams
Grow mellow and soft as a virgin's
dreams,
Through the vine-leaf shadows steal coy-
ly down,
And she wears his light like a bridal
crown.

Let the songster trill, and the breezes
sigh,
And the sun weave crowns of his light i'
the sky;
She heeds them not, for a step is heard,
And her soul leaps up like a startled
bird —

Her soul leaps up, but it is not fear:
He is coming, sweet! he is here! is here!
And she flies to his bosom, (ah! panting
dove),
And is folded home on the heart of love!

WHENCE?

Eerily the wind doth blow
Through the woodland hollow;
Eërily forlorn and low,
Tremulous echoes follow!

Whence the low wind's tortured plaint?
Burden hopeless, dreary,
As the anguished tones that faint
Down the *Miserere.*

Whence? From far-off seas its moan!
Darksome waves and lonely,
Where the tempest, overblown,
Leaves a death-calm only.

Thence it caught the awful cry
Of some last pale swimmer,
O'er whose drowning brain and eye
Life grows dim and dimmer —

Ere the billows claim their prey,
Settling stern and lonely.
Where the storm-clouds, rolled away,
Leave death-silence only!

So with pain the wind-heart sighs;
Through its sad commotion
Weary sea-tides sob, and rise
Wailing hints of Ocean!

Hist! oh hist! as spreads the mist,
  Wood and hill-slope doming,
By no grace of starlight kissed,
  'Mid the shadowy gloaming,

Drearier grows the wind, more drear
  Echoes shuddering follow,
Till a place of doom and fear
  Seems that haunted hollow!

"Uplift and bear me where the wild flowers grow,
By many a golden dell-side, sweet and low."

SONNET.

ENOUGH, this glimpse of splendor wed to shame;
Enough this gilded misery, this bright woe.
Pause, genial wind! that even here dost blow
Thy cheerful clarion; and from dust and flame
The noonday pest, the night-enshrouded blame,
Uplift and bear me where the wild flowers grow
By many a golden dell-side sweet and low,
Shrined in the sylvan Eden whence I came.
O woodland water! O fair-whispering pine!
Loved of the dryad none but I have viewed!
O dew-lit glen, and lone glade, breathing balm,
Receive and bless me, till this tumult rude
Merged in your verdant solitudes divine,
My soul once more hath found her ancient calm!

VIOLETS.

"Rare wine of flowers." — FLETCHER.

A GUSTY wind o'ersweeps the garden close,
And, where the jonquil, with the white-rod glows,
Riots like some rude hoyden uncontrolled.
But here, where sunshine and coy shadows meet,
Out gleam the tender eyes of violets sweet,
Touched by the vapory noontide's fleeting gold.

What subtlest perfume floats serenely up!
Ethereal wine that brims each delicate cup,
Rifled by viewless Ariels of the air,
And lo! methinks from out these fairy flowers
Rise the strange shades of half forgotten hours,
Pale, tearful, mute, and yet, O heaven, how fair!

Yea, fair and marvellous, gliding gently nigh.
Some with raised brows and eyes of constancy,
Fixed with fond meanings on a goal above.
And some faint shades of weary, drooping grace,
Each with a nameless pathos on its face,
Breathing of heart-break and sad death of love.

Slowly they vanish! while these odors steep
Spirit and sense, as if in waves of sleep,
Mysterious and Lethean; languid streams
Flowing through realms of twilight thought apart,
Whereon the half-closed petals of the heart
Pulse flower-like o'er a whispering tide of dreams: —
Nor wakes the soul to outward sound or sight,
Till, noonday beams declining, warm and light,
A wood-breeze fans the dreamer's forehead calm;
Who feels as one long wrapped from pain and drouth,
By magic dreams dreamed in the fervid south,
Beneath the golden shadows of the palm.

BY THE GRAVE OF HENRY TIMROD.

WHEN last we parted — thy frail hand in mine —
Above us smiled September's passionless sky,
And touched by fragrant airs, the hillside pine
Thrilled in the mellow sunshine tenderly;
So rich the robe on nature's slow decay,
We scarce could deem the winter tide was near,
Or lurking death, masked in imperial grace;
Alas! that autumn day
Drew not more close to winter's empire drear
Than thou, my heart! to meet grief face to face!

I clasped thy tremulous hand, nor marked how weak
Its answering grasp; and if thine eyes did swim
In unshed tears, and on thy fading cheek
Rested a nameless shadow, gaunt and dim, —
My soul was blind; fear had not touched her sight
To awful vision; so, I bade thee go,
Careless, and tranquil as that treacherous morn;
Nor dreamed how soon the blight

Of long-implanted seeds of care would throw
Their nightshade flowers above the springing corn.

Since then, full many a year hath risen and set,
With spring-tide showers, and autumn pomps unfurled
O'er gorgeous woods, and mountain walls of jet —
While love and loss, alternate, ruled the world;
Till now once more we meet — my friend and I —
Once more, once more — and thus, alas! we meet —
Above, a rayless heaven; beneath, a grave;
Oh, Christ! and dost thou lie
Neglected here, in thy worn burial-sheet?
Friend! were there none to shield thee, none to save?

Ask of the winter winds — scarce colder they
Than that strange land — thy birth-place and thy tomb:
Ask of the sombre cloud-wracks trooping gray,
And grim as hooded ghosts at stroke of doom;
At least, the winds, though chill, with gentler sweep
Seem circling round and o'er thy place of rest,
While the sad clouds, as clothed in tenderer guise,
Do lowly bend, and weep
O'er the dead poet, in whose living breast
Dumb nature found a voice, how sweet and wise!

Once more we meet, once more — my friend and I —
But ah! his hand is dust, his eyes are dark;
Thy merciless weight, thou dread mortality,
From out his heart hath crushed the latest spark
Of that warm life, benignly bright and strong;
Yet no; we have *not* met — my friend and I —
Ashes to ashes in this earthly prison!
Are these, O child of song,
Thy glorious self, heir of the stars and sky?
Thou art not here, not *here*, for thou hast risen!

Death gave thee wings, and lo! thou hast soared above
All human utterance and all finite thought;
Pain may not hound thee through that realm of love,
Nor grief, wherewith thy mortal days were fraught,
Load thee again — nor vulture want, that fed
Even on thy heart's blood, wound thee; idle, then,
Our bitter sorrowing; what though bleak and wild
Rests thine uncrownèd head?
Known art thou now to angels and to men —
Heaven's saint and earth's brave singer undefiled.

Even as I spake in broken under-breath
The winds drooped lifeless; faintly struggling through
The heaven-bound pall, which seemed a pall of death,
One cordial sunbeam cleft the opening blue;
Swiftly it glanced, and settling, softly shone
O'er the grave's head; in that same instant came
From the near copse a bird-song half divine;
"Heart," said I, "hush thy moan,

List the bird's singing, mark the heaven-born flame,
God-given are these — an omen and a sign!"

In the bird's song an omen *his* must live!
In the warm glittering of that golden beam,
A sign his soul's majestic hopes survive,
Raised to fruition o'er life's weary dream.
So now I leave him, low, yet, restful here;
So now I leave him, high-exalted, far
Beyond all memory of earth's guilt or guile:
Hark! tis his voice of cheer,
Dropping, methinks, from some mysterious star;
His face I see, and on his face — a smile!

SONNET.

As one who strays from out some shadowy glade,
Fronting a lurid noontide, stern, yet bright,
O'er mart and tower, and castellated height,
Shrinks slowly backward, dazed and half afraid —
So I, whose household gods their stand have made
Far from the populous city's life and light,
Its roar of traffic and its stormy might,
Shrink as I pass beyond my woodland shade.
The wordy conflict, the tempestuous din
Of these vast capitals, on ear and brain
Beat with the loud, reiterated swell
Of one fierce strain of passion and of sin,
Strange as in nightmare dreams the mad refrain
Of some wild chorus of the vaults of Hell.

ARIEL.

"My dainty Ariel." —*Tempest.*

A voice like the murmur of doves,
Soft lightning from eyes of blue;
On her cheek a flush like love's
First delicate, rosebud hue;

Bright torrents of hazel hair,
Which, glittering, flow and float
O'er the swell of her bosom fair,
And the snows of her matchless throat;

Lithe limbs of a life so fine,
That their rhythmical motion seems
But a part of the grace divine
Of the music of haunted dreams;

Low gurgling laughter, as sweet
As the swallow's song i' the South,
And a ripple of dimples that, dancing, meet
By the curves of a perfect mouth;

O creature of light and air!
O fairy sylph o' th' sun!
Hearts whelmed in the tidal gold of her hair
Rejoice to be *so* undone!

SONNET.

The glorious star of morning would we blame
Because it burns not on the front of night?
Or the calm evening planet, that her light
Foretells not sunrise, with its herald-flame?
All things that are should subtly own the same
Eternal law! the stars shine on aright,
Each in his sphere; the souls of Love and Might
Their separate bounds of grace or grandeur claim;

Not on the low or lofty, great or small,
Should justice fix for judgment; the true soul,
Which sways its own world in serene control,
Highest or humblest — such the Master's call
Shall summon upward, with its deep "well done,"
And the just Father crown his faithful son!

THE CLOUD-STAR.

A FABLE.

FAR up within the tranquil sky,
Far up it shone;
Floating, how gently, silently,
Floating alone!

A sunbeam touched its loftier side
With deepening light:
Then to its inmost soul did glide,
Divinely bright.

The cloud transfigured to a star,
Thro' all its frame
Throbbed in the fervent heavens afar,
One pulse of flame:

One pulse of flame, which inward turned,
And slowly fed
On its own heart, that burned, and burned,
'Till almost dead,

The cloud still imaged as a star,
Waned up the sky;
Waned slowly, pallid, ghost-like, far,
Wholly to die;

But die so grandly in the sun —
The noonfire's breath —
Methinks the glorious death it won,
Life! life! not death!

Meanwhile a million insect things
Crawl on below,
And gaudy worms on fluttering wings
Flit to and fro;

Blind to that cloud, which grown a star,
Divinely bright,
Waned in the deepening heavens afar,
Till — lost in light!

SWEETHEART, GOOD-BYE!

A SONG.

SWEETHEART, good-bye! Our varied day
Is closing into twilight gray,
And up from bare, bleak wastes of sea
The north-wind rises mournfully;
A solemn prescience, strangely drear,
Doth haunt the shuddering twilight air;
It fills the earth, it chills the sky —
Sweetheart, good-bye!

Sweetheart, good-bye! Our joys are passed,
And night with silence comes at last;
All things must end, yea, — even love —
Nor know we, if reborn above,
The heart-blooms of our earthly prime
Shall flower beyond these bounds of time.
"Ah! death alone is sure!" we cry —
Sweetheart, good-bye!

Sweetheart, good-bye! Through mists and tears
Pass the pale phantoms of our years,
Once bright with spring, or subtly strong
When summer's noontide thrilled with song;
Now wan, wild-eyed, forlornly bowed,
Each rayless as an autumn cloud
Fading on dull September's sky —
Sweetheart, good-bye!

Sweetheart, good-bye! The vapors rolled
Athwart yon distant, darkening wold
Are types of what our world doth know
Of tenderest loves of long ago;
And thus, when all is done and said,
Our life lived out, *our* passion dead,
What can their wavering record be
But tinted mists of memory?
Oh! clasp and kiss me ere we die —
Sweetheart, good-bye!

SONNET.

COMPOSED ON A MARCH MORNING IN THE WOODS.

THE winds are loud and trumpet-clear to-day;
They seem to sound an onset, half in ire,
Half in the wildness of a vague desire
To force spring's fairy vanguard to delay;
For here, methinks, worn winter stands at bay,
Yet stands how vainly! spring-time's subtlest fire
Melts his cold heart to nothingness, while nigher
Draw April hosts, and rearward powers of May —
All maiden verdures, concords of sweet air,
Stealing as dawn steals gently on the world;
Breezes, balm-laden, blown from distant seas,
With armies of blush-roses, dew-impearled,
Till Earth reclaimed from winter's grim despair
Blooms as once bloomed the fair Hesperides.

FRIDA AND HER POET.

A BRAVE young poet born in days of Eld,
Dwelt 'mid the frozen Northlands; he beheld,
And wondering, sung the marvels of the ice,
The swirl of snow-flakes, and the quaint device
Wrought on the fir-trees by the glittering sleet;
And loved on stormy heights, cloud-girt, to greet
The gray ger-falcon towering o'er the sea;
To watch the waves, and mark the cloud-drifts flee,
Big with the wrath of tempests; yet his heart,
Soft as the inner rose-leaves of the spring,
Rich with young life, and love's sweet blossoming,
Too soon, alas! from life and love did part:
Veiled was the fate that smote him; unaware
What sudden, blasting doom had drawn so near,
A strange blight breathed upon him, and he died!

On earth to die, in heaven be glorified,
Such was the Minstrel's portion; still he went
Through all the heavenly courts in discontent
And sombre grief, the pathos of his woe
Rising at times to such wild overflow
As forced its wailful utterance into song.
That passionate rush of music, the heart's wrong
Set to the sweetness of harmonious chords,
The All-Father, Odin, o'er the clash of swords,
And din of heroes feasting at the boards
Of loud Valhalla, heard: thereon he sought
This lonely soul, in highest heaven o'erfraught
With mortal memories. "Wherefore lift'st thou here,"
The All-Father asked, "these measures of despair?"
"Because my mortal Love," the Poet said,
"With time grows gray and wrinkled; on her head,
So golden bright in youth's benignant prime,
Chill frosts of age have left their hoary rime;

Her eyes are dimmed, her soft cheeks' rosy red
Hath with the flowers of many a spring-time fled;
And so when Heaven shall claim her — ah! the pain! —
I shall not know mine earthly love again!"

To whom the God, "But doth she love thee still?"
"Her love, like mine, nor years, nor change can kill,"
The Minstrel answered: "Faith, a ceaseless shower,
Keeps fair and bright our love's immaculate flower."
"I loose thy heavenly bonds, — I bid thee go!"
The All-Father cried, "and seek thy Love below!"
To earth he came: drear waste and flowery lea
Beheld his search 'mid fettered folk and free;
Yet all his toils but brought the direful stress
Of lone heart-yearning, grief and weariness,
Till hope died out and all his soul was dark.

At last, when aimless as an autumn leaf
Borne on November's idle winds afar,
He roamed a sea-beach wild, by moon or star
Unlighted in its dreariest hour of grief
And desolate longing, on his eyes a spark
Of tiny radiance through the clouded night
Flashed from a cottage window on a height,
Next the dim billows of the moaning main.

There broke a sudden lightning on his brain
Of prescient expectation, — then, before
Its glow could fade, he trod the cottage floor,
And saw in tattered raiment, wan and dead,
An ancient withered woman on a bed,
Of whom a crone, as shrunk almost as she,
Said with drawn lips and blinking wearily
"Lo! here thine old Love! Hast thou come so far
To find how cares may blight us, death may mar?"
As ebbs a flood-tide, so his eager breath
Sank slowly. "Oh, the awful front of death!"
He moaned. "Yet wherefore shudder? Thou, my love,
Art precious still; nor shalt thou move above,
An alien soul, albeit no longer fleet,
Nor fair, thou roam'st through Heaven with tottering feet,
Bent, aged form, and face bedimmed by tears;
I only ask to *know* thee, while the years
Eternal roll!"

He bids a last farewell
To this world's life, again prepared to dwell
On heights celestial, in whose golden airs
The heart, at least, shall shed earth's wintry cares,
And blooming, breathe the vernal heats of Heaven.

Twice ransomed soul! thou spirit that hast striven
With countless ills, and conquered all thy foes,
Rise with the might of morning, the repose
Of moonlit night, and entering Heaven once more —
Behold! who first doth meet thee by the door,

With smiling brow, and gently parted lips,
And eyes wherein no vestige of eclipse
From pain, or death, or any evil thing,
Lies darkly, but whose passionate triumphing,
In peace attained, and true love crowned at last,
Hath such rare joy and sweetness round her cast,
She seems an angel on the heights of bliss.
And yet a mortal maid 'twere heaven to kiss!

To whom the singer, in a voice that seems
Vague, and half-muffled in the mist of dreams:—
"Art thou the little Frida that I knew
So long—ah! long ago? Thine eyes are blue,
Deep blue like hers, and brimmed with tender dew,
Through which love's starlight smiles—art thou, in sooth,
The sweet, true-hearted Frida of my youth?"

She drew more closely to the poet's side,
And nestling her small hand in his, replied,
As half in tremulous wonder, half delight:—
"I *am* thy little Frida, in thy sight
Fair once, and well beloved—Ah me! ah me!
Hast thou forgotten?" "Nay; but whose" (quoth he,)
"Yon withered corse, on which I gazed below,
With pale shrunk limbs, and furrowed face of woe?
Thy corse, *thy* face, they told me!" "Yea, but know,
O Love! that earth, and things of earth, are past:
That here, where, soul to soul, we meet at last,
The merciful gods have made this wise decree:—
Love, in heaven's tongue, means immortality
Of youth and joy; then, wheresoe'er we go,
Loving and loved through these high courts divine,
Mine eyes eternal youth shall drink from thine;
And thou forevermore shalt find in me
The tender maid who walked the world with thee,
Thy little Frida, loved so long ago!"

PREËXISTENCE.

WHILE sauntering through the crowded street,
Some half-remembered face I meet,

Albeit upon no mortal shore
That face, methinks, hath smiled before.

Lost in a gay and festal throng,
I tremble at some tender song—

Set to an air whose golden bars
I must have heard in other stars.

In sacred aisles I pause to share
The blessings of a priestly prayer—

When the whole scene which greets mine eyes
In some strange mode I recognize

As one whose every mystic part
I feel prefigured in my heart.

At sunset, as I calmly stand,
A stranger on an alien strand—

Familiar as my childhood's home
Seems the long stretch of wave and foam.

One sails toward me o'er the bay,
And what he comes to do and say

"While sauntering through the crowded street.
Some half-remembered face I meet."

I can foretell. A prescient lore
Springs from some life outlived of yore.

O swift, instinctive, startling gleams
Of deep soul-knowledge! not as *dreams*

For aye ye vaguely dawn and die,
But oft with lightning certainty

Pierce through the dark, oblivious brain,
To make old thoughts and memories plain —

Thoughts which perchance must travel back
Across the wild, bewildering track

Of countless æons; memories far,
High-reaching as yon pallid star,

Unknown, scarce seen, whose flickering grace
Faints on the outmost rings of space!

SONNET.

TO ———

Fair Muse, beloved of all, thou art no high
Imperious goddess of the mount or main,
But a sweet maiden of the pastoral plain,
To whom the hum of bees, the west wind's sigh,
The lapse of waters murmuring tranquilly,
Come, like soft music of a May-tide dream.
Yet, times there are when some imperial theme,
Born of a stormy sunset's marvellous sky,
And heralded by thunder and fierce flame,
Sweeps o'er thy vision with a mien sublime,
And mighty voices, calling on thy name:
Then dost thou rise, exultant, thrilled, inspired,
Thy song a clarion lay that stirs our time,
Hot from the soul some secret god hath fired!

A THOUSAND YEARS FROM NOW.

I sat within my tranquil room;
The twilight shadows sank and rose
With slowly flickering motions, waved
Grotesquely through the dusk repose;
There came a sudden thought to me,
Which thrilled the spirit, flushed the brow —
A dream of what our world would be
A thousand years from now!

If science on her heavenward search,
Rolling the stellar charts apart,
Or delving hour by hour to win
The secrets of earth's inmost heart —
If that her future apes her past,
To what new marvels men must bow,
Marvels of land, and air, and sea,
A thousand years from now!

If empires hold their wonted course,
And blind republics will not stay
To count the cost of laws which lead
Unerring to the State's decay —
What changes vast of realm and rule,
The low upraised, the proud laid low,
Shall greet the unborn ages still,
A thousand years from now!

Our creeds may change with mellowed times
Of nobler hope, and love increased,
And some new Advent flood the world
In glory from the haunted East —
While souls on loftier heights of faith
May mark the mystic pathway grow
Clearer between their stand and heaven's,
A thousand years from now!

These things *may be!* but what, perforce,
Must with the ruthless epochs pass?
The millions' breath, the centuries' pomp,
Sure as the wane of flowers or grass;
The earth so rich in tombs to-day,
There scarce seems space for death to sow,
Who, who shall count her churchyard wealth
A thousand years from now?

And we — poor waifs! whose life-term seems,
When matched with *after* and *before*,
Brief as a summer wind's, or wave's,
Breaking its frail heart on the shore,
We — human toys — that Fate sets up
To smite, or — spare I marvel how
These souls shall fare, in what strange sphere,
A thousand years from now?

Too vague, too faint for mortal ken
That far, phantasmal future lies;
But sweet! one sacred truth I read,
Just kindling in your tear-dimmed eyes,
That states may rise, and states may set,
With age earth's tottering pillars bow,
But hearts like ours can ne'er forget,
And though we know not *where*, nor *how*,
Our conscious love shall blossom yet,
A thousand years from now!

SONNET.

I STOOD in twilight by the winter's sea;
The spectral tides with hollow, hungry roar,
Broke massed and mighty on the shrinking shore.
The sea-birds wailed; the foam flew wild and free.
Ruthless as fate, upborne victoriously,
A fierce wind clove the billows urged afar
With vengeful rhythm toward the western star,
Just risen beyond a gaunt gray cypress tree.
Then twilight waned in cloud-descending night,
The sole star died, as if some phantom hand
Wiped out its radiance; in the void profound
The wind and waters (blended in one sound,
Awful, mysterious), with invisible might
Thrilled the blank heavens, and smote the affrighted strand!

THUNDER AT MIDNIGHT.

AT midnight wakening, through my startled brain
The sudden thunder crashed a chord of pain;

I rose, and, awe-struck, hearkened. Overhead
In one long, loud, reverberant peal of dread,

Ceaseless it rolled, till as a sea of fire,
The climax gained, must wave by wave retire;

So, half-reluctant, up the heights of space
The refluent thunder softened into grace,

Its deep, harsh menace changed to murmurs low
As the lost south wind's, muffled in the snow;

Waning through whisperous echoes less and less
Till the last echo sleeps in gentleness.

Thus 'minded am I of that law of old
Which down the slopes of awful Sinai rolled,

Smote men with judgment terrors; yet, at last,
The lightning flame and mystic tumult passed,

Lapsed down the ages, echoing less and less
Jehovah's wrath, till, changed to tenderness,

The vengeful law, which once man's faith sufficed,
Melts into mercy on the heart of Christ!

ON THE DEATH OF CANON KINGSLEY.

MORTALS there are who seem, all over, flame,
Vitalized radiance, keen, intense, and high,
Whose souls, like planets in a dominant sky,
Burn with full forces of eternity:

Such was his soul, and such the light which came
From that pure heaven he lived in; holiest worth
Of will and work was his, to brighten earth,
Heal its foul wounds, and beautify its dearth.

He dwelt in clear white purity apart,
Yet walked the world; through many a sufferer's door
He shone like morning; comfort streamed before
His footsteps; on the feeble and the poor

He lavished the rich spikenard of his heart.
Christ's soldier! To his trumpet-call he sprung,
Eager, elate; valiant of pen and tongue,
Grand were the words he spake, the songs he sung.

Still, hero-priest! born out of thy due time —
Thou should'st have lived when on thine England's sod
Giants of faith and seers of freedom trod,
Daring all things to break the oppressor's rod.

Great in thine own age, thou hadst been sublime
In theirs — that age of fervent, fruitful breath,
When, scorning treachery, and defying death,
Her true knights girt their loved Elizabeth,

Seeing on her the centuries' hopes were set;
Then hadst thou ranged with Raleigh land and sea,
Bible and sword in hand, gone forth with Leigh,
The tyrant smote, the heathen folk made free!

Yea! but to God and grace thou hast paid thy debt,
In measure scarce less glorious and complete
Than theirs who bearded on his chosen seat
The bloody Antichrist; or, fleet to fleet,

Thundered through storms of battle-wrack and fire
At Britain's Salamis;* the heroic strain
Ran purpling all thy nature like a vein
Oped from God's heart to thine; the loftiest plane

Of thought and action, purpose and desire
Thou trod'st on triumphing; thy Viking's face
Showed granite-willed, yet softened into grace
By effluence of good deeds, the angelic race

---

* Alluding to the defeat of the "Invincible Armada."

Of prayers to prompt, and aid them! Fare thee well,
Clear spirit and strong! thy life-work nobly done,
Shines beautiful as some unsetting sun
O'er arctic summers; chords of victory run
Even through the mournful boom of thy deep funeral knell!

WHEN ALL HAS BEEN SAID AND DONE.

TO RICHARD HENRY STODDARD.

(In reply to his poem called "Wishing and Having.")

"Perhaps it will all come right at last;
It may be, when all is done,
We shall be together in some good world,
Where to *wish* and to *have* are one."
—STODDARD.

O FRIEND! be sure that a spirit came,
In the gloom of your saddened hour,
To plant that hope in your hopeless heart,
Like the seed of an Eden flower.
The seed may rest in your brooding breast,
Half stifled in cold and night,
Or be only felt as a yearning dim
Toward comforting peace and light;
But 'twill burst some day into perfect bloom,
And fruition be brightly won;
For the earth-life fades like a dream o' the dark
When all has been said and done!

The earth-life fades in its sin and pain;
But whatever of sweet and pure
Breathed over its pallor and flushed its gloom,
Surviveth for evermore.
O, not as the ghost of a mortal joy,
But as Joy herself from the dead
Upraised to the clear, calm courts of Heaven,
With a halo around her head;
'Tis only the vile and the sad shall die
With the wane of an earthly sun,
And pass like a vision as man awakes
When all has been said and done!

Do you think you have lost your days for aye
In the heart of the woods of spring,
By that seaside town that is glimpsed through mist,
Like the white of a petrel's wing?
Do you think that the patter of tiny feet
Shall never come back again,
And that those whom the rage of Death had killed
Are in sooth forever slain?
Look up! look up! as the hope commands,
From the ruth of the angels won;
The earth-woe fades like a dream o' the night,
When all has been said and done!

O God, we wander in devious ways,
Till the end comes, stern and stark;
We lift our voices of useless wail
From the depths of the hollow dark;
Yet the Christ is there, though we see him not.
But only when sorrow lowers
Wildest, we feel through the hollow dark
A strange, warm hand in ours;
And a voice is heard in the music of heaven,
Saying: "Courage and hope, O, son!"
The earth-woe fades like a dream o' the night,
When all has been said and done!

THE VISION IN THE VALLEY.

AMID the loveliest of all lonely vales,
Couched in soft silences of mountain calm,
And broadly shadowed both by pine and palm,

O'er which a tremulous golden vapor sails
Forever, though unbreathed on by a breeze
Or any wind of heaven, serenely sleeps
A lucid fountain, from whose fathomless deeps
Come murmurs stranger than the twilight sea's.

That golden vapor, buoyed without a breath,
Tints to its own fair bloom the limpid tide,
Through which erewhile the solemn vision rose
Of a calm face, benignly glorified
By all we dream or yearn for of pure rest,
Profound, Lethéan, passionless repose.
Still through the silence mystic murmurs sighed,
Fraught with far meanings, vague and unexpressed,
Till at the last, upbreathing, weird and near,
The voice of that pale phantom thrilled mine ear —
"*Behold the face, the marvellous face, of Death!*"

THE ARCTIC VISITATION.

Some air-born genius, with malignant mouth,
Breathed on the cold clouds of an Arctic zone—
Which o'er long wastes of shore and ocean blown
Swept threatening, vast, toward the amazèd South:

Over the land's fair form at first there stole
A vanward host of vapors, wild and white;
Then loomed the main cloud cohorts, massed in might,
Till earth lay corpse-like, reft of life and soul;

Death-wan she lay, 'neath heavens as cold and pale;
All nature drooped toward darkness and despair;
The dreary woodlands, and the ominous air
Were strangely haunted by a voice of wail.

The woeful sky slow passionless tears did weep,
Each shivering rain-drop frozen ere it fell;
The woodman's axe rang like a muffled knell;
Faintly the echoes answered, fraught with sleep.

The dawn seemed eve; noon, dawn eclipsed of grace;
The evening, night; and tender night became
A formless void, through which no starry flame
Touched the veiled splendor of her sorrowful face;

Like mourning nuns, sad-robed, funereal, bowed,
Day followed day; the birds their quavering notes
Piped here and there from feeble, querulous throats.
Fierce cold beneath — above, one riftless cloud

Wrapped the mute world — for now all winds had died —
And, locked in ice, the fettered forests gave
No sign of life; as silent as the grave
Gloomed the dim, desolate landscape far and wide.

Gazing on these, from out the mist one day
I saw, a shadow on the shadowy sky,
What seemed a phantom bird, that faltering nigh,
Perched by the roof-tree on a withered spray;

With drooping breast he stood, and drooping head;
This fateful time had wrought the minstrel wrong;
Even as I gazed, our southland lord of song
Dropped through the blasted branches, breathless, dead!

Yet chillier grew the gray, world-haunting shade,
Through which, methought, quick, tremulous wings were heard;
Was it the ghost of that heartbroken bird
Bound for a land where sunlight cannot fade?

THE WIND OF ONSET.

With potent north winds rushing swiftly down,
Blended in glorious chant, on yesternight
Old Winter came with locks and beard of white,
The hoarfrost glittering on his ancient crown:

He sent his icy breathings through the pane,
He raved and rattled at the close-shut doors,
Then waned with hollow murmur down the moors,
To rise, revive and sweep the world again.

The chorus of great winds which gird him round
Hold many voices — the deep trumpet's swell,
The air harp's mournful burden of farewell,
The fife's shrill tones, the clarion's silvery sound:

But o'er the roof-tree, 'round the gable rings
Loudest his wind of onset, hour by hour,
Till a new sense of almost rapturous power
Comes on the mighty waftage of his wings;

Sense of fresh hope and faith's rekindled glow,
The awakened aim, the brain drawn tense and high,
To shoot its fiery thoughts against the sky,
Like arrows launched from some deft archer's bow!

All latent forces of our being start
To marshalled order, ranged in battle line,
While the roused life-blood with a thrill divine
Runs tingling thro' the chambers of the heart.

Summer is rich with dreams of languid tone;
October sunsets feed the soul with light;
But give *me* winter's war wind in his might,
O'er the scourged lands and turbulent oceans blown.

THE VISIT OF MAHMOUD BEN SULEIM TO PARADISE.

Beneath the shadow of a breezeless palm
Mahmoud Ben Suleim, in the evening calm,
Sat, with his gravely meditative eyes
Turned on the waning wonder of the skies;
What time beside him paused a brother sage,
Whose flowing locks, like his, were white with age:
His gaze a half-veiled fire, seemed sadly cast
Inward, to scan the records of his past —

"On yesternight
Old Winter came with locks and beard of white."

Perchance the past of man — and thence to draw
From far experience, sanctified by awe
Of God's mysterious ways, some hint to tell
Who of the dead in heaven and who in hell
Dwelt now in endless bliss or endless bale.

Thus, while he mused, the old man's face grew pale
With stringent memories; on his laboring thought
Vague speculations, dim and doubtful, wrought
From out the fragments of the vanished years.
At length he said: "Ben Suleim, lend thine ears
To that I fain would ask thee. Thou art wise
In sacred lore, in pure philosophies;
So tell me now thine inmost thought of heaven
And heaven's fair habitants."

"Whoe'er hath striven,"
Ben Suleim answered, "to the extremest verge
Of spiritual power, across death's dreary surge
Hath passed to find the fathomless peace of God!"

"Yea," quoth the other, smiting on the sod
His staff impatiently. "I know! I know!
But who of all *we* have seen or loved below
Think'st thou in Aidenn?"

Slowly from his lips,
Wrapped by the smoke-wreaths in a half-eclipse,
Ben Suleim's pipe was lowered: "My friend," said he,
"Hark to this vision of eternity,
Which in the long-gone time of youth did seem
To rise before me in a twilight dream.
Methought the life on earth had passed away,
That near me spread the new, immortal day
Of Paradise; but yet mine eyes looked back
On this our clouded world, and marked the track
My waning life-course still left glimmering there.
Behold! all dues of funeral dole and prayer
Mine heirs had paid me; through the cypress gloom
I saw the glitter of my new-made tomb,
Whereon so many a blazoned virtue shone,
A blush seemed gathering o'er the hardened stone,
And I, albeit a spirit, flushed with shame.
Nathless, just then to Eden gates I came,
And, at the outmost wicket thundering loud,
Summoned full soon an angel from the cloud
Which girds those heavenly portals, blent with mist
Of shifting rainbow arcs of amethyst,
Who, somewhat harshly for an angel, said
I knocked as if an hundred thousand dead,
Not *one* poor soul, besieged the heavenly door.
He raised his luminous hands, which hovered o'er
For a brief moment, like a flash of stars,
The sapphire brilliance of the circling bars,
Then one by one unclosed them. Entered in
The realm celestial, safe from pain and sin,

I stretched at ease, with shadows cool and dim
Floating about me, thus did question him:
'Fair Seraph, speak. Is not this land divine,
Rife with pure souls, once faithful friends of mine?'
'Nay! be content if wandering here and there,
Thou meet'st a *few*—none in the loftiest sphere.'
'Where, then,' I cried, 'is holy Ibn Becár?
If not the highest he, surely not far
Beneath the highest that clear spirit beams?'
'Ah! thou art muffled still in earthly dreams,'
The angel answered. 'If on *him* thou'dst call,
Pass downward, for he's not in Heaven at all!'
'Dread Allah! can it be? So just a man
Walked not, methought, the streets of Ispahan.
Morn after morn, year after year his feet,
Alike in summer's bloom and winter's sleet,
Bore him to worship in the sacred place;
What righteous zeal burned hotly in his face!
And when inspired his heavenly vows he made,
Or 'neath the innermost mosque devoutly prayed,
Why, even the roaring Dervish, robed and cowled,
Shrank from those pious lungs, which almost howled
Creation deaf. A saint we deemed him—one
Pure as the snow, yet ardent as the sun,
Who, not content with turning toward the light
His own blest feet, must set on paths of right
All erring brethren!' 'True,' the angel cried;
'But Ibn Becár, down to the day he died,
Kept on his neighbor's ways so keen an eye
He lost at length his own straight course thereby;
And though the purblind world hath guessed it not,
He bides in Eblis' kingdom; fierce and hot
The waves of Hades roll above him now.'
Amazed, I bowed my head, just whispering low
An '*Allah Kebur*.' Next: 'How fares it, then,'
I asked, 'with Hafiz, the wise scribe, whose pen
Signed many a deed of gift, and scored his name
High on the roll of charitable hearts?'
Clear came the answer: ''Mid thy public marts
No soul more sordid strove with heaven to drive
Its wicked bargains. Largely would he give
To general charities; but, sooth to say,
Whene'er he 'scaped the broad, bright gaze of day,
He stamped with cruel heel the writhing poor,
Would turn the perishing beggar from his door,
And wring from friendless widows the last crust
Saved for their half-starved children. God is just;
So Hafiz dwells not here.'

In faltering tone,
As dropped from one who deals with things unknown,
I questioned next: 'Abdallah, *he* is saved?'
'Nay; for, albeit with seeming truth he braved

Temptation, and each wise and sacred saw
Wrought from the precepts of our prophet's law,
Fell soft as Hybla's honey from his mouth,
Yet his whole nature withered in the drouth
Of drear hypocrisy. By stealth he bought
Strong waters of the Giaour, and nightly sought
Oblivion from sweet opiates of the South.
Sickness he feigned, to gain in these his cure:
And once, that he might tipple more and more,
Moved to a province rife with serpents dread,
Because, by such as knew his wiles, 'twas said
He drank the poison of each treacherous throat,
To seek in fiery wine an antidote.
Nathless, a serpent slew him, and his home
Is far from ours.'
My thoughts began to roam
Vaguely, in loose disorder. Yet again:
'What of Kalkarri, he whose songs of pain
And joy alike forever struck the key,
The under-note of golden purity,
Virtue his theme and heavenly love his muse?'
'Thou fool and blind! Kalkarri could not choose
But sing mellifluous verses; yet in him
The light of truth was always blurred and dim.
A tireless trick of tinkling rhymes he had,
And naught he cared what spirit, good or bad,
O'erruled his lay. The good, perchance, *paid* best;
Therefore he sang of heavenly joy and rest,
But sang of that whereof he shall not taste.'
'Just Allah!' sighed I, 'see what barren waste
Drinks up my hopes. Since none of all I named
Here for the sacred roll hath Allah claimed,
I pray thee tell me *whom* his will hath blessed.'
'Dost thou remember Saädi?' 'What, that wretch
Who shod the Bactrian camels — who would fetch
Strange oaths from far to sow our wholesome air
With moral poison?' 'True, the man did swear,'
Confessed the Bright One, sadly. 'Yet so strong
His penitent sorrow o'er the hateful wrong
Done his own soul and Allah, and so rife
With tireless effort his whole earnest life
To smite the giant tempters in his soul,
To kill them outright, or with firm control
Hold them in native darkness chained and cowed —
At last he conquered and our Lord allowed
His weary soul to quaff the founts of balm!'

Amazement held me dumb. Within the palm
Waving above, just then a whispering breeze
Rose, and passed up the long-ranked, radiant trees
Which lined the hills of heaven. It seemed a sigh
Born of soft Mercy's immortality
Wafted toward the throne! The Bright One then,
Lifting his voice harmonious, spake again:

'Ferdusi, the small merchant by the quays
Too poor to give, but with a heart as broad
As the broad sky, reverent of faith and God;
Islal-ed-Din, who, though he could not make
The commonest prayer, would yet exclaim Amen!
To those who did, so warmly, for the sake
Of truth and fervent worship, all might see
His generous spirit's large sincerity —
Both *these* are with us,'
'But Wassaf,' said I,
The blameless teacher, who methinks came nigh
Virtue as pure as frail humanity
On earth may compass?' 'Yea; his soul *is* here,
But his soul wanders in the humblest sphere.
For, mark thee, though no damning sin did stain
This Wassaf's record, still in blood and brain
So weak was he, his pale life-currents flowed
So like dull streamlets through a wan abode
Of windless deserts, that he lived and died
Ne'er by a sharp temptation terrified;
And if his course the Prophet's law fulfilled
And near his path all passionate gusts were stilled,
What credit to him? His to coldly live,
Act, fade — a creature tamely negative.
But lo! in flaming contrast the hot stir
Of Agha's fate — Agha, the flute player,
Glutton on earth, wine-bibber, and the rest,
He still is held in heaven a nobler guest
Than all your Wassafs — proper, crimeless, cool,
And soulless, almost, as a stagnant pool,
For Agha's blood a furious torrent ran;
Half brutal he, half tiger and half man,
In health and power, the body's lustful force,
Whose strength to fetter in its turbulent course
Had taxed an angel's will. His nature sore
Tormented him; yet o'er and o'er and o'er
From some vast fall he lifted prayerful eyes,
And like a Titan strove to *storm* the skies,
Which, through unequalled strife and travails passed,
His hero-soul hath grandly won at last!

No more! no more! the glorious presence said.
'In light to come thy knowledge perfected
Shall bloom in flower and fruit; but, Suleim, say,
Hast thou beheld the swift sky-rocket's ray
Burn up the heavens? How beautiful at first
Its splendors gleamed, too soon, alas! to burst
And die in outer darkness! Thus it is
With many a soul, soaring, men dream, to bliss.
Awhile they mount, clear, dazzling, drunk with light,
To sink in ruin and the desolate night.
Would'st know the true believer? *He* is one
Whose faith in deeds shines perfect as the sun.
His soul, a shaft feathered by works of grace,
Death, the grim archer, launches forth in space;
It cleaves the clouds, o'ershoots the vaporous wall
That waves 'twixt earth and heaven its mystic pall,

To light, at last, unerring, strong and fleet,
In the deep calm which lies at Allah's feet!'"

MY DAUGHTER.

Thou hast thy mother's eyes, my child —
Her deep dark eyes: the undefiled
Sweetness which breathes around her mouth,
A perfect rosebud of the south,
And the broad brow, as smooth to-day
As when on life's auspicious May
I clasped her to an ardent breast
With yearnings of divine unrest.

Thou hast thy mother's voice, as low
And soft as happy winds that blow
At springtime o'er the wild-bloom beds,
When the blue harebells lift their heads
To hearken to those strains of peace,
And through the lustrous day's decease
Drink in the sunset-beams that float
Downward from glittering airs remote.

Thou hast thy mother's heart, no less
Than all her body's loveliness —
A heart as firmly brave and true,
O'er-brimming now with morning dew
Of hopeful light as doth a flower;
Yet strong to meet misfortune's hour,
And for the sake of loving ruth
Lie down and perish in its youth.

Child! child! so fair, so good thou art,
Sometimes an awful pang my heart
Pierces as thus I gaze on thee.
Too rare a thing thou seem'st to be
Long in this barren world to smile;
Methinks, with many a heavenly wile,
Unseen, but felt, the angels stray
Near thee, to tempt thy soul away.

Oh! heed them not. Why should they cull
My one sweet blossom? Heaven is full
Of just such spirits. Leave her here,
Kind seraphs! our poor joys to share,
Our griefs to brighten by her love;
Pass on to your calm homes above,
And thus in mercy spare to earth
The angel of my heart and hearth.

'Tis strange, but yet so fresh and whole,
So radiant in my brain and soul
Doth this enchanting image dwell,
This pure, unrivalled miracle
Of maidenhood and modest grace,
I vow that I behold her face,
Hear her low tones, and mark her mien
So gentle, virginal, serene,

Clearly, as if her voice and brow,
In softest sooth, beguiled me now;
As if, incarnate and benign,
She placed her little hand in mine,
And her long midnight tresses rare
Were mingling with my snow-touched hair.
And yet she only lives for me
In golden realms of fantasie,
A creature born of air and beam,
The delicate darling of a dream.

OUR "HUMMING-BIRD."

Ah, well I know the reason why
They called her by that graceful name:
She seems a creature born with wings,
O'er which a rainbow spirit flings
Fair hues of softly shifting flame;
Light is she as the changeful air,
Borne on gay humors everywhere,
Bewitchingly.

Her soul hath seldom breathed a sigh;
No hint of care hath ever stirred
Her being; sunshine and the breeze
Have been the fairy witnesses
Of all those joys our happy bird
Hath from the golden fountains drawn
Of youth unsullied as the dawn,
So lavishly.

Full many a flower, just hovering nigh,
In life's broad garden, rife with sweets,
She deftly drains of nectar dew;
Then, sylph-like, sweeps o'er pathways new
To taste some balmier bliss she meets;
Now flashing fast through myrtle bowers,
Now clinging to red lips of flowers,
Capriciously.

Forbear, rash heart! forbear to try
Our bird to capture with your wiles,
For, lo! she glimmers like a beam
Of fancy, on from dream to dream:
Vain are a lover's tears or smiles
To check her flight bewildering,
To tame her soul, or chain her wing
Submissively.

Nay! let the dazzling fairy fly
From flower to flower, so gladly whirled;
Cruel it were her matchless light
By one rude touch to dim or blight,
To see her luminous pinions furled
In grosser airs than those which stray
Round the fresh rosebuds of the May,
Deliciously.

LATER POEMS.

LATER POEMS

OF IMAGINATION, SENTIMENT, AND DESCRIPTION.

UNVEILED.

I CANNOT tell when first I saw her face;
Was it athwart a sunset on the sea,
When the huge billows heaved tumultuously,
Or in the quiet of some woodland place,
Wrapped by the shadowy boon
Of breezeless verdures from the summer noon?
Or likelier still, in a rock-girdled dell
Between vast mountains, while the midnight hour
Blossomed above me like a shining flower,
Whose star-wrought petals turned the fields of space
To one great garden of mysterious light?

Vain! vain! I cannot tell
When first the beauty and majestic might
Of her calm presence, bore my soul apart
From all low issues of the grovelling world; —
About me their own peace and grandeur furled, —
Filling the conscious heart
With vague, sweet wisdom drawn from earth or sky, —
Secrets that glance towards eternity,
Visions divine, and thoughts ineffable!

But ever since that immemorial day,
A steadfast flame hath burned in brain and blood,
Urging me onward in the perilous search
For sacred haunts our queenly mother loves;
By field and flood,
Thro' neighboring realms, and regions far away,
Have I not followed, followed where she led,
Tracking wild rivers to their fountain head,
And wilder desert spaces, mournful, vast,
Where Nature, fronting her inscrutable past,
Holds bleak communion only with the dead;
Yearning meanwhile, for pinions like a dove's,
To waft me further still,
Beyond the compass of the unwinged will;
Yea; waft me northward, southward, east, or west,
By fabled isles, and undiscovered lands,
To where enthroned upon his mountain-perch,
The sovereign eagle stands,
Guarding the unfledged eaglets in their nest,
Above the thunders of the sea and storm?

Oh! sometimes by the fire
Of holy passion, in me, all subdued,
And melted to a mortal woman's mood,
Tender and warm, —
She, from her goddess height,
In gracious answer to my soul's desire,

Descending softly, lifts her Isis veil,
To bend on me the untranslated light
Of fathomless eyes, and brow divinely pale:
She lays on mine her firm, immortal hand;
And I, encompassed by a magical mist,
Feel that her lips have kissed
Mine eyes and forehead; — how the influence fine
Of her deep life runs like Arcadian wine
Through all my being! How a moment pressed
To the large fountains of her opulent breast,
A rapture smites me, half akin to pain;
A sun-flash quivering through white chords of rain!

Thenceforth, I walked
The earth all-seeing; — not her stateliest forms
Alone engrossed me, nor her sounds of power;
Mountains and oceans, and the rage of storms;
Fierce cataracts hurled from awful steep to steep,
Or, the gray water-spouts, that whirling tower
Along the darkened bosom of the deep;
But all fair, fairy forms; all vital things,
That breathe or blossom 'midst our bounteous springs;
In sylvan nooks rejoicingly I met
The wild rose and the violet;
On dewy hill-slopes pausing, fondly talked
With the coy wind-flower, and the grasses brown,
That in a subtle language of their own
(Caught from the spirits of the wandering breeze),
Quaintly responded; while the heavens looked down
As graciously on these
Titania growths, as on sublimer shapes
Of century-moulded continents, that bemock
Alike the earthquake's and the billows' shock
By Orient inlands and cold ocean capes!

The giant constellations rose and set:
I knew them all, and worshipped all I knew;
Yet, from their empire in the pregnant blue,
Sweeping from planet-orbits to faint bars
Of nebulous cloud, beyond the range of stars,
I turned to worship with a heart as true,
Long mosses drooping from the cypress-tree;
The virginal vines that stretched remotely dim,
From forest limb to limb;
Network of golden ferns, whose tracery weaves
In lingering twilights of warm August eves,
Ethereal frescoes, pictures fugitive,
Drawn on the flickering and fair-foliaged wall
Of the dense forest, ere the night shades fall:
Rushes rock-tangled, whose mixed colors live
In the pure moisture by a fountain's brim;
The sylph-like reeds, wave-born, that to and fro
Move ever to the waters' rhythmic flow,
Blent with the humming of the wild-wood bee,
And the winds' under thrills of mystery;
The twinkling "ground-stars," full of modest cheer,
Each her cerulean cup
In humble supplication lifting up,
To catch whate'er the kindly heavens may give

Of flooded sunshine, or celestial dew;
And even when, self-poised in airy grace,
Their phantom lightness stirs
Through glistening shadows of a secret place
The silvery-tinted gossamers;
For thus hath Nature taught amid her All, —
The complex miracles of land and sea,
And infinite marvels of the infinite air,
No life is trivial, no creation small!

Ever I walk the earth,
As one whose spiritual ear
Is strangely purged and purified to hear
Its multitudinous voices; from the shore
Whereon the savage Arctic surges roar,
And the stupendous bass of choral waves
Thunders o'er "wandering graves,"
From warrior-winds whose viewless cohorts charge

"Have I not followed, followed where she led,
Tracking wild rivers to their fountain head."

The banded mists through Cloudland's vaporous dearth,
Pealing their battle bugles round the marge
Of dreary fen and desolated moor;
Down to the ripple of shy woodland rills
Chanting their delicate treble 'mid the hills,
And ancient hollows of the enchanted ground, —
I pass with reverent thought,
Attuned to every tiniest trill of sound,
Whether by brook or bird
The perfumed air be stirred.
But most, because the unwearied strains are fraught
With Nature's freedom in her happiest moods,
I love the mock-bird's, and brown thrush's lay,
The melted soul of May.
Beneath those matchless notes,
From jocund hearts upwelled to fervid throats,
In gushes of clear harmony,
I seem, oft-times I seem
To find remoter meanings; the far tone
Of ante-natal music faintly blown
From out the misted realms of memory;
The pathos and the passion of a dream;
Or, broken fugues of a diviner tongue

That e'er hath chanted, since our earth was young,
And o'er her peace-enamored solitudes
The stars of morning sung!

MUSCADINES.

Sober September, robed in gray and dun,
Smiled from the forest in half-pensive wise;
A misty sweetness shone in her mild eyes,
And on her cheek a shy flush went and came,
As flashing warm between
The autumnal leaves of slowly dying green,
The sovereign sun
Tenderly kissed her; then (in ruthful mood
For the vague fears of modest maidenhood)
Behold him gently, lovingly retire;
Beneath the foliaged screen,
Veiling his swift desire—
Even as a king, wed to some virgin queen,
Might doom his sight to blissful, brief eclipse,
After his tender lips
Had touched the maiden's trembling soul to flame.

Through shine and shade,
Thoughtful I trod the tranquil forest glade,
Up-glancing oft
To watch the rainless cloudlets, white and soft,
Sail o'er the placid ocean of the sky.
The breeze was like a sleeping infant's sigh,
Measured and low, or, in quick, palpitant thrills
An instant swept the sylvan depths apart
To pass and die
Far off, far off, within the shrouded heart
Of immemorial hills,

Through shade and shine
I wandered, as one wanders in a dream,
Till, near the borders of a beauteous stream
O'erhung by flower and vine,
I pushed the dense, perplexing boughs aside,
To mark the temperate tide
Purpled by shadows of the Muscadine.

Reclining there at languid length I sank,
One idle hand outstretched beyond the bank,
With careless grasp
The sumptuous globes of these rare grapes to clasp.
Ah! how the ripened wild fruit of the South
Melted upon my mouth!
Its magic juices through each captured vein
Rose to the yielding brain,
Till, like the hero of an old romance,
Caught by the fays, my spirit lapsed away,
Lost to the sights and sounds of mortal day.

Lost to all earthly sights and sounds was I,
But blithesomely,
As stirred by some new being's wondrous dawn,
I heard about me, swift though gently drawn,
The footsteps of light creatures on the grass.
Mine eyelids seemed to open, and I saw,
With joyance checked by awe,
A multitudinous company
Of such strange forms and faces, quaint, or bright
With true Elysian light,
As once in fairy fantasies of eld

"Sober September, robed in gray and dun,
Smiled from the forest in half-pensive wise."

High-hearted poets through the wilds beheld
Of shadowy dales and lone sea beaches pass,
At spring-tide morn or holy hush of night.

Then to an airy measure,
Low as the sea winds when the night at noon
Clasps the frail beauty of an April moon,
Through woven paces at soft-circling leisure,
They glided with elusive grace adown
The forest coverts — all live woodland things,
Black-eyed or brown,
Firm-footed or up-poised on changeful wings.
Glinting about them 'mid the indolent motion
Of billowy verdures rippling slow
As the long, languid underflow
Of some star-tranced, voluptuous Southern ocean.

The circle widened, and as flower-wrought bands,
Stretched by incautious hands,
Break in the midst with noiseless wrench asunder.
So brake the dancers now to form in line
Down the deep glade — above the shifting lights,
Through massive tree-boles, on majestic heights;
The blossoming turf thereunder,
Whence, fair and fine,
Twinkling like stars that hasten to be drawn
Close to the breast of dawn,
Shone, with their blue veins pulsing fleet,
Innumerable feet,
White as the splendors of the milky way,
Yet rosy warm as opening tropic day,
With lithe, free limbs of curvature divine,
And dazzling bosoms of unveilèd glow,
Save where the long, ethereal tresses stray
Across their unimaginable snow.

One after one,
By sun-rays kissed or fugitive shades o'errun,
All vision-like they passed me. First there came
A Dryad coy, her sweet head bowed in shame,
And o'er her neck and half-averted face
The faintest delicate trace
Of the charmed life-blood pulsing softly pure.
Next, with bold footsteps, sure,
And proudly set, from her untrammelled hills,
Fair-haired, blue-eyed, upon her lofty head
A fragrant crown of leaves, purple and red,
Chanting a lay clear as the mountain rills,
A frank-faced Oread turned on me
Her cloudless glances, laughter-lit and free
As the large gestures and the liberal air
With which I viewed her fare
Down the lone valley land, —
Pausing betimes to wave her happy hand
As in farewell; but ere her presence died
Wholly away,
Her voice of golden swell
Breathed also a farewell.
Farewell, farewell, the sylvan echoes sighed,
From rock-bound summit to rich blossoming bay —
Farewell, farewell!

Fauns, satyrs flitted past me — the whole race
Of woodland births uncouth —
Until I seemed, in sooth,
Far from the garish track

Of these loud days to have wandered, joyful, back
Along the paths, beneath the crystal sky
Of long, long-perished Arcady.
But last of all, filling the haunted space
With odors of the flower-enamored tide,
Whose wavelets love through many a secret place
Of the deep dell and breezeless bosk to glide,
Stole by, lightsome and slim
As Dian's self in each swift, sinuous limb,
Her arms outstretched, as if in act to swim
The air, as erst the waters of her home,
A naiad, sparkling as the fleckless foam
Of the cool fountain-head whereby she dwells.

O'er her sloped shoulders and the pure pink bud
Of either virginal breast is richly rolled
(O rare, miraculous flood!)
The torrent of her freed locks' shimmering gold,
Through which the gleams of rainbow-colored shells,
And pearls of moon-like radiance flash and float
Round her immaculate throat.

Clothed in her beauty only wandered she,
'Mid the moist herbage to the streamlet's edge,
Where, girt by silvery rushes and brown sedge,
She faded slowly, slowly, as a star
Fades in the gloaming, on the bosom bowed
Of some half-luminous cloud,
Above the wan, waste waters of the sea.

Then, sense and spirit fading inward too,
I slept oblivious; through the dim, dumb hours,
Safely encouched on autumn leaves and flowers,
I slept as sleep the unperturbèd dead.
At length the wind of evening, keenly chill,
Swept round the darkening hill;
Then throbbed the rush of hurried wings o'erhead,
Blent with aerial murmurs of the pine,
Just whispering twilight. On my brow the dew
Dropped softly, and I woke to all the low,
Strange sounds of twilight woods that come and go
So fitfully; and o'er the sun's decline,
Through the green foliage flickering high,
Beheld, with dreamy eye,
Sweet Venus glittering in the stainless blue.

. . . . . .

Thus the day closed whereon I drank the wine —
The liquid magic of the Muscadine.

IN A SPRING GARDEN.

When Heaven was stormy, Earth was cold,
And sunlight shunned the wold and wave, —
Thought burrowed in the churchyard mould,
And fed on dreams that haunt the grave: —

But now that Heaven is freed from strife,
And Earth's full heart with rapture swells,
Thought soars the realms of endless life
Above the shining asphodels!

What flower that drinks the south wind's breath,
What sparkling leaf, what Hebe-Morn,
But flouts the sullen graybeard, Death,
And laughs our Arctic doubts to scorn?

Pale scientist! scant of healthful blood,
Your ghostly tomes, one moment, close;
Pluck freshness with a spring-time bud,
Find wisdom in the opening rose:

From toil which, blindly delving, gropes
When time but plays a juggler's part,
Ah go! and breathe the dew-lit hopes
That cluster round a violet's heart:

Mark the white lily whose sweet core
Hath many a wild-bee swarm enticed,
And draw therefrom a honeyed lore
Pure as the tender creed of Christ:

Yea! even the weed which upward holds
Its tiny ear, past bower and lawn,
A lovelier faith than yours enfolds,
Caught from the whispering lips of dawn!

IN DEGREE.

Thy life is full of motion, perfume, grace;
Mine, a low blossom in a shaded place,
Whereto the zephyrs whisper, only they,
Through the long lapses of the lonesome day.

Thy lordly genius blooms for all to see
On the clear heights of calm supremacy;
My humbler dower they only find who pass
With eyes that seek for violets mid the grass.

THE SKELETON WITNESS.

Rooted in soil dull as a dead man's eye,
Dank with decay, yon ghastly oak aspires,
As if in mockery, to the alien sky,
Frowning afar through clouded sunset fires.

No garb of summer greenery girds it now:
Stripped as some naked soul at Judgment-morn,
It rears its blasted arms, its sullen brow,
Defiant still, though wasted, scarred, forlorn!

Not all its ruin came through storm or time;
Ages ago, 'mid winter's dreariest blight,
It saw and strove to shroud an awful crime,
But slowly withered from that fateful night!

An evil charm its many-centuried rings
Robbed of their pith; no more with healthful start
Its lusty life-sap, nursed by countless springs,
Coursed through great veins, and warmed its giant heart.

Now all men shun the gaunt accursèd thing—
Only the raven with monotonous croak,
Tortures the silence, staining with black wing
The leprous whiteness of the rotting oak!

STORM-FRAGMENTS.

The storm had raved its furious soul away;
O'er its wild ruins Twilight, spectral, gray,

Stole like a nun, 'midst wounded men and slain,
Walking the bounds of some fierce battle-plain.

The ghost of thunder muttered faintly by;
While down the uttermost spaces of the sky,

Just where the sunset's glimmering verge grew pale,
The baffled winds outbreathed their dying wail!

The sombre clouds that thronged a shadowy west
Writhed, as if tortured monsters of unrest,

Whose depths the keen sheet-lightnings rent apart,
To show what fiery torment throbbed at heart!

Where raged of late the war of elements dread,
Brooded a solemn silence overhead,

Through which, beyond the cloud-strewn, heavenly field,
The moon shone gory as a warrior's shield,

Dipped in the veins of many a vanquished foe;
Blood-red, I marked the wandering vapors flow

Vaguely about her, while her lurid light
Scared the vague vanguard of the shades of night;

Their banded hosts retreating, wild and dim,
In shattered cohorts o'er the horizon's rim:

Yet, the broad empire of those baleful beams
Heaved with strange shapes and hues of nightmare dreams!

Here, as from cloud-born Himalayas rolled,
I saw what seemed a cataract's rush of gold,

Hurled between shores of darkness, dense and dire,
Down to a seething mountain-lake of fire;

There, dismal catacombs, whose nether glooms
Yawned, to reveal their loathsome place of tombs:

Caverns of mystic depth, whence bubbling came
The blue-tinged horror of sulphureous flame;

Fragments of castles, with fresh blood besprent,
Gaunt, ruined tower, and blasted battlement—

On which, flame-clad, and tottering to their fall,
Dark eyes of frenzy flashed o'er cope and wall!

With awful ocean-spaces, limitless, grand,
Where spectral billows lashed a viewless land;

Their mountainous floods a frowning zenith kissed,
But glimpsed, at times, 'twixt folds of phantom-mist,

I viewed, as faintly touched by muffled stars,
The semblance of dead forms, on shipwrecked spars

Whirled upward, and dead faces, a white spume
Smote to false life against that turbulent gloom,

Where mournful birds, on pinions gray or dun,
Circled, methought, o'er some half-perished sun,

Whose feeble lustre, faltering upward, flings
A sad-hued radiance round their pallid wings;

Yea! all fantastic shapes of terror, wrought
'Twixt errant fancy and dream-haunted thought,

Until I seemed with Dante's soul to fly,
Through new Infernos, shifted to—the sky!

ABOVE THE STORM.

THE winds of the winter have breathed their dirges
Far over the wood and the leaf-strown plain;
They have passed, forlorn, by the mountain verges
Down to the shores of the moaning main;
And the breast of the smitten sea divides,
Till the voice of winds and the voice of tides
Seem blent with the roar of the central surges,
Whose fruitless furrows are sown with rain.

The pines look down, and their branches shiver
On the misty slopes of the mountain wall,
And I hear the shout of a mountain river
Through the gloom of the ghostly gorges call;
While from drifting depths of the troubled sky
Outringeth the eagle's wild reply,
So shrill that the startled echoes quiver;
And the veil of the tempest is over all.

O groaning forest! O wind that rushes
Unfettered and fierce as a doom malign!
How the pulses leap, how the heart-tide flushes
The temples and brow like the flush of wine,
As I pause, as I hearken the vast commotion
Of the air, of the earth, of the wakened ocean;
And my soul goes forth with the storm that crushes,
With the battling foam and the blinding brine.

Yea, my soul is rent by a tempest stronger
Than ever was Nature's, with ruin rife,
And the flame of its lightnings can bide no longer,
Ensheathed at the core of a clouded life;
And its pent-up thunders, unloosed at last,
Keep time to the rhythmic rage of the blast,
For my spirit, half-maddened by Fates that wrong her,
Is shaken by passion, and hot with strife!

Ah, God! for the wings of the eagle above me,
With their steadfast vigor and royal might;
Ah, God! for an impulse like theirs to move me
In endless courses of upward flight;
The clouds may billow, the vapors heave,
But still his pinions the darkness cleave;
And proudly serene, in those realms above me
He is soaring from conquered height to height:

Till at length, his great, broad vans at even
And stately poise on the airy stream,
I mark, through the rifts of the turbid heaven
His form outflashed like a wingèd beam;
And I ask, "Shall *my* spirit soar like his?
Shall it ever soar in the peace and bliss
Of the shining heights and the glory given
To the will unvanquished, the faith supreme?"

UNDERGROUND—A FANTASY.

MAJESTIC dreams of heavenly calms,
Bright visions of unfading palms,
Wherewith the brows of saints are crowned,—

Awhile my soul resigns them all,
Content to rest death's dreamless thrall,
Safe underground!

Rest! rest! oblivious rest I crave,
Though narrowed to a pine-clad grave,
With sylvan shadows shimmering round;
The peace of Heaven, if fair and deep,
Scarce wooes me like Earth's ebon sleep,
Far underground.

By infinite weariness oppressed
Of soul and senses, blood and breast,
Where can such Gilead balm be found
As that which breathes from out the sod
Baptized by rain and dews of God,
Deep underground?

A century's space I yearn to be
Untroubled, slumbering tranquilly,
There, by the haunted woodlands bound;
What suns shall set, what planets rise
O'er pulseless brain and curtained eyes,
Dark underground!

A century's sleep might bring redress
To these dull wounds of weariness,
Till the soothed spirit, hale and sound,
Grow conscious of the sacred trust
Which holds immortal bloom in dust,
Safe underground.

Yea! conscious grow of rustling wings,
And keen, mysterious whisperings,
Blown flame-like o'er the burial-mound:
My soul would feel thy Orient kiss,
Angel of Palingenesis,
Thrilled underground!

THE DRYAD OF THE PINE.

Ah, forest sweetheart! over land and sea
I come once more, once more to stand by thee;
My sylvan darling! set 'twixt shade and sheen,
Soft as a maid, yet stately as a queen!

Thy loyal head, crowned by one lonely star,
Flickers thro' twilight, coldly fine, and far;
But thy earth-yearning branches bend to greet
The lowliest wood-grass tangled round my feet.

Leaning on thee, I feel the subtlest thrill
Stir thy dusk limbs, tho' all the heavens are still;
And 'neath thy rings of rugged fretwork, mark
What seems a heart-throb muffled in the dark!

Here lingering long, amid the shadowy gleams,
Faintly I catch (yet scarce as one that dreams)
Low words of alien music, softly sung,
And rhythmic sighs in some sweet unknown tongue.

And something rare, I cannot clasp or see,
Flits vaguely out from this mysterious tree —
A viewless glory, an ethereal grace,
Which make Elysian all the haunted place!

Ethereal! viewless! yet divinely dear!
Ah me! what strange enchantment hovers near.
What breaths of love the old, old dreams renew!
What kisses fall, like charmed Thessalian dew!

My Dryad-Love hath slipped the imprisoning bark,
Her heart on mine, unmuffled by the dark.

WELCOME TO FROST.

O Spirit! at whose wafts of chilling breath
Autumn unbinds her zone, to rest in death;
Touched by whose blight the light of cordial days
Is lost in sombre browns and sullen grays;
Thou seemest of all sad things a mournful part:
Yet now we greet thee with exultant heart.
Not as a thief, at night-time bearing doom,
But a brave messenger of grace and bloom;
Thy flickering robe and footsteps soft we mark
Down the dim borders of the tremulous Dark;
And though before thee flowers and foliage wane,
Thou layest a magic hand on human pain.

Red Fever, soothed by thy cool finger-tips,
Ebbs from hot cheek and wildly-muttering lips;
Delirious dreams and frenzied fancies fade
Into fine landscapes of enchanted shade,
With low of kine and lapse of lyric rills
Through the cleft channel of Arcadian hills;
Till the worn patient feels his languid eyes
Flushed with what seems an earthly Paradise,
And life's old blissful tide, with lustier strain,
Revels in music through each ransomed vein.

Therefore, O monarch of all cold device,
Wrought in strange temples of Siberian ice!
Lord of fair realms and watery worlds grotesque!
Majestic afreet of weird Arabesque!
We hail thee sovereign in these fevered lands.
No more with alien hearts and folded hands,
But as an angel from the fadeless palms,
And the great River of God's central calms,
Whose silent charm must work benign release,
Whose touch is healing, and whose breath is — peace!

THE PINE'S MYSTERY.

I.

Listen! the sombre foliage of the Pine,
  A swart Gitana of the woodland trees,
Is answering what we may but half divine,
  To those soft whispers of the twilight breeze!

II.

Passion and mystery murmur through the leaves,
  Passion and mystery, touched by deathless pain.
Whose monotone of long, low anguish grieves
  For something lost that shall not live again!

TO A BEE.

Small epicurean, would to heaven that I
  Could borrow your lithe body and swift wing
To speed, a lightning atom through the sky,
  The blithest courier on the winds of spring!

O blissful mite! native of light and air!
In eager zeal you haste your spoils to win;
From half-blown bud to flower all matron-fair,
Sucking the nectared sweetness shrined within!

The jonquil wooes you with her golden blush,
And blossoming quince (each flower a fairy Mars,
That tints its heaven of green with crimsoned flush),
While the pure "white-rod" blooms in silvery stars,

Open to yield their delicate richness up.
But most you love on vernal noons, to dart
'Mid jasmine bowers, and drain each petalled cup
With fervid lip and warm voluptuous heart.

There, safely couched, you hum a low refrain,
Of such supreme and rare contentment born,
Its happy monotone mocks our human pain,
And subtly stings us with unconscious scorn.

Thence, honey-freighted, you steal lazily out,
Pausing a moment on some leafy brink,
As if enmeshed by viewless webs of doubt
From what next fount of luscious life to drink—

A moment only. Soon your matchless flight
Cleaves the far blue; your elfin thunder booms
In elfin echoes from yon glimmering height,
To fall and die amid these ravished blooms.

Gone, like a vision! Yet, be sure that he
Hath only flown through lovelier flowers to stray,
Anacreon's soul, thus prisoned in a bee,
Still sips and sings the springtide hours away!

THE FIRST MOCKING-BIRD IN SPRING.

Winged poet of vernal ethers!
Ah! where hast thou lingered long?
I have missed thy passionate, skyward flights
And the trills of thy changeful song.
Hast thou been in the hearts of woodlands old,
Half dreaming, and, drowsed by the winter's cold,
Just crooning the ghost of thy springtide lay
To the listless shadows, benumbed and gray?
Or hast thou strayed by a tropic shore,
And lavished, O sylvan troubadour!
The boundless wealth of thy music free
On the dimpling waves of the Southland sea?
What matter? Thou comest with magic strain,
To the morning haunts of thy life again,
And thy melodies fall in a rhythmic rain.

The wren and the field-lark listen
To the gush from their laureate's throat;
And the blue-bird stops on the oak to catch
Each rounded and perfect note.
The sparrow, his pert head reared aloft,
Has ceased to chirp in the grassy croft,
And is bending the curves of his tiny ear
In the *pose* of a critic wise, to hear.
A blackbird, perched on a glistening gum,
Seems lost in a rapture, deep and dumb;
And as eagerly still in his trancèd hush,

'Mid the copse beneath, is a clear-eyed thrush.
No longer the dove by the thorn-tree root
Moans sad and soft as a far-off flute.
All Nature is hearkening, charmed and mute.

We scarce can deem it a marvel,
For the songs *our* nightingale sings
Throb warm and sweet with the rhythmic beat
Of the fervors of countless springs.
All beautiful measures of sky and earth
Outpour in a second and rarer birth
From that mellow throat. When the winds are whist,
And he follows his mate to their sunset tryst,
Where the wedded myrtles and jasmine twine,
Oh! the swell of his music is half divine!
And I vaguely wonder, O bird! can it be
That a human spirit hath part in thee?
Some Lesbian singer's, who died perchance
Too soon in the summer of Greek romance,
But the rich reserves of whose broken lay,
In some mystical, wild, undreamed-of way,
Find voice in thy bountiful strains today!

THE RED AND THE WHITE ROSE.

The Red Rose bowed one golden summer's night,
The Red Rose bent, low whispering to the White,

"Thou pallid shadow of a beauteous flower,
Unchanged from purpling dawn to sunset hour;
Whose calm, cold heart beneath all lights that beam,
Seems centred always in an Arctic dream;

Prim, puritanic, passionless, austere,
What would'st thou give my opulent life to share?

To every breeze — the daintiest breeze that blows,
Each petalled curve of mine more richly glows; —

And all the countless tints of heaven-born grace
But touch to make more bright my Hebe face!"

"Ah! well, fulfil thy fate!" the White Rose said;
"List to the wooing winds! uplift thy head

In sovereign pride through every radiant phase
Of star-illumined nights and cloudless days;

Let wingèd lovers thy warm leaves dispart,
To find voluptuous shelter next thy heart.

Fulfil thy fate, O Queen! but leave to me
My stainless calm and cloistral sanctity;

Those passionate airs that trembling round thee meet,
Sink in soft worship at my veilèd feet;

The reverent sun-rays shimmering gently down,
Weave o'er my brows a halo for a crown;

And while I muse in star, or moonshine faint,
The flowers seem murmuring, 'Lo! our garden saint!'"

The Red Rose heard, but ere she spoke, her mouth
Thralled by the light, quick kisses of the South,

Passed from arch wonder, blent with gay disdain,
Back to its dimpled mirthfulness again;

And she,—the garden's empress—proud yet fond,—
Of summer flowers, the matchless Rosamond,—

Looked at her pale-hued sister, dew-impearled,
As that fair marvel of the island world,

Might, in her ruddier nature's Tropic glow,
Have viewed a calm St. Agnes' brow of snow,

With some dim sense of mystic space between
The heaven-bound votaress and the earthly queen!

BEFORE THE MIRROR.

WHERE in her chamber by the Southern sea,
Her taper's light shone soft and silvery,
Fair as a planet mirrored in the main,
Fresh as a blossom bathed by April rain,
A maiden robed for restful sleep aright,
Stood in her musing sweetness, pure and white
As some shy spirit in a haunted place:
Her dew-bright eyes and faintly flushing face
Viewed in the glass their delicate beauty beam,
Strange as a shadowy "dream within a dream"
With fingers hovering like a white dove's wings,
'Mid little, tender sighs and murmurings
(Joy's scarce articulate speech), her eager hands
Loosed the light coif, the ringlet's golden bands,
Till, by their luminous loveliness embraced,
From lily-head to lithe and lissome waist,
Poured the free tresses like a cascade's fall.
Her image answered from the shimmering wall,
Answered and deepened, while the gracious charms
Of brow and cheek, bared breast and dimpling arms,
To innocent worship stirred her happy heart:
Her lips—twin rosebud petals blown apart—
Quivered, half breathless; then, subdued but warm,
Around her perfect face, her pliant form
A subtler air seemed gathering, touched with fire
By many a fervid thought and swift desire,
With dreams of love, that, bee-like, came and went,
To feed the honeyed core of life's content!
Closer toward her mirrored self she pressed,
With large child-eyes, and gently panting breast,
Bowed as a flower when May-time breezes pass,
And kissed her own dear Image in the glass!

TWO EPOCHS.

LOVERS by a dim sea strand
Looking wave-ward, hand in hand;
Silent, trembling with the bliss
Of their first betrothal kiss:

Lovers still, tho' wedded long!
(Time true love can never wrong!
Gazing — faithful hand in hand,
O'er a darker sea and strand:

Ah! one lover's face is wan
As a wave the moon shines on;
But those strange tides stretched afar
Know not sun, nor moon, nor star!

"O masterful wind and cruel! at thy sweep,
From the bold hill-top to the valley deep,
Surprise and fear through all the woodlands run."

*WIND FROM THE EAST.**

THE Spring, so fair in her young incompleteness,
Of late the very type of tender sweetness;
Now, through frail leaves and misty branches brown,
Looks forth, the dreary shadow of a frown
Chasing the frank smile from her innocent face;
What marvel this? for the East Wind's disgrace
Smites, like a buffet, April's tingling cheek,
Whence the swift, outraged blood doth ebb to seek
The affrighted heart!
The Earth, herself so gay,
Buoyant, and happy, at the dawn of day,
Thrills, shivering low with every flaw increased,
And fraught with salt-sea coldness from the East!

O masterful wind and cruel! at thy sweep,
From the bold hill-top to the valley-deep,
Surprise and fear through all the woodlands run,
Till the coy nestling-places of the sun
Are ruffled up, from shine to shade, as when
At the first note of storm the moorland hen
Ruffles her wings ere yet their warmth be spread
About each tremulous nestling's dusky head.

On the tall trees the foremost buds, half bare,
Stared, as wild-eyed, on the keen, rasping air;

* This piece is (for the most part) a rhymed version of an exceedingly graphic description of the East wind, which occurs in Mr. Blackmore's admirable novel, "Cripps, the Carrier." Mr. Blackmore is a poet, although he writes in prose.

Then shook — but not with softly-palpitant thrills,
As when, o'erlooking the freed mountain-rills,
They felt their life by loving arms caressed —
Warm, viewless arms of zephyrs of the West —
But with the sense, the cold and shivery stress
Of utter and forlornest nakedness.
The twigs that bore them flattened upward, lost
To all but rigid consciousness of frost;
And their full-foliaged branches which so blindly
Bowed in meek homage when the winds were kindly
Strained upward, too, in stiff, rebellious fashion,
With throes of anguish and deep moans of passion,
Wrung from them by wild beatings of the gale!

Then many a tiny leaf, though waxing pale,
Cloud-shadowed; all unfrayed, yet quivering, shrunk
Behind the mosses of some giant trunk,
To wait till the shrewd tempest hurtling by
Left Spring once more empress of earth and sky —
While many a large leaf, almost riven apart,
Piped a sad dirge from out its fluted heart,
And knowing what sombre selvage must be seen —
Alas, too soon! — to film its glow of green,
Bewailed the hour whose treacherous brightness came
To warm its life-blood into genial flame
Only to send the blissful-flowing tide
Back through the baffled veins unsatisfied,
Its nascent joy nipped by the arctic breath
And merciless waftage of this Wind of Death!

PEACH BLOOMS.

O! tenderly beautiful, beyond compare,
Flushed from pale pink to deepest rosebud hue —
Nurslings of tranquil sunshine and mild air,
Of shadowless dawn, and silvery twilight dew —
Ye blush and burn, as if your flickering grace
Were love's own tint on Spring's enamored face!

And day by day — yea, golden hour by hour
Your subtle fragrance and rich beauty tell
(Each fairy blossom rounded into flower),
How matchless once that lost Arcadian spell,
Which dwelt in leafy bowers and vernal dyes
Whence coyly peeped the Dryad's fawn-like eyes!

And yet, while all so fair and bounteous seems,
While the birds carol — each his daintiest part,
Veiled in soft brightness, and like musical dreams
In some blithe soul — the bee-swarms haunt your heart.
Lo! severed slowly from yon roseate crown,
A scarlet snowdrift, silent, falters down.

The reign of these rich blooms is almost done;
Soon to the languid Zephyr's feeblest breath,
Their loosened petals, yielding one by one,

Must find the Lethe of unwakening death.
Ah me! of all the bourgeoned buds that shoot
Even to full flower, how few shall bear us fruit!

Their little day is closing fast in gloom;
Nor will they reck — poor wilted waifs, and blind!
What germs of richness wax from faded bloom,
To charm the pampered taste of human kind;
Forever dropped from off their parent stem,
What have man's thoughts or tastes to do with them?

So let them rest, I pray you, let them rest,
Small, perishing sweethearts of the sun and rain:
O! mother-earth, thou hast a ruthful breast,
Which yearns to fold thy humblest child from pain.
Men fall like flowers; both claim the self-same balm,
The equal peace of thy majestic calm!

THE AWAKENING.

From day to day the dreary heaven
Outpoured its hopeless heart in rain;
The conscious pines, half shuddering, heard
The secret of the East wind's pain.

Mist veiled the sun — the sombre land,
In floating cloud-wracks densely furled,
Seemed shut forever from the bloom
And gladness of the living world.

From week to week the changeless heaven
Wept on — and still its secret pain
To the bent pine-trees sobbed the wind,
In hollow truces of the rain.

Till in a sunset hour, whose light
Pale hints of radiance pulsed o'erhead,
Afar the moaning East wind died,
And the mild West wind breathed instead.

Then the clouds broke, and ceased the rain;
The sunset many a kindling shaft
Shot to the wood's heart; nature rose,
And through her soft-lipped verdures laughed.

Low to the breeze; as some fair maid,
Love wakes from troublous dreams, might rise,
Half dazed, yet happy — mists of sleep
Still hovering in her haunted eyes.

LOVE'S AUTUMN.

[To My Wife.]

I would not lose a single silvery ray
Of those white locks which like a milky way
Streak the dusk midnight of thy raven hair;

I would not lose, O sweet! the misty shine
Of those half-saddened, thoughtful eyes of thine,
Whence Love looks forth, touched by the shadow of care;

I would not miss the droop of thy dear mouth,
The lips less dewy-red than when the South, —
The young South wind of passion sighed o'er them;

I would not miss each delicate flower that blows
On thy wan cheeks, soft as September's rose
Blushing but faintly on its faltering stem;

I would not miss the air of chastened grace
Which breathed divinely from thy patient face,
Tells of love's watchful anguish, merged in rest;

Naught would I miss of all thou hast, or art,
O! friend supreme, whose constant, stainless heart,
Doth house unknowing, many an angel guest;

Their presence keeps thy spiritual chambers pure;
While the flesh fails, strong love grows more and more
Divinely beautiful with perished years;

Thus, at each slow, but surely deepening sign
Of life's decay, we will not, Sweet! repine,
Nor greet its mellowing close with thankless tears;

Love's spring was fair, love's summer brave and bland,
But through love's autumn mist I view the land,
The land of deathless summers yet to be;

There, I behold thee, young again and bright,
In a great flood of rare transfiguring light,
But there as here, thou smilest, Love! on me!

THE SPIREA.

[This exquisite plant blooms in the Southern States as early as the middle of February.]

Of all the subtle fires of earth
Which rise in form of spring-time flowers,
Oh, say if aught of purer birth
Is nursed by suns and showers

Than this fair plant, whose stems are bowed
In such lithe curves of maiden grace,
Veiled in white blossoms like a cloud
Of daintiest bridal lace?

So rare, so soft, its blossoms seem
Half woven of moonshine's misty bars,
And tremulous as the tender gleam
Of the far Southland stars.

Perchance — who knows? — some virgin bright,
Some loveliest of the Dryad race,
Pours through these flowers the kindling light
Of her Arcadian face.

Nor would I marvel overmuch
If from yon pines a wood-god came,
And with a bridegroom's lips should touch
Her conscious heart to flame;

While she, revealed at that strange tryst,
In all her mystic beauty glows,
Lifting the cheek her Love had kissed,
Paled like a bridal rose.

COQUETTE.

[Among the family portraits.]

I.

Yes! there from out the gallery gloom,
Retaining still a flush of bloom,
I mark our bright ancestress glow —
The maiden Rose of long ago.
She lived in times of sumptuous dress,
And rich colonial stateliness;
But through the strong restraints of art
I seem to view her heaving heart,
As if a protest warm it made
'Gainst that stiff bodice of brocade,
While in her fair cheeks' deepening dyes,
Her lifted brows and roguish eyes,
Her swan-like neck and dimpled chin—
Cleft for small Loves to ambush in —

"Ah! many a gallant loved her well
In those old days."

I can not fail (who could ?) to see
All potent charms of coquetry —
The wiles whose glamour, swift and sure,
Smote hapless victims by the score;
And even now (although they be
Discerned in pictured phantasy)
Not all innocuous, but possessed
Of power to pierce the manly breast,
If frosted to its shivering core
By forty arctic years or more.

II.

Ah! many a gallant loved her well
In those old days! Her features tell
The world-wide story o'er again,
Of *others'* passion, *her* disdain;
Of hearts that spent their best to make
Her own more tender for love's sake,
Only in time to find, perchance,
Dull ending to a life's romance,
Since trivial natures are not stirred
Save by the lightly trivial word;
And much I fear, despite the fine
Rare beauty of each faultless line —
Her face, of gay *insouciance*, shows
No golden gulfs of pure repose
Deep in her inmost being shrined —
But shallow thoughts and purpose blind.
And yet who knows ? My erring sight
May not have read its meanings right,
And something of ethereal grace
May lurk beneath that careless face,
Which masks with inconsiderate mirth
A soul not wholly wed to earth!

III.

Therefore, sweet flesh and blood, I trust
That, ere ye passed to senseless dust,
Your beauty played a worthier part —
The love-*rôle* of the loyal heart.

. . . . . .

No answer comes; for time doth mar
Our records. Only, like a star
Scarce touched by vapors vague and chill,
Your gracious image haunts us still.
But none, alas! may truly guess
What fate befell your loveliness.

SKATING.

I CHASED the maid with rapid feet,
Where ice and sunbeam quiver;
But still beyond me, shyly fleet,
She flashed far down the river.

Sometimes, blown backward in the chase,
With balmy, soft caresses,
I felt across my glowing face
The waft of perfumed tresses.

Sometimes a glance she shot behind,
O'er graceful shoulders turning
A cheek whose tints the eager wind
Had set like sunrise burning.

Then, in a sudden onward glide,
She rushed with even motion,
As a long wave the restless tide
Drives shoreward fast from ocean;

And swift as some winged creature sped
Far down the crystal river,
Until the shining form that fled
I dreamed might fly forever.

THE WORLD WITHIN US.

A FANTASY.

PERCHANCE our *inward* world may partly be
But *outward* Nature's fine epitome;

Now, o'er it floats some cloud of tender pain
Too frail to hold the sad reserves of rain;

And now behold some breezy impulse run
O'er Thought's bright surface, glittering in the sun;

Whereon, like birds, the flocks of fancy throng,
And all is peace and sweetness, light and song:

Anon, dim moods like shadowy woodlands rise
As 'twere between the spirit's earth and skies:

All fair suggestions, hints of twilight grace,
Safe harborage seek within the spell-bound space;

Music is there, low laughter, and the sound
Of fairy voices, echoing gently round

The cool recesses of the veilèd mind:
While on the surge of memory's phantom wind,

Ghosts of dead loves, swathed in a silvery mist
Pass by us; and the lips our lips had kissed,

In youth's glad prime, unutterable things
Whisper, through wafts of visionary wings.

Ah, yes! our *inward* world but mirrors true,
This *outward* world of sense; — it hath its dew,

Its sunshine, and fresh roses, white and red;
It holds a tender moonlight over head;

The dews of yearning, mild, or fiery-bright,
The flowers of peace, or passion; the calm light

Of reasoning thought, and retrospection fine,
All merged in subtlest beauty — half divine!

It hath its mounts of vision, and its vales
Of contemplation, where fond nightingales,

Born of the brain, and 'gainst some thorns of woe,
Setting their breasts — but sing more sweetly so:

Fountains it owns of shyest fantasie;
Glad streams of inspiration, swift and free,

Rolling toward Thought's central ocean vast
Wherein all lesser forms of thought, at last

Sink, as the rivulets perish in a sea; —
Thus, rounded, whole, our spirit-landscapes be,

Our spirit-world thus perfect; over all,
No clouds of doubt hang, stifling as a pall;

But if the soul be healthful, noble, high,
God's promise lights it, like a sleepless eye!

FOREST QUIET.

[In the South.]

So deep this sylvan silence, strange and sweet,
Its dryad-guardian, virginal Peace, can hear
The pulses of her own pure bosom beat;

And her low voice echoed by elfin rills,
And far-off forest fountains, sparkling clear
'Mid haunted hollows of the hoary hills;

No breeze, nor wraith of any breeze that blows,
Stirs the charmed calm; not even yon gossamer-chain,
Dew-born, and swung 'twixt violet and wild rose,

Thrills to the airy elements' subtlest breath;
Such marvellous stillness almost broods like pain
O'er the hushed sense, holding dim hints of death!

What shadows of sound survive, the waves' far sigh,
Drowsed cricket's chirp, or mock-bird's croon in sleep,
But touch this sacred, soft tranquillity

To yet diviner quiet: the fair land
Breathes like an infant lulled from deep to deep
Of dreamless rest, on some wave-whispering strand!

THE MOCKING-BIRD.

[At night.]

A GOLDEN pallor of voluptuous light
Filled the warm southern night:
The moon, clear orbed, above the sylvan scene
Moved like a stately queen,
So rife with conscious beauty all the while,
What could she do but smile
At her own perfect loveliness below,
Glassed in the tranquil flow
Of crystal fountains and unruffled streams?
Half lost in waking dreams,
As down the loneliest forest dell I strayed,
Lo! from a neigboring glade,
Flashed through the drifts of moonshine, swiftly came
A fairy shape of flame.
It rose in dazzling spirals overhead,
Whence to wild sweetness wed,
Poured marvellous melodies, silvery trill on trill;
The very leaves grew still
On the charmed trees to hearken; while for me,
Heart-trilled to ecstasy,
I followed — followed the bright shape that flew,
Still circling up the blue,
Till as a fountain that has reached its height,
Falls back in sprays of light
Slowly dissolved, so that enrapturing lay,
Divinely melts away
Through tremulous spaces to a music-mist,
Soon by the fitful breeze
How gently kissed
Into remote and tender silences.

A STORM IN THE DISTANCE.

[Among the Georgian Hills.]

I SEE the cloud-born squadrons of the gale,
Their lines of rain like glittering spears deprest
(While all the affrighted land grows darkly pale),
In flashing charge on earth's half-shielded breast;

Sounds like the rush of trampling columns float
From that fierce conflict; volleyed thunders peal,
Blent with the maddened wind's wild bugle-note;
The lightnings flash, the solid woodlands reel!

Ha! many a foliaged guardian of the height,
Majestic pine or chestnut, riven and bare,
Falls in the rage of that aerial fight,
Led by the Prince of all the powers of air!

Vast boughs, like shattered banners hurtling fly
Down the thick tumult: while, like emerald snow,

Millions of orphaned leaves make wild the sky,
Or drift in shuddering helplessness below.

Still, still, the levelled lances of the rain
At earth's half-shielded breast take glittering aim;
All space is rife with fury, racked with pain,
Earth bathed in vapor, and heaven rent by flame!

At last the cloud-battalions through long rifts
Of luminous mists retire; . . . the strife is done;
And earth once more her wounded beauty lifts,
To meet the healing kisses of the sun.

THE VISION BY THE SEA.

"A thing of beauty is a joy forever."

I.

A HAUNTING face! with strange, ethereal eyes,
Deep as unfathomed gulfs of tranquil skies
When o'er their brightness a vague mist is drawn,
Breathed from the half-veiled lips of melting dawn;
A mouth whose passionate love and sweetness seem
But just released from kisses in a dream;
A brow like Psyche's, pensive, broad, and low
And white as winter's whitest wreath of snow;
While round that gracious forehead, calmly fair,
Ripples an April rain of golden hair.

II.

For some rapt moments, on the ocean strand,
Unconscious, beautiful, I saw her stand,
As tremulous wave on wave, with freightage sweet
Of murmured music, fawned about her feet,
Then died in one divine, harmonious sigh;
The breeze bewitched, could only falter nigh,
And in shy delicate wafts of homage play
With her rare tresses; like incarnate May,
She seemed the earth, the tides, the heaven, to bless:
For once I gazed on Beauty's perfectness.

III.

I gazed for some rapt moments, but no more;
Then lowered mine eyes and slowly left the shore
Made marvellous by that vision of delight;
Yet evermore its beauty, day and night,
Standing between the blue sky and the sea,
Shines like a star of immortality
Through all my being; it becomes a part
Of the deep life that quickens soul and heart
To sense of things ideal and supreme —
A palpable bliss, yet wedded to a dream.

THE VISIONARY FACE.

I AM happy with her I love,
In a circle of charmed repose;
My soul leaps up to follow her feet
Wherever my darling goes;
Whether to roam through the garden walks,
Or pace the sands by the sea; —
There's never a shadow of doubt or fear
Brooding 'twixt her and me: —
But through memory's twilight mists,
Sometimes, I own, in sooth,
Falters the face of one I loved
In the fervent years of youth; —

The soft pathetic brow is there,
  With its glimmer and glance of golden hair,
And scarcely shadowed by death's eclipse
The delicate curve of the faultless lips,
The tremulous, tender lips I kissed,
So coyly raised at the sunset tryst,
As we stood from the restless world apart,
'Mid the whispering foliage, heart to heart,
  In the fair, far years of youth.
Yet, the vision is pure as heaven,
  Untouched by a hint of strife
From the passion that moved itself to sleep,
  On the morning strand of life;
And I know that my living Love would feel
  The tremor of ruthful tears,
If I told of the sweetness and hope that drooped,
  So soon in the vanished years:
She would not banish the phantom sad
  Of a beauty discrowned and low; —
Can jealousy rest in the rose's breast
  Of a lily under the snow ?
Can the passion so warm and strong to-day
  Envy a ghost from the cypress shades
    For an hour astray ?
Or, the love that waned like a blighted May,
  In the dead days, long ago,
    Ah! long, how long ago!

THE ROSE AND THORN.

She's loveliest of the festal throng
  In delicate form and Grecian face;
A beautiful, incarnate song:
  A marvel of harmonious grace;
And yet I know the truth I speak:
  From those gay groups she stands apart,
A rose upon her tender cheek,
    A thorn within her heart.

Though bright her eyes' bewildering gleams,
  Fair tremulous lips and shining hair,
A something born of mournful dreams,
  Breathes round her sad enchanted air;
No blithesome thoughts at hide and seek
  From out her dimples smiling start;
If still the rose be on her cheek,
    A thorn is in her heart.

Young lover, tossed 'twixt hope and fear,
  Your whispered vow and yearning eyes
Yon marble Clytie pillared near
  Could move as soon to soft replies;
Or, if she thrill at words you speak,
  Love's memory prompts the sudden start;
The rose has paled upon her cheek,
    The thorn has pierced her heart.

THE RED LILY.

I call her the Red Lily. Lo! she stands
  From all her milder sister flowers apart;
A conscious grace in those fair-folded hands,
  Pressed on the guileful throbbings of her heart!

I call her the Red Lily. As all airs
  Of North or South, the Lily's leaves that stir,
Seem lost in languorous sweetness that despairs
  Of blissful life or hope, except through her;

So this Red Lily of maids, this human flower,
  Yielding no love, all sweets of love doth take,
Twining such spells of passion's secret power
  As, woven once, what lordliest will can break ?

LAKE WINNIPISEOGEE.

One day the River of Life flowed o'er
The verge of heaven's enchanted shore,
And falling without lapse or break.
Its waters formed this wondrous lake.

Hence the far sheen of Eden palms
Is mirrored in its silvery calms,
And all its rich cerulean dyes
Are deep as Raphael's splendid eyes.

And hence the unimagined grace
Which sanctifies this lonely place,—
A subtle, soft, ethereal spell
Of light and sound ineffable.

Surely such tempered glory paints
The mystic City of the Saints;
Such music breathes its dying falls
Above the heavenly palace walls.

O lake of peace! whose still expanse
Gleams through a golden-misted trance,
Earth holds thee sacred and apart,
The cloistered darling of her heart.

LAKE MISTS.

[Composed near Lake Winnipiseogee.]

As I gazed on the prospect enchanted,
On waves the sun-glory had kissed,
There slowly swept down from the distance,
The phantom-like bands of the mist.

On their feet that were spectrally soundless,
They glided fantastic and chill,
While a prescient pallor crept over
The beauty of lake-side and hill!

All nature grew cold at their advent!
Like Thugs of the air, demon-born,
With their coils of blue vapor they strangled
The virgin effulgence of morn.

By that ambush of darkness was girdled
Each bright beam in dreary embrace,
Till the fairest young dawn of September
Lay wan on her death-shadowed face.

When wildly and weirdly from sea-ward,
A low wind how mournfully stole!
Like an anthem outbreathed for the morning,
Thus sternly divorced from her soul!

THE INEVITABLE CALM.

The sombre wings of the tempest,
In fetterless force unfurled,
Buffet the face of beauty,
And scar the grace of the world;

But they fade at length with the darkness,
And softly from sky to sod
Peace falls like the dew of Eden,
From the opened palm of God!

Earthquake, the angered Titan,
A continent cleaves apart;
Yet soon the glamour of quiet heals
Earth's smitten and tortured heart.

And soon o'er the ruin of cities
The sun-bright virginal grass
Courtesies and curves into dimples,
At the kiss of the winds that pass.

One lesson all nature teaches,
As balm to the troubled breast,
That after the turmoil of passion
There cometh a time of rest.

For the anguish of life wanes downward
Like fire unfanned by a breath;
And deep is the ashen stillness
On the hearthstone cold of death!

THE DEAD LOOK.

Lo! in its still, soft-shrouded place,
The pathos of a death-pale face!

I view the marks of mortal care
Time's hopeless sorrows branded there.

Waning beneath the noiseless glide
Of Lethe's dim, ethereal tide,

As furrows on some twilight lea
Fade in calm wave-sweeps of the sea!

Across that bare, unbended brow
The chrism of peace has fallen now,

And, lightening life's austere eclipse,
A star-soft smile hath touched the lips:

Though his sealed sight the death-mists mar,
He hath a strange look, fixed afar:—

As if wan folds of curtained eyes
Trembled almost in act to rise,

And show where each cold-lidded sheath
Now veils the wide, weird orbs beneath,

The mirrored glow, the blest surprise
Of some first glimpse of Paradise!

"While grimly down the moonlit bay,
The wrecked hull gleamed from far."

JETSAM.

Beside the coast for many a rood
Were fragments of a shipwreck strewn;
And there in sad and sombre mood
I walked the sands alone.

Torn bales and broken boxes lay,
Heaped high 'mid shattered sails and spar,
While grimly down the moonlit bay
The wrecked hull gleamed from far.

Well had the storm its mission wrought,
With thunder crash and billowy roar;
For not one precious waif was brought
Safe to the rugged shore.

Yet stay! what tiny sparkling thing
Shines faintly in the moonbeams cold?
I stooped, and wondering, grasped a ring,
A fairy ring of gold.

Of great and small, of rich and rare,
Of all yon stranded vessel bore,
Only this gem the waves would spare
To cast unharmed ashore.

With what a deep and tender thrill
I put the modest gem away,
And while the silvery vapors chill
Crept ghost-like up the bay,

I dreamed of shivering human lives
Wrecked on Fate's cold and cruel lee,
Trusting that some small hope survives,
Spared to them from the sea!

FAMELESS GRAVES.

I WALKED the ancient graveyard's ample round,
Yet found therein not one illustrious name
Wedded by Death to Fame.

The sea-winds moaned by each deserted mound,
Where mouldering marbles shed their pungent must
O'er that worn human dust.

Thin cloudlets passed, with purpled skirts of rain
Grazing the sentinel pine-trees, gaunt and tall;
Some trembling to their fall.

From out the misty marsh-lands next the main,
Long lines of curlews in the sunset flame,
With dissonant noises came;

O'erswept the tombs in slow, high-wheeling flight,
And while the sunset verged on evening's gray,
Faded, ghostlike, away.

Yet down the dusky, shimmering, weird twilight
(Though lost their forms beyond the outmost hill),
Their strange cries sounded still;—

Prolonged by elfin echoes, 'mid the rocks,
Or lapsing in sad, plaintive wails to die
'Twixt darkling wave and sky.

The garrulous sparrows, in home-wending flocks,
Sought their rude nests among those shattered tombs,
Veiled now in vesper glooms;

Till o'er the scene a mystic influence stole;
The wave-enamored winds their pinions furled;
Pale Silence clasped the world.

Beside a grave, the lowliest of the whole
Obscure republic of the fameless dead,
Pausing, I mused, and said:—

All graves are equal! His, the laurelled, great,
Miraculous Shakspeare's, some far day shall rest
As level on Earth's breast,—

And all unknown—through stern behests of Fate—
As this, round which the rustling dock-leaves meet
Here, tangled at my feet.

All graves are equal to all-conquering Time;
Scornful, he laughs at monumental stones,—
Wasting a great man's bones,

A great man's sepulchre, though reared sublime
Toward heaven, until both stone and record pass,
Mocked by the flippant grass;

The feeblest weeds in Nature flaunting high
Above a Shakespeare's or a Dante's dust:—
Just then a gentle gust

Breathed from beyond the gloaming: Night's first sigh
Of conscious life touched the awakened trees,
And blended with the sea's

Monotonous murmur, seemed to whisper low:
"I rise, and sink, am born, and lose my breath,
Yet am not held by Death.

"For since the world began — when sunset's glow
Melts in the western tides — my air of balm
Rises, if earth be calm.*

"My spell is sacred, wheresoe'er it falls;
The dreariest graves grow brighter at my voice,
And human hearts rejoice,

"Because that I, winged from these twilight halls,
In this, my life renewed, would subtly seem
A sweet, half-uttered dream

"Of immortality, made bright by love:
That love which binds the humblest human clod
Fast to the throne of God."

I left the graves; but now my gaze above
Ranged through the heavenly spaces, clear and far;
I marked the vesper star

Silver the edges of the wavering mist,
And centred in an air-wrought, luminous isle
Of lambent glory, smile; —

Smile like an angel whom the Lord hath kissed,
And freed from arms divine, in soft release,
To bless our earth with peace.

* What dweller by the ocean can have failed to remark the almost invariable rising, just after sunset on quiet evenings, of this gentle air, a very sigh of tranquillity, a breath, as it were, from God?

WINTER ROSE.

God's benison upon each happy day
Dead now and gone! — its gentle ghost our feet
Doth follow, singing faintly; and how sweet —
Tenderly sweet, as through a luminous mist —
Its shadowy lips draw near us, to be kissed!
And though they melt upon the yearning mouth
Like fairy balm from some phantasmal south,
Their touch is magic; and we feel the start
As of an unsealed fountain, close at heart —
Till, warmed, restored, breathing a fine repose,
Our innermost nature, wakening, glows anew;
While, gemmed by sunset memory's radiant dew,
Lo! the heart blossoms, like a Winter Rose!

TRISTRAM OF THE WOOD.

Once, when the autumn fields were dim and wet,
The trumpets rang; the tide of battle set
Toward gray Broceliande, by the western sea.

In the fore-front of conflict grimly stood,
Clothed in dark armor, Tristram of the Wood,
And round him ranged his knights of Brittany.

Of lordlier frame than even the lordliest there,
Firm as a tower, upon his vast *destrere*,
He looked as one whose soul was steeped in trance.

Ne'er spake nor stirred he, though the trumpet's sound
Echoed abroad, and all the glittering ground
Shook to the steel-clad warriors' swift advance;

Ne'er spake nor stirred he, for the mystic hour
Closed o'er him then; the glamour of its power
Dream-wrought, and sadly beautiful with love —

Love of the lost Iseult. In marvellous stead
Of thronging faces, with looks stern and dread,
Through the dense dust, the hostile plumes above,

He saw his fair, lost Iseult's passionate eyes,
And o'er the crash of lances heard her cries,
Shrill with despair, when last they twain did part.

While others thrilled to strife, he, thrilled with woe,
Felt his life-currents shuddering cold and low
Round the worn bastions of his broken heart.

Then rolled his way the battle's furious flood;
Squadrons charged on him blindly; blows and blood
Showered down like hail and water; vainly drew

The whole war round him; still his broadsword's gleam
Flashed in death's front, and still, as wrapped in dream,
He fought and slew, witting not whom he slew,

Nor knew whose arm had smitten him deep and sore —
So deep that Tristram never, never more
Shone in the van of conflict; but the smart

Of his fierce wound tortured him night and day,
Till, through God's grace, his life-blood ebbed away,
And death's sweet quiet healed his broken heart.

HINTS OF SPRING.

[COMPOSED IN SICKNESS.]

"When the hill-side breaks into green, every hollow of blue shade, every curve of tuft, and plume and tendril, every broken sunbeam on spray of young leaves is *new! No spring is a representation of any former spring!*" — GOETHE.

A SOFTENING of the misty heaven,
A subtle murmur in the air;
The electric flash through coverts old
Of many a shy wing, touched with gold;
The stream's unmuffled voice, that calls,
Now shrill and clear, now silvery low,
As if a fairy flute did blow
Above the sylvan waterfalls;
Each mellowed sound, each quivering wing
Heralds the happy-hearted Spring:
Earth's best beloved is drawing near.

Amid the deepest woodland dells,
So late forlornly cold and drear,
Wafts of mild fervor, procreant breaths
Of gentle heat, unclose the sheaths
Of fresh-formed buds on bower and tree;
A spirit of soft revival looks
Coyly from out the young-leaved nooks,
Just dimpling into greenery;
Through flashes of faint primrose bloom,
Through delicate gleam and golden gloom,
The wonder of the world draws near.

On some dew-sprinkled, cloudless morn,
She, in her full-blown joyance rare,
Will pass beyond her Orient gate,
Smiling, serene, calmly elate,
All garmented in light and grace:
Her footsteps on the hills shall shine
In beauty, and her matchless face
Make the fair vales of earth divine.
O goddess of the azure eyes,
The deep, deep charm that never dies,
Delay not long, delay not long!
Come clad in perfume, glad with song,
Breathe on me from thy perfect lips,
Lest mine be closed, and death's eclipse
Rise dark between
Me and thine advent, tender queen,
Albeit thou art so near, so near!

THE HAWK.

Ambushed in yonder cloud of white,
Far-glittering from its azure height,
He shrouds his swiftness and his might!

But oft across the echoing sky,
Long-drawn, though uttered suddenly,
We hear his strange, shrill, bodeful cry.

Winged robber! in his vaporous tower
Secure in craft, as strong in power,
Coolly he bides the fated hour,

When thro' cloud-rifts of shadowy rise,
Earthward are bent his ruthless eyes,
Where, blind to doom, the quarry lies!

And from dense cloud to noontide glow,
(His fiery gaze still fixed below),
He sails on pinions proud and slow!

Till, like a fierce, embodied ray,
He hurtles down the dazzling day,—
A death-flash on his startled prey;

And where but now a nest was found,
Voiceful, beside its grassy mound,
A few brown feathers strew the ground!

OVER THE WATERS.

I.

Over the crystal waters
She leans in careless grace,
Smiling to view within them
Her own fair happy face.

II.

The waves that glass her beauty
No tiniest ripple stirs:
What human heart thus coldly
Could mirror grace like hers?

THE TRUE HEAVEN.

The bliss for which our spirits pine,
That bliss we feel shall yet be given,
Somehow, in some far realm divine,
Some marvellous state we call a heaven.

Is not the bliss of languorous hours
A glory of calm, measured range,
But life which feeds our noblest powers
On wonders of eternal change?

A heaven of action, freed from strife,
With ampler ether for the scope
Of an immeasurable life
And an unbaffled, boundless hope.

A heaven wherein all discords cease,
Self-torment, doubt, distress, turmoil,
The core of whose majestic peace
Is godlike power of tireless toil.

Toil, without tumult, strain or jar,
With grandest reach of range endued,
Unchecked by even the farthest star
That trembles thro' infinitude;

In which to soar to higher heights
Through widening ethers stretched abroad,
Till in our onward, upward flights
We touch at last the feet of God.

Time swallowed in eternity!
No future evermore; no past,
But one unending NOW, to be
A boundless circle round us cast!

THE BREEZES OF JUNE.

OH! sweet and soft,
Returning oft,
As oft they pass benignly,
The warm June breezes come and go,
Through golden rounds of murmurous flow,
At length to sigh,
Wax faint and die,
Far down the panting primrose sky,
Divinely!

Though soft and low
These breezes blow,
Their voice is passion's wholly;
And ah! our hearts go forth to meet
The burden of their music sweet,
Ere yet it sighs,
Faints, falters, dies,
Down the rich path of sunset skies —
Half glad, half melancholy!

Bend, bend thine ear!
Oh! hark and hear
What vows each blithe new-comer,
Each warm June breeze that comes and goes,
Is whispering to the royal rose,
And star-pale lily, trembling nigh,
Ere yet in subtlest harmony
Its murmurs die,
Wax faint and die,
On thy flushed bosom, passionate sky,
Of youthful summer!

A MOUNTAIN FANCY.

[Respectfully inscribed to Mrs. R. S. Storrs.]

CLOSE to each mountain's towering peak
A white cloud leans its tearful cheek,
Till all its soul of mystic pain
Dissolves in slow, soft, vaporous rain.

Thus, when our heart-griefs seek aright
Some heavenly Thought's majestic height,
Their passion, touched by loftier air,
Dissolves in tender mists of prayer!

Jefferson Hill House, White Mountains, N.H., September, 1879.

ABSENCE AND LOVE.

WE need the clasp of hand in hand,
The light flashed warm from neighboring eyes:
Or else as weary seasons pass —
Alas! alas!
Our tenderest love grows wan and dies.

The fatal years like seas expand
'Twixt souls that long have dwelt apart,
Till, broadening o'er our being's verge,
The ruthless surge
Love's memory sweeps from out the heart.

O Absence! thou unreverenced Death!
Thy dense, unconsecrated clay
Inurns affection past regret;
No hint is set
Thereon of Resurrection Day.

THE FALLEN PINE-CONE.

I LIFT thee, thus, thou brown and rugged cone,
Well poised and high,
Between the flowering grasses and the sky;
And, as sea-voices dwell
In the fine chambers of the ocean-shell,
So fancy's ear
Within thy numberless, dim complexities
Hath seemed ofttimes to hear
The imprisoned spirits of all winds that blow;
Winds of late autumn that lamenting moan

Across the wild sea-surges' ebb and flow;
Storm-winds of winter mellowed to a sigh,
Long-drawn and plaintive; or—how lingeringly!—
Soft echoes of the spring-tide's jocund breeze,
Blent with the summer south wind, murmuring low!

What wonder, fairy cone, that thou should'st hold
The semblance of these voices? day and night,
Proudly enthroned upon the wavering height
Of yon monarchal pine, thou did'st absorb
The elemental virtues of all airs,
Timid or bold,
Measures of gentle joys and wild despairs,
Breathed from all quarters of our changeful orb;
Whether with mildness freighted or with might,
Into thy form they entered, to remain
Each the strange phantom of a perished tone.
An eerie, marvellous strain
Pent in this tiny Hades made to fold
Ghosts of the heavenly couriers long ago,
Sunk as men dreamed by ocean and by shore,
Into the void of silence evermore!

STERN TRUTHS TRANSFIGURED.

THOSE mountain forms of giant girth
Are rooted deep in moveless earth;
But lo! their yearning heights withdrawn,
Are melting in soft seas of dawn.

What golden lights and shadows kiss
Brown ledge and Titan precipice!
Till all the rock-bound, sullen space
Glows like a visionary face:
Thus frowning truths whose roots are furled
Round bases of some granite world,
May lift their mellowed light afar,
Transfigured by love's morning-star.

DISTANCE.

WHY is it that yon far-off, mellowed horn
Sounds like an antique story, half-forlorn,
Half-sweet, with iterance of rare echoes sent
Up the serenely listening firmament?

I thrill, soul-smitten by each melting tone
About the golden distant spaces blown,
As if soft pathos came on rhythmic sighs
From out the heart of vanished centuries.

Distance is magic! in its fairy hold
Are alchemies that change even dross to gold,—
While beauty's nymph, too closely seen or pressed,
Melts to mere shadow from the enamored quest!

HORIZONS.

I LOVE to gaze along the horizon's verge—
To strain my sight where steeped in golden-gray
The sun-illumined vapors gently surge,
To melt in measureless distances away.

I gaze and gaze, till tears bedim my eyes,
And tongueless fancies haunt me, vague and fond;
Ethereal boundary! blending earth and skies,
Ah! dost thou veil some marvellous realm beyond?

Deep spirit of mine! thou, too, art strangely bound
By far horizons, vaporous, dim, and vast;
Beyond the range of whose enchanted round,
Not even the genii of weird dreams have passed!

IN THE GRAY OF THE EVENING.

AUTUMN.

When o'er yon forest solitudes
The sky of autumn evening broods —
A heaven whose warp, but palely bright,
Shot through with woofs of crimson light,
So slowly wanes with waning day —
Whatever thoughts, pathetic, sweet
Are wont to fawn round Memory's feet,
Pleading with soft and sacred stress
To be upcaught in tenderness;
Whatever thoughts like these there are,
Choose the weird hour 'twixt sun and star,
Of failing breeze, and whisperous sea,
And that still heaven o'er leaf and lea,
To come — each thought a temperate bliss —
Embracing the calmed soul, to kiss
The pallor of old cares away.

O twilight sky of mellow gray,
Flushed with faint hues! O voiceful trees,
Lilting low ballads to the breeze!
O all ye mild amenities
Wherewith the solemn eve is rife,
At this strange hour 'twixt death and life;
The death of beauteous day, whose last
Dim tints are almost overpast,
Who lives alone in odors blent
Of every subtlest element,
Borne on a fairy rain-like dew,
Exhaled, not dropped from out the blue;
The life of stars that one by one
Are mustering o'er the sunken sun,
And wafts of vague earth-perfume blown
Up to the pine-tree's quivering cone,
From heath-flowers hidden in cool grass, —
Like spells of delicate balm, ye pass
Into my wearied heart and brain.

What room for any sordid pain
Within me now? Ah! Nature seems
Through something sweeter than all dreams,
To woo me; yea, she seems to speak
How closely, kindly, her fond cheek
Rested on mine, her mystic blood
Pulsing in tender neighborhood,
And soft as any mortal maid,
Half veilèd in the twilight shade,
Who leans above her love to tell
Secrets almost ineffable!

THE VISION AT TWILIGHT.

[To E. R., October, 1879.]

Without the squares of misted pane,
I saw the wan autumnal rain,
And heard, o'er tufts of churchyard grass,
The wind's low *miserere* pass.

Within, more bright for outward gloom,
I saw her wild-rose cheeks abloom,
And, deep as stars in uppermost skies,
The lustre of dark Syrian eyes!

Without, still drearier grew the sigh
Of the chill east wind shuddering by,
Wilder the sad, strange moaning made
Beneath the elm-trees' rayless shade.

Within, as if the embodied south
Had opened her enchanted mouth,
I caught, through twilight's gray eclipse,
The music from her gracious lips.

It breathed such sweetness, purely deep,
On my dull pain it dropped like sleep.
"How vain," I thought, "this gathering gloom;
Some heavenly presence fills the room!"

"O twilight sky of mellow gray,
Flushed with faint hues."

And when her warm hand, pulsing youth,
On mine she pressed in guileless ruth,
One moment, charmed through blood and brain,
I felt my own lost youth again!

With quickened heart and lifted head
I viewed the vision near my bed,
But lovelier for that envious gloom,
Her heavenly presence blessed the room!

AN HOUR TOO LATE.

I HAVE loved you, oh, how madly!
I have wooed you softly, sadly,
As the changeful years went by;
Yet you kept your haughty distance,
Yet you scorned my brave persistence,
While the long, long years went by.

Now that colder lovers leave you,
Now that Fate and Time bereave you
(For the cruel years *will* fly),
In your beauty's pale declension
You would grace with condescension
The love that touched you never
When your bloom and hopes were high.

Ah! but what if I discover
That too long in antique fashion
I have nursed a fruitless passion,
Whose rage and reign (thank Heaven!)
Are passed at length and over—
That fate hath locked forever love's golden Eden gate?
There's a wrong beyond redressing,
There's a prize not worth possessing,
And a lady's condescension
May come an hour *too late!*

"TOO LOW AND YET TOO HIGH!"

HE came in velvet and in gold;
He wooed her with a careless grace;
A confidence too rashly bold
Breathed in his language and his face.
While she—a simple maid—replied:
"No more of love 'twixt thee and me!
These tricks of passion I deride,
Nor trust thy boasted verity.
Thy suit, with artful smile and sigh,
Resign, resign:
No mate am I for thee or thine,
Being too low, and yet too high!"

His spirit changed; his heart grew warm
With genuine passion; morn by morn
More perfect seemed the virgin charm
That crowned her 'mid the ripening corn.
And now he wooed with fervent mien,
With soul intense, and words of fire,
But reverence-fraught, as if a queen
Were hearkening to his heart's desire.
She brightly blushed, she gently sighed,
Yet still the village maid replied
(Though in sad accents, wearily):
"Thy suit resign,
Resign, resign!
Lord Hugh, I never can be thine.
Too low am I, and yet too high!"

THE LORDSHIP OF CORFU.

A LEGEND OF 1516.

WHAT time o'er gory lands and threatening seas
Fair fortune, wearied, fled the Genoese—
What time from many a realm the waters woo
In the warm south, "*Who now shall rule Corfu?*"
Rose with the eager passion and fierce greed
Of those who preyed on every empire's need,—
There fell upon that isle's disheartened brave
A wild despair, such as in one dark grave
Might well have whelmed the prostrate nation's pride,
Her honor, strength, traditions—all beside

Which crowns a race with sovereignty. Sublime
Above the reckless purpose of his time
Their Patriarch stood, and such wise words he spake
The basest souls are thrilled, the feeblest wake
To some high aim, some passion grand and free,
Some cordial grace of magnanimity:
By such unwonted power they yield their all
To him that came, as if at Godhead's call,
To save the state, whose stricken pillars reel.

How works the Patriarch for his people's weal?
Calmly he bids them launch their stanchest keel—
A gorgeous galley: on her decks they raise
Great golden altars, girt by lights that blaze
Divinely, and by music's mystic rain,
Blent of soft spells, half sweetness and half pain,
Fallen from out the highest heaven of song.

And there, to purify all souls of wrong
And latent sin, he calls from far and near
Nobles and priests and people. Every where
The paths are full, which, sloping steeply down
From the green pasture and the wallèd town,
Lead oceanward, where, anchored near the quay,
That sacred galley heaved along the sea—
Her captain no rude mariner, with soul
Tough as the cordage his brown hands control,
But the gray Patriarch, lifting eyes of prayer,
While o'er the reverent thousands, calm in air,
The sacred host shone like an awful star.

"Children!" the Patriarch cried, "If strong ye are
To trust in heaven—albeit heaven's message sent
This day through me, seem strange, and strangely blent
With chance-fed issues—swear, whate'er betide,
When once our unmoored bark doth fleetly glide
O'er the blue spaces of the midland sea—
What flag soe'er first greets our eager view,
Our own to veil, and humbly yield thereto
The faith and sovereign claims of fair Corfu."

They vowed a vow methinks ne'er vowed before,
The while their galley, strangely laden, bore
Down the south wind, which freshly blew from shore.

Past Vido and San Salvador they sped,
Past stormy heights and capes whose rock-strewn head
Baffled the surges; still no ship they met,
Till, sailing far beyond the rush and fret
Of shifting sand-locked bars, at last they gain
The open and illimitable main.

There in one line two gallant vessels rode;
From this the lurid Crescent banner glowed,
From that the rampant Lion of St. Mark's!

Much, much they wondered when
athwart them drew,
With glittering decks, the galley from
Corfu,
Lighted by tapers tall of myriad dyes,
And echoing chants of holy litanies.

Soon unto both the self-same message
came;
For loud o'er antique hymn and altar
flame
Thrilled the chief's voice, "Hearken, ye
rival powers!
Whichever first may touch our armèd
towers*
Thenceforth shall be the lords of fair
Corfu!"

Changed was the wind, and landward
now it blew:
Smiting the waves to foam-flakes wild
and white.
All sails were braced, the rowers rowed
with might,
But soon the island men turned pale to
see
The Turk's prow surging vanward stead-
ily,
Till five full lengths ahead, careering
fast,
With flaunting flag and backward-swoop-
ing mast,
And scores of laboring rowers bent as one
Toward oars which made cool lightnings
in the sun,
The Paynim craft — unless some mar-
vellous thing
Should hap to crush her crew or clip her
wing —
Seemed sure as that black Fate which
urged her on
Victor to prove, and that proud island
race
To load with sickening burdens of dis-
grace!

* These "Towers," we must remember, were built in with the substance of the city walls, which rose abruptly out of the waters of the sea.

And now on crowded decks and crowd-
ed shore
Naught but the freshening sea wind's
hollow roar
Was heard, with flap of rope and clang
of sail,
Veering a point to catch the changing
gale,
Or furious lashes of the buffeting oar!

Just then the tall Venetian strangely
changed
Her steadfast course, with open port-
holes ranged
'Gainst the far town. Across the sea-
waste came,
First, a sharp flash and lurid cloud of
flame,
Then the dull boom of the on-speeding
ball,
Followed by sounds which to the isles-
men seem
Sweet as the wakening from some night-
mare dream —
The sounds of splintered tower and
crashing wall!
Then rose a shrill cry to the shivering
heaven —
"*Thus, thus to us your island realm is
given!*"
Burst as one voice from out the conquer-
ing crew:
"*Thus Venice claims the lordship of
Corfu!*"

TALLULAH FALLS.

ALONE with nature, where her passion-
ate mood
Deepens and deepens, till from shadowy
wood,
And sombre shore the blended voices
sound
Of five infuriate torrents, wanly crowned
With such pale-misted foam as that
which starts
To whitening lips from frenzied human
hearts!

Echo repeats the thunderous roll and boom
Of these vexed waters through the foliaged gloom
So wildly, in their grand reverberant swell
Borne from dim hillside to rock-bounded dell,
That oft the tumult seems
The vast fantastic dissonance of dreams;
A roar of adverse elements, torn and riven
In dark recesses of some billowy hell,
But sending ever through the tremulous air,
Defiance laden with august despair
Up to the calm and pitiful face of heaven!

From ledge to ledge the impetuous current sweeps
Forever tortured, tameless, unsubdued,
Amid the darkly humid solitude.
Through waste and turbulent deeps
It cleaves a terrible pathway, overrun
Only by doubtful flickerings of the sun.
To meet with swift cross-eddies, whirlpools set
On verges of some measureless abyss,
Above the stir and fret,
The lion's hollow roar, or serpent hiss
Of whose unceasing conflict waged below
The gorges of the giant precipice,
Shines the mild splendor of a heavenly bow.

But blinded to the rainbow's glory shed
Fair as the aureole 'round an angel's head
Still with dark vapors all about it furled
The demon spirit of this watery world,
Through many a maddened curve, and stormy throe,
Speeds to its last tumultuous overflow,
When downward hurled, from 'wildering shock to shock,
Its wild heart breaks upon the outmost rock
That guards the empire of this rule of wrath!
Henceforth, beyond the shattered cataract's path,
The tempered spirit of a gentler guide
Enters, methinks the unperturbèd tide;
Its current sparkling in the blest release
From wasting passion, glides through shores of peace, —
O'er brightened spaces and clear confluent calms,
Float the hale breathings of near meadow balms,
And still by silent cove and silvery reach,
The murmurous wavelets pass;
Lip the green tendrils of the delicate grass,
And tranquil hour by hour,
Uplift a crystal glass,
Wherein each lithe Narcissus-flower,
May mark its slender frame and beauteous face
Mirrored in softly visionary grace,
And still, by fairy-bight and shelving beach,
The fair waves whisper low as leaves in June
(Small gossips lisping in their woodland bower),
And still, the ever-lessening tide
Lapses, as glides some once imperious life
From haughty summits of demoniac pride,
Hatred and vengeful strife,
Down through time's twilight-valleys purified;
Yearning, alone, to keep
A long-predestined tryst with night and sleep,
Beneath the dew-soft kisses of the moon!

DIVIDED.

As not a bud that burgeons 'mid the bowers;
As not a leaf on any tree that grows,
But to its neighbor some unlikeness shows,
Made clearer still through all the blossoming hours.

Thus hath it chanced that, since the world began,
No soul hath found its fellow; fates may blend
In the close ties of lover, husband, friend,
Yet through some subtle difference, man from man
Severed, sees not his brother's innermost life;
The lover his sweet mistress knows in part,
And each to other half revealed in heart,
Pass deathward, the true husband and true wife.

Shall heaven make all things plain?
Nay, who can tell?
Only, sick heart! like the sore-wounded dove
Seeking her distant nest, *hold fast to love,*
Till death's deep curfew tolls its vesper bell.

"Gurgle, gurgle, gurgle,
Over ledge and stone."

THE MEADOW BROOK.

Gurgle, gurgle, gurgle,
Over ledge and stone;
How I'm going, flowing,
Westward, all alone;
All alone, but happy,
Happy and hale am I,
Clasped by the emerald meadows,
Flushed by the golden sky!

No kindred brook is calling,
To woo these tides in glee;
I hear no neighboring voices
Of inland rill, or sea;
But the sedges thrill above me,
And where I blithely pass,
Coy winds, like nymphs in ambush,
Seem whispering through the grass.

Tinkle, tinkle, tinkle;
Hark! the tiny swell
Of wavelets softly, silverly
Toned like a fairy bell,
Whose every note, dropped sweetly
In mellowed glamour round,
Echo hath caught and harvested
In airy sheaves of sound!

THE VALLEY OF ANOSTAN.

[In Ælian's "Various History," book iii., chapter xviii., the following legend, or parable, will be found. How vividly it recalls to us the words of the Master: "Unless ye be converted, and *become as little children*, ye cannot enter into the kingdom of heaven!"]

AN Orient legend, which hath all the light
And fragrance of the asphodels of heaven,
Smiles on us from old Ælian's mellowed page;
And thus it runs, smooth as the stream of joy
Whereof it tells, yet with some discord blent,
Which, hearkened rightly, makes the music true
To man's mysterious instincts and his fate:

In the strange valley of Anostan dwelt
The far Meropes, through whose murmurous realm
Two mighty rivers — one a stream of joy,
Divine and perfect; one a stream of bale —
Flowed side by side, 'twixt forest shades and flowers
(Bright shades and sombre, poison flowers and pure),
Down to a distant and an unknown sea.

On either bank were fruit-trees and ripe fruit,
Whereof men plucked and ate; but whoso ate
Of the wan fruitage of the stream of bale
Went ever after weeping gall for tears,
Till death should find him; but whoe'er partook
Of the rare fruitage of the stream of joy
Straightway was lapped in such ecstatic peace,
Such fond oblivion of all base desires,
His soul grew fresh, dew-like, and sweet again,
And through his past, his golden yesterdays,
He wandered back and back, till youth, regained,
Shone in the candid radiance of his eyes,
That still waxed larger, holier, crystal-clear,
With resurrection of life's tenderest dawn
Of childlike faith; by which illumed and warmed,
He walks, himself a dream within a dream,
Yearning for infancy. This found at last,
Gently he passes upward unto God,
Not through death's portal, wrapped in storms and wrath,
But the fair archway of the gates of birth!

TWO SONGS.

FIRST SONG.

LET me die by the sea!
When his billows are haughty and high,
And the storm-wind's abroad, —
When his dark passion grasps at the sky
With the power of a god, —
When all his fierce forces are free —
Let me die by the sea.

Let me die by the sea!
To his rhythms of tempest and rain,
I would pass from the earth,
Through death that is travail and pain,
Through death that is birth;
'Mid the thunders of waves and of lea,
Let me die by the sea.

Let me die by the sea!
When the great deeps are sundered and stirred,
And the night cometh fast,
Let my spirit mount up like a bird,
On the wings of the blast.

O'er the tumults of wave and of lea,
O'er their ravage and roar,
She would soar, she would soar,
Where peace waits her at last:
Oh! Fate, let me die by the sea.

SECOND SONG.

Ah, no! Ah, no! I would not go
While earth and heaven are black:—
When all is wildly drear and dark,
Guard, guard, O God! this vital spark!

But I would go when winds are low,
And distant, dreamy rills
Are heard to lapse with lingering flow,
Between the twilight hills:
With earth, and wave, and heaven at peace,
Then let these outworn pulses cease.

SONNETS.

ON VARIOUS THEMES.

I.

FRESHNESS OF POETIC PERCEPTION.

Day followed day; years perish; still mine eyes
Are opened on the self-same round of space;
Yon fadeless forests in their Titan grace,
And the large splendors of those opulent skies.
I watch, unwearied, the miraculous dyes
Of dawn or sunset; the soft boughs which lace
Round some coy dryad in a lonely place,
Thrilled with low whispering and strange sylvan sighs:
Weary? the poet's mind is fresh as dew,
And oft re-filled as fountains of the light.
His clear child's soul finds something sweet and new
Even in a weed's heart, the carved leaves of corn,
The spear-like grass, the silvery rim of morn,
A cloud rose-edged, and fleeting stars at night!

II.

LAOCOON.

A gnarled and massive oak log, shapeless, old,
Hewed down of late from yonder hillside gray,
Grotesquely curved, across our hearthstone lay;
About it, serpent-wise, the red flames rolled
In writhing convolutions; fold on fold
They crept and clung with slow portentous sway
Of deadly coils; or in malignant play,
Keen tongues outflashed, 'twixt vaporous gloom and gold.
Lo! as I gazed, from out that flaming gyre
There loomed a wild, weird image, all astrain
With strangled limbs, hot brow, and eyeballs dire,
Big with the anguish of the bursting brain:
Laocoon's form, Laocoon's fateful pain.
A frescoed dream on flickering walls of fire!

III.

AT LAST.

In youth, when blood was warm and fancy high,
I mocked at death. How many a quaint conceit
I wove about his veilèd head and feet.
Vaunting aloud. *Why need we dread to die?*
But now, enthralled by deep solemnity.
Death's pale phantasmal shade I darkly greet:
Ghostlike it haunts the hearth, it haunts the street,
Or drearier makes drear midnight's mystery.

Ah, soul-perplexing vision! oft I deem
That antique myth is true which pictured death
A masked and hideous form all shrank to see;
But at the last slow ebb of mortal breath,
Death, his mask melting like a nightmare dream,
Smiled, — heaven's high-priest of Immortality!

IV.

A PHANTOM IN THE CLOUDS.

All day the blast, with furious ramp and roar,
Sweeps the gaunt hill-tops, piles the vapors high,
Thro' infinite distance, up the tortured sky —
Till to one nurtured on the ocean-shore,
It seems — with eyes half-shut to hill and moor —
The anguished sea waves' multitudinous cry —
It changes! deepening . . Christ! what agony
Doth some doomed spirit on these wild winds outpour!
At last a lull! stirred by slow wafts of air!
When lo! o'er dismal wastes of stormy wreck,
Cloud-wrought, an awful form and face abhorred!
Thine, thine, Iscariot! smitten by mad despair,
With lurid eyeballs strained, and writhing neck,
Round which is coiled a blood-red phantom cord!

V.

JAPONICAS.

Beneath the sullen slope of shadowy skies,
Midmost this flowerless, wind-bewildered space
(Once a fair garden, now a desert-place)
Ah! what voluptuous hues are these that rise
In sudden lustre, on my startled eyes?
They glow like roses on an orient face,
Glimpsed in swift flashes of enchanting grace,
'Twixt the shy harem's gold-wrought tapestries!
Ye bright Japonicas! your glorious gleam
Tints with strange light the enamored waves of air,
And wafts of such coy fragrance round you float
Fancy transcends these boundaries blanched and bare,
For beauty lures her in a ravishing dream
Of roseate lips, dark locks, and swan-white throat!

VI.

THE USURPER.

For weeks the languid southern wind had blown,
Fraught with Floridian balm; thro' winter skies
We seemed to catch the smile of April's eyes;
A queenly waif, from her far temperate zone
Wayfaring — half bewildered and alone.
Yet, by the delicate fervor of her grace,
And the arch beauty of her changeful face,
Making an alien empire all her own.
So day by day that sweet usurper's reign
Gladdened the world. One eve the south wind sighed
Her soft soul out; the north wind raved instead;
All night he raved; when morning dawned again,
Winter, rethroned, looked down with scornful pride
Where April, dying, bowed her golden head!

VII.

DECEMBER SONNET.

ROUND the December heights the clouds are gray —
Gray, and wind-driven toward the stormy west,
They fly, like phantoms of malign unrest,
To fade in sombre distances away.
A flickering brightness o'er the wreck of day,
Twilight, like some sad maiden, grief-oppressed,
Broods wanly on the farthest mountain crest;
All nature breathes of darkness and decay
Now from low meadow land and drowsy stream.
From deep recesses of the silent vale,
Night-wandering vapors rise formless and chill,
When, lo! o'er shrouded wood and shadowy hill,
I mark the eve's victorious planet beam,
Fair as an angel clad in silver mail!

VIII.

A COMPARISON.

I THINK, ofttimes, that lives of men may be
Likened to wandering winds that come and go,
Not knowing whence they rise, whither they blow
O'er the vast globe, voiceful of grief or glee.
Some lives are buoyant zephyrs sporting free
In tropic sunshine; some long winds of woe
That shun the day, wailing with murmurs low,
Through haunted twilights, by the unresting sea;
Others are ruthless, stormful, drunk with might,
Born of deep passion or malign desire:
They rave 'mid thunder-peals and clouds of fire.
Wild, reckless all, save that some power unknown
Guides each blind force till life be overblown,
Lost in vague hollows of the fathomless night.

IX.

FATE, OR GOD?

BEYOND the record of all eldest things,
Beyond the rule and regions of past time,
From out Antiquity's hoary-headed rime,
Looms the dread phantom of a King of kings:
Round His vast brows the glittering circlet clings
Of a thrice royal crown; behind Him climb,
O'er Atlantean limbs and breast sublime
The sombre splendors of mysterious wings;
Deep calms of measureless power, in awful state,
Gird and uphold Him; a miraculous rod,
To heal or smite, arms His infallible hands:
Known in all ages, worshipped in all lands,
Doubt names this half-embodied mystery — Fate,
While Faith, with lowliest reverence, whispers — God!

X.

SONNET.

Written on a fly-leaf of "The Rubaiyat" of Omar Kháyyám, the astronomer-poet of Persia.

WHO deems the soul to endless death is thrall,
That no life breathes beyond that moment dire,
When every sense *seems* lost as outblown fire; —

Must walk, clothed round with darkness like a pall,
Or on false gods of sensual rapture call;
Pluck the rich rose-leaves! lift the wine cup higher!
Wed delicate Instinct to malign Desire,
(Like some Greek girl clasped by a barbarous Gaul!)
Thus Omar preached, thus practised, centuries since;
Wine, beauty, idlesse, orgies crowned by lust;
All these he chanted in voluptuous song;
Yet who shall vow, deep Thinker! poet Prince!
Thy rhythmic creed the unnatural voice of wrong,
If man, dust-born, shall still return to dust?

XI.

EARTH ODORS — AFTER RAIN.

LIFE-YIELDING fragrance of our mother earth!
Benignant breath exhaled from summer showers! —
All Nature dimples into smiles of flowers,
From unclosed woodland, to trim garden girth; —
These perfumes softening the harsh soul of dearth,
Are older than old Shinar's arrogant towers,—
And touched with visions of rain-freshened hours,
On Syrian hill-slopes 'ere the patriarch's birth!
Nay! the charmed fancy plays a subtler part!—
Lo! banished Adam, his large, wondering eyes
Fixed on the trouble of the first dark cloud!
Lo! tremulous Eve,— a pace behind, how bowed,—
Not dreaming, 'midst her painful pants of heart,
What balm shall fall from yonder ominous cloud!

XII.

SONNET.

I LAY in dusky solitude reclined,
The shadow of sleep just hovering o'er mine eyes,
When from the cloudland in the western skies
Rose the strange breathings of a tremulous wind.
As sound upborne o'er water, through some blind,
Mysterious forest, so this wind did rise.
Laden, methought, with half-articulate sighs,
Wafted like spirit-memories o'er the mind.
Then the night deepened; through my window-bars
I saw the gray clouds billowing fast and free,
Smit by the splendor of the solemn stars.
Then the night deepened; wind and cloud became
A blended tumult, crossed by spears of flame,
While the great pines moaned like a moaning sea.

XIII.

POVERTY.

ONCE I beheld thee, a lithe mountain maid,
Embrowned by wholesome toils in lusty air;
Whose clear blood, nurtured by strong, primitive cheer,
Through Amazonian veins, flowed unafraid.
Broad-breasted, pearly-teethed, thy pure breath strayed,
Sweet as deep-uddered kine's curled in the rare
Bright spaces of thy lofty atmosphere,
O'er some rude cottage in a fir-grown glade.
Now, of each brave ideal virtue stripped,
O Poverty! I behold thee as thou art,

A ruthless hag, the image of woeful dearth
Or brute despair, gnawing its own starved heart.
Thou ravening wretch! fierce-eyed and monster-lipped,
Why scourge forevermore God's beauteteous earth?

XIV.

WASTE.

How many a budding plant is born to fade!
How many a May bloom wilt with quick decay!
Ofttimes the ruddiest rose holds briefest sway,
While heart and sense are evermore betrayed
Alike in nature's shine and nature's shade.
Vainly earth-tendered seeds have sought the day,
And countless threads of rivulets wind astray,
For one that joins the vast main unembayed.
O prodigal nature, why this spendthrift waste
Of light, strength, beauty given to earth or man?
Thy richest realm may lie in trackless seas,
Thy tenderest loves, perchance, die unembraced;
While faith and reason watch thy 'wildering plan,
The baffled soul's cloud-compassed Hyades!

XV.

A MORNING AFTER STORM.

ALL night the north wind blew; the harsh north rain
Lashed like a spiteful whip at roof and sill.
Now the pale morning lowers, bewildered, chill,
Leaning her cheek against the misted pane,
Like some worn outcast, sick in heart and brain.
The wind that raved all night, though muttering still,
Moans fitfully, with faint, irresolute will,
Through dreary interludes, its low refrain.
In desolate mood I turn to rest once more,
Closing my senses to this hopeless morn,
This dismal wind. Still must the morning gloom,
Still the low sighing pass sleep's muffled door,
Till her veiled life is filled with dreams forlorn,
With hollow sounds and bodeful shapes of doom.

XVI.

DEAD LOVES.

WHENE'ER I think of old loves wan and dead,
Of passion's wine outpoured in senseless dust,
Of doomed affection's and long-buried trust,
Through all my soul an arctic gloom is shed;
And ah! I walk the world disquieted.
Thou, my own love! white lily of April! must
Thy beauty, perfume, radiance, all be thrust
Earthward, to crumble in a grass-grown bed?
Yea, sweet, 'tis even so! How long, how long
The dust of her who once was tender Ruth,
Hath mouldered dumbly! And how oft the clod,
Which binds, like hers, all perished love and truth,

Strives with pale weeds to veil death's hopeless wrong,
Or through chill lips of flowers appeals to God!

XVII.

NATURE AT EASE.

I FEEL the kisses of this lingering breeze,
Warm, close, and ardent as the lips of love,
I quaff the sunshine streaming from above,
Like mellow wine of antique vintages;
Now, serene nature, at luxurious ease,
Her deep toils perfected, and richly rife
With subtlest meanings — all her opulent life
Reveals in tremulous brakes and whispering seas.
If, then, the reverent soul doth lean aright,
Close to those voices of wood, wind, and wave,
What wondrous secrets bless the spiritual ear,
Born, as it were, of music winged with light,
Sweeter than those strange songs which Orpheus gave
To earth and heaven, while both grew dumb to hear!

XVIII.

THE CNYDIAN ORACLE.

"*What though the Isthmus lacks an ocean-gate,*
Delve not the soil! If Jove had willed it so,
His watchful power had opened long ago
The channelled pathways of a billowy strait."
Thus spake the Cnydian Oracle but too late;
For men are blinder than blind winds that blow
Round midnight waves, yet idly dream they know
Some Hermes' trick to steal the goods of fate.
Fools! trench your Isthmus, delving fast and deep;
And as ye toil uplift your boastful breath
O'er swift inrushings of the turbulent sea —
Too swift, by heaven! for, lo! its treacherous sweep
O'erwhelms the graded dykes, the opposing lea,
While ye that mocked at fate, fate whirls to death!

XIX.

THE HYACINTH.

HERE in this wrecked storm-wasted garden-close
The grave of infinite generations fled
Of flowers that now lay lustreless and dead,
As the gray dust of Eden's earliest rose.
What bloom is this, whose classical beauty glows
Radiantly chaste, with the mild splendor shed
Round a Greek virgin's poised and perfect head,
By Phidias wrought 'twixt rapture and repose?
Mark the sweet lines whose matchless ovals curl
Above the fragile stem's half shrinking grace,
And say if this pure hyacinth doth not seem
(Touched by enchantments of an antique dream)
A flower no more, but the low drooping face
Of some love-laden, fair Athenian girl?

XX.

THE WOOD FAR INLAND.

I CLOSE mine eyes in this lone inland place,
This wood, far inland, thronged with sombrous trees —

"Now, serene nature, at luxurious ease,
. . . all her opulent life
Reveals in tremulous brakes and whispering seas."

Our southland pines — in whose dark boughs the breeze
Mourns like a spirit shorn of joy and grace;
The same wild genius whose half-veilèd face
Dawns on the barren brink of wave-washed leas,
Fraught with the ancient mystery of the seas,
Whose hoary brow bears many a storm-bolt's trace;
I close mine eyes; but lo! a spiritual light
Steals round me: I behold through foam and mist
A dreary reach of wan, slow-shifting sand,
By transient glints of flickering star-beams kissed,
And hear upborne athwart the desolate strand
Voices of ghostly billows of the night.

XXI.

[Composed just after midnight on the 31st of December, 1878.]

A MOMENT since his breath dissolved in air!
And now divorced from life's last hectic glow,
He joins the old ghostly years of long ago,
In some cloud-folded realm of vague despair;
Ah me! the unsceptred years that wander there!
With cold, wan hands, and faces white as snow,
And echoes of dead voices quavering low
The phantom-burden of long-perished care!
Perchance all unsubstantialized and gray,
Time's earliest year now greets his last, deceased;
Or he that dumbly gazed on Adam's fall,
Palely emerging from the shadowy east,
With flickering semblance of cold crown and pall,
Clothes the dim ghost of him just passed away!

XXII.

MAGNOLIA GARDENS.

YES, found at last, — the earthly paradise!
Here by slow currents of the silvery stream
It smiles, a shining wonder, a fair dream,
A matchless miracle to mortal eyes:
What whorls of dazzling color flash and rise
From rich azalean flowers, whose petals teem
With such harmonious tints as brightly gleam
In sunset rainbows arched o'er perfect skies!
But see! beyond those blended blooms of fire,
Vast tier on tier the lordly foliage tower
Which crowns the centuried oaks' broad crested calm:
Thus on bold beauty falls the shade of power;
Yet beauty still unquelled, fulfils desire,
Unfolds her blossoms, and outbreathes her balm!

XXIII.

ENGLAND.

CLOUD-GIRDED land, brave land beyond the sea!
Land of my father's love! how oft I yearn
Toward thy famed ancestral shores to turn,
Roaming thy glorious realm in liberty;
All English growths would sacred seem to me,
From opulent oak to flickering wayside fern;
Much from her delicate daisies could I learn,
And all her home-bred flowers by lake or lea.

But most I dream of Shropshire's meadow grass,
Its grazing herds, and sweet hay-scented air;
An ancient hall near a slow rivulet's mouth;
A church vine-clad; a graveyard glooming south;
These are the scenes through which I fain would pass;
There lived my sires, whose sacred dust is there.

XXIV.

DISAPPOINTMENT.

Ah! phantom pale, why hast thou come with pace
Thus slow, and such sad deprecating eyes?
What! dost thou dream *thy* presence could surprise
One the born vassal of thy realm and race?
I looked in boyhood on thy clouded face;
In youth dissevered from all cordial ties,
Heard the deep echoes of thy murmured sighs
In many a shadowy, grief-enshrouded place;
Therefore, O sombre Genius, be not coy!
When have we dwelt so alien and apart
I could not faintly feel thy muffled heart?
Till even should hope's fruition softly shine,
I well might deem beneath the mask of joy
Lurked that sad brow, those twilight eyes of thine!

XXV.

THE LAST OF THE ROSES.

A royal rose! A rose how darkly red!
A proud, voluptuous, full blown flower, that sways
Her sceptre o'er the wind-swept garden-ways,
With mantling cheek and bold, imperious head!
Alone she lifts above yon desolate bed
A beauty past all terms of raptured praise,
The statelier that she rules in autumn days,
When every rival flower is dimmed or dead!
A haughty Cleopatra! there she smiles,
Unwitting that her sovereign love is lost —
Her Antony! a gorgeous sunflower bloom!
Ah! vain henceforth her beauty and sweet wiles!
Queen! art thou blind? Thy lord hath met his doom;
His Actium came with winter's vanguard — Frost!

XXVI.

THE AXE AND PINE.

All day, on bole and limb the axes ring,
And every stroke upon my startled brain
Falls with the power of sympathetic pain;
I shrink to view each glorious forest-king
Descend to earth, a wan, discrownèd thing.
Ah, Heaven! beside these foliaged giants slain,
How small the human dwarfs, whose lust for gain
Hath edged their brutal steel to smite and sting!
Hark! to those long-drawn murmurings, strange and drear!
The wail of Dryads in their last distress;
O'er ruined haunts and ravished loveliness
Still tower those brawny arms; tones coarsely loud
Rise still beyond the greenery's waning cloud,
While falls the insatiate steel, sharp, cold and sheer!

XXVII.

BETROTHAL NIGHT.

THROUGH golden languors of low glimmering light,
Deep eyes, o'erbrimmed with passion's sacred wine,
Heart-perfumed tears—yearning towards me, shine
Like stars made lovelier by faint mists at night;
Her cheeks, sweet lilies change to roses bright,
Blown in love's realm, fed by his breath divine;
And even those virginal tremors seem the sign
Of perfect joy through love's unchallenged right:
O happy breast, that heavest soft and fair
Through silvery clouds of luminous silk and lace!
O, gracious hands, O flower-enwoven head,
O'er which hope's charm its delicate warmth has shed!
While smiles and blushes wreathe her dimpling face,
Set in the splendor of dark Orient hair!

XXVIII.

"THE OLD MAN OF THE SEA."

GRIEVOUS, in sooth, was luckless Sindbad's plight,
Saddled with that foul monster of the sea;
But who of some soul-harrowing weight is free?
And though we veil our woe from public sight,
Full many a weary day and dismal night,
It chafes our spirits sorely! Yet, for thee,
Whate'er, O friend, thy special grief may be,
Range thou against it all thy manhood's might.
Thus, though thou may'st not smite on brow or breast
That irksome incubus, be sure some day
The load that blights shall droop and fall away,
And thou, because of torture borne so well,
Shall pass from out thy long, malign unrest
And walk thy future paths invincible!

XXIX.

TWO PICTURES.

SHE stood beneath the vine-leaves flushed and fair;
The dimpling smiles around her tender mouth,
Seemed born of mellow sunshine of the South;
A light breeze trembled in her unbound hair;
No young Greek goddess, in the violet air
Of vales immortal, shone with purer grace;
A delicate glory touched her form and face,
Whence the sweet soul looked on us, nobly bare, —
As Heaven itself, unclouded: — thus she stood,
But when I saw her next (O God! the woe!)
Love, mirth, and life had fled forever more;
Prostrate she lay, about her a dark wood,
And many a helpless mourner, wailing low;
The cruel waves which drowned her lapped the shore.

XXX.

THE MIGHT HAVE BEEN.

ONCE in the twilight hour there stole on me
A strange, sweet spirit! In her tender eyes

Shone a far beauty, like the morning skies,
And tranquil was she as a summer sea;
An air of large, divine benignity
Breathed, like a living garb of spiritual dyes
About her — with the gentle fall and rise
Of her heart pulses tuned to mystery —
But, as I gazed, a sadness deep as death
Crept o'er the beauty of her brow serene
And a faint tremor stirred her shadowy lips;
"Thou know'st me not, "she sighed, with mournful breath;
"How can'st thou know me? Lo, through Fate's eclipse,
Thou seest, too late, too late, thy MIGHT HAVE BEEN!"

XXXI.

NIGHT-WINDS IN WINTER.

WINDS! *are* they winds? — or myriad ghosts, that shriek?
Ghosts of poor mariners, drowned in Northern seas,
Beside the surf-tormented Hebrides,
Whose voices now of tide-born terror speak
In tones to blanch the boldest listener's cheek?
Hark! how they thunder down the far-off leas,
Sweep the scourged hills, and smite the woodland trees,
To die where towers yon glittering mountain-peak!
A moment's stillness! Then with lustier might
Of wing and voice, these marvellous wraiths of air
Fill with dread sound the ominous heights of night.
Athwart their stormful breath the star-throngs fade:
How dimmed is Cassiopæia's radiant chair,
While Perseus droops, touched by transfiguring shade!

XXXII.

TO THE QUERULOUS POETS.

THROW by the trappings of your tinsel rhyme!
Hush the crude voice, whose never-ending wail
Blights the sweet song of thrush, or nightingale, —
Set to the treble of our querulous time;
Is earth grown dim? Hath heaven her grace sublime,
Her pomp of clouds, and winds, and sunset showers
Merged in the twilight of funereal hours,
And Time's death-signal struck its iron chime?
O! false, frail dreamer! not one tiniest note
From yonder green-girt copse, but whispers "shame!" —
Love, beauty, rapture, swell the warbler's throat, —
The self-same joy, the passion blithe and young,
Thrilled by the force of whose immaculate flame,
The first glad stars, the stars of morning, sung!

XXXIII.

IN THE PORCH.

IN this old porch, fast mouldering to decay,
But wreathed in vines and girt by shadowy trees,
All day I hear the dreamful hum of bees,
Soft-rustling foliage, and the fragrant sway
Of breezes borne from some far ocean bay;
And oft with half-closed eyelids, stretched at ease —
The pines above me voiced like distant seas —
I seem to mark a coy young Dryad stray
Out from the tangled greenery overhead,

"Winds! *are* they winds?—or myriad ghosts, that shriek? . . .
Hark! how they thunder down the far-off leas."

Her brow leaf-crowned, her eyes of twilight fire
Deep with Arcadian mysteries softly shed;
And near her, wafted from the ambrosial South,
A white-limbed Nereid, round whose balmy mouth
Breathe the wave's freshness and the wind's desire.

XXXIV.

THE PHANTOM — SONG.

In museful hours, when thoughts of grace divine
Roll wave-like up the stormless strand of dreams; —
When that which *is* grows vague as that which *seems*, —
I mark, far-off, a radiant shade incline
From heaven to earth, — whose face of marvellous shine,
(Half veiled in mystic beauty), softly beams
With delicate lustres, and elusive gleams,
Caught from some viewless Eden — hyaline: —
Ethereal, as the wavering hues that start
From chorded rainbows; — lingering scarce so long
As the last sun-ray flashed in twilight's eye,
I hail this phantom of a perfect song; —
And I, some day, shall pass the phantom by. —
To feel the embodied music next my heart!

XXXV.

SMALL GRIEFS AND GREAT.

How oft by trivial griefs our spirits tossed
Drift vague and restless round this changeful world!
Yet when great sorrows on our lives are hurled,
And fate on us has wreaked his uttermost,
O'er wounded breasts our steadfast arms are crossed;
We front the blast, silent, with unbowed head
And stoic mien; for fear with hope is dead;
And calm the voice which whispers: *"All is lost!"*
Thence to the end, our being, stripped and bare
Of love, and peace, and gracious joys of of earth,
Like some storm-shattered tree, its withered might
May lift defiant, dauntless in its dearth,
Seeming Death's bolt, that final stroke, to dare,
A dreary watcher on a blasted height!

XXXVI.

THE SHALLOW HEART!

"Pity her," say'st thou, "pity her!" nay, not I!
Her heart is shallow as yon garrulous rill
That froths o'er pebbles: grief, *true* grief is still,
Deathfully solemn as eternity
Thro' whose dread realm its silent fancies fly
Seeking the lost and loved; sorrows that kill
Life's hope, are like those poisons which distil
Their noiseless dews beneath the midnight sky: —
Their venom works in secret! gnaws the heart,
And withers the worn spirit, albeit no sign
Shows the sad inward havoc, till some day,
(Pledging our calm friend o'er the purpling wine),
Sudden, he falls amongst us, and we start
At a low whisper, "He has passed away!"

XXXVII.

THE STORMY NIGHT.

[Written on a stormy Christmas night (1873).]

How roars this wintry tempest, fierce and loud,
Borne from far passes of the ice-locked hills!
How raves this desolate rain, whose tumult fills
The whole dark heaven up-piled with cloud on cloud;
While yonder quivering pine-trees, drenched and bowed,
Blend their strange moaning with the noise of rills,
And one swift stream, whose angry clarion shrills,
Piercing the mists which o'er it cling and crowd!
Roar, mighty wind! rave on, thou merciless rain!
Uproot, and madly ravage — whilst ye may;
Your furious voices smite mine ears in vain,
For, housed and warmed by this bright fireside cheer, —
Safe as on some calm springtide's calmest day,
I mock your ire, nor heed your wild despair.

PERSONAL SONNETS.

I.

TO HENRY W. LONGFELLOW.

I THINK earth's noblest, most pathetic sight
Is some old poet, round whose laurel-crown
The long gray locks are streaming softly down: —
Whose evening, touched by prescient shades of night,
Grows tranquillized, in calm, ethereal light: —
Such, such art *thou*, O master! worthier grown
In the fair sunset of thy full renown, —
Poising, perchance, thy spiritual wings for flight!
Ah, heaven! why shouldst thou from thy place depart?
God's court is thronged with minstrels, rich with song;
Even now, a new note swells the immaculate choir, —
But thou, whose strains have filled our lives so long,
Still from the altar of thy reverent heart
Let golden dreams ascend, and thoughts of fire!

II.

TO GEORGE H. BOKER.

Addressed to George H. Boker, of Philadelphia — after the perusal of Sonnets contained in his "Plays and Poems."

IT hath been thine to prove what use and power,
What sweetness, and what glorious strength belong
To the brief compass of that slandered song
We term the Sonnet. Thine hath been the dower
Whereby its richly fruitful, fairy shower
Of poesy hath flooded o'er our hearts;
And thine the dominant magic which imparts
Life to its thrilling music. Hour by hour,
My soul from this small fountain, in whose deep
The sunshine of thy passionate genius plays,
Doth drink delight, till fancy melts in sleep,
Charmed by the witchery of thy perfect lays, —
Not dreamless, but flushed through with joys that keep
Some fervent gleam of youth's voluptuous days.

III.

TO ALGERNON CHARLES SWINBURNE.

Not since proud Marlowe poured his potent song
Through fadeless meadows to a marvellous main,
Has England hearkened to so sweet a strain —
So sweet as thine, and ah! so subtly strong!
Whether sad love it mourns, or wreaks on wrong
The rhythmic rage of measureless disdain,
Dallies with joy, or swells in fiery pain,
What ravished souls the entrancing notes prolong!
At thy charmed breath pale histories blush once more:
See! Rosamond's smile! drink love from Mary's eyes;
Quail at the foul Medici's midnight frown.
Or hark to black Bartholomew's anguished cries!
Blent with far horns of Calydon widely blown
O'er the grim death-growl of the ensanguined boar!

But crowned by hope, winged with august desire,
Thy muse soars loftiest, when her breath is drawn
In stainless liberty's ethereal dawn,
And "songs of sunrise" her warm lips suspire:
High in auroral radiance, high and higher,
She buoys thee up, till, earth's gross vapors gone,
Thy proud, flame-girdled spirit gazes on
The unveiled fount of freedom's crystal fire.
When thou hast drained deep draughts divinely nurst
'Mid lucid lustres, and hale haunts of morn,
On lightning thoughts thy choral thunders burst
Of rapturous song! Apollo's self, new-born,
Might thus have sung from his Olympian sphere;
All hearts are thrilled; all nations hushed to hear!

IV.

TO EDGAR FAWCETT.

Art thou some reckless poet, fiercely free,
Singing vague songs an errant brain inspires?
Mad with the ravening force of inward fires,
Whose floods o'erwhelm him like a masterless sea?
No! art and nature wisely blend in thee!
Thy soul has learned from lays of loftiest lyres
What laws should bind weird fancy's wild desires,
Rounded to rhythmic immortality!
Thus golden thoughts in golden harmonies meet:
Thy fairy conceptions reel not with false glow,
Through frenzied realms by metrical motley swayed;
But passion-curbed, with voices strong and sweet,
Born of regret or rapture, love or woe,
Pass from rich sunshine to dew-haunted shade!

V.

CARLYLE.

O granite nature; like a mountain height
Which pierces heaven! yet with foundations deep,
Rooted where earth's majestic forces sleep,
In quiet breathing on the breast of night: —

Proud thoughts were his that sealed the infinite
Of loftiest grasp, and calm Elysian sweep;
Fierce thoughts were his that burnt the donjon keep
Of ancient wrong, to flood its crypts with light:
Yet o'er his genius, firm as Ailsa's rock,
Large, Atlantean, with grim grandeur dowered, —
Love bloomed, and buds of tender beauty flowered: —
Yet down his rugged massiveness of will
Unscarred by alien passion's fiery shock,
Mercy flowed melting like an Alpine rill!

VI.

TO JEAN INGELOW.

BRAVE lyrist! like the sky-lark, heaven-possessed,
Thy glance is sunward; and thy soul grown wise,
Fronts the full splendor of Apollo's eyes,
While following still thy muse's high behest:
Strength, sweetness, subtlety, are all expressed
In thy clear lays, — whether they dare the skies,
O'ertopping radiant dawns, or rill-like rise,
To thread with rhythmic pulse earth's pastoral breast!
Proud inspiration, hand in hand with act
Hath made thy winged feet beautiful along
The haloed heights of thine eternal song:
So near our human love, though born afar,
Its mellow concord on the listener's heart
Melts with the softness of a falling star!

VII.

TO M. I. P.

YOUR gracious words steal o'er like the breeze
That blows from far-off southland isles benign, —
All steeped in perfume, sweet as fairy wine,
Yet touched with salt keen breathings of the seas!
What smiling thoughts of tender ministries
Passionless service, and strong faith divine,
Rest with this pictured sister's face of thine,
And sister's love: — (blent fire and balms of ease!)
O love! a two-faced shield of light thou art,
Whose golden-sided glamour long hath shone,
In wedded bliss and affluence on my life;
A sister's love — the fair shield's silvery zone,
Turns on me now! — thy deathless fervor, wife,
Blends with the sweetness of this new found heart!

MACDONALD'S RAID. — *A.D.* 1780.

AS NARRATED MANY YEARS AFTER BY A VETERAN OF "MARION'S BRIGADE."

[The hero of the following ballad, though a Scotchman by birth, was a determined, enthusiastic Whig. Marion's men, among whom he served during the whole of the war for Independence, regarded him with an admiration bordering sometimes upon awe. His gigantic size and strength, and a species of "Berserker rage" which came over him in battle, were the means by which he performed many a feat of "derring-do," characteristic rather of the Middle Ages than the times of practical "Farmer George." Of all his desperate escapades, the raid through Georgetown, South Carolina, with a force of only four troopers (Georgetown being a fortified post, defended by a garrison of three hundred English regulars), proved, naturally enough, the most notorious. Authorities differ as to the origin and details of this remarkable affair. Some inform us that Sergeant Macdonald had been commanded by Marion to take a small party of his men and merely reconnoitre the enemy's lines, and that he chose to exceed his orders; while others affirm that Macdonald himself, acting independently, as he often did, proposed the mad scheme of "bearding the British lion in his den," as a charming relief to the *ennui* of camp life. The latter authorities have furnished the groundwork of our ballad. "Nothing," observes Horry, in his Life of General Marion, "ever so mortified the British as did this mad frolic. 'That half a dozen d——d young rebels,' they exclaimed, 'should thus dash in among us, in open daylight, and fall to cutting and slashing the *king's troops* at this rate! And after all, to gallop away without the least harm in hair and hide! 'Tis high time to turn our bayonets into pitchforks, and go to foddering the cows.'"]

I REMEMBER it well; 'twas a morn dull and gray,
And the legion lay idle and listless that day,
A thin drizzle of rain piercing chill to the soul,
And with not a spare bumper to brighten the bowl,
When Macdonald arose, and unsheathing his blade,
Cried, "Who'll back me, brave comrades? I'm hot for a raid.
Let the carbines be loaded, the war harness ring,
Then swift death to the Redcoats, and down with the King!"

We leaped up at his summons, all eager and bright,
To our finger-tips thrilling to join him in fight;
Yet he chose from our numbers *four* men and no more.
"Stalwart brothers," quoth he, "you'll be strong as fourscore,
If you follow me fast wheresoever I lead,
With keen sword and true pistol, stanch heart and bold steed.
Let the weapons be loaded, the bridle-bits ring,
Then swift death to the Redcoats, and down with the King!"

In a trice we were mounted; Macdonald's tall form
Seated firm in the saddle, his face like a storm
When the clouds on Ben Lomond hang heavy and stark,
And the red veins of lightning pulse hot through the dark;
His left hand on his sword-belt, his right lifted free,
With a prick from the spurred heel, a touch from the knee,
His lithe Arab* was off like an eagle on wing —
Ha! death, death to the Redcoats, and down with the King!

* Macdonald owned a magnificent horse, named Selim, of pure Arabian blood, which he obtained possession of through a cunning trick played at the expense of a certain wealthy Carolina Tory.

'Twas three leagues to the town, where, in insolent pride,
Of their disciplined numbers, their works strong and wide,
The big Britons, oblivious of warfare and arms,
A soft *dolce* were wrapped in, not dreaming of harms,
When fierce yells, as if borne on some fiend-ridden rout,
With strange cheer after cheer, are heard echoing without,
Over which, like the blast of ten trumpeters, ring,
" Death, death to the Redcoats, and down with the King!"

Such a tumult we raised with steel, hoof-stroke, and shout,
That the foemen made straight for their inmost redoubt,
And therein, with pale lips and cowed spirits, quoth they,
" Lord, the whole rebel army assaults us to-day.
Are the works, think you, strong? God of heaven, what a din!
'Tis the front wall besieged — have the rebels rushed in?
It must be; for, hark! hark to that jubilant ring
Of 'death to the Redcoats, and down with the King!'"

Meanwhile, through the town like a whirlwind we sped,
And ere long be assured that our broadswords were red;
And the ground here and there by an ominous stain
Showed how the stark soldier beside it was slain:
A fat sergeant-major, who yawed like a goose,
With his waddling bow-legs, and his trappings all loose,
By one back-handed blow the Macdonald cuts down,
To the shoulder-blade cleaving him sheer through the crown,
And the last words that greet his dim consciousness ring
With "Death, death to the Redcoats, and down with the King!"

Having cleared all the streets, not an enemy left
Whose heart was unpierced, or whose headpiece uncleft,
What should we do next, but — as careless and calm
As if we were scenting a summer morn's balm
'Mid a land of pure peace — just serenely drop down
On the few constant friends who still stopped in the town.
What a welcome they gave us! One dear little thing,
As I kissed her sweet lips, did I dream of the King? —

Of the King or his minions? No; war and its scars
Seemed as distant just then as the fierce front of Mars
From a love-girdled earth; but, alack! on our bliss,
On the close clasp of arms and kiss showering on kiss,
Broke the rude bruit of battle, the rush thick and fast
Of the Britons made 'ware of our rash *ruse* at last;
So we haste to our coursers, yet flying, we fling
The old watch-words abroad, " Down with Redcoats and King!"

As we scampered pell-mell o'er the hard-beaten track
We had traversed that morn, we glanced momently back,
And beheld their long earth-works all compassed in flame:
With a vile plunge and hiss the huge musket-balls came,
And the soil was ploughed up, and the space 'twixt the trees
Seemed to hum with the war-song of Brobdingnag bees;
Yet above them, beyond them, victoriously ring
The shouts, "Death to the Redcoats, and down with the King!

Ah! *that* was a feat, lads, to boast of! What men
Like you weaklings to-day had durst cope with *us* then?
Though I say it who should not, I am ready to vow
I'd o'ermatch a half score of your fops even now—

"I remember it well; 'twas a morn cold and gray, . . .
A thin drizzle of rain piercing chill to the soul."

The poor puny prigs, mincing up, mincing down,
Through the whole wasted day the thronged streets of the town:
Why, their dainty white necks 'twere but pastime to wring—
Ay! *my* muscles are firm still; *I* fought 'gainst the King!

Dare you doubt it? well, give me the weightiest of all
The sheathed sabres that hang there, uplooped on the wall;
Hurl the scabbard aside; yield the blade to my clasp;
Do you see, with one hand how I poise it and grasp
The rough iron-bound hilt? With this long hissing sweep
I have smitten full many a foeman with sleep—
That forlorn, final sleep! God! what memories cling
To those gallant old times when we fought 'gainst the King.

THE BATTLE OF KING'S MOUNTAIN.

Supposed to have been narrated by an aged volunteer, who had taken part in the fight, to certain of his friends and neighbors, upon the fiftieth anniversary of the conflict, viz. Oct. 7. 1830.

[Written for the Centennial Celebration of the battle on Oct. 7, 1880.]

OFTTIMES an old man's yesterdays o'er his frail vision pass,
Dim as the twilight tints that touch a dusk-enshrouded glass;
But, ah! youth's time and manhood's prime but grow more brave, more bright,
As still the lengthening shadows steal toward the rayless night.

So deem it not a marvel, friends, if, gathering fair and fast,
I now behold the gallant forms that graced our glorious past,
And down the winds of memory hear those battle bugles blow,
Of strifeful breath, or wails of death, just fifty years ago.

Yes, fifty years this self-same morn, and yet to me it seems
As if time's interval were spanned by a vague bridge of dreams,
Whose cloud-like arches form and fade, then form and fade again,
Until a beardless youth once more, 'mid stern, thick-bearded men,

I ride on Rhoderic's bounding back, all thrilled at heart to feel
My trusty "smooth-bore's" deadly round, and touch of stainless steel—
And quivering with heroic rage—that rush of patriot ire
Which makes our lives from head to heel, one seething flood of fire.

There are some wrongs so blackly base, the tiger strain that runs,
And sometimes maddens thro' the veins, of Adam's fallen sons,
Must mount and mount to furious height, which only blood can quell,
Who smite with hellish hate must look for hate as hot from hell!

And hide it as we may with words, its awful need confessed,
War is a death's-head thinly veiled, even warfare at its best;
But *we*—heaven help us!—strove with those by lust and greed accurst,
And learned what untold horrors wait on warfare at its worst.

You well may deem my soul in youth dwelt not on thoughts like these;
Timed to strong Rhoderic's tramp my pulse grew tuneful as the breeze,
The hale October breeze, whose voice, borne from far ocean's marge,
Pealed with the trumpet's resonance, which sounds "To horse, and charge!"

A mist from recent rains was spread about the glimmering hills;
Far off, far off, we heard the lapse of streams and swollen rills,
While mingling with them, or beyond, from depths of changeful sky,
Rose savage, sullen, dissonant, the eagle's famished cry.

We marched in four firm columns, nine hundred men and more,
Men of the mountain fortresses, men of the sea-girt shore;

Rough as their centuried oaks were these, those fierce as ocean's shocks,
When mad September breaks her heart across the Hatteras rocks.

We marched in four firm columns, till now the evening light
Glinted through rifting cloud and fog athwart the embattled height,
Whereon, deep-lined, in dense array of scarlet, buff or dun,
The haughtiest British "regulars" outflashed the doubtful sun.

Horsemen and footmen centred there, unflinching rank on rank,
And the base Tories circled near, to guard each threatened flank;
But, pale, determined, sternly calm, our men, dismounting, stood,
And at their leader's cautious sign, crouched in the sheltering wood.

What scenes come back of ruin and wrack, before those ranks abhorred!
The cottage floor all fouled with gore, the axe, the brand, the cord;
A hundred craven deeds revived, of insult, injury, shame—
Deeds earth nor wave nor fire could hide, and crimes without a name.

Such thoughts but hardened soul and hand. Ha! "dour as death" were we,
Waiting to catch the voice which set our unleashed passion free.
At last it came deep, ominous, when all the mountain ways
Burst from awed silence into sound, and every bush ablaze.

Sent forth long jets of wavering blue, wherefrom, with fatal dart,
The red-hot Deckhard bullets flew, each hungering for a heart;
And swift as if our fingers held strange magic at their tips,
Our guns, reloaded, spake again from their death-dealing lips,

Again, again, and yet again, till in a moment's hush,
We heard the order, "Bay'nets charge!" when, with o'ermastering rush,
Their "regulars" against us stormed, so strong, so swift of pace,
They hurled us backward bodily for full three furlongs' space.

But, bless you, lads, we scattered, dodged, and when the charge was o'er,
Felt fiercer, pluckier, madder far, than e'er we had felt before;
From guardian tree to tree we crept, while upward, with proud tramp,
The British lines had slowly wheeled to gain their 'leaguered camp.

Too late; for ere they topped the height, Hambright and Williams strode
With all their armèd foresters, across the foeman's road,
What time from right to left there rang the Indian war-whoop wild,
Where Sevier's tall Waturga boys through the dim dells defiled.

"Now, by God's grace," cried Cleaveland (my noble colonel he),
Resting (to pick a Tory off) quite coolly on his knee—
"Now, by God's grace, we have them! the snare is subtly set;
The game is bagged; we hold them safe as pheasants in a net."

And thus it proved; for galled and pressed more closely hour by hour,
Their army shrank and withered fast, like a storm-smitten flower;
Blank-eyed, wan-browed, their bravest lay along the ensanguined land,
While of the living, few had 'scaped the bite of ball or brand.

Yet sturdier knave than Ferguson ne'er ruled a desperate fray:
By heaven! you should have seen him ride, rally, and rave that day,
His fleet horse scoured the stormy ground from rock-bound wall to wall,
And o'er the rout shrilled wildly out his silvery signal call.

"That man must die before they fly, or yield to us the field."
Thus spake I to three comrades true beneath our oak-tree shield;
And when in furious haste again the scarlet soldiers came
Beside our fastness like a fiend, hurtling through dust and flame,

Their sharp demurrers on the wind our steadfast rifles hurled,
And one bold life was stricken then from out the living world.
But, almost sped, he reared his head, grasping his silver call,
And one long blast, the faintest, last, wailed round the mountain wall.

Ah, then the white flags fluttered high; then shrieks and curses poured
From the hot throats of Tory hounds beneath the avenger's sword —
Those lawless brutes who long had lost all claims of Christian men,
Whereof by sunset we had hanged the worst and vilest ten.

. . . . .

We slept upon the field that night, 'midmost our captured store,
That seemed in gloating eyes to spread and heighten more and more.
Truly the viands ravished us; our clamorous stomachs turned
Eager toward the provender for which they sorely yearned.

Apicius! what a feast was there blended of strong and sweet,
Cured venison hams, Falstaffian pies, and fat pigs' pickled feet:
While here and there, with cunning leer, and sly Silenus wink,
A stoutish demijohn peered out, and seemed to gurgle, "Drink!"

Be sure we revelled merrily, till eyes and faces shone;
Our lowliest felt more lifted up than any king on throne;
Our singers trolled; our jesters' tongues were neither stiff nor dumb;
And, by Lord Bacchus! how we quaffed that old Jamaica rum!

Perchance (oh, still, through good and ill, his honest name I bless!) —
Perchance my brother marked in me some symptoms of excess;
For gently on my head he laid his stalwart hand and true,
And gently led me forth below the eternal tent of blue;

He led me to a dewy nook, a soft, sweet, tranquil place,
And there I saw, upturned and pale, how many a pulseless face!

"That man must die before they fly, or yield to us the field."

Our comrades dead — they scarce seemed fled, despite their ghastly scars,
But wrapped in deep, pure folds of sleep beneath the undying stars.

My blood was calmed; all being grew exalted as the night,
Whence solemn thoughts sailed weirdly down, like heavenly swans of white,
With herald strains ineffable, whose billowy organ-roll —
Thrilled to the loftiest mountain peaks and summits of my soul.

Then voices rose (or seemed to rise) close to the raptured ear,
Yet fraught with music marvellous of some transcendent sphere,
While fancy whispered: These are tones of heroes, saved and shriven,
Who long have swept the harps of God by stormless seas in heaven!

Heroes who fought for right and law, but, purged from selfish dross,
Above whose conquering banners waved a shadowy Christian cross:
Whose mightiest deed no ruthless greed had smirched with sad mistrust,
And whose majestic honors scorn all taint of earthly dust.

Doubt, doubt who may! but, as I live, on the calm mountain height
Those voices soared, and sank, and soared up to the mystic night.
A dream! perhaps; but, ah! such dreams in ardent years of youth
Transcend, as heaven transcends the earth, your sordid daylight truth.

The voices soared, and sank, and soared, till, past the cloud-built bars,
They fainted on the utmost strand and silvery surge of stars.
Then *something* spoke: Your friends who strove the battle tide to stem,
Who died in striving, have passed up beyond the stars with them.

. . . . .

What, lads! you think the old man crazed to talk in this high strain,
Or deem the punch of years gone by still buzzes in his brain?
Down with such carnal fantasy! nor let your folly send
Its blunted shafts to smite the truth you may not comprehend.

Would ye be worthy of your sires who on King's Mountain side
Welcomed dark death for freedom's sake as bridegrooms clasp a bride?
Then must your faith be winged above the world, the worm, the clod,
To own the veiled infinitudes and plumbless depths of God!

The roughest rider of my day shrank from the atheist's sneer,
As if Iscariot's self were crouched and whispering at his ear;
The stormiest souls that ever led our mountain forays wild
Would ofttimes show the simple trust, the credence, of a child.

True faith goes hand in hand with power — faith in a holier charm
Than fires the subtlest mortal brain, the mightiest mortal arm;
And though 'tis right in stress of fight "to keep one's powder dry,"
What strength to feel, beyond our steel, burns the great Captain's eye!

THE HANGING OF BLACK CUDJO.

(1780.)

A DIALECT BALLAD.

The incidents of this Ballad are literally true. Our readers will find them circumstantially recorded in Horry's "Life of Marion." Captain Snipes (Phoebus! *what* a name) was a notable patriot during the Revolutionary war, but is likely to be known to the future, rather as the master of Cudjo, than as an active member of a Partisan Band.

He resided in the low country of South Carolina; and Cudjo's quaint *patois* is an *exact* representation of the broken English spoken by the slaves of that section in the *ante bellum* times:

"WELL, Maussa! if you wants to heer, I'll tell you 'bout um 'true.
Doh de berry taut ob dat bad time is fit to tun me blue;
A sort ob brimstone blue on black, wid jist a stare o' wite,
As when dem cussed Tory come fur wuck deir hate dat nite!

"Mass Tom and me was born, I tink, 'bout de same year and day,
And we was boys togedder, Boss! in ebbery sport and play —
Ole missis gib me to Mass Tom wid her las' failin bret:
And so I boun' — in conscience boun', fur stick to him till det.

"At las' ole Maussa, *he* teck sick wid chill and feber high,
And de good Dokter shake 'e head, and say he sur fur die,
And so true 'nuff de sickness bun' and freeze out all he life,
And soon ole Maussa sleep in peace long side e' fateful wife.

"Den ebbery ting de lan' could show, de crap, de hoss, de cows,
Wid all dem nigger in de fiel', and all dem in de house,
Dey b'long to my Mass Tom fur true, and so dat berry year,
He pick *me* out from all de folks to meck me Obersheer!

"I done my bes', but niggars, sir — dey seems a lazy pack,
One buckra man will do mo' wuck dan five and twenty black,
I jeered dem and I wolloped dem, and cussed dem too — but law!
De Debble self could nebber keep dem rascal up to tau!

"But still we done as good as mose, wid cotton, rice and corn,
Till in de year dat '*Nuttin' tall*' * (my oldest chile) was born,
De Tory war, de bloody war, 'bout which you've heerd dem tell,
Come down on all de country yeh, as black and hot as hell!

"Mass Tom he jine de Whig, you know; in course I follow him,
And Gor' a mighty! how he slash dem Tory limb from limb,
When fust I heer the war-cry shout and see de flow ob blood'—
I long fur hide this woolly head like cootah in de mud!

---

* The negro is a humorous creature. We have credibly heard of a negro father whose son being *abnormally small*, at birth, coolly had the ebony youngster christened, "*Nuttin' Tall* (*Nothing at all*). We have borrowed so characteristic a name, and bestowed it upon Cudjo's supposititious "son and heir."

This is the single touch of fancy in the whole ballad.

"But Lawd! I soon git n'used to blood, de broadswed and de strife,
And nebber care a pig tail eend fur 'tudder folks's life;
Only, I heerd my Maussa yell thro' all dem battle-call,
And sneaked dis big fat karkiss up betwixt him and de ball!

"Well, sir! one day Mass Tom come home, 'e close and hoss blood red,
And say sense all dem Tory kill, he gwine dat once to bed;
'I needs a long fine snooze,' sez he, 'so don't you wake me soon,
'But Cudjo! let me snore oncalled till late to-morrow noon!';

"Somehow, my mine misgib me dem; so by de kitchin light,
I sot and smoked, with open ears, a listenen' true de nite:
And when de fus cock crow, I heer a fur soun, down de road,
And knowed 'um fur de hosses' trot, and de clash ob spur and sword:

"Quick I run outside in de yad, and quick outside de gate —,
And there I see de Tory come as fas' and sho' as fate;
I run back to my Maussa room, and den wid pull and push
I shub 'um by de side way out, and hide 'um in de bush!

"He only hab he nite shut on, and how he rabe and cuss!
'But Maussa! hush,' sez I, 'before you meck dis matter wuss;'
I tun to fin' some hidin' too, but de moon shine bright as sun,
And de d—d Tory ride so swif', dey ketch me on de run.

"Den, dey all screech togedder, loud, 'Boy, is your Boss widin?
'Say where he hide, or by de Lawd! your life not wut a pin!'
I trembled at dese horrid tret, but sweer my Boss was fled,
Yet when, or where, poor Cudjo knowed no better dan de dead.

"One Tory debble teck my head, another teck my foot
To drag me like a Chrismass hog to de ole oak tree root;
Dey fling a tick rope roun' my neck, dey drawed me quick and high,
I seed a tousan' million star a-flashin' from de sky.

"And den I choke, and all de blood keep rushin' to my head
I tried to yell, but only groaned, and guggled low enstead;
Till ebbery ting growed black as nite, and my last taut was, sho,
Dis nigger is a gone coon now, he'll see de wuld no mo'!

"But, Boss! I was a hale man den, and tough as tough could be;
Dey loose de rope and let me down quite safely from de tree;
But when I seed and heered agen, come de same furious cry,
'Say where your Maussa hide, you dog, quick, quick, or else you die!'

"I gib dem de same answer still, and so, dey hang me higher;
I feel de same hot chokin' sob; see de same starry fire;
Dey heng me twice, tree time dey heng; but de good Lawd was dere,
And Jesus self, *he* bring me safe from all de pain and fear.

"Mose dead dey lef' me, stiff and cole, stretched on de swashy groun'
While all de house, big house and small, was blazin', fallin' roun'.
When pore Mass Tom from out de briar creep in he half-torn shut,
To bless and ring me by bote han' dere in de damp and dut!

"And when de war was ober, Boss, Mass Tom, he come to me,
And say, I sabe he life dat time, and so he meck me free;
'I'll gib you house and lan' (sez he,) 'and wid dem plough and mule,'
I tenk him kind, 'but Boss,' (says I,) 'wha' meck you tink me fool?'

"'If you, Mass Tom, was like," (sez I,) *some* buckra dat I know,
Cudjo bin run and hug de swamp — Lawd bless you! — long ago,
But I got all ting dat I want, wid not one tax to pay;
Now go long, Maussa! why you wish for dribe ole Cuj away?

"'I nebber see free nigger yet, but what he lie and steal,
Lie to 'e boss, 'e wife, 'e chile, in de cabin, and de fiel' —
And as for tieffin', dem free cuss is all like 'lightfoot Jack,'
Who carry de lass blanket off from he sick mudder back!

"'I stays wid you, (sez I again,) I meck de nigger wuck,
I wuck myself, and may be, Boss, we'll bring back de ole luck;
But don't you pizen me no more wid talk ob "freedom sweet,"
But sabe dat gab to stuff de years of de next fool you meet!'"

CHARLESTON RETAKEN.

DEC. 14, 1782.

As some half-vanquished lion,
  Who long hath kept at bay
A band of sturdy foresters
  Barring his blood-stained way —
Sore-smitten, weak and wounded —
  Glares forth on either hand;
Then, cowed with fear, his cavernous lair
  Seeks in the mountain land:

So when their stern Cornwallis,
  On Yorktown heights resigned,
His sword to our great leader,
  Of the stalwart arm and mind —
So when both fleet and army
  At one grand stroke went down
And Freedom's heart beat high once more
  In hamlet, camp and town; —

Through wasted Carolina,
  Where'er from plain to hill
The Briton's guarded fortresses
  Uprose defiant still,
Passed a keen shock of terror,
  And the breasts of war-steeled men
Quailed in the sudden blast of doom
  That smote their spirits then.

"Our cause is lost!" they muttered,
  Pale browed, with trembling lips;
"Our strength is sapped, our hope o'erwhelmed,
  In final, fierce eclipse;
And what to us remaineth
  But to blow our earthworks high,
And hurl our useless batteries
  In wild fire to the sky?"

'Twas done! each deadly fastness
  In flaming fragments driven
Farther than e'er *their* souls could climb
  Along the path to heaven —
Coastward the Britons hurried,
  In reckless throngs that flee
Wild as December's scattered clouds
  Storm-whirled toward the sea.

In Charleston streets they gathered,
  Each dazed wiseacre's head
Wagging, perchance in prophecy,
  Or more perchance in dread.
Horsemen and footmen mingled,
  They talked with bated breath
Of the shameful fate that stormed the gate,
  Of wrack, and strife, and death!

"Three hundred noble vessels
  Rose on the rising flood,
Wherein with sullen apathy
  Embarked those men of blood."

Meanwhile our squadrons hastened,
  Keen as a sleuth-hound pack
That near their destined quarry
  By some drear wild-wood track,
Ah, Christ! what desolation
  Before us grimly frowned!
The roadways trenched and furrowed,
  The gore-ensanguined ground,
With many a mark (oh! deep and dark!)
  Made ghastlier by the star-white frost,
'Twixt broken close and thorn-hedge-row,
Of desperate charge and mortal blow
  In conflicts won or lost!

Proud manors once the centre
  Of jubilant life and mirth,
Now silent as the sepulchre,
  Begirt by ruin and dearth;
Their broad domains all blackened
  With taint of fire and smoke,
And corpses vile with a death's-head smile,
  Swung high on the gnarlèd oak.

No sportive flocks in the pasture,
  No aftermath on the lea;
No laugh of the slaves at labors
  No chant of birds on the tree;
But all things bodeful, dreary,
  As a realm by the Stygian flood,
With odors of death on the uplands,
  And a taste in the air of blood!

On, on our squadrons hastened,
  Sick with the noisome fumes
From man and beast unburied,
  Through the dull funeral gloom

Till in unsullied sunshine
One glorious morn we came
Where far aloof, o'er tower and roof,
We viewed our brave St. Michael's spire
Flushed in the noontide flame!

Without their ruined ramparts,
Beyond their shattered lines,
Just where the soil, bent seaward,
In one long slope declines,
The foe had sent their messengers,
Who vowed the vanquished host
Would leave unscathed our city,
Would leave unscathed our coast!

Only due time they prayed for
(Meek, meek our lords had grown)
To range their broken legions,
And rear ranks overthrown —
So that, though smirched and tainted
Their martial fame might be,
In order meet their stately fleet
Should bear them safe to sea.

Who win, may well be gracious;
We did not stint their boon,
Though the white 'kerchiefs of our wives
Were fluttered in the noon,
On house-top and on parapet
Each token fair and far
Shone through the golden atmosphere
Like some enchanted star!

Next morn their signal-cannon
Roared from the vanward wall,
And to the ranks right gleefully
We gathered, one and all,
Our banners scarred in many a fight,
Could still flash back the winter light,
And proud as knights of old renown,
With sunburnt hands and faces brown,

Borne through the joyous, deepening hum,
'Mid ring of fife and beat of drum,
'Mid purpling silk and flowery arch,
Our long, unwavering columns march;
And yet (good sooth!) we almost seem
Like weird battalions of a dream;
Our souls bewildered scarce can deem
We tread once more,
Released, secure,
With fetterless footsteps as of yore,
The pathways of the ancient town!

And still, as borne through dreamland,
We glanced from side to side,
While mothers, wives and daughters rushed
To greet us, tender-eyed;
Each hoary patriot proudly
Lifted his brave, gray head,
And the forms of careworn captives rose
Like spectres from the dead —

Like spectres whom the trumpets
Of freedom's cohorts call
To burst their grave-like dungeon,
And spurn their despot's thrall;
To take once more the image
Of manhood's loftier grace,
And, chainless now, the universe
Look boldly in the face!

And the young girls scattered flowers,
And the lovely dames were bright
With something more than beauty,
In their faithful hearts' delight;
The very babes were crowing
Shrill welcome to our bands,
And, perched on matron shoulders, clapped
Blithely their dimpled hands:

And naught but benedictions
Lightened that sacred air,
Freed from the awful burden
Of two long years' * despair —
Two years so thronged with anguish,
So fraught with bitter wrong,
They seemed in mournful retrospect
Well nigh a century long.

* The precise period of the British occupation of Charleston was two years, seven months and two days.

But if years of mortal being
Trebled threescore and ten,
At the last, our souls exultant,
Would recall that scene again,
With its soft "God bless you, gentlemen?"
Its greetings warm and true,
And the tears of bliss our lips did kiss
From dear eyes black or blue.

Nathless, despite our rapture,
Down to the harbor-mouth
We dogged the Britons doomed to fly
Forever from our South!
They left as some foul vulture
Might leave his mangled prey,
And pass with clotted beak and wing
Reluctantly away.

Three hundred noble vessels
Rose on the rising flood,
Wherein with sullen apathy
Embarked those men of blood;
Then streamed their admiral's pennant —
The northwest breeze blew free;
With sloping mast, and current fast,
Out swept their fleet to sea.

We strained our vision waveward,
Watching the white-winged ships,
Till the vague clouds of distance
Wrapped them in half eclipse:
And still we strained our vision
Till, dimmer and more dim,
The rearmost sail, a phantom pale,
Died down the horizon's rim.

Thus, o'er the soul's horizon,
Did thoughts of blood and war,
Through time's enchanted distances
Receding, fade afar,
Thus o'er the soul's horizon,
Our strife's last ghastly fear,
Like all the rest, down memory's west
Did slowly disappear.

TO THE AUTHOR OF "THE VICTORIAN POETS."

So keen, so clear thy genius, that no mist
Of subtlest phrase can baffle or delay
The lance-like, swift illuminating ray,
Wherewith, O art-enamored annalist,
Thy lightning logic cleaves the elusive gist
Of thoughts Protean; or, in lowlier play,
Smites tinselled weakness to a red dismay—
As swordsmen smite by one deft turn of wrist.
Yet oft that glittering and remorseless blade
Thy logic wields is dropped that thou may'st take
Some gracious lyre, and sing with liquid breath
By many a haunted dell and shadowy lake,
Where faun and naiad wander undismayed,
Lays of Arcadian love, or painless death.

HERA.

(IN THE HERAEUM.)

Once between Argos and Mycaenæ shone
Half-veiled in myrtle and mysterious pine,
The ivory splendors of that holy shrine,
Wherein embowered, majestic, and alone
Her sculptured brow with wavering locks o'erblown,
As if by airs ethereal and divine,
Smiled the calm goddess of Olympian line,
Girt by awed silence, like a sacred zone:

Save that mild murmurings sounding vague and far,
From suppliant women—through frail-hearted dread
Touched the shy pulses of that strange repose,
Till the last petal dropped from sunset's rose,

And gleamed through twilight, like a flawless star,
The chastened glory of proud Hera's head!

BELOW AND ABOVE.

I SEE in the forest coverts
The sheen of shimmering lights;
They gleam from the dusky shadows,
They flash from the ghostly heights:

No lights of the tranquil homestead
Or the hostel warm are they;
But warring flames of the Titan fire
Which stormed through the woods to-day.

Each darts with an aimless passion,
Or sinks into lurid rest
Like the crest of a wounded serpent drooped
On the scales of its treacherous breast.

Let them idly dart and quiver,
Or sink into lurid rest —
Above, like a child-saint's face in heaven,
There's a sole, sweet star in the west.

Ah! slowly the earth-lights wither;
But the star, like a saintly face,
Shines on, with the steadfast strength of peace,
In its God-appointed place.

THE WOODLAND GRAVE.

WE roam, my love and I,
'Mid the rich woodland grasses,
Where, through dense clouds of greenery,
The softened sunshine passes;
But near a rivulet's lonely wave
We come half startled, on — a grave!

We pause, my love and I,
Each thinking, "*Who* reposes
Here, in the forest tranquilly,
Beneath these sylvan roses?"
When, 'twixt the wild flowers' tangled flame,
Wind-parted, we beheld — a name.

We mark, my love and I,
With thoughts that swiftly vary,
Of doubt, surprise, solemnity,
The flickering name of "Mary;"
My love's own name! — but flickering *there*,
Each letter burns a hint of fear.

We shrink, my love and I,
Pierced by prescient sorrow,
"To think, my sweet! that *thou* may'st die
To-night or else to-morrow!"
Each murmurs sadly, under breath:
"O love, malignly watched by death!"

We turn, my love and I,
From that strange grave together,
And o'er our spirits' darkened sky
Roll mists of mournful weather;
With boding grief our hearts are rife —
Death's shadow steals 'twixt love and life!

A CHARACTER.

"The most impenetrable mask for a malicious design is — well-acted candor." — *From the French of De Larrimère.*

YES, madame, I know you better, far better than those can know
Whose plummet of judgment never is dropped to the depths below;

Whose test is a surface-seeming, the glitter of lights that gleam
With a moment's rainbow lustre on the shifting face of the stream.

"We turn, my love and I,
From that strange grave together."

Because you have bold, blunt manners, because you can broadly smile,
With the devil's own art in veiling your infinite gulfs of guile,

There are some who bring you homage, who vow your nature is free
And frank as the life of summer, when fullest on land and sea:

And yet your soul is a charnel where many a ruined name
Rots, festering vile and loathsome in burial-shrouds of shame;

A sepulchre dark, that's crowded with ashes of old and young,
Dead fames you have foully poisoned with your pitiless serpent's tongue!

Beware! by the God above us, who parteth the false from true,
There's a curse in the future, *somewhere*—an ambushed curse for you.

It will burst from the wayside fiercely, when least you dream of a blow.
A tigerish fate in its fury, to rend, and to lay you low!

But ere it has sucked your heart's blood, and stifled your latest breath,
The thought of *your* victims, woman! will sharpen the sting of death!

LYRIC OF ACTION.

'Tis the part of a coward to brood
O'er the past that is withered and dead:
What though the heart's roses are ashes and dust?
What though the heart's music be fled?
Still shine the grand heavens o'erhead,
Whence the voice of an angel thrills clear on the soul,
"Gird about thee thine armor, press on to the goal!"

If the faults or the crimes of thy youth
Are a burden too heavy to bear,
What hope can rebloom on the desolate waste
Of a jealous and craven despair
Down, down with the fetters of fear!
In the strength of thy valor and manhood arise,
With the faith that illumes and the will that defies.

"*Too late!*" through God's infinite world,
From his throne to life's nethermost fires,
"*Too late!*" is a phantom that flies at the dawn
Of the soul that repents and aspires.
If pure thou hast made thy desires.
There's no height the strong wings of immortals may gain
Which in striving to reach thou shalt strive for in vain.

Then, up to the contest with fate,
Unbound by the past, which is dead!
What though the heart's roses are ashes and dust?
What though the heart's music be fled?
Still shine the fair heavens o'erhead;
And sublime as the seraph who rules in the sun
Beams the promise of joy when the conflict is won!

BY A GRAVE.

IN SPRING.

Ah, mother! canst thou feel her? . . . spring has come!
Birds sing, brooks murmur, woods no more are dumb;

And for each grief that vexed thine earthly hour,
Nature has kissed thy grave! and lo! . . a flower.

Here wails no nightingale against her thorn,
But like the incarnate soul of May-flushed morn,
The mocking-bird above thy splendor sings,
With rapturous throat, and upraised quivering wings;

Half drowsed between brief glooms and mellowed gleams,
The sun smiles gently, like a god in dreams;
His sacred light across thy place of rest,
Steals with the softness of a hand that blessed!

Thro' magic ministers of spring-tide grace,
Thy grave transfigured lifts a radiant face,
O'er which elusive golden shadows run,
A waft of wind-wrought dimples in the sun;

Ah! if thy soul, that loved all beauty here,
May yet look earthward from her holier sphere,
'Twill joy to mark, from even those heights august,
In what a mantle Nature wraps thy dust.

And still the brown bird rears his poet-head,
And pours his matchless music o'er the dead,
'Till touched and wakened by the marvellous flow,
I seem to hear a thrilled heart throb below!

SEVERANCE.

Ah! who can tell how strong the tie
Which subtly binds us, heart to heart,
Till the dark master, Death, comes nigh,
To wrench our kindred lives apart?

Then, pondering on the sombre bed,
Where one we cherished dumbly lies,
With pulseless hands, low-smitten head,
And the wan droop of curtained eyes,

The torpor of the death-sleep cold,
The mystic quiet's awful spell,
Whose fathomless silence seems to hold
Such pathos of supreme farewell,

Our clouded spirits throb and reel,
As if some viewless power in air
Had driven a keen ethereal steel
Through quivering heart-depths of despair!

Paled is the dream of heavenly grace,
The jasper sea, the unwaning calms;
We can but mark that breathless face,
Those sightless orbs and folded palms!

A moment since, she softly spake,
Her soul looked forth still hale and clear;
Now, who her wondrous sleep can break?
And she! where hath she vanished, — where?

Ah, Christ! yon shape of ice-locked clay,
Yon fading image, frail and thin,
Touched, as we gaze, by swift decay,
Shrivelled without, and wan within,

What is it but an empty husk,
O'er which (at Death's mysterious kiss)
Freed Psyche soars from doubt and dusk
Beyond earth's crumbling chrysalis?

Ay! "dust to dust!"—the soil she trod
Claims soon her outworn fleshly dress;
But her true life puts forth, with God,
Fresh blooms of everlastingness!

TWO GRAVES.

I.

It glooms forlornly 'mid wan ocean dunes,
A desolate grave-mound on a dreary lea,
Touched by sad splendors of gray-misted moons,
Or veiled by shivering spray-drifts from the sea.

There, all unmarked, the dim days come and go;
No tender hand renews its crumbling turf,
On which the o'erwearied sea-winds faintly blow,
Blent with far murmurings of the mournful surf.

Vaguely the uncompanioned hours flit by,
Wrapped in pale clouds that sometimes mutely weep
Some ghost of Lethe haunts that hollow sky,
Where even the doubtful noontides seem asleep,

Save when autumnal tempests fiercely rise,
Baring the harbor-mouth's black teeth of rocks,
And like a Maenad, with wild hair and eyes,
Raves from the North the infuriate Equinox.

II.

Here, peace divine, o'er glimmering grove and grass,
Hallows the sunshine in the noon's warm lull;
Ethereal shadows gently pause, or pass,
Flecking with gold the hill-slope beautiful.

This grave, all wreathed with flowers and glad with spring
Looks skyward like a half-veiled, museful eye,
Which answers subtly while the wood-birds sing
Heaven's smile of forecast immortality.

Can deathly dust pervade a spot so sweet?
Or hath the form it guarded stolen away,
And ere its hour of ransom, gone to meet
The unborn soul of Resurrection Day?

THE WORLD.

QUATRAINS.

The world is older than our earliest dates;
All thoughts, all feelings, all desires, all fates,
Were known and tested, long ere Adam's crime
Set the keen sword of flame at Eden-gates!

Billions of years on billions more have fled,
Since first love's kiss a maiden cheek turned red;
Since the first mother nursed her innocent babe—
The first wild mourner wept above his dead.

These ancient clods our vagrant feet displace,
May once have held the loftiest soul of grace;

This dateless dust that dims our garden flowers,
May once have smiled — a beauteous woman's face!

Older than all man's wisdom and his dreams,
Older than all which is, than all which seems,
Our world rolls on, where wrapped in cloud-like fire,
Phantasmal, pale, her awful death-morn gleams!

THE MAY SKY.

O sky! O lucid sky of May!
O'er which the fleecy clouds have stolen,
In bands snow-white, and glimmering-gray,
Or heart-steeped in a lustre golden.

O sky! that tak'st a thousand moods,
Enshadowed now, and now out-beaming,
Swept by low winds like interludes
Of music 'twixt soft spells of dreaming,

Type of the poet's soul thou art
In spring-time of his teeming fancies,
When heavenly glamours brim his heart,
And heavenly glory lights his glances;

As morning's dubious vapors form
In wavering lines and circlets tender,
Pure as an infant's brow, or warm
With tintings of a primrose splendor;

Thus o'er the poet's soul his thought
Pale first as mist-wreaths scarce created,
With fire-keen breaths of ardor fraught,
From radiance born, to beauty mated,

Takes shape like yonder cloud outspanned
Above the murmurous woodland spaces,
Whose brightening rifts, methinks, are grand
With mystic lights and marvellous faces;

Or, merges in some fancy vain,
Yet rare beyond the worldling's measure;
Some delicate cloudlet of the brain
That melts far up its quivering azure!

A LYRICAL PICTURE.

COMPOSED NEAR THE SEA-COAST.

See! see!
How the shadows steal along,
Blending in a golden throng,
Softly, lovingly;
From each mossed and quaint tree-column,
Stretched toward the dimpling river,
How they quiver!
While in low, pathetic tone
Twilight's herald-breeze is blown
Down the sunset solemn!

Hear! hear!
Dropped from gray mists, circling high,
The sea-wending curlew's cry,
Strangely wild and drear;
Echoed by a voice that thrills us,
From the murmurous verge of ocean —
Voice that fills us
With a sense of mystery old,
And vague memories which enfold
Many a weird emotion.

Turn! turn!
From yon loftier cloud-land dun;
Mark what splendors of the sun
Westward throb and burn —
Burn as if some glorious angel
Blessed the air and land and river
With his mute evangel:
All things own so rich a grace
That in Heaven's divine embrace
Earth seems clasped forever!

LAMIA UNVEILED.

Her step is soft as a fay's footfall,
And her eyes are wonderful founts of blue;
But I've seen that small foot spurning hearts,
And the soul that burns so strangely through
Those orbs of blue,
O! is't a *human* soul at all?

I never have gazed on their cloudless light,
But there came a chill to my blood and brain,
And their ominous beauty hath struck me dumb
With a secret and nameless pain:
Ay, blood and brain
Grew cold as with spells of a witch's blight.

Is't true? Can it be that a mortal frame
Of the tenderest mould, of the fairest grace,
May hold but a serpent's soul in sooth?
That the white and red of the daintiest face
May mask the trace
Of subtle guile, that shall wake to flame

And smite with the sting of a poisoned jest,
Or the sudden flashing of deadly scorn,
If it be, I know that your Charmian there,
In her fragile grace, is a Lamia, born
To blight the morn
Of the passion that clings to her faithless breast!

Why, look! As we speak, she has turned her wiles
On the gilded wooer her eyes had sought,
While *you* were steeped in the roseate gulf
Of a sweet, voluptuous thought:
Some loves are bought,
And you'll yearn in vain for her 'wildering smiles.

From this night forth, until placid and meek,
(Oh! meek as a saint, as an angel bland!)
With a faint rose flushing her brow and cheek,
She whispers, "*Adieu! I must give my hand,*
At the heart's command.
Win a worthier love; you have only to seek!"

RACHEL.

INSCRIBED TO MRS. M. D., OF GEORGIA.

"A more desolate Rachel than she of old, because, although her children 'are not,' yet the fountain of her tears is sealed."

The wan September moonbeams, struggling down
Through the gray clouds upon her desolate head,
The coldness of their muffled radiance shed
Faintly above her like a spectral crown:

So, glimmering ghostlike in the dreary light,
Recounting her strange sorrows o'er and o'er,
Her words rang hollow as far waves ashore
Rolled through the sombre void of windless night.

Nor in her mortal weakness could she win
Even brief redemption from the soul's eclipse.
She looked like suffering Patience, on whose lips
Cold fingers press to keep the wild grief in.

Suddenly on the pathos and the woe
 Of that sad vision broke the gleeful noise
 From the near playground of blithe girls and boys,
Through shine and shadow hurrying to and fro.

A wearier shade the pallid face o'er-crossed;
 She shivered, drooping; but through flowery bars
 Of the rude trellis sought the distant stars,
Saying, low: "*Where dwell in heaven my loved and lost?*

Dear Christ, I thought, if soft and ruthful, thou
 Still reign'st beyond us,— ah! assuage the pain
 Of this worn soul, more laden than hers of Nain;
Ope thy deep heavens for one swift moment now;

And, while her very heart-throbs seem to cease
 For rapture, let those hungering eyes behold
 Her lost beloved transfigured in thy fold,
Crowned with the palm, walking the fields of peace!

THE SNOW-MESSENGERS.

Dedicated to John Greenleaf Whittier and Henry Wadsworth Longfellow, with pen portraits of both.

THE pine-trees lift their dark bewildered eyes —
Or so I deem — up to the clouded skies;
No breeze, no faintest breeze, is heard to blow:
In wizard silence falls the windless snow.

It falls in breezeless quiet, strangely still;
'Scapes the dulled pane, but loads the sheltering sill.
With curious hand the fleecy flakes I mould,
And draw them inward, rounded, from the cold.

The glittering ball that chills my finger-tips
I hold a moment's space to loving lips;
For from the northward these pure snow-flakes came,
And to *my* touch their coldness thrills like flame.

Outbreathed from luminous memories nursed apart,
Deep in the veiled *adytum* of the heart,
The type of Norland dearth such snows may be:
They bring the soul of summer's warmth to me.

Beholding them, in magical light expands
The changeful charm that crowns the northern lands,
And a fair past I deemed a glory fled
Comes back, with happy sunshine round its head.

For Ariel fancy takes her airiest flights
To pass once more o'er Hampshire's mountain heights,
To view the flower-bright pastures bloom in grace
By many a lowering hill-side's swarthy base;

The fruitful farms, the enchanted vales, to view,
And the coy mountain lakes' transcendent blue,
Or flash of sea-waves up the thunderous dune,
With wan sails whitening in the midnight moon;

The cataract front of storm, malignly rife
With deathless instincts of demoniac strife.
Or, in shy contrast, down a shaded dell,
The rivulet tinkling like an Alpine bell;
And many a cool, calm stretch of cultured lawn,
Touched by the freshness of the crystal dawn,
Sloped to the sea, whose laughing waters meet
About the unrobed virgin's rosy feet.

"To pass once more o'er Hampshire's mountain heights, . . .
The fruitful farms, the enchanted vales, to view,
And the coy mountain lakes' transcendent blue."

But, tireless fancy, stay the wing that roams,
And fold it last near northern hearts and homes.

These tropic veins still own their kindred heat,
And thoughts of thee, my cherished South, are sweet —
Mournfully sweet — and wed to memories vast,
High-hovering still o'er thy majestic past.

But a new epoch greets us; with it blends
The voice of ancient foes now changed to friends.
Ah! who would friendship's outstretched hand despise,
Or mock the kindling light in generous eyes?

So, 'neath the Quaker-poet's tranquil roof,
From all dull discords of the world aloof,
I sit once more, and measured converse hold
With him whose nobler thoughts are rhythmic gold;

See his deep brows half puckered in a knot
O'er some hard problem of our mortal lot,
Or a dream soft as May winds of the south
Waft a girl's sweetness round his firm-set mouth.

Or should he deem wrong threats the public weal,
Lo! the whole man seems girt with flashing steel;

His glance a sword thrust, and his words of ire
Like thunder-tones from some old prophet's lyre.

Or by the hearth-stone when the day is done,
Mark, swiftly launched, a sudden shaft of fun;
The short quick laugh, the smartly smitten knees,
And all sure tokens of a mind at ease.

Discerning which, by some mysterious law,
Near to his seat two household favorites draw,
Till on her master's shoulders, sly and sleek,
Grimalkin, mounting, rubs his furrowed cheek;

While terrier Dick, denied all words to rail,
Snarls as he shakes a short protesting tail,
But with shrewd eyes says, plain as plain can be,
"*Drop that sly cat. I'm worthier far than she.*"

And he who loves all lowliest lives to please,
Conciliates soon his dumb Diogenes,
Who in return his garment nips with care,
And drags the poet out, to take the air.

God's innocent pensioners in the woodlands dim,
The fields and pastures, know and trust in him;
And in *their* love his lonely heart is blessed,
Our pure, hale-minded Cowper of the West!

. . . . .

The scene is changed; and now I stand again
By one, the cordial prince of kindly men,
Courtly yet natural, comrade meet for kings,
But fond of homeliest thoughts and homeliest things.

A poet too, in whose warm brain and breast
What birds of song have filled a golden nest,
Till in song's summer prime their wings unfurled,
Have made Arcadian half the listening world,

Around whose eve some radiant grace of morn
Smiles like the dew-light on a mountain thorn.
Blithely he bears Time's envious load today:
Ah! the green heart o'ertops the head of gray.

Alert as youth, with vivid, various talk
He wiles the way through grove and garden walk,
Fair flowers untrained, trees fraught with wedded doves,
Past the cool copse and willowy glade he loves.

Here gleams innocuous of a mirthful mood
Pulse like mild fire-flies down a dusky wood,
Or keener speech (his leonine head unbowed)
Speeds lightning-clear from thought's o'ershadowing cloud.

O deep blue eyes! O voice as woman's low!
O firm white hand, with kindliest warmth aglow!
O manly form, and frank, sweet, courteous mien,
Reflex of museful days and nights serene!

Still are ye near me, vivid, actual still,
Here in my lonely fastness on the hill;
Nor can ye wane till cold my life-blood flows,
And fancy fades in feeling's last repose.

What! snowing yet? The landscape waxes pale;
Round the mute heaven there hangs a quivering veil,
Through whose frail woof like silent shuttles go
The glancing glamours of the glittering snow.

Yes, falling still, while fond remembrance stirs
In these wan-faced, unwonted messengers.
Dumb storm! outpour your arctic heart's desire!
Your flakes to me seem flushed with fairy fire!

TO ALEXANDER H. STEPHENS.

Last of a stalwart time and race gone by,
That simple, stately, God-appointed band,
Who wrought alone to glorify their land,
With lives built high on truth's eternity,
While placemen plot, while flatterers fawn or lie,
And foul corruptions, wave on wave, expand,
I see thee rise, stainless of heart as hand,
O man of Roman thought and radiant eye!

Through thy frail form, there burn divinely strong
The antique virtues of a worthier day;
Thy soul is golden, if thy head be gray,
No years can work that lofty nature wrong;
They set to concords of ethereal song
A life grown holier on its heavenward way.

THE ENCHANTED MIRROR.

FROM THE PERSIAN.

What time o'er Persia ruled that upright Khan
Khosru the Good, in Shiraz lived a man,
A beggar-carle, to whose rough hands were given—
I know not how—a mirror clear as heaven
On beauteous, vernal mornings, and more bright
Than streamlets sparkling in midsummer's light;
And, strange to say, whoso should look therein,
Though uglier than a nightmare dream of sin,
Grew comely as the loveliest shapes we know;
The while—oh, wonder! a fair form and face
Caught straightway somewhat of celestial grace.

Where'er in twilight dusk, or noontide glow
With swift, firm pace or footstep sad and slow,
Where'er he walked through the broad land of palms,
Or yet his lips unclosed to plead for alms,
The beggar held his mystic treasure high
To glass the forms of those who passed him by;
And all who came within that marvel's range,
Paused spell-bound by the strangely-dazzling change;

Lords, ladies, gazed! the prospect pleased them well;
"Ah, heavens!" they sighed, "how irresistible!"
E'en the coarse hag, foul, wrinkled, and unclean,
Beamed like a blushing virgin of sixteen.

Hearts are transformed with faces; outward beauty
Seems to make quick the inward sense of duty;
For none, of all the charmèd throng that pass
Revivified within the fairy glass,
But pours upon the beggar pence with praise,
Invoking on his head long, golden days,
And every joy that lights our mortal ways.

In vain! — the beggar sickened. While he lay
In death's cold shadow, prostrate and forlorn,
He bade his wife call to him, on a morn,
His only son: "Guard well when I am dead,"
Feebly, with fluttering breath, the old man said;
"This mystic glass, whereby great things are won —
Be shrewd, be watchful; do as I have done,
And thou shalt prosper likewise, O my son!"

He took the precious gift — that brainless wight —
But, scorning to employ its powers aright,
Returned all pale and penniless at night.

"Fool!" cried the angry father, "well I guess
Why thus thou seek'st me, pale and penniless:
O stupid dolt! vain peacock! arrant ass!
Thou hast watched all day thine own face in the glass;
Go to! this foolish fruit of idle pride
No human heart hath ever satisfied,
Far less an empty pocket lined with gold;
Thy coxcomb pate to base self-love is sold!
Yet hearken once again: *he's only wise*
Who dupes the world through flattery's mirrored lies;
But past all terms of scorn the insensate elf
Who holds its glass therein to view — himself!"

THE IMPRISONED SEA-WINDS.

VOICES of strange sea breezes caught,
Half tangled in the pine-tree tall,
With ocean's tenderest music fraught,
Serenely rise, and sweetly fall.

They charm the lids of wearied eyes,
And all the dreamy senses bless
With breath of wave-born symphonies,
And balms of mild forgetfulness,

'Till o'er the fragrant calms of peace,
My soul, scarce moved, benignly glides,
Or in all sorrows' soft surcease,
Rocks trancèd on the phantom tides:

But still those faint sea voices speak,
Those prisoned sea winds rise and fall,
The ghost of sea foam sweeps my cheek,
And the sea's mystery sighs through all.

BLANCHE AND NELL.

A BALLAD.

OH, Blanche is a city lady,
Bedecked in her silks and lace:
She walks with the mien of a stately queen,
And a queen's imperious grace.

But Nell is a country maiden,
  Her dress from the farmstead loom:
Her step is free as a breeze at sea,
  And her face is a rose in bloom.

The house of Blanche is a marvel
  Of marble from base to dome;
It hath all things fair, and costly and rare,
  But alas! it is not — home!

Nell lives in a lonely cottage
  On the shores of a wave-washed isle;
And the life she leads with its loving deeds
  The angels behold and smile.

Blanche finds her palace a prison,
  And oft, through the dreary years,
In her burdened breast there is sad unrest,
  And her eyes are dimmed with tears.

But to Nell her toils are pastime,
  (Though never till night they cease);
And her soul's afloat like a buoyant boat
  On the crystal tides of peace.

Ah! Blanche hath many a lover,
  But she broodeth o'er old regret;
The shy, sweet red from her cheek is fled
  For the star of her heart has set.

Fair Nell! but a single lover
  Hath she in the wide, wide world;
Yet warmly apart in her glowing heart
  Love bides, with his pinions furled.

To Blanche all life seems shadowed,
  And she but a ghost therein;
Thro' the misty gray of her autumn day
  Steal voices of grief and sin.

To Nell all life is sunshine,
  All earth like a fairy sod,
Where the roses grow, and the violets blow,
  In the softest breath of God.

What meaneth this mighty contrast
  Of lives that we meet and mark?
One bright as the flowers from May-tide showers,
  One rayless, sombre, and dark?

O, folly of mortal wisdom,
  That neither will break nor bow,
That riddle hath vexed the thought perplexed
  Of millions of souls ere now!

O, folly of mortal wisdom!
  From your guesses what good can come?
We can learn no more than the wise of yore;
  'Tis better to trust, and — be dumb!

THE DARK.

A FANTASY.

The passionless twilight slowly fades
Beyond the gray, grim woodland glades,
Till now, with mournful eyes, I mark
    The approaching dark:

A clouded spirit, borne from far,
Whose sombre front no delicate star
Brightens, — to tint with silvery light
    Her realms of night:

An *awful* spirit! her pale lips
Low whispering down the drear eclipse,
Send thro' those rayless spaces chill
    An ominous thrill:

Her tongue's strange language none may know;
We only feel it ebb and flow
In murmurs of half-muffled sighs,
    And vague replies:

All hail! akin to me thou art,
Dim angel of the veilèd heart —
Ah! wrap me close, ah! fold me deep!
    I fain would sleep!

IN THE STUDIO.

You walk my studio's modest round,
With slowly supercilious air;
While in each lifted eyebrow lurks,
The keenness of an ambushed sneer.

You lift your glass, and scan the walls,
Between the pictures — with a glance
Which takes the curtained drapery in,
But views the art-work all askance:

A sigh! a shrug! and then you turn
Homeward — your judgment fixed as fate —
The labors of a life-time gauged,
Serenely in your shallow pate!

WASHINGTON!

Feb. 22, 1732.

Bright natal morn! what face appears
Beyond the rolling mist of years? —
A face whose loftiest traits combine
All virtues of a stainless line
Passed from leal sire to loyal son;
The face of him whose steadfast zeal
Drew harmonies of law and right
From chaos and anarchic night:
Who with a power serene as Fate's
Wrought from rude hordes of turbulent States
The grandeur of our commonweal: —
All hail! all hail! to Washington!

Freedom he wooed in such brave guise,
Men gazing in her luminous eyes
Beheld all heaven reflected shine
Far down those sapphire orbs divine:
And, worshipped her so chastely won;
If still she panted, fresh from strife,
And blood-stains flecked her garment's rim,
They could not make its whiteness dim;
For, shed by hearts sublimely true,
Such drops are changed to sacred dew.
The chrism of patriot light and life, —
Baptizing first our Washington.

For cloudless years, benignant still.
This Freedom worked her bounteous will; —
Mingling with homespun man and maid,
Her pale cheek caught a browner shade
In fields where harvest toils were done;
To theirs she tuned her rhythmic tongue
Veiling in part her goddess-mien:
The woman smiled above the queen;
While stationed always by her side,
Men saw — as bridegroom near his bride.
(O bride, forever fair and young!) —
Her chosen hero — Washington!

She wove for him a civic crown;
She made so pure his hale renown,
All glories of the antique days,
Waned in the clear, immaculate blaze
Poured from his nature's noontide sun;
No slave of folly's catchword school,
His instincts proud of blood and race
She tempered with sweet, human grace,
Till his broad being's rounded flow
Sea-like, embraced the high and low,
Swayed by the golden-sceptred rule,
The equal will of Washington.

His influence spread so wide and deep,
Earth's fettered millions stirred in sleep;
And murmurs born of wakening flame
On the wild winds of twilight came
From lands by despot-swarms o'errun;
They too would win the priceless boon
Of Freedom's dower; — they too would see,
And clasp the robes of Liberty;
But, throned within the virgin west,
She heard them not; — she loved to rest
In dew-lit dawn and tranquil noon,
Next the strong heart of Washington!

Through shower and sun the seasons rolled,
November's gray and April's gold;
They only raised (more calmly grand)
His genius of supreme command,

"You walk my studio's modest round, . . .
While in each eyebrow lurks
The keenness of an ambushed sneer."

Whose course, in blood and wrath begun,
Grew gentler, as the mellowing lights
Of peace made beauteous sky and sod;
His evening came; — he walked with God;
And down life's gradual sunset-slope,
He hearkened to a heavenly hope; —
"Look up! behold the fadeless heights
Which rise to greet thee, — Washington!"

He dies! the nations hold their breath!
He dies! but is he thrall to Death? —
Thousands who quaff earth's sunshine free,
Are less alive on earth than he;
Lacking that power which thrills through none
But God's elect, that wingèd spell
Which like miraculous lightning darts
Electric to all noble hearts;—
Flashed from his soul's sublimer sphere,
'Tis still a matchless influence here!
Majestic spirit! all is well,
Where'er thou rulest, — Washington!

IN AMBUSH.

THE crescent moon, with pallid glow,
Swept backward like a bended bow:
Across, a shaft of phantom light
Thrilled, like an arrow winged for flight.

Just when that flickering shaft was aimed
Venus in mellow radiance flamed,
Unmindful of the treacherous dart
Which seemed upreared to pierce her heart;

For, fain to smite her through and through,
Dian lay ambushed in the blue:
Half veiled from sight, still, still below,
She aimed her shaft, she clasped her bow.

For ever thus, since time was born,
Cold virtue points *her* shaft of scorn
At passionate love, in whose warm beam
Her own but seems a crescent dream.

*SOUTH CAROLINA TO THE STATES OF THE NORTH.**

ESPECIALLY TO THOSE THAT FORMED A PART OF THE ORIGINAL THIRTEEN.

Dedicated to His Excellency, Wade Hampton.

I LIFT these hands with iron fetters banded:
Beneath the scornful sunlight and cold stars
I rear my once imperial forehead branded
By alien shame's immedicable scars;
Like some pale captive, shunned by all the nations,
I crouch unpitied, quivering and apart —
Laden with countless woes and desolations,
The life-blood freezing round a broken heart!

About my feet, splashed red with blood of slaughters,
My children gathering in wild, mournful throngs;
Despairing sons, frail infants, stricken daughters,
Rehearse the awful burden of their wrongs;
Vain is their cry, and worse than vain their pleading:

* This Poem was composed at a period when it seemed as if all the horrors of misgovernment, so graphically depicted by Pike in his "*Prostrate State*," would be perpetuated in South Carolina.

It was a significant and terrible epoch; a time American statesmen would do well to remember occasionally as a warning against patchwork political re-constructions.

I turn from stormy breasts, from yearning eyes,
To mark where Freedom's outraged form receding,
Wanes in chill shadow down the midnight skies!

I wooed her once in wild tempestuous places,
The purple vintage of my soul outpoured,
To win and keep her unrestrained embraces,
What time the olive-crown o'ertopped the sword;
O! northmen, with your gallant heroes blending,
Mine, in old years, for this sweet goddess died;
But now — ah! shame, all other shame transcending!
Your pitiless hands have torn her from my side.

What! 'tis a tyrant-party's treacherous action —
Your hand is clean, your conscience clear, ye sigh;
Ay! but ere now your sires had throttled faction,
Or, pealed o'er half the world their battle-cry;
Its voice outrung from solemn mountain-passes
Swept by wild storm-winds of the Atlantic strand,
To where the swart Sierras' sullen grasses,
Droop in low languors of the sunset-land!

Never, since earthly States began their story,
Hath any suffered, bided, borne like me:
At last, recalling all mine ancient glory,
I vowed my fettered commonwealth to free:

Even at the thought, beside the prostrate column
Of chartered rights, which blasted lay and dim —
Uprose my noblest son with purpose solemn,
While, host on host, his brethren followed *him*:

Wrong, grasped by *truth*, arraigned by *law*, (whose sober
Majestic mandates rule o'er change and time) —
Smit by the *ballot*, like some flushed October,
Reeled in the autumn rankness of his crime;
Struck, tortured, pierced — but not a blow returning.
The steadfast phalanx of my honored braves
Planted their bloodless flag where sunrise burning,
Flashed a new splendor o'er our martyrs' graves!

What then? O, sister States! what welcome omen
Of love and concord crossed our brightening blue,
The foes we vanquished, are they not *your* foemen,
Our laws upheld, your sacred safeguards, too?
Yet scarce had victory crowned our grand endeavor,
And peace crept out from shadowy glooms remote —
Than — as if bared to blast all hope forever,
Your tyrant's sword shone glittering at my throat!

Once more my bursting chains were reunited,
Once more barbarian plaudits wildly rung
O'er the last promise of deliverance blighted,

The prostrate purpose, and the palsied tongue:
Ah! faithless sisters, 'neath my swift undoing,
Peers the black presage of your wrath to come;
Above your heads are signal clouds of ruin,
Whose lightnings flash, whose thunders are not dumb!

There towers a judgment-seat beyond our seeing;
There lives a Judge, whom none can bribe or blind;
Before whose dread decree, your spirit fleeing,
May reap the whirlwind, having sown the wind:
I, in that day of justice, fierce and torrid,
When blood — *your* blood — outpours like poisoned wine,
Pointing to these chained limbs, this blasted forehead,
May mock your ruin, as ye mocked at mine!

THE STRICKEN SOUTH TO THE NORTH.

[Dedicated to Oliver Wendell Holmes.]

"We are thinking a great deal about the poor fever-stricken cities of the South, and all contributing according to our means for their relief. Every morning as the paper comes, the first question is 'What is the last account from Memphis, Grenada, and New Orleans.'" — *Extract from a private letter of Dr. Holmes.*

When ruthful time the South's memorial places —
Her heroes' graves — had wreathed in grass and flowers;
When Peace ethereal, crowned by all her graces,
Returned to make more bright the summer hours;
When doubtful hearts revived, and hopes grew stronger;
When old sore-cankering wounds that pierced and stung,
Throbbed with their first, mad, feverous pain no longer,
While the fair future spake with flattering tongue;
When once, once more she felt her pulses beating
To rhythms of healthful joy and brave desire;
Lo! round her doomed horizon darkly meeting,
A pall of blood-red vapors veined with fire!

O! ghastly portent of fast-coming sorrows!
Of doom that blasts the blood and blights the breath,
Robs youth and manhood of all golden morrows —
And life's clear goblet brims with wine of death! —
O! swift fulfilment of this portent dreary!
O! nightmare rule of ruin, racked by fears,
Heartbroken wail, and solemn *miserere*,
Imperious anguish, and soul-melting tears!
O! faith, thrust downward from celestial splendors,
O! love grief-bound, with palely-murmurous mouth!
O! agonized by life's supreme surrenders —
Behold her now — the scourged and suffering South!

No balm in Gilead? nay, but while her forehead
Pallid and drooping, lies in foulest dust,
There steals across the desolate spaces torrid,
A voice of manful cheer and heavenly trust,
A hand redeeming breaks the frozen starkness
Of palsied nerve, and dull, despondent brain:

Rolls back the curtain of malignant darkness,
And shows the eternal blue of heaven again —
Revealing there, o'er worlds convulsed and shaken,
That face whose mystic tenderness enticed
To hope new-born earth's lost bereaved, forsaken!
Ah! still beyond the tempest smiles the Christ!

Whose voice? Whose hand? Oh, thanks, divinest Master,
Thanks for those grand emotions which impart
Grace to the North to feel the South's disaster,
The South to bow with touched and cordial heart!
Now, now at last the links which war had broken
Are welded fast, at mercy's charmed commands;
Now, now at last the magic words are spoken
Which blend in one two long-divided lands!
O North! you came with warrior strife and clangor;
You left our South one gory burial ground;
But love, more potent than your haughtiest anger,
Subdues the souls which hate could only wound!

THE RETURN OF PEACE.

[Written by request of the committee of arrangements, for the opening ceremonies of the International Cotton Exposition, in Atlanta, Georgia, Oct. 5, 1881.

I HAD a vision at that mystic hour,
When in the ebon garden of the Night,
Blooms the Cimmerian flower
Of doubt and darkness, cowering from the light.
I seemed to stand on a vast lonely height,
Above a city ravished and o'erthrown,
The air about me one long lingering moan
Of lamentation like a dreary sea
Scourged by the storm to murmurous weariness;
Then, from dim levels of mist-folded ground
Borne upward suddenly.
Burst the deep-rolling stress
Of jubilant drums, blent with the silvery sound
Of long-drawn bugle notes — the clash of swords
(Outflashed by alien lords) —
And warrior-voices wild with victory.

They could not quell the grieved and shuddering air,
That breathed about me its forlorn despair:
It almost seemed as if stern Triumph sped
To one whose hopes were dead,
And flaunting there his fortune's ruddier grace,
Smote — with a taunt — wan Misery in the face!

Lo! far away,
(For now my dream grows clear as luminous day,)
The victor's camp-fires gird the city round;
But she, unrobed, discrowned —
A new Andromeda, beside the main
Of her own passionate pain;
Bowed, naked, shivering low —
Veils the soft gleam of melancholy eyes,
Yet lovelier in their woe, —
Alike from hopeless earth and hopeless skies.
No Perseus, for her sake, serenely fleet,
Shall cleave the heavens with winged and shining feet: —
Ah me! the maid is lost —
For sorrow, like keen frost

Shall eat into her being's anguished
core —
Atlanta (not Andromeda in this),
What outside helper can bring back her
bliss?
Can re-illume, beyond its storm-built
bar,
Her youth's auroral star,
Or wake the aspiring heart that sleeps
forever more.

O! lying prophet of a sombre mood,
This city of our love
Is no poor, timorous dove,
To crouch and die unstruggling in the
mire;
If, for a time, she yields to force and fire,
Blinded by battle-smoke, and drenched
with blood,
Still must that dauntless hardihood
Drawn to her veins from out the iron
hills,
(Nerving the brain that toils, the soul
that wills,)
Shake off the lotus-languishment of
grief!
I see her rise and clasp her old belief,
In God and goodness — with imperial
glance,
Face the dark front of frowning Circum-
stance, —
While trusting only to her strong right
arm
To wrench from deadly harm,
All civic blessings and fair fruits of
peace!
High-souled to gain (despite her
ravished years),
And dragon-forms of monstrous doubts
and fears,
The matchless splendor of Toil's "golden
fleece!"

I see her rise, and strive with strenuous
hands firmly to lay
The fresh foundations of a nobler
sway —
War-wasted lands
Laden with ashes, gray and desolate —
Touched by the charm of some regener-
ate fate —
Flush into golden harvests prodigal;
Set by the steam-god's fiery passion free,
I hear the rise and fall
Of ponderous iron-clamped machinery,
Shake, as with earthquake thrill, the
factory halls;
While round the massive walls
Slow vapor, like a sinuous serpent
steals —
Through which revolve in circles,
great or small,
The deafening thunders of the tireless
wheels!

Far down each busy mart
That throbs and heaves as with a human
heart
Quick merchants pass, some debonair
and gay,
With undimmed, youthful locks —
Some wrinkled, sombre, gray —
But all with one accord
Dreaming of him — their lord —
The mighty monarch of the realm of
stocks!
And year by year her face more frankly
bright,
Glows with the ardor of the bloodless
fight
For bounteous empire o'er her
cherished South.
More sweet the smile upon her maiden
mouth,
Just rounding to rare curves of woman-
hood:
Because all unwithstood
The magic of her power and stately pride
Hath called from many a clime
Of tropic sunshine and of winter rime,
The world's skilled art and science to
her side;
Hence from her transient tomb,
Three lustra since, a hideous spot to
see —
Grows the majestic tree
Of heightened and green-leaved pros-
perity.

Hence, her broad gardens bloom
With rose and lily, and all flowers of balm.
And hence above the lines
Of her vast railways, droop the laden vines —
A luscious largess thro' the summer calm!

. . . . .

Feeling her veins so full of lusty blood,
That pulsed within them like a rhythmic flood,
And eager for sweet sisterhood, — the bond
Blissful and fond,
That yet may hold all nations in its thrall,
Atlanta — from a night of splendid dreams,
Roused by soft kisses of the morning beams,
Decreed a glorious festival
Of art and commerce in her brave domain;
She sent her summons on the courier breeze;
Or thro' the lightning wingèd wire
Flashed forth her soul's desire: —
Swiftly it passed,
O'er native hills and streams and prairies vast, —
And o'er waste barriers of dividing seas
'Till from all quarters, like quick tongues of flame,
That warm, but burn not, — cordial answers came,
And waftage of benignant messages.

Thus, thus it is a mighty concourse meets
O'erflowing squares and streets —
Borne at flood-tide toward the guarded ground,
Where treasures of two hemispheres are found,
To tax the inquiring mind, the curious eye!
Grain of the upland and damp river-bed,
In yellow stalks, or sifted meal for bread;
Unnumbered births of Ceres clustered nigh;
Beholding which — as touched by tropic heat, —
(The old-world picture never *can* grow old,
Nor the deep love that thrills it dumb and cold) —
Clear fancy looks on Boaz in the wheat,
And in her simple truth,
The tender eyes of Ruth
Holding the garnered fragments at his feet!

But piled o'er all, thro' many an unbound bale
Peering to show its snow-white softness pale,
— Snow-white, yet warm, and destined to be furled
In some auspicious day,
For which we yearn and pray,
Round half the naked misery of the world,
A fleece more rich than Jason's, glances down.
Ah! well we know no monarch's jewelled crown,
No marvellous koh-i-noor,
Won, first perchance, from gulfs of human gore,
Or life-toil of swart millions, gaunt and poor,
Hath e'er outshone its peerless sovereignty.

. . . . .

The wings of song unfold
Towards thy noontide-gold;
The eyes of song are clear,
(Turned on thy broadening sphere)
To mark, oh! city of the midland-weald,
And follow thy fair fortunes far afield —
The years unborn,
Doubtless must bring to thee
Trials to test thy spirit's constancy;
(While unthrift aliens wear the mask of scorn),

Financial shocks without thee and within:
Wrought by shrewd moneyed Shylocks hot to win
Their brazen game of monstrous usury;
Ravage of bandit "rings" whose boundless maw
Can swallow all things glibly, save — the law!
And many a subtler ill
Sudden and subtle as the ambush laid,
By black-browed "stranglers" 'mid an Orient glade:
But thou, with keenest will,
Shalt cut the bonds of stealthy fraud apart,
And if force fronts thee with a murderous blade,
Pierce the rash son of Anak to the heart!

Oh! queen! thy brilliant horoscope
Was cast by Helios in the halls of hope;

"War-wasted lands . . .
Touched by the charm of some regenerate fate —
Flush into golden harvests prodigal."

And hope becomes fulfilment, as thy tread —
Firm, placed between the living and the dead —
Wins the high grade which owns a heavenward slope:
For force and fraud undone,
And stormless summits won,
In thee I view heaven's purpose perfected:
Thou shalt be empress of all peaceful ties,
All potent industries,
All world-embracing magnanimities:
A warrior-queen no more, but mailed in love,
Thy spear a fulgent shaft of sun-steeped grain;
Thy shield a buckler, the field-fairies wove
Of strong green grasses, in the silvery noon
Of some full harvest-moon,
Thy stainless crown, red roses, blent with white!
Now, throned above the half-forgotten pain

Of dreadful war, and war's remorseless blight,
Thy heart-throbs glad and great,
Sending through all thy Titan-statured state,
Fresh life and gathering tides of grander power
From glorious hour to hour,
Thousands thy deeds shall bless
With strenuous pride, toned down to tenderness:
Shall bless thy deeds, exalt thy name;
Till every breeze that sweeps from hill to lea,
And every wind that furrows the deep sea,
Shall waft the fragrance of thy soul abroad
The sweetness and the splendor of thy fame:—
For thou, midmost a large and opulent store,
Of all things wrought to meet a nation's need,
Thou, nobly pure,
Of any darkening taint of selfish greed,—
Wert pre-ordained to be
Purveyor of divinest charity,—
The love-commissioned almoner of God.

YORKTOWN CENTENNIAL LYRIC.

[Written at the request of the Yorktown Centennial Commission, appointed by Congress, to conduct the celebration of the surrender of Lord Cornwallis, to the combined forces of France and America, upon the 19th of Oct. 1781, at Yorktown, Va.]

Hark, hark! down the century's long reaching slope
To those transports of triumph, those raptures of hope,
The voices of main and of mountain combined
In glad resonance borne on the wings of the wind,
The bass of the drum and the trumpet that thrills
Through the multiplied echoes of jubilant hills.
And mark how the years melting upward like mist
Which the breath of some splendid enchantment has kissed,
Reveal on the ocean, reveal on the shore
The proud pageant of conquest that graced them of yore,
When blended forever in love as in fame
See, the standard which stole from the starlight its flame,
And type of all chivalry, glory, romance,
The lilies, the luminous lilies of France.

Oh, stubborn the strife ere the conflict was won!
And the wild whirling war wrack half stifled the sun.
The thunders of cannon that boomed on the lea,
But re-echoed far thunders pealed up from the sea,
Where guarding his sea lists, a knight on the waves,
Bold De Grasse kept at bay the bluff bull-dogs of Graves.
The day turned to darkness, the night changed to fire,
Still more fierce waxed the combat, more deadly the ire,
Undimmed by the gloom, in majestic advance,
Oh, behold where they ride o'er the red battle tide,
Those banners united in love as in fame,
The brave standard which drew from the star-beams their flame,
And type of all chivalry, glory, romance,
The lilies, the luminous lilies of France.

No respite, no pause; by the York's tortured flood,
The grim Lion of England is writhing in blood.

Cornwallis may chafe and coarse Tarleton aver,
As he sharpens his broadsword and buckles his spur,
"*This blade, which so oft has reaped rebels like grain,*
Shall now harvest for death the rude yeomen again."
Vain boast! for ere sunset he's flying in fear,
With the rebels he scouted close, close in his rear,
While the French on his flank hurl such volleys of shot
That e'en Gloucester's redoubt must be growing too hot.
Thus wedded in love as united in fame,
Lo! the standard which stole from the starlight its flame,
And type of all chivalry, glory, romance,
The lilies, the luminous lilies of France.

O morning superb! when the siege reached its close;
See! the sundawn outbloom, like the alchemist's rose!
The last wreaths of smoke from dim trenches upcurled,
Are transformed to a glory that smiles on the world.
Joy, joy! Save the wan, wasted front of the foe,
With his battle-flags furled and his arms trailing low;—
Respect for the brave! In stern silence they yield,
And in silence they pass with bowed heads from the field.
Then triumph transcendent! so Titan of tone
That some vowed it must startle King George on his throne.

When Peace to her own, timed the pulse of the land,
And the war weapon sank from the war-wearied hand,
Young Freedom upborne to the height of the goal
She had yearned for so long with deep travail of soul,
A song of her future raised, thrilling and clear,
Till the woods leaned to hearken, the hill slopes to hear:—
Yet fraught with all magical grandeurs that gleam
On the hero's high hope, or the patriot's dream,
What future, tho' bright, in cold shadow shall cast
The proud beauty that haloes the brow of the past.
Oh! wedded in love, as united in fame,
See the standard which stole from the starlight its flame,
And type of all chivalry, glory, romance,
The lilies, the luminous lilies of France.

ON THE PERSECUTION OF THE JEWS IN RUSSIA.

"Be advised! Do not trample upon my people. *Nations and men that oppress us do not thrive.*"—*From Charles Reade's "Never Too Late to Mend.*"

What murmurs are these that so wofully rise
Into heart-storms of agony borne from afar?
A tempest of passion, a tumult of sighs?
There is dread on the earth, and stern grief in the skies,
While the nations, appalled, watch the realm of the Czar!

Can humanity's sun have gone down in an hour,
Or a fiend have struck mercy's soft key-note ajar,
That upwhirled on the fierce winds of madness and power,
This cloud—with its hail of harsh hatreds—should lower
O'er those who still call on their "father," the Czar?

Can hell have burst upward, and spawned from its womb
The worst of all demons that menace and mar?
O God! see an empire reeking in gloom—
Hark! the death-shock, the shriek, the wild volleys of doom—
Ay! the riot of hell shakes the land of the Czar!

The fields are flame-girdled, the rivers roll red
Through the sulphurous fumes and swift ravage of war,
A war on the helpless, unhelmeted head,
Which tortures the living and spares not the dead;
Is he sleeping, or dumb, their "good father" the Czar?

Ah, no!—through the corridors stately and vast
Of his palace that gleams like a pale polar star,
On a gale from the south these black tidings have passed:
He hears! and the lightnings of justice at last
Quiver hissing and hot in the hand of the Czar!

The world holds its breathing to mark them in flame
On their limitless course that no bulwark can bar;
But instead, through his wily state parasite came
A rescript so false, its unspeakable shame
Should haunt to his death the dark dreams of the Czar!

No word for the victims, all butchered and bare,
By the hearth-stone defiled, and the blood-tainted lar;
For the poor ravished maid, whose sole shroud is her hair;
For the mother's lament, or the father's despair:
No pity for such thrills the thought of the Czar;

But his spirit leans, tender and yearning, above
The mad helots who riot, rage, murder afar;
To them he is soft as a nest-brooding dove;
But the *murdered!* alas! *they* are stinted of love,
Right, justice, or ruth, in the creed of the Czar!

Shall grim carnage goad onward, embruted and base,
The black coursers that strain at her iron-wrought car,
While those of high purpose and fetterless race
Idly gaze on the foul mediæval disgrace
Which poisons all earth from yon realm of the Czar?

Wake, England, your thunders! America, fling
To the wind the shrewd statecrafts that hamper, or mar!
Blend your voices of wrath! your deep warnings outring,
To smite the dulled ears, and blind soul of the king—
Who rules—Heaven help them! those realms of the Czar!

ASSASSINATION.

O BLINDED readers of the scroll of time,
Think ye that freedom yields her hand to crime?

Or the fair whiteness of her virginal bud
Of heavenly hope, would desecrate with blood?

Her eyes are chastened lightnings, and
the fire
Of her divinely purified desire

Burns not in ambush by assassins
trod.
But on the holiest mountain heights of
God!

So, ye that fain would meet her fond
embrace,
Purge the base soul, unmask the
treacherous face,

Drop bowl or dagger while ye bring her
naught
But the grand worship of a selfless
thought!

ENGLAND.

LAND of my father's love, my father's
race,
How long must I in weary exile
sigh
To meet thee, O my empress, face to
face,
And kiss thy radiant robes before I
die?

O England! in my creed, the humblest
dust
Beside thy haunted shores and shadowy
streams,
Is touched by memories and by thoughts
august,
By golden histories and majestic
dreams.

O England! to my mood thy lowliest
flower
Feeds on the smiles of some transcen-
dent sky:
Thy frailest fern-leaf shrines a spell of
power!
Ah! shall I walk thy woodlands ere I
die?

Thy sacred places, where dead heroes
rest
By temples set in ivy-twilight deep;
Thy fragrant fields topped by the sky-
lark's crest;
Thy hidden waters breathing balms of
sleep:

Thy castled homes, and granges veiled
afar
In antique dells; thy ruins hoar and
high;
Thy mountain tarns, each like a glitter-
ing star,
Shall I behold their marvels ere I die?

Thine opulent towns, throned o'er the
subject-main,
Girt by brave fleets, their weary canvas
furled,
Deep-laden argosies through storm and
strain,
Borne from the utmost boundaries of
the world

O'er all, thy London! every stone with
breath
Indued to question, counsel, or reply;
City of mightiest life and mightiest
death,
Shall I behold thy splendors ere I die?

But most I yearn, in body as heart, to
bow
Before our England's poets, strong and
wise,
Watch some grand thought uplift the
laureate's brow,
And flash or fade in Swinburne's fiery
eyes.

And other glorious minstrels would I
greet
Bound to my life by many a rhythmic
tie,
When shall I hear their welcomes frankly
sweet,
And clasp those cordial hands, before
I die?

Fair blow the breezes; high are sail and steam;
Soon must I mark brave England's brightening lea;
Fulfilled at length, the large and lustrous dream
Which lured me long across the summer sea!

Alas! a moment's triumph! — false as vain!
O'er dreary hills the gaunt pines moan and sigh;
Pale grows my dream, pierced through by bodeful pain;
England! I shall not see thee ere I die!

TO LONGFELLOW.

(ON HEARING HE WAS ILL.)

O THOU, whose potent genius (like the sun
Tenderly mellowed by a rippling haze)
Hast gained thee all men's homage, love and praise,
Surely thy web of life is not outspun,
Thy glory rounded, thy last guerdon won!
Nay, poet, nay! — from thought's calm sunset ways
May new-born notes of undegenerate lays
Charm back the twilight gloom ere day be done!

But past the poet crowned I see the friend —
Frank, courteous, true — about whose locks of gray,
Like golden bees, some glints of summer stray;
Clear-eyed, with lips half poised 'twixt smile and sigh;
A brow in whose soul-mirroring manhood blend
Grace, sweetness, power and magnanimity!

"PHILIP MY KING." *

"PHILIP, my king," ay, still thou art a king,
Though storms of sorrow on thy suffering head
Have flashed and thundered through the midnight's dread;
Ah, lofty soul! fraught with the sky-lark's wing
To capture heaven, the sky-lark's voice to sing
Such notes ethereal through veiled brightness shed
Their gracious power to liquid pathos wed,
Thrills like the soft rain-pulses of the spring:

Banned from earth's day — thine *inward* sight expands
Above the night-bound senses' birth or bars;
Lord of a larger realm, of subtler scope,
Where thou at last shalt press the lips of Hope,
And feel God's angel lift in radiant hands
Thy life from darkness to a place of stars!

Meanwhile, alas! despite these inward spells
Of voice and vision, and fond hope to be,
Perchance,—though vaguely shadowed forth to thee,—
Oft-times thy thought but echoes the deep knells
Of buried joy; oft-times thy spirit swells
With moaning memories, like a smitten sea,
When the worn tempest wandering up the lea,
Leaves a low wind to breathe its wild farewells.

---

* "*Philip my King*," Miss Mulock's exquisite song, all lovers of poetry must recall. The little hero of that lyric was Philip Marston, the author's god-son.

O brother! — pondering dreary and apart
O'er the dead blossoms of deciduous years:
O poet! fed too long on bitter tears!
I waft, o'er seas, a white-winged courier-dove,
Bearing to thee this balmy spray of love,
Warm from the nested fragrance of my heart.

"Old passions may be purged of blood,
Old memories cannot die."

A PLEA FOR THE GRAY.

[A discussion has recently been inaugurated in the city of Mobile, Ala., among the military companies, as to the propriety of changing the *Gray* for the *Blue* or some other uniform.]

When the land' s martyr, mid her tears,
Outbreathed his latest breath,
The discord of long, festering years,
Lay also dumb in death:
Our souls a new-born friendship drew
With spells of kindliest sway;
At last, at last, the conquering Blue
Blent with the vanquished Gray!

Yet, *who* thro' this south-land of ours,
While faith and love are free,
But still must cast memorial flowers
Across the grave of Lee?
And oft their ancient grief renew
O'er "Stonewall's" cherished clay?
The heart that's pledged to guard the Blue
Must honor still the Gray!

O veterans of Potomac's flood,
Or Vicksburg's lurid sky,
Old passions may be purged of blood,
Old memories cannot die!
They fill your eyes with fiery dew,
Revive your manhood's May,
And past the bright victorious Blue,
Bring back the stainless Gray!

O martyrs of the desperate fight,
All weak and broken now,
With shattered nerves, or blasted sight,
Frail arms and furrowed brow!
What think ye of the *patriot* view
Flashed on your minds to-day?
Too old to don the prosperous Blue,
Ye clasp your tattered Gray!

From many a worn and wasted mound,
And dust-encumbered clod,
The voices of dead heroes sound,
Rising from earth to God!
"Our doom was dark, our lives were true,
Ah! cast not quite away,
What time ye hail the favored Blue —
Old dreams that crowned the Gray!"

Can honor in his sacred grave
Less fair and glorious be?
Can faith on fortune's fickle wave,
Change with the changeful sea?
Beware lest what ye rashly do
Should end in shamed dismay,
And all pure champions of the Blue,
Scorn traitors to the Gray!

UNION OF BLUE AND GRAY.

[Suggested by the recent visit of Governor Bigelow and the Connecticut companies to Charleston, South Carolina.]

THE Blue is marching south once more,
With serried steel and stately tread;
Their martial music pealed before,
Their flag of stars flashed overhead.
Ah! not through storm and stress they come,
The thunders of old hate are dumb,
And frank as clear October's ray
This meeting of the Blue and Gray.

A Phœnix from her outworn fires,
Her gory ashes, rising free,
Fair Charleston with her stainless spires
Gleams by the silver-stranded sea.
No hurtling hail nor hostile ball
Breaks through the treacherous battle-pall;
True voices speak from hearts as true,
For strife lies dead 'twixt Gray and Blue.

Grim Sumter, like a Titan maimed,
Still glooms beyond his shattered keep;
But where his bolts of lightning flamed
There broods a quiet, mild as sleep;
His granite base, long cleansed of blood,
Is circled by a golden flood,
Type of that peace whose sacred sway
Enfolds the Blue, exalts the Gray.

The sea-tides faintly rise afar,
And — wings of all the breezes furled,
Seem slowly borne o'er beach and bar,
Dream-murmurings from a spirit world,
Through throbbing drum and bugle-trill
The distant calm seems deeper still —
Deep as that faith whose cordial dew
Hath soothed the Gray and charmed the Blue.

O'er Ashley's breast the autumn smiles,
All mellowed in her hazy fold,
While the white arms of languid isles
Are girdled by ethereal gold.
All Nature whispers: war is o'er,
Fierce feuds have fled our sea and shore;
Old wrongs forget, old ties renew,
O heroes of the Gray and Blue!

The southern Palm and northern Pine
No longer clash through leaf and bough;
Tranquillities of depth benign
Have bound their blending foliage now,

Or, tranced by cloudless star and moon.
Serene they shine in sun-lit noon.
Their equal shadows softly play
Above the Blue, across the Gray.

THE KING OF THE PLOW.

The sword is re-sheathed in its scabbard.
  The rifle hangs safe on the wall;
No longer we quail at the hungry
  Hot rush of the ravenous ball,
The war-cloud has hurled its last lightning,
  Its last awful thunders are still,
While the demon of conflict in Hades
  Lies fettered in force as in will:
Above the broad fields that he ravaged,
  What monarch rules blissfully now?
Oh! crown him with bays that are bloodless,
  The king, the brave king of the plow!

A king! ay! what ruler more potent
  Has ever swayed earth by his nod?
A monarch! aye, *more* than a monarch,
  A homely, but bountiful God!
He stands where in earth's sure protection
  The seed-grains are scattered and sown,
To uprise in serene resurrection
  When spring her soft trumpet hath blown!
A monarch! yea, *more* than a monarch,
  Though toil-drops *are* thick on his brow;
O! crown him with corn-leaf and wheat-leaf,
  The king, the strong king of the plow!

Through the shadow and shine of past ages,
  (While tyrants were blinded with blood)
He reared the pure ensign of Ceres
  By meadow, and mountain, and flood,
And the long, leafy gold of his harvests
  The earth-sprites and air-sprites had spun,
Grew rhythmic when swept by the breezes,
  Grew royal, when kissed by the sun;
Before the stern charm of his patience
  What rock-rooted forces must bow!
Come! crown him with corn-leaf and wheat-leaf,
  The king, the bold king of the plow!

Through valleys of balm-drooping myrtles,
  By banks of Arcadian streams,
Where the wind-songs are set to the mystic
  Mild murmur of passionless dreams;
On the storm-haunted uplands of Thule,
  By ice-girdled fiords and floes,
Alike speeds the spell of his godhood,
  The bloom of his heritage glows;
A monarch! yea, *more* than a monarch,
  All climes to his prowess must bow;
Come crown him with bays that are stainless,
  The king, the brave king of the plow.

Far, far in earth's uttermost future,
  As boundless of splendor as scope,
I see the fair angel!—fruition,
  Outspeed his high heralds of hope;
The roses of joy rain around him,
  The lilies of sweetness and calm,
For the sword has been changed to the plowshare,
  The lion lies down with the lamb!
O! angel-majestic! We know thee,
  Though raised and transfigured art thou,
This lord of life's grand consummation
  Was once the swart king of the plow!

IN MEMORIAM.

I.

LONGFELLOW DEAD.

Ay, it is well! Crush back your selfish tears;
For from the half-veiled face of earthly spring
Hath he not risen on heaven-aspiring wing
To reach the spring-tide of the eternal years?

With life full-orbed, he stands amid his peers,
The grand immortals! a fair, mild-eyed king,
Flushing to hear their potent welcomes ring
Round the far circle of those luminous spheres.

Mock not his heavenly cheer with mortal wail,
Unless some human-hearted nightingale,
Pierced by grief's thorn, shall give such music birth
That he, the new-winged soul, the crowned and shriven,
May lean beyond the effulgent verge of heaven,
To catch his own sweet requiem, borne from earth!

Such marvellous requiem were a pæan too —
(Woe touched and quivering with triumphant fire);
For him whose course flashed always high and higher,
Is lost beyond the strange, mysterious blue:
Ah! yet, we murmur, *can* this thing be true?
Forever silent here, that tender lyre,
Tuned to all gracious themes, all pure desire,
Whose notes dropped sweet as honey, soft as dew?

No tears! you say — since rounded, brave, complete,
The poet's work lies radiant at God's feet.
Nay! nay! our hearts with grief *must* hold their tryst:
How dim grows all about us and above!
Vainly we grope through death's bewildering mist,
To feel once more his clasp of *human* love!

II.

ON THE DEATH OF PRESIDENT GARFIELD.

I see the Nation, as in antique ages,
Crouched with rent robes, and ashes on her head:
Her mournful eyes are deep with dark presages,
Her soul is haunted by a formless dread!

"O God!" she cries, "why hast Thou left me bleeding,
Wounded and quivering to the heart's hot core?
Can fervid faith, winged prayer, and anguished pleading
Win balm and pity from thy heavens no more?

"I knelt, I yearned, in agonizing passion,
Breathless to catch thy 'still small voice' from far;
Now thou *hast* answered, but in awful fashion,
And stripped our midnight of its last pale star.

"What tears are given me in o'ermastering measure,
From fathomless floods of Marah, darkly free,
While that pure life I held my noblest treasure
Is plunged forever in death's tideless sea!

"Hark to those hollow sounds of lamentation,
The muffled music, the funereal bell;
From far and wide on wings of desolation
Float wild and wailful voices of farewell.

"The North-land mourns her grief in full libation,
Outpoured for him who died at victory's goal;
And the great West, in solemn ministration,
May not recall her hero's shining soul.

"Yea, the North mourns; the West; a stricken mother,
Droops as in sackcloth with veiled brow and mouth;
And what old strifes, what waning hates, can smother
The generous heart-throbs of the pitying South?

"Did doubt remain? — *She* crushed its latest ember
At that stern moment when the victim's fall
Changed loveliest summer to a grim December,
Paled by the hiss of Guiteau's murderous ball.

"Thus by the spell of one vast grief united
(Where cypress boughs their death-cold shadows wave),
My sons, I trust, a holier faith have plighted,
And sealed the compact by *his* sacred grave."

. . . . .

'Twas thus she spoke; but still in prostrate sorrow,
While lowlier earthward drooped her brow august.
To-day is dark; vague darkness clouds to-morrow.
Ah! in God's hand the nations are but — dust!

III.

DEAN STANLEY.

DEAD! dead! in sooth his marbled brow is cold,
And prostrate lies that brave, majestic head;
True! his stilled features own death's arctic mould,
Yet, by Christ's blood, I know he is not dead!

Here fades the cast-off vestment that he wore,
The robe of flesh, whence his true self hath fled;
Whate'er be false, one faith holds fast and sure,
Great souls like his abide not with the dead:

Eyried with God, beyond all mortal pain,
Breathing the effluence of ethereal birth,
Through deeds divine, his spirit walks again,
On rhythmic feet the mournful paths of earth!

In heaven immortal, yet on earth supreme,
The glamour of his goodness still survives,
Not in vain glimpses of a flattering dream,
Bnt flower and fruit of ransomed human lives.

His hopes were ocean-wide, and clasped mankind;
No Levite plea his mercy turned apart,
But wounded souls — to whom all else were blind —
He soothed with wine and balsam of the heart.

With stainless hands he reared his Master's cross;
His Master's watchword pealed o'er land and sea;
And still through days of gain, and days of loss,
Proclaimed the golden truce of charity.

All men were brethren to his larger creed,
But given the thought sincere — the earnest aim:
God's garden will not spurn the humblest weed
That yearns for purer air and loftier flame.

This sweet evangel of the unborn years,
Seer-like he spake, as one that viewed his goal,
While the world felt through darkness and through tears,
Mysterious music thrill its raptured soul.

Dead! nay, not dead! while eagle thoughts aspire,
Clothed in winged deeds across the empyreal height,
And all the expanding space is flushed with fire,
And deep on deep, heaven opens to our sight,—

He *cannot* die! yet o'er his dust we shed
Our rain of human sorrow; on his breast
Cross the pale palms; and pulseless heart and head
Leave to the quiet of his cloistered rest.

Sleep, knightly scholar! warrior-saint, repose!
Thy life-force folded like an unfurled sail!
Spent is time's rage —its foam of crested woes —
And thou hast found, at last, the Holy Grail!

IV.

HIRAM H. BENNER.

[Dedicated to the Wife of this Hero and Martyr.]

WHEN the war-drums beat and the trumpets blare,
When banners flaunt in the stormy air,
When at thought of the deeds that must soon be done,
The hearts of a thousand leap up as one,
Who could not rush through the din and smoke,
The cannon's crash and the sabre stroke,
Scarce conscious of ebbing blood or breath,
With a laugh for wounds and a scoff at death?

But when on the sullen breeze there comes
No thrill of trumpets nor throb of drums,
But only the wail of the sick laid low
By the treacherous blight of a viewless foe —
Who, then, will upgird his loins for fight
With the loathsome pest in the poisoned night,
No martial music his pulse to start,
But the still, small voice of the ruthful heart?
Who then? Behold him, the calm, the brave,
On his billowy path to an alien grave!
Serene in the charm of his God-like will,
This soldier is armored to save, not kill.
Ah! swiftly he speeds on the mist-bound stream
This pilgrim wrapped in his tender dream,
His vision of help for the sick laid low
By the evil spell of an ambushed foe.

Ah! swiftly he speeds 'mid the hollow boom
Of bells that are tolling to death and doom.

Till even the sounds of the bells grow
still;
For the hands of their ringers are lax
and chill.
And the hum of the mourners is heard
no more
On the misty slope and the vacant shore,
And the few frail creatures that greet
him seem
But the ghosts of men by a phantom
stream.

Still the hero his own great soul enticed
To suffer and toil in the name of Christ,
He follows wherever his Lord had led,
To the famished hut or the dying bed.
He medicines softly the fevered pain;
To the starving he bringeth his golden
grain:
And ever before him and ever above
Is the sheen of the unfurled wings of
love.

Meanwhile, in his distant home are those
That his going has robbed of their sweet
repose.
The days pass by them like leaden years;
The nights are bitter with tears and
fears —
Till at last, by the lightning glamour
sped,
Comes a name and date, with the one
word, "Dead!"
And the arms of the smitten are lifted
high,
And the heavens are rent by an anguished
cry!

Dead! dead! Vain word for the wise to
hear!
How false its echo on heart and ear!
To the earth and earth's he may close
his eyes,
But who dares tell us a martyr dies?
And of him just gone it were best to say
That in some charmed hour of night or
day —
Having given us all that his soul could
give —
Brave Hiram Benner began to live.

V.

W. GILMORE SIMMS.

A POEM

Delivered on the night of the 13th of December, 1877 "at the Charlestown Academy of Music," as prologue to the "Dramatic Entertainment" in aid of the "Simms Memorial fund."

THE swift mysterious seasons rise and
set;
The omnipotent years pass o'er us,
bright or dun; —
Dawns blush, and mid-days burn, 'till
scarce aware
Of what deep meaning haunts our
twilight air,
We pause bewildered, yearning for the
sun;
Only to find in that strange evening-
tide,
By the last sunset pathos sanctified,
Pale memory near us, and divine re-
gret!

Then memory gently takes us by the
hand;
And doubtful boundaries of a faded
time,
Half veiled in mist and rime,
Emerge, grow bright, expand;
The past becomes the present to our
eyes;
Poor slaves of dust and death,
(As if some trump of resurrection
clear
Somewhere outpealed, *our* senses could
not hear)
Rise, freed from churchyard taint and
mortal stain;
Old friends! dear comrades! *have* we
met again?
God! how these dismal years
Of anguished desolation, and veiled
tears,
Of fettered feeling, and despondent
sighs,
Wither and shrivel like a parchment
scroll

Seized by the fury of consuming fire,
Before the rapture of the illumined soul,
Lifted and lightened by our love's desire!

Old friends! dear comrades! *have* we met once more?
Come! let us fondly mark
In this weird truce, whose moments soon must flee,
'Twixt the charmed heart and dread reality,
Those well-belovéd features that ye wore
Once on this earthly shore,
Now rescued from the void and treacherous dark!
O! faces soft or strong,
Familiar faces! how ye press and throng
Closely about us, while the enchanted light
Changes to noonday our long spiritual night!
The faithful eyes that beamed in ours of yore,
Shine on us in their ancient guileless way,
Undimmed, unshorn of *one* beneficent ray,
And vital seeming as our own, to-day;
Lips smile, as once they smiled with innocent zest,
When round the social board
The impetuous flood-tide poured
Of curbless mirth, and keen sparkling jest
Vanished like wine-foam on its golden crest!
We feel the loyal grasp
Of many a warm hand, yielding clasp for clasp:
But may not stay, alas! we may not stay
To greet ye one by one,
Comrades! returned from realms beyond the sun:
For lo! in rightful precedence of power,
"A Saul amongst his brethren," than the rest
Loftier, if ruder in his natural might,
The man who toiled through fortune's bitterest hour,
As calmly steadfast and supremely brave,
As if above a fair life's tranquil wave,
Brooded the halcyon with unruffled breast:
The man whose sturdy frame upheld aright,
We meet, (O friends), to consecrate to-night!

All pregnant powers that wait
On intellectual state,
Favored and loved him: earliest, dearest came
Imagination, robed in mystical flame;
Her clear eyes searching all created things
Heavenly and earthly; with vast breadth of wings
Engirdled by the magic of a spell ineffable:
And like the sportive nymph of woodland bowers,
Fancy stole on him coyly, pranked with flowers,
Whereof the fairest her white fingers shed,
To crown his bended head.
Bluff humor true, if broad,
Placed in his hand a mirth-evoking rod,
While satire, from the heights of reason proud,
Flashed a keen gleam, like lightning from a cloud
The levin-bolt so sheerly cuts in two,
The cloud disparts, to leave — a luminous blue!

All that he was, all that he owned, we know
Was lavished freely on *one* sacred shrine,
The shrine of home and country! from the first
Fresh blush of youth, when merged in sanguine glow,

His life-path seemed a shadowless steep to shine,
Leading forever upward to the stars;
Through many a desperate and embittered strife
That raging, rose and burst
Above the storm-wracked waste of middle-life,
Down to the day, a few sad years ago,
When a grave veteran with his age's scars,
He moved among us, like a Titan maimed;
Only *one* glorious goal,
Through fate, grief, change, the pure allegiance claimed

"Pale memory near us."

Of his unconquered and majestic soul;
The goal of honor; not that *he* might rise
Alone and dominant; *but that all men's eyes*
Might view, perchance through much brave toil of his,
His country stripped of every filthy weed
Of crime imputed ; in thought, word and deed,
A noble people, none would dare despise
In their unsullied *Palingenesis,*
(Which he with blissful awe,
And all a poet's prescient faith foresaw;)
A *noble people,* o'er their subject-lands
Ruling with constant hearts and stainless hands;
Their feet firm planted as McGregor's were,
Deep in the herbage of their native sod,
And every honest forehead free to rear
A front unquelled by fear,
Untouched by shame, unfurrowed by despair, —
High in man's sight, or bowed alone to God!

So, let us rear the shaft, and poise the bust
Above the mouldering, but ah! priceless dust
Of vanished genius! Let our homage be
Large as that splendid prodigality
Of force and love, wherewith he stanchly wrought
Out from the quarries of his own deep thought,
Unnumbered shapes; whether of good or ill,
No puny puppets whose false action frets
On a false stage, like feeble *Marionettes;*
But life-like, human still;
Types of a by-gone age of crime and lust;
Or, grand historic forms, in whom we view
Re-vivified, and re-created stand,
The braves who strove through cloud-encompassed ways,
Infinite travail, and malign dispraise,
To guard, to save, to wrench from tyrant hordes,
By the pen's virtue, or the lordlier sword's
Unravished Liberty,
The virgin huntress on a virgin strand!

I, through whose song your hearts have spoken to-night,
Soul-present with you, yet am far away;
Outside my exile's home, I watch the sway
Of the bowed pine-tops in the gloaming gray,
Casting across the melancholy lea,
A tint of browner blight;
Outside my exile's home, borne to and fro,
I hear the inarticulate murmurs flow
Of the faint wind-tides breathing like a sea;
When, in clear vision, softly dawns on me,
(As if in contrast with yon slow decay),
The loveliest land that smiles beneath the sky,
The coast-land of our Western Italy;
I view the waters quivering; quaff the breeze,
Whose briny raciness keeps an *under* taste
Of flavorous tropic sweets (perchance swept home,
Across the flickering waste
Of summer waves, capped by the Ariel foam),
From Cuba's perfumed groves, and garden spiceries!

Along the horizon-line a vapor swims,
Pale rose and amethyst, melting into gold;
Up to our feet the fawning ripples rolled,
Glimmer an instant, tremble, lapse, and die;
The whole rare scene, its every element
Etherealized, transmuted subtly, blent
By viewless alchemy,
Into the glory of a golden mood,
Brings potent exaltations, while I walk,
(A joyful youth again),
The snow-white beaches by the Atlantic Main!
Ah! *not* alone! the carking curse of Time
Far from him yet; his bold hopes unsubdued
By the long anguish of the woes to be,
Midmost his years, in mellow-hearted prime,
Beside me stands our stalwart-statured *Simms!*

See! what a Viking's mien!
Half tawny locks in careless masses curled
Over his ample forehead's massive dome!
Eyes of bold outlook, that sometimes beneath
Their level-fronted brows, shine lambent, deep,
With inspirations scarce aroused from sleep;

And sometimes rife with ire,
Sent forth as sword-blades from an unbared sheath,
Flashes of sudden fire!
His whole air breathes of combat, unserene
Profounds of feeling, by a scornful world
Too early stirred to impotent disdains;
Generous withal: bound by all liberal ties
Of lordly-natured magnanimities;
Whereof we mark the sign
In the curved fullness of a mobile mouth,
Almost voluptuous; hinting of the south,
Whose suns high summer shed through all his veins:
Blending the mildness of a cordial grace
With sterner traits of his Berserker face,
Firm-set as granite, haughty, leonine.

No prim Precisian he! his fluent talk
Roved thro' all topics, vivifying all;
Now deftly ranging level plains of thought,
To sink, anon in metaphysical deeps;
Whence, by caprice of strange transition brought
Outward and upward, the free current sought
Ideal summits, gathering in its course,
Splendid momentum and imperious force,
Till, down it rushed as mighty cataracts fall,
Hurled from gaunt mountain steeps!

Sportive he could be as a gamesome boy!
By heaven! as 'twere but yesterday, I see
His tall frame quake with throes of jollity;
Hear his rich voice that owned a jovial tone,
Jocund as Falstaff's own;
And catch moist glints of steel-blue eyes o'errun
Sideways, by tiny rivulets of fun!

Alas! this vivid vision slowly fades!
Its serious beauty, and its flush of joy
Pass into nothingness! . . . Stern Death resumes
His sombre empire in the dusk of tombs;
And the deep umbrage of the cypress glades
Is wanly, coldly cast
In lengthening gloom o'er the reburied past!
What then? the spirit of him
We mourn and fain would honor, grows not dim;
On earth will live with consummated toil
Worthily wrought, despite the hot turmoil
Of open enmity, the secret guile,
That mole-like burrowed 'neath the fruitful soil
Of his broad mental acres, but to show
Marks of its crawling littleness between,
Each far-extended row
Of those hale harvests, glittering gold or green!

And somewhere, *somewhere* in the infinite space,
Like all true souls by our Soul-Father prized,
It dwells *forever individualized;*
No ghost bewildered 'midst a "No Man's Land;"
Outlawed and banned
Of fair identity's redeeming grace,
Shivering before its wretched phantom self,
Marred by Lethean moonshine — a pale elf,
A passionless shadow, but in mind and heart,
The mortal creature's marvellous counterpart;
Only exalted, nobler; down on us
Gazing thro' fathomless ethers luminous;
Watching the earth and earth-ways from afar,

Perhaps with somewhat of a scornful smile;
Yet tempered by the tolerance which beseems
One long translated from *our* sphere of dreams,
Hollow illusions, vacant vanities,
To that vast actual, which beyond us lies,
Where who may guess? midst yonder opulent skies;
Clear "coigns of vantage," in some deathless star!

VI.

DICKENS.

Methinks the air
Throbs with the tolling of harmonious bells,
Rung by the hands of spirits; everywhere
We feel the presence of a soft despair
And thrill to voices of divine farewells.

Sweet Fancy lost,
Wandering in darkness, now makes silvery moan;
While Pathos, pale, and shadowy, like a ghost,
Sobs upon Humor's breast, that mourns him most,
The wizard king who leaves them all— alone.

Wan genii throng,
From earth's four quarters hurrying, mount and mart,
Pure woodland peace, the city's din and wrong,
Each breathing low a fond funereal song,
Each sadly bowed o'er that grand, silent heart.

The children's tears
Mingle with manhood's woe, that falls like rain;
Low lieth one who towered above his peers,
And nevermore, through all the fruitful years,
Our eyes shall greet the master's like again.

Creations fine,
His prodigal offspring, crowd so thickly round
That Wit falls foul of Sorrow, Cupids twine
Warm arms with Avarice, and Love's strength divine
Hath vanquished Hate on Hate's own chosen ground.

Though gone, his art
Triumphant spans the threatening clouds of death;
Its rainbow hues forever pulse and start,
Steeped in the life-blood of the human heart,
And woven on heavens beyond Time's stormy breath.

VII.

TO BAYARD TAYLOR BEYOND US.

A VISION OF CHRISTMAS EVE, 1878.

As here within I watch the fervid coals,
While the chill heavens without shine wanly white,
I wonder, friend! in what rare realm of souls,
You hail the uprising Christmas-tide to-night!

I leave the fire-place, lift the curtain's fold,
And peering past these shadowy window-bars,
See through broad rifts of ghostly clouds unrolled,
The pulsing pallor of phantasmal stars.

Phantoms they seem, glimpsed through the clouded deep,
Till the winds cease, and cloudland's ghastly glow

Gives place above to luminous calms of sleep,
Beneath, to glittering amplitudes of snow!

Some stars like steely bosks on blazoned shields,
Stud constellations measureless in might;
Some lily-pale, make fair the ethereal fields,
In which, O friend, art thou ensphered to-night?

Where'er mid yonder infinite worlds it be,
Its souls, I know, are clothed with wings of fire;
How wouldst *thou* scorn even Immortality,
In whose dull rest thou couldst not still aspire!

There, Homer raised where genius cannot nod,
Hears the orbed thunders of celestial seas;
And Shakespeare, lofty almost as a God,
Smiles his large smile at Aristophanes;

With earth's supremest souls, still grouped apart,
Great souls made perfect in the eternal noon,
There thy loved Goethe holds thee to his heart,
Re-born to youth and all life's chords in tune.

While in the liberal air of that wide heaven,
He whispers: "Come! we share the self-same height;
To me on earth thy noblest toils were given,
Brothers, henceforth, we walk these paths of light."

Clear and more clear the radiant vision gleams!
More bright grand shapes and glorious faces grow:
While like deep fugues of victory, heard in dreams,
A thousand heavenly clarions seem to blow!

VIII.

BAYARD TAYLOR (UPON DEATH).

"More than once I have met death, but without fear! Nor do I fear now! Without being able to demonstrate it, I KNOW that my soul cannot die. . . . Indeed, to me the infinite is more comprehensible than the finite!"

These words occur in a letter of Bayard Taylor's to me, written not many weeks before his death. They have suggested the following sonnet: —

"OFT have I fronted Death, nor feared his might!
To me immortal, this dim Finite seems
Like some waste low-land, crossed by wandering streams
Whose clouded waves scarce catch our yearning sight:
Clearer by far, the imperial Infinite!
Though its ethereal radiance only gleams
In exaltations of majestic dreams,
Such dreams portray God's heaven of heavens aright!"
Thou blissful Faith! that on death's imminent brink
Thus much of heaven's mysterious truth hast told!
Soul-life aspires, though all the stars should sink;
Not vain our loftiest instinct's upward stress,
Nor hath the immortal hope shone clear and bold,
To quench at death, his torch in nothingness!

IX.

RICHARD H. DANA, SEN.

O DEEP grave eyes! that long have seemed to gaze
On our low level from far loftier days,
O grand gray head! an aureole seemed to gird,
Drawn from the spirit's pure, immaculate rays!

At length death's signal sounds! From weary eyes
Pass the pale phantoms of our earth and skies;
The gray head droops; the museful lips are closed
On life's vain questionings and more vain replies!

Like some gaunt oak wert thou, that lonely stands
'Mid fallen trunks in outworn desert lands;
Still sound at core, with rhythmic leaves that stir
To soft swift touches of aerial hands.

Ah! long we viewed thee thus, forlornly free,
In that dead grove the sole unravished tree;
Lo! the dark axe man smites! the oak lies low
That towered in lonely calm o'er land and sea!

X.

BRYANT DEAD!

Lo! there he lies, our Patriarch Poet, dead!
The solemn angel of eternal peace
Has waved a wand of mystery o'er his head,
Touched his strong heart, and bade his pulses cease.

Behold in marble quietude he lies!
Pallid and cold, divorced from earthly breath,
With tranquil brow, lax hands, and dreamless eyes,
Yet the closed lips would seem to smile at death.

Well may they smile; for death, to such as he,
Brings purer freedom, loftier thought and aim;
And, in grand truce with immortality,
Lifts to song's fadeless heaven his star-like fame!

XI.

THE POLE OF DEATH.

IN MEMORY OF SIDNEY LANIER.

How solemnly on mournful eyes
The mystic warning rose,
While o'er the Singer's forehead lies
A twilight of repose.

The twilight deepens into night, —
That night of frozen breath,
The rigor of whose Arctic blight,
We recognize as — death!

But since beyond the polar ice
May shine bright baths of balm;
Past its grim barriers' last device,
A crystal-hearted calm, —

Thus, ice-bound Death that guards so well
His far-off, secret goal,
May clasp a peace ineffable,
For some who reach his pole!

My poet — is it thus with thee,
Beyond this twilight gray, —
This frozen blight, this sombre sea, —
Ah! hast thou found the Day ?

XII.

THE DEATH OF HOOD.*

THE maimed and broken warrior lay,
By his last foeman brought to bay.

No sounds of battlefield were there —
The drum's deep bass, the trumpet's blare.

* During the terrible yellow fever season of 1878, General Hood and his wife died at very nearly the same time. They left a large family of children unprovided for, under circumstances which aroused the sympathy of the public, north and south. At the South, a considerable fund was subsequently raised for their support; while northern philanthropists, we understand, adopted two of the children.

No lines of swart battalions broke
Infuriate, thro' the sulphurous smoke.

But silence held the tainted room
An ominous hush, an awful gloom,

Save when, with feverish moan, he stirred,
And dropped some faint, half-muttered word,

Or outlined in vague, shadowy phrase,
The changeful scenes of perished days!

What thoughts on his bewildered brain,
Must then have flashed their blinding pain!

The past and future, blent in one, —
Wild chaos round life's setting sun.

But most his spirit's yearning gaze
Was fain to pierce the future's haze,

And haply view what fate should find
The tender loves he left behind.

"O God! outworn, despondent, poor,
I tarry at death's opening door,

While subtlest ties of sacred birth
Still bind me to the lives of earth.

How *can* I in calm courage die,
Thrilled by the anguish of a cry

I know from orphaned lips shall start
Above a father's pulseless heart?"

His eyes, by lingering languors kissed,
Shone like sad stars thro' autumn mist;

And all his being felt the stress
Of helpless passion's bitterness.

When, from the fever-haunted room,
The prescient hush, the dreary gloom,

A blissful hope divinely stole
O'er the vexed waters of his soul,

That sank as sank that stormy sea,
Subdued by Christ in Galilee.

It whispered low, with smiling mouth,
"She is not dead, — thy queenly South.

And since for her each liberal vein
Lavished thy life, like vintage rain,

When round the bursting wine-press meet
The Ionian harvesters' crimsoned feet;

And since for her no galling curb
Could bind thy patriot will superb.

Yea! since for her thine all was spent,
Unmeasured, with a grand content, —

Soldier, thine orphaned ones shall rest,
Serene, on her imperial breast.

Her faithful arms shall be their fold,
In summer's heat, in winter's cold;

And her proud beauty melt above
Their weakness in majestic love!"

Ah! then the expiring hero's face,
Like Stephen's, glowed with rapturous grace.

Mad missiles of a morbid mood,
Hurled at his heart in solitude,

No longer wounding, round it fell;
Peace sweetened his supreme farewell!

For sure the harmonious hope was true,
O South! he leaned his faith on you!

And in clear vision, ere he died,
Saw its pure promise justified.

MEDITATIVE AND RELIGIOUS.

I.

CHRIST ON EARTH.

HAD we but lived in those mysterious days,
When, a veiled God 'mid unregenerate men,
Christ calmly walked our devious mortal ways,

Crowned with grief's bitter rue in place of bays. —
Ah! had we lived but then:

Lived to drink in with every wondering breath,
A consciousness beyond all human ken,
That clothed in flesh, as long conceived in faith,
We viewed the Lord of life and Lord of death, —
Ah! had we lived but then:

To mark all Nature quickening where He trod,
Whether thro' golden field, or shadowy glen,
While a strange sweetness breathed from leaf and clod,
As thro' man's image they divined their God; —
Ah! had we lived but then!

Wild birds above him passed on reverent wing,
And savage sovereigns of dark dune or den,
Out stole to greet Him with mild murmuring,
Soft as a nested dove's song in the spring —
Ah! had we lived but then!

At "peace: be still!" the storm-wind ceased to roar,
And the lulled waters seemed to sigh "amen!"
Fear — the soul's mightier tempest — surged no more,
But a strange stillness fell on sea and shore; —
Ah! had we lived but then!

With our own ears to hear the words He said,
(Their music pondering o'er and o'er again!)
The wine of wisdom quaff from wisdom's head,
View the lame leap, and watch the uprising dead:
Ah! had we lived but then!

The world grows old. Faith, once a mountain stream,
Now crawls polluted down a poisonous fen;
The Bethlehem star hath lost its morning beam;
Thy face, dear Christ, wanes like a wasted dream, —
How changed, how cold since then.

Ah! 'tis our sordid lives whose promise fails:
These languorous lives of low, lost, aimless men;
Thro' mockery's mist our Lord's pure aureole pales,
Yet tenderer than the Syrian nightingales,
His voice sounds *now* as *then*.

II.

HARVEST-HOME.

O'ER all the fragrant land this harvest day,
What bounteous sheaves are garnered, ear and blade!
Whether the heavens be golden-glad, or gray, —
And the swart laborers toil in sun or shade: —

Like some fair mother in time's morning beams,
When mortal beauty lured immortal eyes,
Here, Earth lies smiling in ethereal dreams,
While her deep-bosomed breathings fall and rise!

Through half-closed lids she views o'er lawn and lea,
Rich-fruited trees, vast piles of glimmering grain, —

"O'er all the fragrant land this harvest day,
What bounteous sheaves are garnered, ear and blade."

And from the mountain boundaries to the sea,
Hears the low rumbling of the loaded wain.

A magical murmur born of ocean-deeps,
Blent with the pine-tree's lingering music thrills
Up the brown pastures to the trackless steeps,
And ancient caverns of the lonely hills.

Far-flashing insects flicker thro' the grass;
The humble-bee with burly bass drones by;
Afar the plover pipes; the curlews pass
In long lithe lines across the violet sky:

A mellowed radiance rings creation round;
Plenty and peace the auspicious season bless;
The full year pauses proudly, clothed and crowned
In consummation of high queenliness:

All nature seems to throb with rhythmic fires;
Dawns rise harmonious; splendid sunsets roll
Down to the chorus of invisible choirs—
Strange winds in tune with Earth's victorious soul!—

Thus, on the verge of winter's dreary rest,
Nature rejoices in rare pomps of power;
To breeze and sunbeam bares her prodigal breast,
And robes in purple her last shadowless hour.

Ah, when Life's autumn nears the eternal main,
May the heart's granary its rich depths unfold,—
Brimmed with immaculate sheaves of heavenly grain,
And flushed with fruitage of unfading gold!

III.

RECONCILIATION.

[From the South to the North. Written in view of the new year.]

LAND of the North! I waft to thee
The South's warm *benedicite!*
Thou camest when all was grief and pain,
The feverish blood, the tortured brain,
When through hot veins delirium ran,
Thou cam'st, the true Samaritan!

The charm of ruthful grace divine,
The golden oil and perfumed wine,
Have soothed far deeper wounds than those
Which harmed the body's hale repose;
On anguished souls dropped purely calm,
And sweet as Mary's "spikenard" balm!

Lo! now o'er all the world are drawn
Clear splendors of the New-year's dawn!
O North! O South! let warfare cease!
Hark! to *that* prince whose name is peace!
And ere time's new-born child departs,
Be joined in hands and joined in hearts!

Once wedded thus, O North! O South!
Should discord ope her Marah mouth,
Smite the foul lips so basely fain
To outpour hate's salt tides again:
Long raged the storm, long lowered the night,—
O faction, fly our morning light!

IV.

A VERNAL HYMN.

THE fresh spring burgeons into bloom—
And Earth with all her vernal charms
Lies like a queenly bride enclasped
Within her heavenly bridegroom's arms;

The storms that raved have sunk to
peace;
Freed rivulets weave a blithesome lay,
And blissful Nature softly sings
Preludings of her perfect day!

Meanwhile there's not a breeze that
thrills
Leaf, bud, and flower with genial
kiss, —
Which does not breathe *thy* mystic hope,
Oh, soul of Palingenesis: —

Glance where we may, the symbols rise
Of loftier loves and lives to be: —
*This marvellous spring-time seems to
grasp
The skirts of immortality!*

V.

CHRISTIAN EXALTATION.

O CHRISTIAN soldier! shouldst thou rue
Life and its toils, as others do —
Wear a sad frown from day to day,
And garb thy soul in hodden-gray?
O rather shouldst thou smile elate,
Unquelled by sin, unawed by hate, —
Thy lofty-statured spirit dress
In moods of royal stateliness; —
For say, what service so divine
As that, ah! warrior heart, of thine,
High pledged alike through gain or loss,
To thy brave banner of the cross?

Yea! what hast *thou* to do with gloom,
Whose footsteps spurn the conquered
tomb?
Thou that through dreariest dark can
see
A smiling immortality?

Leave to the mournful doubting slave,
Who deems the whole wan earth a grave,
Across whose dusky mounds forlorn
Can rise no resurrection morn,
The sombre mien, the funeral weed,
That darkly match so dark a creed;
But be *thy* brow turned bright on all,
Thy voice like some clear clarion call,
Pealing o'er life's tumultuous van
The keynote of the hopes of man,
While o'er thee flames through gain,
through loss, —
That fadeless symbol of the cross.

VI.

SOLITUDE; IN YOUTH AND AGE.

IN youth we shrink from solitude!
Its quiet ways we shun,
Because our hearts are fain to dance
With others' in the sun; —
Life's nectar bubbling brightly up,
O'erfloweth toward our brother's cup.

In age we shrink from solitude,
Because our God is there;
And something in his "still, small voice"
Doth bid our souls "beware!"
Who flies from God and conscience, can
But seek his fellow-sinner — man!

VII.

DENIAL.

WE look with scorn on Peter's thrice-
told lie;
Boldly we say, "Good brother! you
nor I,
So near the sacred Lord, the Christ,
indeed,
Had dared His name and marvellous
grace deny."

Oh, futile boast! Oh, haughty lips, be
dumb!
Unheralded by boisterous trump or
drum,
How oft 'mid silent eves and midnight
chimes,
Vainly to us our pleading Lord hath
come —

Knocked at our hearts, and striven to
enter there;
But we poor slaves of mortal sin and care,
Sunk in deep sloth, or bound by
spiritual sleep,
Heard not the voice divine, the tender
prayer!

Ah! well for us if some late spring-tide hour
Faith still may bring, with blended shine and shower;
If through warm tears a late remorse may shed,
Our wakened souls put forth *one* heavenly flower!

VIII.

LESSON OF SUBMISSION.

BEN YOUSSUF, bound to Mecca, day by day
Toiled bravely o'er the desert's fiery way,
Till its hot sands and flint-sown courses sore
Pressed on the broidered sandals which he wore,
Scorching and cutting! at the last they fell
Loosely abroad; — he seemed to fare through hell,
So blistering now, the flame-hued rocks and dust: —
"O mighty Allah!" cried he, "art thou just,
To let thy faithful pilgrim, serving thee,
Pass onward, thus, in nameless agony?"
With bitter thoughts and half-rebellious mind
He left, at length, the desert sands behind,
And still in that dark temper — far from grace —
Went where his brethren midst the holy place
Kneeled, by the *Caäba's* sanctity enthralled: —
Lo! there he marked a smitten wretch who crawled
Nearer the shrine, on bleeding hands and knees,
Yet his deep eyes were stars of prayer and peace; —
And ah, how Youssuf's heart remorseful beat,
To find *he* lacked not only shoes, but — feet!

IX.

THE SUPREME HOUR.

THERE comes an hour when all life's joys and pains
To our raised vision seem
But as the flickering phantom that remains
Of some dead midnight dream!

There comes an hour when earth recedes so far,
Its wasted wavering ray
Wanes to the ghostly pallor of a star
Merged in the milky way.

Set on the sharp, sheer summit that divides
Immortal truth from mortal fantasie;
We hear the moaning of time's muffled tides
In measureless distance die!

Past passions — loves, ambitions and despairs,
Across the expiring swell
Send thro' void space, like wafts of Lethean airs,
Vague voices of farewell.

Ah, then! from life's long-haunted dream we part,
Roused as a child new-born,
We feel the pulses of the eternal heart
Throb thro' the eternal morn.

X.

A CHRISTMAS LYRIC.

THO' the Earth with age seems whitened,
And her tresses hoary and old
No longer are flushed and brightened
By glintings of brown or gold,
A voice from the Syrian highlands,
O'er waters that flash and stir,
By the belts of their tropic islands,
Still singeth of joy to her!

A song which the centuries hallow!
Though softer than April rain
That soweth on field and fallow,
A spell that shall rise in grain —

Yet deep as the sea-strain chanted
  On the fluctuant ocean-lyre,
By the magical west-wind haunted,
  With the pulse of his soul on fire!

A promise to lift the lowly, —
  To weed the soul of its tares,
And change into harmonies holy
  The discord of fierce despairs:
A glory of high Evangels,
  Of rhythmical storms and calms;
All hail to the voices of angels,
  Heard over the starlit palms!

A hymn of hope to the ages,
  The music of deathless trust,
No frenzy of mortal rages
  Can darken with doubt or dust;
A rapture of high evangels,
  But centred in sacred calms!
Ah! still the chorus of angels
  Thrills over the Bethlehem palms!

Still heralds the day-spring tender,
  That never can melt or close,
Till the noon of its deepening splendor
  Out-blooms, like a mystic rose,
Whose petals are rays supernal
  Of love that hath all sufficed, —
And whose heart is the grace eternal,
  Of the fathomless peace of Christ!

XI.

THE PILGRIM.

THROUGH deepening dust and dreary dearth
I walk the darkened wastes of earth,
A weary pilgrim sore beset,
By hopeless griefs and stern regret.

With broken staff and tattered shoon
I wander slow from dawn to noon —
From arid noon till dew-impearled,
Pale twilight steals across the world.

Yet sometimes through dim evening calms
I catch the gleam of distant palms;
And hear, far off, a mystic sea
Divine as waves on Galilee.

Perchance through paths unknown, forlorn,
I still may reach an orient morn;
To rest when Easter breezes stir,
Around the sacred sepulchre.

XII.

PENUEL.

NEAR Jabbok Ford, endued with sacred might,
The patriarch strove with *one* that silent came,
Obscurely limned against the twilight flame —
Strove thro' slow watches of the marvellous night!

"*Ungird thine arms, for lo! 'tis morning light,*"
Spake the weird stranger! — "*nay, but grant the claim,*
Made good thro' strife divine, and bless my name,
'Ere yet thou goest from doubtful clasp and sight!"

Thus Jacob, in the slowly ebbing swell
Of power and passion, — yearning still to mark
That wrestler's face between the dawn and dark:

Again, "*wilt thou not bless me?*" . . . *yea!* and *yea!*"
Dropped a still voice, what time the new-born day
Haloed an angel's head at Penuel!

XIII.

PATIENCE.

SHE hath no beauty in her face,
  Unless the chastened sweetness there
And meek long-suffering yield a grace
  To make her mournful features fair.

Shunned by the gay, the proud, the young,
  She roams through dim unsheltered ways;

Nor lover's vow, nor flatterer's tongue,
  Brings music to her sober days.

At best, her skies are clouded o'er,
  And oft she fronts the stinging sleet,
Or feels on some tempestuous shore
  The storm-waves lash her naked feet!

Where'er she strays, or musing stands
  By lonesome beach, by turbulent mart, —
We see her pale, half-tremulous hands
  Crossed humbly o'er her aching heart.

Within, a secret pain she bears,
  A pain too deep to feel the balm
An April spirit finds in tears, —
  Alas! all cureless griefs are calm!

Yet in her passionless strength supreme,
  Despair beyond her pathway flies,
Awed by the softly steadfast beam
  Of sad, but heaven-enamored eyes!

Who pause to greet her, vaguely seem
  Touched by fine wafts of holier air,
As those who in some mystic dream
  Talk with the angels unaware!

XIV.

THE LATTER PEACE.

We have passed the noonday summit,
  We have left the noonday heat,
And down the hillside slowly
  Descend our weary feet.
Yet the evening airs are balmy,
  And the evening shadows sweet.

Our summer's latest roses
  Lay withered long ago;
And even the flowers of autumn
  Scarce keep their mellowed glow.
Yet a peaceful season woos us
  Ere the time of storms and snow.

Like the tender twilight weather
  When the toil of day is done,
And we feel the bliss of quiet
  Our constant hearts have won —
When the vesper planet blushes,
  Kissed by the dying sun.

So falls that tranquil season,
  Dew-like, on soul and sight,
Faith's silvery star rise blended
  With memory's sunset light,
Wherein life pauses softly
  Along the verge of night.

XV.

GAUTAMA.

Seven weary centuries ere our star-like Christ
  Rose on the clouded heavens of mortal faith
  Gautama came, the stern high priest of death,
Oblivion's sombre, dark evangelist.
Millions of souls hath this dread creed enticed
  To wander lost through realms of baleful breath,
  Ghoul-haunted, rife with shapes of sin and scath,
Monstrous, yet dim, as births of midnight mist:

All life, he taught, hath been, all life must be
  Accursed! the gift of demons! All delight
Lies at the far-off goal of pulseless peace.

Note. — We yield to none in our cordial admiration of Mr. Edwin Arnold's "Light of Asia;" but we regard that most eloquent, pathetic, and beautiful poem, chiefly as a poem — and by no means as an absolutely authoritative presentation of Gautama's creed, or its tendencies. It even seems to us that Mr. Arnold is himself somewhat in the dark as to these matters. The "prodigious controversy among the erudite in regard to Gautama's doctrines," Mr. Arnold confronts chiefly by his own firm conviction that "a third of mankind would never have been brought to believe in blank abstractions, or in nothingness, as the crown of Being!" *Au contraire*, we cannot fairly ignore the opinion of those Orientalists who maintain, that "Nirvana" is essentially nothingness; and moreover, that the idea involved in it has a peculiar charm for the Hindoo mind.

"Pray," sighed he, "that this breath of men shall cease;
Our hell is earth, our heaven eternal night;
Our only godhead vague Nonentity!"

XVI.

CHRIST.

THE soul's physician thus the soul would kill,
The soul's high priest its heaven-bound pinions stay,
Bring from fresh beauty chaos, night from day,
Despair from trust, from all good promise ill;
The outworn heart and sickened senses still
Must shroud heaven's life in fogs of foul decay,
Veil the swift angel, love, and hide the ray
Born of God's smile with masks of morbid will: —

But Truth, and Truth's great Master cannot die;
While Love, the seraph, free of wings and eyes,
Upsweeps the realm of calm immensity.
A thousand times our buried Christ shall rise
In prayerful souls to hush their anguished sighs,
And dawn, not darkness, rule o'er earth and sky.

XVII.

A WINTER HYMN.

O WEARY winds! O winds that wail!
O'er desert fields and ice-locked rills!
O heavens that brood so cold and pale
Above the frozen Norland hills!

Nature is like some sorrowing soul,
Robed in a garb of dreariest woe; —
She cannot see her vernal goal
Through ghostly veils of mist and snow: —

Her pulse beats low; through all her veins
Scarce can the sluggish life-blood start;
What feeble, faltering heat sustains
The half-numbed forces of her heart!

Above, despondent eyes she lifts,
To view the sun-ray's dubious birth;
Beneath she marks the storm-piled drifts
About a waste bewildering earth!

Ah, stricken Mother! hast thou lost
All memory of the germs that rest
Untouched by tempest, rain, or frost,
Shrined in thine own immortal breast?

Bend, bend thine ear; yea, bend and hear, —
Despite the winds' and woodlands' strife, —
Deep in Earth's bosom, faint and clear,
The far-off murmurous hints of life: —

The sound of waves in whispering flow;
Of seeds that stir in dreams of light,
Whose sweetness mocks the shrouded snow,
Whose radiance smiles at death and night;

So, Christian spirit! wrapt in grief, —
Beneath *thy* misery's frozen sod,
Love works, to burst in flower and leaf,
On some fair spring-dawn fresh from God!

XVIII.

THE THREE URNS.

LIST to an Arab parable, wherein
The beauty of the Orient fancy shrines
A star-like truth, the iconoclastic West
Is blind to see, its shrewd material vision
Bent over on the foulest soils of earth,
If only gold may gild them! Hear and learn!

Nimroud, the king to whom his four-score years
Had brought a wisdom pure as his white locks,

"O weary winds! O winds that wail,
O'er desert fields and ice-locked rills."

(And spotless they as snow on Caucasus!)
One morn commanded his three sons to grace
His presence chamber; there in front of each
A mighty urn, sealed with a mystic seal,
Was duly set — the one of burnished gold,
Blazed like an August noon — of amber fair
The other — but the third (dull as a cloud
Seen 'gainst the bright flash of a distant wave,
Or 'twixt the glittering tree-tops), seemed, in form,
A rugged mould wrought from the common earth.

"Choose thou, my eldest," said the king, deep-breathed,
"Choose thou amongst these urns, the urn which seems
To thee most precious," — whereupon he chose
The Vase of Gold, which bore in jewelled flame,
Clear leaping, the word "EMPIRE," — opened it,
And found beneath a deadly, vaporous fume,
(Which on the instant sickened heart and sense), —
Nought but a bubbling tide of vital blood,
Hot, as appeared, that moment from the veins
Of murdered manhood. The fair amber vase,
With "GLORY" written on it — "this for me!"
Exclaimed the second prince, with eager eyes,
And feverish hands clasping his treasure close,—
Too close, alas! for as he spake, the urn
Crashed on his breast, and bruised and tortured it,
And a rare dust, the ashes of great men,
Dead centuries since, rose from its shattered bulk
Pungent, and yet so light the feeblest puff
Of failing wind hath shorn and scattered them
Into vague air. One vase alone remained,
Which the third son unsealing, found therein,
Deep-graven, glittering like a planet keen,
Thro' gulfs of envious darkness the sole name
Of GOD, — "which name, O! princes," said the king,
"Doth sanctify yon vase of common earth
Above all precious metals sought of men,
Since but one letter of that sacred three,
Outweighs all worlds, from the mild star of eve,
Shining on love, to those mysterious orbs,
Which gird the pathway of the Pleiades."

XIX.

ON THE DECLINE OF FAITH.

As in some half-burned forest, one by one,
We catch far echoes on the doleful breeze,
Born of the downfall of its ruined trees;
While even thro' those which stand, slow shudderings run,
As if Fate's ruthless hand were laid thereon;
So, in a world sore-smitten by foul disease,
— That Pest, called Doubt — we mark by slow degrees,
The fall of many a faith that wooed the sun:
Some, with low sigh of parting bough, or leaf,

Strain, quivering downward to the abhorrèd ground;
Some totter feebly, groaning toward their doom;
While some broad-centuried growths of old Belief,
Sapped as by fire, defeatured, charred, discrowned,
Fall with a loud crash, and long reverberant boom!

Thus, fated hour by hour, more gaunt and bare,
Gloom the wan spaces, whence, a power to bless,
Up burgeoned once, in grace or stateliness,
Some creed divine, offspring of light and air;
What then? and must we yield to blank despair,
Beholding God Himself wax less and less,
Paled in the skeptical storm-cloud's whirl and stress,
Till all is lost — love, reverence, hope, and prayer.
O man! when faith succumbs, and reason reels,
Before some impious, bold iconoclast,
Turn to thy heart that *reasons* not, but *feels;*
Creeds change! shrines perish! *still* (*her* instinct saith),
Still the soul lives, the soul must conquer Death.
Hold fast to God, and God will hold thee fast!

XX.

THE ULTIMATE TRUST.

Though in the wine-press of thy wrath divine,
My crushed hopes droop, like crude and worthless must,
That love and mercy, Father! still are thine,
With reverent soul, I trust!

Though all my life be shattered by thine ire,
The mystic whirlwind of thy will august,
Still, from the din, the darkness and the fire,
I lift my song of trust!

Tho' foes assail me! yea, within, without!
Harrow my heart, and hurl its joys in dust,
No forceful fear, nor fraud of treacherous doubt,
Disarms my bucklered trust!

Though my lost years be wrapped in Arctic cloud,
And Grief on me hath wreaked her ruthless lust,
Still, like an angel's face above a shroud
Smiles my celestial trust!

Tho', Lord! thou wear'st a mask of hate ('twould seem),
And for a time, I think — as mortals must —
That mask shall melt, as melts a nightmare dream,
Before my Orient trust!

Yea! tho' Thou slay me, and supine, I cower,
Heart-pierced and bleeding from the fiery thrust, —
I know there bides in heaven a glorious hour,
To crown my sacred trust!

XXI.

"A LITTLE WHILE I FAIN WOULD LINGER YET."

A little while (my life is almost set!)
I fain would pause along the downward way,
Musing an hour in this sad sunset-ray,
While, Sweet! our eyes with tender tears are wet;
A little hour I fain would linger yet.

A little while I fain would linger yet,
All for love's sake, for love that cannot tire;
Though fervid youth be dead, with youth's desire,
And hope has faded to a vague regret,
A little while I fain would linger yet.

A little while I fain would linger here:
Behold! who knows what strange, mysterious bars
'Twixt souls that love, may rise in other stars?
Nor can love deem the face of death is fair;
A little while I still would linger here.

A little while I yearn to hold thee fast,
Hand locked in hand, and loyal heart to heart;
(O pitying Christ! those woeful words, "*We part!*")
So ere the darkness fall, the light be past,
A little while I fain would hold thee fast.

A little while, when night and twilight meet;
Behind, our broken years; before, the deep
Weird wonder of the last unfathomed sleep.
A little while I still would clasp thee, Sweet;
A little while, when night and twilight meet.

A little while I fain would linger here;
Behold! who knows what soul-dividing bars
Earth's faithful loves may part in other stars?
Nor can love deem the face of death is fair:
A little while I still would linger here.

XXII.

TWILIGHT MONOLOGUE.

CAN it be that the glory of manhood has passed,
That its purpose, its passion, its might,
Have all paled with the fervor that fed them at last,
As the twilight comes down with the night?

Can it be I have lived, dreamed, and labored in vain —
That above me, unconquered and bright,
The proud goal I had aimed at is taunting my pain,
As the twilight comes down with the night?

Can it be that my hopes, which *seemed* noble and fair,
Were predestined to mildew and blight?
Ah! sad disenchantment! that bids me beware
Of a twilight which heralds the night!

The glad days, the brave years that were lusty and long —
How they fade on vague memory's sight!
And their joys are like echoes of jubilant song,
As the twilight comes down with the night!

All the past is o'ershadowed, the present is dim,
And could earth's fairest future requite
The worn spirit that swoons, the racked senses that swim,
In this dread of the twilight and night?

There is dew on my raiment; the sea winds wail low,
As lost birds, wafted wave-ward in flight,

And all Nature grows cold, as my heart in its woe,
At the advent of twilight and night!

From the realm of dead sunset scarce darkened as yet —
Over hills mist-enshrouded and white,
A deep sigh of ineffable, mournful regret,
Seems exhaled 'twixt the twilight and night!

O! thou genius of art! I have worshipped and blessed;
O! thou soul of all beauty and light!
Lift me up in thine arms, give me warmth from thy breast,
Ere the twilight be merged in the night!

Let me draw from thy bosom miraculous breath,
And for once, on song's uppermost height,
I may chant to the nations such music in death
As shall mock at the twilight and night!

XXIII.

THE SHADOW OF DEATH.

I PRAY you, when the shadow of death draws nigh,
To bear me out beneath the unmeasured heaven;
I fain would hear the pine-trees' slumberous sigh,
And watch the cloud flotillas drifted high,
By slow, soft breezes driven
Due south, perchance toward realms of tropic balms,
And the warm fragrance of the Syrian palms.

I pray you, when the shadow of death comes down,
Oh! lay me close to nature's pulses deep,
Whether her breast with autumn tints be brown,
Or bright with summer, or hale winter's crown
Press on her brows in sleep;
So nigh the dawn of some new, marvellous birth,
I'd look to heaven, still clasped in arms of earth!

I pray you, when the shadow of death draws near,
Give, give me freedom for my last, faint breath;
Beneath God's liberal heaven I could not fear,
His merciful winds would dry my latest tear,
His sunshine soften death,
And some fair shreds of our dear earth's delight
Cling round the spirit in her upward flight.

XXIV.

FINIS.

A MOMENT'S gleam, a hint of sunnier weather,
Borne from the storm-clouds and the mists of fate;
Dawned, with a tender "Peradventure" hither,
A soft "Perchance it is not yet too late!"

And so a transient omen magnifying,
My soul would fain pass brightened, unto thine;
But to my half-formed thought comes truth replying:
"No life mounts backward from its wan decline."

Would'st thou expect, drear winter, ashen, sober,
To burn with blushes of a spring-tide noon?
Would'st thou expect the hectic-cheeked October
To catch the virginal freshness of young June?

All mortal lives like the year's seasons ever
Pass from their May dawn and rare summer's bloom,
Down to the day when autumn winds dissever
Life's latest sheaves to strew them near a tomb.

And then death looms, that pitiless grim December.
Bringing cold tears, a winding sheet like snow,
Last, a carved stone, which bids the world remember
One of its countless myriads sleeps below.

"My thoughts are wandering on the verge of dreams, . . .
While lower, feebler, flit the fireside gleams."

XXV.

THE SHADOWS ON THE WALL.

WHAT mournful influence chills my soul to-night ?
I watch the expiring flames that fade and fall.
From which outleap vague shafts of arrowy light,
Pursued by spectral shadows on the wall.

My thoughts are wandering on the verge of dreams,
Mist-laden, gray, and sombre as a pall,
While lower, feebler, flit the fireside gleams,
And darker those quaint shadows on the wall.

The old sad voice (fraught with the centuries' tears)
  That seems through infinite space and time to call,
Faint with the doubts and grief of antique years,
  Years that are dim as shadows on the wall;

The old sad voice is whispering to my heart:
  Man's life, phantasmal, vain, illusive all,
Beholds too soon its cloud-foundations part,
  Melting like midnight shadows on the wall.

Too soon the noblest passions, worn and old,
  Die, or grow dulled and languid past recall;
Even love may wane in memory's twilight cold,
  Sad, wavering, wan, as shadows on the wall.

And oft the loftiest nature's loftiest aim,
  Heaven-soaring once, wide as this earthly ball,
Sinks, a tamed eagle o'er whose eyes of flame
  The death-films steal like shadows on the wall.

A subtler voice whispers the conscious soul,
  "What of high hopes which held *thy* youth in thrall?
Where flash *thy* chariot wheels, where shines *thy* goal?"
  The mocking shadows answer from the wall.

With deepening dusk and faded flame they grow
  Fantastic phantoms, hovering over all
The tremulous space, or flickering to and fro
  In wild unearthly antics on the wall.

Till as the last slow ember drops in gloom,
  Like vassals hurrying through some wizard's hall,
Whirling they pass, and darkness haunts the room,
  No life, not even a shadow on the wall!

XXVI.

CONSUMMATUM EST.

I've done with all the world can give,
  Whate'er its kind or measure.
(O Christ! what paltry lives we live
  If toil be lord, or pleasure!).
Alas! *I* only yearn for sleep,
  Calm rest for fevered riot —
The sacred sleep, the shadows deep,
  Of death's majestic quiet.

I've done with all our earth-life lends —
  False hopes and wild ambitions,
Brilliant beginnings, futile ends,
  And long-postponed fruitions,
Those hollow shows dissembling truth,
  Vain myths that mock the real,
The dreary wrecks of peace and youth
  Above a crushed ideal.

I've done with heavenly dreams that wane
  At touch of earth-born dawnings,
With fervid passion, useless pain,
  Brave aims and dim forewarnings;
I've done with alien tears or smiles,
  Past days and vague to-morrows;
I've done with earth's unhallowed wiles,
  Brief joys and helpless sorrows.

I've done with compacts sealed in dust,
  Dull cares that overweighed me,
With promise of the Judas-trust,
  That, while it kissed, betrayed me;
With *all* save love, whose matchless face
  Midmost a life's undoing
Smiles in its tender angel's grace
  To sanctify the ruin.

I've done with all beneath the stars,
O world! so wanly fleeting!
How long against time's ruthless bars
Have the soul's wings been beating,
Till even the soul but yearns for sleep,
Calm rest for fevered riot —
The sacred sleep, the shadows deep,
Of death's majestic quiet!

XXVII.

THE BROKEN CHORDS.

Like a worn wind-harp on a barren lea,
Unstirred by subtle breathings of the sea,
Though sweet south-breezes swell the floodtide's flow,
The lyric power in this worn heart of mine
Droops in the twilight of life's wan decline,
While the loosed chords of song grown lax and low,
Are dumb to all the heavenly airs that blow!

Only, sometimes along each shattered string
I hear the ghost of Memory murmuring
Old strains, as half in sadness half in scorn,
So faint, so far, they scarcely pass the bound
'Twixt sullen silence and ethereal sound, —
Mere wraiths of murmurous tone, that die forlorn
Ere yet we deem those faltering notes are born!

So, smitten chords, sink, wane, and pass away!
Yet have ye made soft music in your day
On many a sea-swept strand or breezy lawn.
Once more I hear that yearning music rise;
Once more I see deep tears in tender eyes;
And all my soul melts in me, fondly drawn
Back to youth's love and youth's Arcadian dawn!

XXVIII.

THE RIFT WITHIN THE LUTE.

A tiny rift within the lute
May sometimes make the music mute!
By slow degrees, the rift grows wide,
By slow degrees, the tender tide —
Harmonious once — of loving thought
Becomes with harsher measures fraught,
Until the heart's Arcadian breath
Lapses thro' discord into death!

XXIX.

IN HARBOR.

I think it is over, over,
I think it is over at last,
Voices of foeman and lover,
The sweet and the bitter have passed: —
Life, like a tempest of ocean
Hath outblown its ultimate blast:
There's but a faint sobbing sea-ward
While the calm of the tide deepens leeward,
And behold! like the welcoming quiver
Of heart-pulses throbbed thro' the river,
Those lights in the harbor at last,
The heavenly harbor at last!

I feel it is over! over!
For the winds and the waters surcease;
Ah! — few were the days of the rover
That smiled in the beauty of peace!
And distant and dim was the omen
That hinted redress or release: —
From the ravage of life, and its riot
What marvel I yearn for the quiet
Which bides in the harbor at last?
For the lights with their welcoming quiver
That through the sanctified river
Which girdles the harbor at last,
This heavenly harbor at last?

I *know* it is over, over,
  I know it is over at last!
Down sail! the sheathed anchor uncover,
For the stress of the voyage has passed:
Life, like a tempest of ocean
  Hath outbreathed its ultimate blast:
There's but a faint sobbing sea-ward,
While the calm of the tide deepens lee-
    ward;
And behold! like the welcoming quiver
Of heart-pulses throbbed thro' the river,
  Those lights in the harbor at last,
  The heavenly harbor at last!

XXX.

FORECASTINGS.

When I am gone, what alien steps shall
    tread
  This flowery garden-close?
What alien hands shall pluck the violets
    sweet,
Or gather the rich petals of the rose,
  When I — drear thought! — am dead?

When I am gone, toward doubtful dark-
    ness led,
  What voices, false or true,
Shall echo round these old, familiar
    haunts
My happiest days of tranquil manhood
    knew,
  Ah me! when I am dead?

When I am gone, what museful eyes
    instead
  Of these dimmed eyes of mine,
Beneath yon trellised porch shall mark
    thro' heaven,
On cloudless eves the summer sunsets
    shine,
  When I, alas! am dead?

When I am gone, and all is done and
    said,
  One life had wrought below —
'Mid these fair scenes what other souls
    shall thrill,
In turn, to love and anguish, joy and
    woe —
  Dear Christ! when I am dead?

Though I be dead, perchance when
    Spring has shed
  Her gentlest influence round —
Here, where love reigned, my ghostly
    feet may tread
The old accustomed paths without a
    sound, —
Perchance — when I am dead!

Though I be dead, earth's fragrant
    white and red
  Here in spring roses met,
May to strange spiritual senses bring the
    balms
Of tender memory and divine regret,
  Yea! even to me — though dead!

Though I be dead, with faded hands and
    head
  Laid in unbreathing rest —
Dear cottage roof! thou still mayst lure
    me back,
Among the unconscious living a wan
    guest,
  Veiled, as Fate veils the dead:

A guest of shadowy frame, ethereal
    tread,
  Amongst them, yet apart —
A sombre mystery! in whose bosom
    throb
The faint, slow pulses of its phantom
    heart,
  Ah, heaven! not wholly dead!

XXXI.

APPEAL TO NATURE OF THE SOLITARY HEART.

Dear mother, take me to thy breast!
I have no other place of rest
  In all this weary world of men:
  Ah! fold me in thy love again,
Sweet mother; clasp me to thy breast!

From out thy womb, long since, I came,
A creature wrought of dust and flame;
I knew no mortal mother's grace,
But only viewed *thy* mystic face,
That softly went, and softly came!

I knew thee in the sunset grand,
The waveless calm, the silvery strand;
From out the shimmering twilight-bars
I saw thee smile between the stars,
Divinely sweet, or softly grand!

I heard, beneath the sylvan arch,
Thy battling winds, led on by March,
Sweep where the solemn pine-tops close
About its ravaged, dim repose —
Hushed, awed, beneath the woodland arch!

I heard thee, 'mid some tender hour,
In lisping leaf and rustling flower,
In low lute-breathings of the breeze,
And tidal sighs o'er moonless seas
Star-charmed in midnight's mournful hour!

I thrilled at each far-whispered tone
That touched me from thy vast unknown,
At every dew-bright hint that fell
From out thy soul unsearchable,
Yea, each strange hint and shadowy tone!

I felt, through dim, awe-laden space,
The coming of thy veilèd face;
And in the fragrant night's eclipse
The kisses of thy deathless lips,
Like strange star-pulses, throbbed through space!

Now mine own pulses, beating low,
Whisper the spent life: "*Thou must go;*
Even as a wasted rivulet, pass
Beyond the light, beneath the grass,
For strength grows faint, and hope is low!"

FOUR POEMS FOR SPECIAL OCCASIONS.

I.

TO THE POET WHITTIER.

ON HIS 70th BIRTHDAY.

From this far realm of pines I waft thee now
A brother's greeting, Poet, tried and true;
So thick the laurels on thy reverend brow,
We scarce can see the white locks glimmering through!

O pure of thought! Earnest in heart as pen,
The tests of time have left thee undefiled;
And o'er the snows of threescore years and ten
Shines the unsullied aureole of a child.

II.

TO O. W. HOLMES,

ON HIS BIRTHDAY.

Dear Doctor, whose blandly invincible pen
Has honored so often your great fellow-men
With your genius and virtues, who doubts it is true
That the world owes in turn, a warm tribute to you?

Wheresoever rare merit has lifted its head
From the cool country calm or the city's hotbed —
You were always the first to applaud it by name,
And to smooth for its feet the harsh pathway to fame.

Wheresoever beneath the broad rule of the sun,
By some spirit elect, a grand deed has been done —

Its electrical spell like the lightning's would dart,
Though the globe lay between, to thrill first in *your* heart!

Philanthropist! poet! romancer! combined —
Ay! shrewd scientist too — who shall fathom your mind,
Shall plumb that strange sea to the uttermost deep,
With its vast under-tides, and its rhythmical sweep?

You have toiled in life's noon, till the hot blasting light
Blinds the eyes that would guage your soul stature aright;
But when eve comes at last, 't will be clear to mankind,
By the length of bright shadow your soul leaves behind!

III.

TO EMERSON.

ON HIS 77th BIRTHDAY.

"I do esteeme him a deepe sincere soule; one that seemeth ever to be travailing after the Infinite!" — *Sir Thomas Browne.*

Ah! what to him *our* trivial praise or blame,
Who through long years hath raised half-mournful eyes
Yearning to mark some heaven-descended flame
Light his soul's altar rife with sacrifice?

The offering of far thoughts, profound as prayer,
And starry dreams, still rhythmical of youth,
With travail of brain that pants for loftier air,
To the veiled mystery of immaculate Truth:

No Orient seer — wild woodlands, 'round him furled, —
Building his shrine 'mid virginal vales apart,
E'er watched and waited in the antique world,
For fire divine, with more ethereal heart!

Can life's supreme oblations still remain
All undiscerned? or hath some marvellous levin
Hallowed his gift, and down his rifted pain
Flashed the white splendor of God's grace from heaven?

IV.

TO HON. R. G. H.

UPON HIS 78th BIRTHDAY.

Close to the verge of fourscore crowded years
Your heart is strong, your soul serene and bright;
As when confronting first life's hopes and fears —
The star of manhood crowned your brow with light.

Clear thoughts are spells to keep the life-blood pure,
Brave aims are medicinal, rife with balm;
What wonder then, with *thee* life's joys endure,
And life's majestic sunset smiles in calm!

For thou art one whose brotherhood supreme
Hath touched all circles of benign desire;
Therefore, thy days like some unclouded dream,
Are slowly melting into heavenly fire.

HUMOROUS POEMS.

HUMOROUS POEMS.

VALERIE'S CONFESSION.

TO A FRIEND.

THEY declare that I'm gracefully pretty,
The very best waltzer that whirls;
They say I am sparkling and witty,
The pearl, the queen rose-bud of girls.
But, alas for the popular blindness!
Its judgment, though folly, can hurt:
Since my heart, that runs over with kindness,
It vows is the heart of a flirt!

How, *how*, can I help it, if Nature,
Whose mysteries baffle our ken,
Hath made me the tenderest creature
That ever had pity on men?
When the shafts of my luminous glances
Have tortured some sensitive breast,
Why, I soften their light till it trances
The poor wounded bosom to rest!

Can I help it if, brought from all regions,
As diverse in features as gait,
Rash lovers besiege me in legions,
Each lover demanding his fate?
To be cold to such fervors of feeling
Would pronounce me a dullard or dunce;
And so, the bare thought sets me reeling,
I'm engaged to *six* suitors at once!

The first, — we shall call him "sweet William,"
He's a lad scarcely witty or wise —
The gloom of the sorrows of "Ilium"
Would seem to outbreathe on his sighs.
When I strove, half in earnest, to flout him,
Pale, pale at my footstool he sunk;
But mamma, quite too ready to scout him,
Would hint that "sweet Willie" was drunk!

My second, a florid Adonis
Of forty-and-five, to a day,
Drives me out in his phaeton with ponies,
Making love every yard of the way,
Who so pleasantly placed could resist him?
Had he popped 'neath the moonlight and dew
That eve, I could almost have kissed him
(A confession alone, dear, for you).

Next, a widower, polished and youthful,
Far famed for his learning and pelf:
Can I doubt that *his* passion is truthful,
That he seeks me alone for myself?
Yet I know that some slanderers mutter
His fortune is just taking wings;
But I scorn the backbiters who utter
Such basely censorious things!

Could they hearken his love-whisper, dulcet
As April's soft tide on the strand,
Whose white curves are loath to repulse it,
So sweet is its homage and bland;
Could they hear how his dead wife's devotion
He praises, while yearning for mine —
They would own that his ardent emotion
Is something — yes — almost *divine!*

My fourth — would to heaven I could
paint him
As next the high altar he stands —
A Saint John, all the people besaint
him?
Pale brow and immaculate hands,
Ah! his tones in their wooing seem
holy,
Nor dare I believe it misplaced,
When an arm of the church, stealing
slowly.
Is folded, at length, round my waist;

Behold this long list of my lovers
With a soldier and sailor complete:
Both swear that their hearts were but
rovers
Till fettered and bound at *my* feet.
Oh dear! but these worshippers daunt
me:
Their claims, their vain wishes, appall;
'Tis sad how they harass and haunt
me, —
What, WHAT, *shall I do with them all?*

LATER.

As the foam-flakes, when steadfastly
blowing,
The west wind sweeps reckless and
free,
Are borne where the deep billows, flow-
ing,
Pass out to a limitless sea,
So the gay spume of girlish romances,
Upcaught by true Love on his breath,
With the fretwork and foam of young
fancies,
Was borne through vague distance to
death.

For he came — the true hero — one
morning,
And my soul with quick thrills of de-
light
Leaped upward, renewed, and reborn in
A world of strange beauty and might:
I seemed fenced from all earthly disas-
ter;
My pulses beat tuneful and fast;
So I welcomed my monarch, my master
The *first* real love, and the *last*.

A MEETING OF THE BIRDS.

Of a thousand queer meetings, both
great, sir, and small
The bird-party *I* sing of seemed oddest
of all!

How they come to assemble — a multi-
form show —
From all parts of the earth, is — well
— more than *I* know.

I only can vow that, one fine night of
June,
In a vast, varied garden, made bright by
the moon,

Such bird-throngs I saw, with plumes
brilliant or dark,
As had ne'er met, I deem, since the age
of the ark:

There the phœnix, upborne on a tall
jasper spar,
His fair mate by his side, shone serene
as a star;

With a calm sort of pride glancing down
on all others,
As scorning to claim such *canaille* for
his brothers!

He alone of earth's creatures (more wise
far than Adam),
When Eve tempted *him*, said "Excuse
me, good madam!

"No juice from *that* fruit shall e'er
moisten *my* thrapple!
Delicious! perhaps . . but who gave
you the apple?" *

* Tradition says that when Adam ate of the forbidden fruit, at Eve's instigation, the phœnix, *alone*, of all creatures, equally tempted, did *not* fall.

Then — his tiny red optics upturned to this king
Of all species that court the light air with a wing —

Lo, the rooster! his top-knot bright crimson and blue,
With his impudent strut and his cock-doodle-doo,

Is resolved, one can see, the king's hauteur to balk!
What's a phœnix, forsooth, to such cocks of the walk!

Oh! he bustles along, and he bullies his wife,
Till the poor humbled partlet is weary of life —

When, phew! like a bolt of blue lightning or brown,
Outflashed from the trees, a swift bee-bird whirls down

Upon cocky's great top-knot upreared like a dome,
To cut, just for once, his big highness's comb!

From the rooster's discomfiture, laughing, I turn
To where, 'mid the garden's cool avenues, burn

The fair cinnamon tufts of those hipooes that sold
To King Solomon, once, their true crownlets of gold; *

And beyond where the shadow waves dim by the sheen,
The gay humming-bird darts — a live rainbow — between:

While the parrakeets glitter, the orioles float
Through the moonlighted mist and fine vapors remote;

And by sides of small streams and clear lakelets outspread
Stalks the long-legged flamingo, all scarlet and red:

In sooth, birds of all climes, whether wild birds or tame,
Whether dove-hued and sad, or high-colored like flame,

Walked, wobbled and sauntered, paused, fluttered and flew,
With vast blending of plumes, and, ah! endless ado.

The eagle's loud anger, set deaf'ningly loose,
Shrilled fierce o'er the arrogant hiss of the goose,

And a peacock, who screeched till his gills were half black,
Could not drown, after all, a professional "quack;"

The nightingale pitted his voice and his lore
'Gainst the skylark, that never had trilled *thus* before;

And the cock now recovered, and fresh, sir, as dew,
Strove to bear them *both* down with his cock-doodle-doo:

Till — one volume of strange, contradictory sound,
The air, like a millwheel, whizzed round us and round.

And while still the white moonshine, on vapors of fleece,
Rained down its ineffable splendors in peace,

* The Hipooes originally had *real* crowns of gold on their heads; but so persecuted were they because of this possession that they appealed to Solomon, who (the legend says) exchanged their gold crowns for crowns of feathers, retaining the *former* as a trifling "compliment" for his magic skill and *kindness!*

That bird congregation broke up in a row,
Whose noises, half dreaming, I catch even now.

But the last glimpse of all that flashed quick on my eyes,
Ere the whole meeting faded 'twixt garden and skies,

Was the cuckoo's unwearied, nefarious leg
Scratching fast to discover a phœnix's egg,

Which, if found, I've no doubt, was close-hidden and pressed
By the vile little wretch, with quite mother-like breast.

Yet I've seen other creatures than creatures with wings
Who dared to make free with thrice sanctified things,

From whose false incubation *what* creeds came in vogue!
Even truth's egg is marred if hatched out by a rogue!

A BACHELOR-BOOKWORM'S COMPLAINT OF THE LATE PRESIDENTIAL ELECTION.

[Written during the Hayes and Tilden Controversy].

A MAN of peace, I never dared to marry,
Lover of tranquil hours, I dwelt apart;
Outside the realm where noisy schemes miscarry;
My only handmaids, Science, Learning, Art;
Oh! home of pleasant thought, of calm affection,
All blasted now by this last vile election!

One morn, absorbed in studious contemplation
Of what or whom, I cannot now recall,
A strident voice, "Rise! help to save the nation!"
Roared in mine ear, half bellow and half squall;
"Throw by your books, why, man, there's treason brewing;
Come, come with me, we'll block the march of ruin!"

My neighbor, Dobson—all the gods confound him!
Seized, shook and hauled me from my cushioned seat;
(Just then I could have drugged the wretch, or drowned him;)
But the next moment on bewildered feet,
I trudged with him through dirty streets and weather,
That we might vote at the next poll together.

Vote! vote for whom? I'd not the faintest notion;
Little I recked of modern joys or woes;
Wrapped in Greek wars and ancient Rome's commotion,
What passed beneath my philosophic nose,
Seemed dim as glimmerings of a midnight taper
Marked from afar through autumn clouds and vapor!

At length we paused before a wood-work wicket,
Shrining the grimy guardian of the poll;
Into my hands they thrust a printed ticket,
An ink-besmeared, suspicious-looking scroll,
Which, ne'ertheless, held names of men whose action
Would cow—they swore—the brazen front of faction!

With scarce a glance, in vacant mood, I cast it;
That ticket soiled into as soiled a box;

A box, I thought, half vaguely as I passed it;
Whose guardian "Rough" looked wily as a fox,
Willing, no doubt, for any public hero,
To cheat *ad lib.* — a Brutus, or a Nero!

Well! from that day, my peace of life was shattered;
Dobson *would* come, all lowering or ablaze
With joy, to shout — (as if the issue mattered!)
Now "*Tilden's won!*" now "*glorious Ruthy Hayes!*"
Vainly I argued, vainly vowed that d—n me,
I didn't care three straws for Ruth or— Sammy!

"Have I not Scipio and majestic Cato,
With their grand deeds to ponder yet?" I cried;
"Why, dunder-headed Dobson, *will* you prate so,
Of modern dwarfs of time and fate untried;"
"Untried!" quoth he, aghast at my iniquity;
"I'll back them *both*, by Jove! 'gainst all antiquity!"

And still he came, morning, and noon, and twilight,
Bringing, at last, his party henchmen too;
O! how I yearned to blow them through the skylight,
Or, at the gentlest, beat them black and blue;
Each cursed and threatened like some desperate Lara;
Meanwhile they quaffed and quaffed my best Madeira!

A point there is beyond the soul's defiance,
Which gained, a mortal man must fight, or fly;
Fight, if he knows the wily tricks of "science,"*
Fly, if he knows not *when* to smite, and *why;*
Needless to say, in this disastrous matter,
Of the two ways, I wisely chose — the latter!

I left my home; I fled to shades suburban,
Where an old aunt, as deaf as twenty posts,
(A fine antique, bedecked with lace and turban,)
Lived in a house unknown to rats or ghosts;
There, far from party conflicts, proud or petty,
I dwell at peace, with sober Madame Betty!

At peace! good lack, the universal virus
Of party strife had captive made the air,
The light, the very sun-motes shifting nigh us,
And thus, alas! it entered even there;
Up, down her stairs, how oft had I to stump it,
Shrieking the news through her infernal trumpet.

Baffled, once more I sought the public pass-ways,
But then, from morn to midnight's "witching noon,"
Monotonous as when some blatant ass brays,
The same mixed clamors rose 'neath sun and moon;
Tilden and Hayes in never-ceasing wrangle,
Who the vexed "snarl" shall ever disentangle?

---

* *Ring science*, of course.

Bank, hall, and market, counting-house and alley,
Patrician parlor and low bar-room den,
Echoed, as 'twere, cries of retreat or rally,
From brassy throats of many thousand men;
Such foolish boasts were blent with threats as silly,
Yet even the wise men babbled — *willy nilly.*

The very nurse-maids with their baby charges,
Took sides, and squabbled; newsboys shouting loud,
Scuttled along the slippery pavement marges,
And burst like young bulls through the motley crowd
Of parsons, black-legs, dandies, hack-men, bummers;
Swollen each moment by some rash new comers!

Around the telegraph stands they surged and battled,
Till direful Hades seemed unloosed on earth;
Lies were exchanged, cudgels and brick-bats rattled;
The veriest blackguard scorned the man of birth,
And tweaked his nose, or knocked his beaver double—
Ah me! the noise, the blows, the furious trouble!

I passed a gay "Bazaar," and glanced within it,
Of silks and satins, what a dazzling maze!
Fair tongues were wagging smartly; every minute,
"Of course 'tis Tilden!" "nay, not so, 'tis Hayes!"
Rose, with the rustle of bright garments blending—
A strife of voices, eager and unending!

You'd scarce believe it; but maids fair and tender,
Dancing from school, the merest slips of girls,
Shrilled *Hayes* or *Tilden*, and with fingers slender,
Caught and dragged fiercely at each others' curls;
Ill words they spake—those inconsiderate misses —
From rosebud lips just framed for love and kisses!

. . . . . .

Enough! the die is cast; from rage and riot,
I'll cross o'er mountain walls and ocean streams,
To seek and find again, that gracious quiet,
Whose charm hath left me, save in transient dreams;
In some far land and time, my spirit stilled then—
I may — who knows — forgive both Hayes and Tilden!

COQUETTE AND HER LOVER.

A "PETITE COMEDIE" IN RHYME.

LOVER.

Coquette! coquette! now, is it fair
To weave for me your magic hair,
Binding me thus, all unaware?
Till, wholly meshed in every part,
From dazzled eyes to captured heart,
Scarce can I, thro' your radiant snare,
Inhale one waft of free-born air;
Answer, coquette! now, is it fair?

COQUETTE.

O, foolish querist! what if I,
Beholding your enamored face
And every well-attested trace
Of verdant, young idolatry,
Should, after my own fashion, choose
To play the subtly-amorous muse,

Your inexperienced heart-strings touch,
Wooing the warm chords overmuch!
Or tempt you, 'twixt a smile and sigh,
To enter beauty's luminous net?
Such snares must evermore be set
For blinded human flies like you!
Cease, therefore, this half-feigned ado,
You are a natural victim! I
Am by the same strange law's decree,
Your dear, predestined enemy!

"For full five seconds, it would seem
As if you really thought, coquette,
On something grave."

LOVER.

Is *such* the only comfort, then,
You give to thrice-deluded men?
Suppose our life-plan quite upset,
Reversed in whole, or changed in part;
My sex your own, and feelings strong,
(Wiled by deep passion's syren song);
Yours the blind victim's tangled heart,
And *mine* to weave the tempter's net—
What then, O! honey-tongued coquette?

COQUETTE.

Such questions!—ah! *mon Dieu! mon Dieu!*—
Fancy I've places changed with you!
I cannot! 'tis too hard a task
Of any mortal *belle* to ask!

[ASIDE *with a half-humorous, half-solemn air.*]

Fancy *my* person changed to *his*
By some odd metamorphosis!

My fairy frame to that huge bulk
That might befit red Rory O'Fulke,
Our Irish groom!—six feet, at least,
Of stature—with that boundless waist,
Instead of mine, Titania might
Quite envy on a "round-dance" night,
By all the waltzing beaux adored!
My brow to that great, sabre-scored
Brown forehead; and my cheeks of rose
To bearded *puffs*; my delicate nose—
Quel horreur! 'tis a hideous dream!

LOVER.

For full five seconds, it would seem
As if you really *thought*, coquette,
On something grave! Slowly about
Your flower-like lips' delicious pout,
Came tiny puckerings, lined with doubt;
Your large eyes widened deep and blue,
As May-skies glimpsed thro' morning dew;
And shadows vague as noon-tide trance
Stole o'er your vivid countenance:
Coquette! show pity!—after all,
Have you resolved to free from thrall
Your wretched serf? . . . Close, close your eyes
For one brief, merciful minute; try
To turn your perfect mouth awry;
Let those arch smiles which magnetize
My inmost blood be changed to scorn;
Do all a winsome lady born
To loveliness and witchery, can,
To flout a love-tormented man!

COQUETTE.

You know as well as I
What balms have soothed your slavery;
Besides, *I'm sure, whate'er you say,*
There never yet has dawned the day
On which, in truth ('tis vain to frown),
You longed to lay your fetters down.
Surely but airy chains they are,
And tenuous as the farthest star.
But *should* you break the binding net,
You'd come . . . (ah! graceless, thankless loon!)
'Ere the next wax or wane of moon,
To sigh, or call on "sweet coquette!"

LOVER.

Too much! by heaven! you heartless chit!
I'll *prove* you underrate my wit,
And self-respect, for all that's passed!
I will—will break these bonds at last.
Yes! look! you false, hard-hearted girl!
I dash to earth the dazzling curl
You gave me once! . . . your portrait too! . . .
(O, yes! I *stole* it, . . . what of that?
'Twill soon be shapeless, crushed and flat,
Beneath my stern, avenging heel!
Would it were *flesh*, and so could *feel*,
. . . Where is it! *where?*

[*He searches frantically, but vainly for the likeness in one pocket after another.*]

[COQUETTE—approaching with infinite sweetness, rests one hand upon his shoulder, while the forefinger of the other is archly shaken in his angry face, that changes with ludicrous quickness, from passion to bewilderment, and from bewilderment to rapture]:

. . . Why, Hal, for shame! you prayed just now,
With earnest mien and solemn brow,
That I would sting you with hot scorn;
"*Do all a winsome lady born*
To loveliness and witchery, can,
To flout a love-tormented man."
And lo! because your bidding's done;
Half-way, and mildly; why, I've won
Such rude abuse! . . . I shall not stir,
Till you have begged my pardon, sir!
. . . Hal! *do* you love me? . . .

LOVER.

. . . Angel! saint!
Can this be true! . . . my heart grows faint,
With happiness! . . . so then, despite—

COQUETTE (*interrupting*).

Yes, dear! of feigned contempt and slight,
—I have loved you always! who but *you*

Had failed thus long to read me true?
You dear, delightful, blundering boy.

LOVER.

. . . Cupid be blessed! Oh, love! Oh, joy!
. . . But where's that precious curl I threw
Rashly away? . . . Already flown
On some light wind?

COQUETTE.

—— Yes, yes, 'tis gone!
But then the whole bright, golden net
(*shaking down her curls.*)
You've gained with me! . . . If still unfair
You deem this soft, imprisoning snare;
And self-respect, for all that's passed,
Demands you break your bonds at last,
Give me due warning — if you please —

LOVER (*embracing her*).

Ah! *thus* a loving seal is set
On rosy lips to keep them dumb;
Some other eve beneath the trees
Of golden summer, 'mid the hum
Of forest brooks and hive-bound bees,
I'll hearken, madcap, while you tease.
But now, my heart the future years
Sees through a mist of blissful tears;
My eyes with gracious dew are wet;
I'm dreaming! . . . No! . . . *here* smiles coquette!

SENEX TO HIS FRIEND.

ABOUT THE PERIOD OF A NEW YEAR.

Dedicated to Sam'l Lord, Jr., Charleston, S.C.

YOUR hair is scant, my friend, and mine is scanter,
On heads snowed white by Time, the disenchanter:
In place of joyous beams and jovial twinkles,
Behold, old boy, our faces scored with wrinkles!

Sparkles your legal lore with salt that's Attic!
But, ah! those twinges (gout?), those pangs rheumatic!
With muse of mine no more the public quarrels,
But, Lord! how cold I feel despite the laurels!

If spiced your fame, not so your milk or sago:
Only mild diet suits a sharp lumbago.
While as for me — what critic "puff" avails one
Whose own short breath (asthmatic!) almost fails one?

The world we deemed so rife with fadeless prizes —
Which of us most its hollow show despises?
We'd yield our gains for just one marvellous minute
Of our lost youth, with all youth's glory in it!

Yet from this House of Life, now wrapped in twilight,
Gleams 'mid the shadowy roof Faith's magic skylight;
Whereby as night steals down through weird gradations,
We hail the glow of heavenly constellations.

So, as through darkness only dawn the graces
Of God's calm stars and lofty shining spaces,
That night called death which shrouds our bodies breathless
May flood the heaven of soul with peace made deathless.

THE OBSERVANT "ELDEST" SPEAKS.

"PA vows that all gluttony's wicked;
He's always for docking *my* meat,
And ne'er at dessert will he give me
Enough of what's racy and sweet:

Yet he'll gorge and gorge on at *his* dinners,
As restless in mouth as in hand; —
Now, say, — if all gluttons are sinners,
Where — where does *my* 'governor' stand!

"Oh! pa's most impressive on lying;
('Meanest crime in the annals of sin;')
Yet why does *he* tell folk (through Thomas)
That he's *out* when he knows that he's *in?*
And ma's done the same, when she meant not
From house nor from chamber to stir:
I suppose what is punished in *me*, sir,
Is all right in *him* or in *her!*

"Pa says, that good men must be generous,
Self-denying, benevolent, kind;'
Then why does he give those poor beggars
Just nothing? The lame and the blind,
Small orphan, and wan, pining widow,
The gold-covered head and the gray,
Unsoothed and unhelped in their sorrows,
From *him* turn — how sadly — away!

"Pa counsels fair words of our neighbors; —
Oh! he dotes on the pure 'golden rule;' —
Yet he calls Aunt Selina 'back-biter,'
And he dubs Uncle Reuben 'a fool."
And when *I* said, 'Young Reub's like his father,'
On what text in reply did pa lean?
Why. 'Whoso thou fool shall dare utter,'
Must taste — well, *you* know what I mean!

"Pa says, 'we must reverence our elders;' —
How he harps and he harps upon that; —
Yet grandfather, who's ninety and upward,
He treats like an imbecile 'flat.'
And once when poor grandpa, at breakfast,
Mistook the slop-bowl for his cup,
Pa muttered, 'I wish the old dotard
Were locked — *somewhere* — heedfully up!'

"I don't know what the 'governor's' made of;
But truly, if *he were not he*,
(I mean if he were not *my* 'pater' —
Alack! that *such* fathers should be,)
His name would begin as I spelt it,
With a big blatant H, if you please,
And conclude with the tiniest, meanest,
But most self-sufficient of e's!"

LUCIFER'S DEPUTY.

A MEDIÆVAL LEGEND.

A POET once, whose tuneful soul, perchance,
Too fondly leaned toward sin, and sin's romance,
On a long vanished eve, so calm and clear
None could have deemed an evil spirit near,
Brooding ill deeds, was summoned by a writ,
In the due form of Hades, to the Pit;
A red-nosed, red-haired fiend the summoner,
About whose horrent head his locks did stir
Like half-waked serpents! "Well," in wrath and woe,
The poet cried. "whom the De'il drives *must* go,
Whate'er the goal! Yet much I wish that he
Had sent as guide some nobler fiend than thee,
Thou hideous varlet!"

"Come, keep cool, I say,"
Counselled the other sagely, "while *you may!*"
Whereon, as half in scorn and half in ire,
He haled the poet to the realm of fire.

Arrived in bounds Hadéan, a vast rout
Of fiends they met, who rushed tumultuous out,
To roam the earth and those doomed spirits snare
Who unsuspecting lived and acted there;
Till in a few brief seconds the whole crew
Of crowding demons — black, brown, green and blue —
All but their haughty chief, his form upreared
Through the red mist, had wildly disappeared.

Then said the dark archangel to the bard:
"Thine eye is bright, thou hast a shrewd regard;
And, therefore, ere I likewise o'er the marge
Of Hades wing my way for some brief hours,
To thee I choose to delegate my powers
As chief and sovereign of this kingdom dread,
To which, if well thou guardest, by my head
Thy recompense, when I come back, shall be
A luscious tid bit, garnished daintily —
No meaner *entrée* than a roasted monk,
(Before he's cooked we'll make the rascal drunk,
To spice his juices!); or, if thou'dst prefer
Yon leaner and less succulent usurer,
Why, of our toil and time with trifling loss,
We'll serve *him* up, larded with golden sauce!"

But while the absent fiends their cunning tasked
To trap unwary souls, thick cloaked and masked,
One entered Hades who did soon entice
The heedless bard to play a game at dice,
Staking the souls he held in charge thereon.
The stranger played superbly — played, and won.
So, gathering round him the freed souls, with care
And kind despatch, safe to the outward air
He led them triumphing; and all who now
Looked on his unmasked face and glorious brow
Knew that St. Peter stood amongst them there.
But when the devils, trooping homeward, found
Their kingdom void — its conflagrations drowned
As 'twere by showers from Heaven — such curses rose —
Like thunder bellowing through the strange repose
Which late had reigned — the poet's head whirled round,
Stunned by the tumult. But ere long, with whirr
And furious whizz, his right hand Lucifer
Brought in such stinging contact with one cheek
And then the other, that our minstrel, weak
From pain and fear, sank trembling on the floor.
But sternly Satan pointed to the door,
Where through his faithless guard, with many a kick
And echoing thump, and one swift merciless prick
Of a keen pitchfork, was thrust forth in shame

From out the empire of fierce grief and flame,
In even more woeful plight than when he came!
Then Lucifer upraised his arms and swore
A mighty oath that Hades' lurid door
No poet's form should ever enter more!

So, brother bards, whate'er ye write or do,
Be fearless. Hades holds no place for you:
Since if on earth men deem your worth but small,
Why there, 'tis plain, ye have no worth at all!

POEMS FOR CHILDREN.

POEMS FOR CHILDREN.

LITTLE NELLIE IN THE PRISON.

The eyes of a child are sweeter than any hymn we have sung,
And wiser than any sermon is the lisp of a childish tongue!

HUGH FALCON learned this happy truth one day;
('Twas a fair noontide in the month of May) —
When, as the chaplain of the convicts' jail,
He passed its glowering archway, sad and pale,
Bearing his tender daughter on his arm.
A five years' darling she! The dewy charm
Of Eden star-dawns glistened in her eyes;
Her dimpled cheeks were rich with sunny dyes.

"Papa!" the child that morn while still abed,
Drawing him close toward her, shyly said:
"Papa! oh, won't you let your Nellie go
To see those naughty men that plague you so,
Down in the ugly prison by the wood?
Papa, I'll beg and pray them to be good."
"What, you, my child?" he said, with half a sigh.
"Why not, papa? I'll beg them so to *try*."

The chaplain, with a father's gentlest grace,
Kissed the small ruffled brow, the pleading face:
"Out of the mouths of babes and sucklings still,
Praise is perfected," thought he; thus, his will
Blended with hers, and through those gates of sin,
Black, even at noontide, sire and child passed in.

Fancy the foulness of a sulphurous lake,
Wherefrom a lily's snow-white leaves should break,
Flushed by the shadow of an unseen rose!
So, at the iron gate's loud clang and close,
Shone the drear twilight of that place defiled,
Touched by the flower-like sweetness of the child!
O'er many a dismal vault, and stony floor,
The chaplain walked from ponderous door to door,
Till now beneath a stairway's dizzy flight
He stood and looked up the far-circling height;
But risen of late from fever's torture-bed,
How could he trust his faltering limbs and head?

Just then, he saw, next to the mildewed wall,
A man in prisoner's raiment, gaunt and tall,
Of sullen aspect, and wan, downcast face,
Gloomed in the midnight of some deep disgrace;

He shrank as one who yearned to fade away,
Like a vague shadow on the stone-work gray,
Or die beyond it, like a viewless wind;
He seemed a spirit faithless, passionless, blind
To all fair hopes which light the hearts of men, —
A dull, dead soul, never to wake again!

The chaplain paused, half doubting what to do,
When little Nellie raised her eyes of blue,
And, no wise daunted by the downward stir
Of shaggy brows that glowered askance at her,
Said, — putting by her wealth of sunny hair, —
"Sir, will you kindly take me up the stair?
Papa is tired, and I'm too small to climb."
Frankly her eyes in his gazed all the time;
And something to her childhood's instinct known
So worked within her, that her arms were thrown
About his neck. She left her sire's embrace
Near that sad convict-heart to take her place,
Sparkling and trustful! — more she did not speak;
But her quick fingers patted his swart cheek
Caressingly, — in time to some old tune
Hummed by her nurse, in summer's drowsy noon!

Perforce he turned his wild, uncertain gaze
Down on the child! Then stole a tremulous haze
Across his eyes, but rounded not to tears;
Wherethrough he saw faint glimmerings of lost years
And perished loves! A cabin by a rill
Rose through the twilight on a happy hill;
And there were lithe child-figures at their play
That flashed and faded in the dusky ray;
And near the porch a gracious wife who smiled,
Pure as young Eve in Eden, unbeguiled!

Subdued, yet thrilled, 'twas beautiful to see
With what deep reverence, and how tenderly,
He clasped the infant frame so slight and fair,
And safely bore her up the darkening stair!
The landing reached, in her arch, childish ease,
Our Nelly clasped his neck and whispered:
"Please,
Won't you be good, sir? For I like you so,
And you are such a big, strong man, you know — "
With pleading eyes, her sweet face sidewise set.
Then suddenly his furrowed cheeks grew wet
With sacred tears — in whose divine eclipse
Upon her nestling head he pressed his lips
As softly as a dreamy west wind's sigh,
What time a something, undefined but high,
As 'twere a new soul, struggled to the dawn
Through his raised eyelids. Thence, the gloom withdrawn
Of brooding vengeance and unholy pain,
He felt no more the captive's galling chain;
But only knew a little child had come
To smite despair, his taunting demon, dumb;

"Our Nelly clasped his neck and whispered:
'Please
Won't you be good, sir? For I like you so.'"

A child whose marvellous innocence enticed
All white thoughts back, that from the heart of Christ
Fly dove-like earthward, past our clouded ken,
Child-life to bless, or lives of child-like men!

Thus he went his way,
An altered man from that thrice blessèd day;
His soul tuned ever to the soft refrain
Of words once uttered in a sacred fane:
"The little children, let them come to me,
Of such as these my realm of heaven must be;"
But most he loved of one dear child to tell,
The child whose trust had saved him, tender Nell!

THE CHILDREN.

THE children! ah, the children!
Your innocent, joyous ones;
Your daughters, with souls of sunshine;
Your buoyant and laughing sons.

Look long in their happy faces,
Drink love from their sparkling eyes,
For the wonderful charm of childhood,
How soon it withers and dies!

A few fast-vanishing summers,
A season or twain of frost,
And you suddenly ask, bewildered
"What is it my heart hath lost?"

Perhaps you see by the hearth-stone
Some Juno, stately and proud,
Or a Hebe whose softly ambushed eyes
Flash out from the golden cloud

Of lavish and beautiful tresses
That wantonly floating, stray
O'er the white of a throat and bosom
More fair than blossoms in May.

And perhaps you mark their brothers—
Young heroes who spurn the sod
With the fervor of antique knighthood,
And the air of a Grecian god!

But where, ah, where are the children,
Your household fairies of yore?
Alack! they are dead, and their grace has fled
For ever and ever more!

WILL AND I.

I.

WE roam the hills together,
In the golden summer weather,
Will and I:
And the glowing sunbeams bless us,
And the winds of heaven caress us,
As we wander hand in hand
Through the blissful summer land
Will and I.

II.

Where the tinkling brooklet passes
Through the heart of dewy grasses,
Will and I
Have heard the mock-bird singing,
And the field-lark seen upspringing
In his happy flight afar,
Like a tiny wingèd star,
Will and I.

III.

Amid cool forest closes
We have plucked the wild wood roses,
Will and I;
And have twined, with tender duty,
Sweet wreaths to crown the beauty
Of the purest brows that shine
With a mother-love divine
Will and I.

IV.

Ah! thus we roam together,
Through the golden summer weather,
Will and I;

While the glowing sunbeams bless us,
And the winds of heaven caress us —
As we wander hand in hand
O'er the blissful summer land
Will and I.

JAMIE AND HIS MOTHER — IN THE TROPICS.

JAMIE.

O MOTHER, what country is that I see
Far over the stream and the boulders gray,
Where the wind-song pipes, and the curlews flee,
And the little brown squirrels dance and play
Through the boughs all day?

MOTHER.

Why, only a forest dark and wild,
A savage waste you must shun, my child!

JAMIE.

O mother, what shapes are those that sit
In the deep dun heart of the woodland gloom?
And what those creatures that dip and flit,
Each crowned with a golden and scarlet plume,
O'er the tamarind bloom?

MOTHER.

Why, only the monkeys crouched from sight,
And paroquets flashing in gay-hued flight!

JAMIE.

O mother, what children are those that run
So swift and light 'mid the tree-stems bare?
They seem to twinkle from shade to sun,
And beckon me over their sport to share
In the noontide fair!

"Go not," she cried, with a quivering breath:
"They are Pixies, child, and their sport is death!"

But there came a morn when the mother's words
No longer dwelt in her Jamie's mind;
When he followed the flight of the whirring birds
That circled and soared on the woodland wind,
And mother and home were far behind.

Like one in a golden dream was he,
Far over the stream and the boulders gray;
And the wind-song pipes, and the curlews flee,
And the little brown squirrels dance and play
Through the boughs all day.

But the day grew dim, and the nightshades fell,
And there in the dark, drear, hungry wild,
In the loneliest nook of a mountain dell,
Where never a tender moonbeam smiled,
Lay the weary child!

Like one in an awful trance was he,
In the deep dun heart of the woodland gloom;
But a trance whose shadows can never flee,
Till the mystic trump of the day of doom
Breaks vault and tomb.

And they found him there with his bleeding hands
So humbly crossed o'er the ragged vest,
His spirit had gone to the angel lands,
But his out-worn body they laid to rest
In the last sad smile of the gentle west:
God guard his rest!

THE THREE COPECKS.

CROUCHED low in a sordid chamber,
With a cupboard of empty shelves,
Half starved, and, alas, unable
To comfort or help themselves,

Two children were left forsaken,
All orphaned of mortal care;
But with spirits too close to heaven
To be tainted by earth's despair,

Alone in that crowded city,
Which shines like an arctic star,
By the banks of the frozen Neva,
In the realm of the mighty Czar.

Now. Max was an urchin of seven;
But his delicate sister, Leeze,
With the crown of her rippling ringlets,
Could scarcely have reached your knees.

As he looked on his sister weeping,
And tortured by hunger's smart,
A thought like an angel entered
At the door of his opened heart.

He wrote on a fragment of paper,
With quivering hand and soul,
"*Please send to me, Christ, three copecks.*
To purchase for Leeze a roll!"

Then. rushed to a church, his missive
To drop.—ere the vesper psalms,—
As the surest mail bound Christward,
In the unlocked box for alms!

While he stepped upon tiptoe to reach it,
One passed from the priestly band,
And with smile like a benediction,
Took the note from his eager hand.

Having read it, the good man's bosom
Grew warm with a holy joy;
"Ah! Christ may have heard you already,
Will you come to *my* house, my boy?"

"But not without Leeze?" "No, surely,
We'll have a rare party of three;
Go, tell her that somebody's waiting
To welcome her home to tea."

That night in the cosiest cottage,
The orphans were safe at rest,
Each sang as a callow birdling,
In the depths of its downy nest.

And the next Lord's Day, in his pulpit,
The preacher so spake of these.
Stray lambs from the fold, which Jesus
Had blessed by the sacred seas:

So recounted their guileless story,
As he held each child by the hand,
That the hardest there could feel it,
And the dullest could understand.

O'er the eyes of the listening fathers
There floated a gracious mist;
And oh, how the tender mothers
Those desolate darlings kissed!

"You have given your tears," said the preacher,
"Heart-alms we should none despise;
But the open palm, my children,
Is more than the weeping eyes!"

Then followed a swift collection,
From the altar steps to the door,
Till the sum of two thousand rubles
The vergers had counted o'er.

So you see that the unmailed letter
Had somehow gone to its goal,
And more than three copecks gathered
To purchase for Leeze a roll!

THE REASON WHY.

I'D like, indeed I'd like to know
Why sister Bell, who loved me so,
And used to pet me day and night,
And could not bear me out of sight,

Now always looks so cross and glum,
If to her side I chance to come,
When that great, gawky man is nigh;
I'd like to know the reason why?

That man! I *hate* him! yes, I do,
And, in *my* place, you'd hate him too.
At first, (his common name is John!)
He brought me boxes of *bon bons*,
With books, and dolls, and tiny rings,
And lots on lots of precious things,
And said, of all Miss Pontoon's girls,
Not one could match my flowing curls,
My rosy cheeks and rounded chin,
With one sly dimple nestling in.
But now, he seems so stern and high,
I scarce may catch his scornful eye,
While as for *toys!* — he has ceased to buy!
Tell me, who can, the reason why?

It's mean! dear me! I'm sure it's mean!
Did I not run a "go-between"
From him to sister Bell so long,
(Although I *feared* it might be wrong),
With sweetmeats, flowers, and scented notes,
Sealed by two doves with curving throats?
Of course I thought him kind and nice.
But now, he's cold as arctic ice!
And more than once I've heard him say,
"That chit's forever in the way!"
While Bell — she *snaps!* till I could cry.
Will no one tell the reason why?

LATER.

Think — Mr. John's my friend again.
('Twas yesternight he made it plain),
For most of our big household gone
To Friday's lecture, — left alone,
But Bell and I; *he* came to tea,
(As now he's coming constantly,)
And spoke to me quite warmly — quite:
"Lizzie, you are not looking bright;
And since both Bell and I are here,
Take Nurse, and see the circus, dear;
I'll pay, my love! accept of this."
(A wee gold dollar, and — a kiss!)
"Why don't you come with Bell?" asked I;
He smiled, but would not answer why.

LATER STILL.

Good news! good news! I'm almost mad,
I feel so pleased, so proud and glad.
To-morrow is the wedding-day;
Papa will give our Bell away,
And I'm a bridesmaid!—oh, my dress!
"Soft waves of white silk loveliness,"
Bell says, "with grace in every tuck!"
And isn't Brother John a duck?
(I call him *Brother* now, you see,)
He gave this dainty dress to me,
And said, his "little friend must look
Fair as a picture in a book."
I answered gayly, "I shall try!"
What need to ask the reason why?

THE SILKEN SHOE.

"Hie on the holly-tree!" — *Old Ballad.*

The firelight danced and wavered
In elvish, twinkling glee
On the leaves and crimson berries
Of the great green Christmas Tree;

And the children who gathered round it
Beheld, with marvelling eyes,
Pendant from trunk and branches
How many a precious prize,

From the shimmer of gold and silver
Through a purse's cunning net,
To the coils of a rippling necklace,
That quivered with beads of jet.

But chiefly they gazed in wonder
Where flickered strangely through
The topmost leaves of the holly
The sheen of a silken shoe!

And the eldest spake to her father:
"I have seen — yes, year by year,
On the crown of our Christmas hollies,
That small shoe glittering clear;

"But you never have told who owned it,
 Nor why so loftily set.
It shines through the fadeless verdure,
 You never have told us yet!"

'Twas then that the museful father
 In slow sad accents said,
While the firelight hovered eerily
 About his downcast head:

"My children — you had a sister;
 (It was long, long, long ago),
She came like an Eden rosebud
 'Mid the dreariest winter snow,

"And for four sweet seasons blossomed
 To cheer our hearts and hearth,
When the song of the Bethlehem angels
 Lured her away from earth —

"My shoe, papa, please hang it
Once more on the holly bough."

"For again 'twas the time of Christmas,
 As she lay with laboring breath;
But — our minds were blinded strangely,
 And we did not dream of death.

"A little before she left us,
 We had deftly raised to view,
On the topmost branch of the holly
 Yon glimmering, tiny shoe;

"We knew that no toy would please her
 Like a shoe so fair and neat,
To fold, with its soft caressing
 Her delicate, sylph-like feet!

"Truly, a smile like a sunbeam
 Brightened her eyes of blue,
And once — twice — thrice — she tested
 The charm of her fairy shoe!

"Ah! then the bright smile flickered,
 Faded, and drooped away,
As faintly, in tones that faltered,
 I heard our darling say:

"'My shoe, papa, please hang it
 Once more on the holly bough,
Just where I am sure to see it,
 When I wake — an hour from now.

"But alas! she never wakened!
 Close shut were the eyes of blue;
Whose last faint gleam had fondled
 The curves of that dainty shoe.

"Ah, children, you understand me;
 Your eyes are brimmed with dew,
As they watch on the Christmas holly
 The sheen of a silken shoe."

THE BLACK DESTRIER.

A BALLAD OF THE THIRD CRUSADE.

FIRST 'mid the lion Richard's host,
Sir Aymer fought in Holy Land;
And they loved him well for his honest heart,
And they feared, for his stalwart hand.

Once on a glorious battle eve,
The Paynim legions wildly flying,
Sir Aymer paused from his work of blood,
Where an eastern knight lay dying.

He was the latest guard of one,
The Soldan's fair and favorite bride,
And there on the trampled and crimson sod
She moaned by the warrior's side.

No strength had he to shield his charge;
But mild the Christian victor's face;
And the lady knew, as she gazed thereon,
That his mercy would grant her grace.

The Paynim died: "I am thy guide,"
The brave Sir Aymer softly said;
"By my father's faith thou art safe from scaith,
Wheresoever thou would'st be led."

True to his word, through friend, through foe,
He bore the lady fast and far,
Till the hostile sheen of the Moslem spears
Flashed under the evening star.

The Soldan's self with speechless joy,
With glistening eyes and bated breath,
The queen of his house and heart embraced,
As if claiming his Love from death!

"Now, Christian knight, by this pure light,
No vain nor empty thanks are mine;
So, name thee the guerdon a king may grant,
And believe me, it shall be thine."

"No guerdon, prince, for simple ruth
The Christian warrior deigns to take;
He has vowed to rescue the lorn and weak,
For his own sweet lady's sake.'

"All proofs of zeal the grateful feel,
Surely, fair knight, thou would'st not shun?
An honored guest, thou wilt tarry and rest,
At least till the morrow's sun?"

Thus, in the Soldan's tent he stayed —
What time the queen with passionate eyes,
Struck blind to the harem's splendor, dreamed
Of his beauty with love-sick sighs:

And ere that morrow's sun had set,
With scarce a blush her love she told;
But Sir Aymer hearkened with haughty mien,
And the words that he spake were cold.

Then flushed the imperious forehead high,
A dark flame glittered in her eyes,
And the hate of the deadly orient quelled
The breath of her tender sighs.

"Sir knight, enough; thou scorn'st my love!
But ere thou goest, take instead
This marvellous steed of the jet-black breed,
In the land of the Magi bred.

"O stern in fight! O swift in flight!
This matchless steed will serve thee well,
Whether thy lure be a lady's bower,
Or the vanward war-trump's swell."

He took the gift, he bowed him low,
And gained the Christian camp at noon;
"O courser of might in strife or flight!"
Quoth he, "I shall prove thee soon."

. . . . .

The conflict joins; the hosts are hot;
That gallant Destrier "holds his own;"
Aghast at the rush of his whirlwind course,
Whole legions are overthrown.

In twice three mortal combats more
The same fell ruin marked his path,
Till the Saracens deemed, as their life-blood streamed,
'Twas a fiend of hell in his wrath.

But once, alas! alas! the day!
The Moslem's sudden war-cry rose,
And the knight his "Avè" forgot to say,
Ere he hastened to meet his foes.

St. Paul! what wizard spell is this?
The Destrier spurns the hands that guide,
And full on the front of the *Christian* host
Sweeps back through the battle tide.

Gramercy! 'twas a dreadful sight
Which met the gathering thousands there,
When the war-horse charged like a blazing star,
Through a halo of blood-red air.

With bristling mane, and hot disdain
Against the mail-clad lines he came;
And his red orbs burned with a frenzied ire,
And his nostrils darted flame.

Thus raging from the heathen van,
Strange steed and awful rider rushed,
And the souls of the boldest shrank appalled,
And the wildest voice was hushed;

Till swift towards King Richard's camp
The fiery-fronted portent bore,
From the fetlock firm to the horrent crest
All reeking with Christian gore.

There, on a sudden paused the barb,
Still, as if carved in marble black,
And from silent knight and terrible steed
The pale throng shuddered back:

But now from out the trembling crowd
A priest with holy water passed,
He sprinkled the knight, he sprinkled the steed
With the pure lymph free and fast:

When lo! the fatal charm dissolved —
Prone, with a hollow, rattling sound
In the clasp of his unscathed armor, fell
The knight to the bloody ground:

They loosed his hauberk and his helm,
But dead and wan his eyeballs shone,
As if they had gazed on a nameless dread
Which had frozen their life to stone!

They felt his pulseless heart, his brow
Dim with the death-shade's mystic gloom,
While ruthless and stern are the looks they turn
On the demon that wrought his doom.

But pallid as a waning cloud
Athwart the summer moon-disc blown,
The shadowy form of a demon steed
In the ghost-like eve had grown:

Only — his supernatural eyes
One moment shot a vengeful spark,
Ere the glimmering Syrian twilight closed
On the steps of the sudden dark.

THE ADVENTURES OF LITTLE BOB BONNYFACE.

LITTLE Bob Bonnyface went out one day
Into his father's fields to play;
'Twas a morn undarkened by mist or cloud,

With the thrush and the blackbird piping loud;
The locust, deep in the pine-tree wood,
Shrilled, as only a locust could;
And borne on the waft of a summer breeze,
Swarmed by him an army of honey-bees.
Delighted he saw, delighted he heard
The morn, the bees, and the singing bird;
He also sang, as he roamed through the clover,
Feeling *so* jolly, and free all over!

But Bob — I must tell you the honest truth —
Was a terribly mischievous thoughtless youth;
Whatever he wanted to do or say,
He did and he said in the boldest way,
Not seeming to ponder, even to care
How naughty his words or his actions were;
For the only aim of this reckless elf
Was — everywhere, always, to please — himself!

'Twas to please himself, without license or leave
Nor a thought how his poor sick mother might grieve,
If she missed too long, on her suffering bed,
The golden gleam of his curly head,
That he left his home through the fields to stray,
On that sunny and beautiful summer's day,
As the air breathed over him, blithesome, but calm,
All laden with fragrance and meadow-balm,
And the sunshine warmed his young blood through,
While it dazzled and danced from the stainless blue,
Bob felt that a jollity, wholesome and sweet,
Possessed him wholly, from head to feet.

He looked around, and what should his eye
In an open space 'mid the clover spy,
But an ant-hole, wrought in the sandy drouth.
Out of its busy, populous mouth,
The dwarfish tenants — an endless train,
Emerging, covered the tiny plain;
Eastward and westward, north and south,
They toiled, with a constant will, to gain
The fairy stores of their winter's grain;
Yet Bob in his recklessness deemed it fun
The ants and their mansion to overrun.
By millions down in the crumbling sod
The frightened creatures he swiftly trod;
Filled up with dust, and grasses, and stone,
The entrance-ways to their home, o'erthrown
Not one of the innocent horde, not *one*,
Was left to toil in the laughing sun —
But still Bob shouted, and thought it — fun!

Next on his wandering way he came
To a furze-bush, gleaming like yellow flame;
A spider as ugly and fierce as sin,
Had spread the snares of his web therein;
But — cunning and sly — as Bob rushed up,
He hid himself deep in a thistle's cup,
Leaving above, in his worship's stead,
A bee, caught fast in his poisoned thread!

Now, here was a chance for Bobby to free
From his pain and prison this harmless bee;
But bless you! no! 'twas a finer thing
He thought, to pierce him from wing to wing;
On a pin's keen point to whirl him high,

And behold the quivering insect die,
This, too, when the barbarous act was done,
Seemed nothing to Bob but a moment's — fun.

More gleeful than ever, Bob onward pressed;
In the wayside thickets he found a nest,
The eggs half hatched; but he took them out,
And with rude hand scattered them all about,
Laughing to see how the egg-shells broke.
But hey! what's this? with a buffeting stroke,
The wings of the outraged mother-bird
(Who down from her neighboring perch had whirred,)
So smartly smote him on forehead and eyes,
That Bobby in *his* turn trembling — flies!

(Don't you think that his was a wretched plight?
Just picture a *boy* from a *bird* in flight!
His heart and his knee-joints weak with fright.)

But soon recovered, he trudged along,
Humming the words of a ballad-song,
Till reaching a place where the grasses bred
Tall "hoppers" in thousands, he staid his tread,
And cunningly crouching, as quick as thought,
A "grandfather hopper" was deftly caught.
Bob squeezed his body, and pulled his thighs,
And poked a straw in his winking eyes:
Then, with shrill laughter, and merry scoff,
He wrenched both legs of the creature off;
And next (could the rascal have had a heart?)
Its head from the body was snatched apart,
Till, a pitiful image of death and dearth,
Its carcass lay on the verdant earth!

I haven't the leisure to stop and tell
What other pains and evils befell
The defenceless tenants of wood and dell;
All wrought by an urchin's uncurbed will,
At length as an evening fair and still,
Shone over the wood, Bob strolled beyond
The wooded glades to a quiet pond,
The home of eels, mud-fishes, and things
Half frog, half fish, all covered with stings,
And scaly armor, as bright as brass;
Then and there, reader, it came to pass
That a terrapin, lazily crawling o'er
The moistened ways of its native shore,
Bob shrewdly captured — he turned his back
Heedfully down on the sandy track,
And — need we say it? — at once began
To practise as ever, his teasing plan.
He pinched the flesh of the terrapin sore
Racked it behind, and racked it before;
And strove — tho' just with a touch of awe,
The reptile's head from its shell to draw.
When hark! the sound of a vicious snap!
And the juvenile's fingers were in a trap
As ruthless as fate, and as sharp as steel;
Then, followed a piteous discord! Squeal,
Bellow, and shriek, the echoes around,
Woke up from the startled wave and ground.
Bob struggled and panted, kicked and cried,
Yet, his enemy's hold all efforts defied;

He thought to rise, but he would not do it,
For fear that his mangled flesh might rue it;
And still more agonized, angry, and loud,
His yells went up to a whirling cloud,
Which in a moment from out the blue,
(*Or such was his fancy*), darker grew,
Whence peered a head and a face to fear;
But what shall I say of the monster's leer,
His huge mouth stretching from ear to ear?

"You have tortured," (it said) "and torn all day
God's helpless creatures in wanton play;
Now, learn, oh! cruel and coward elf!
A useful lesson of pain, yourself!
Does it burn and sting to the deepest nerve?
What less do your brutal deeds deserve?
How! groaning again! for shame! be done!
You only tortured, you know, — in fun!"

. . . . .

When he gained from the terrapin's clutch release
While resting, that night, on his couch in peace,
There softly dawned thro' the twilight gloom,
A face more fair than a white-rose bloom;
And a voice that seemed like the under speech
Of the waters that swoon on a breezeless beach,
Whispered as low as low could be;
"Look up! I charge thee! and worship me;
And yet *not* me, but the Master — Christ!
"My name is Pity! — I am enticed
From even the Heaven of Heavens to bring
Soft balms for mortal suffering;
And whosoever the frailest thing
With strength within it to feel or love,
Wounds *here* — he is torturing me above;
And worse — for the pangs of that anguish dart
Through mine, to the tender Saviour's heart!"

Silence! — but just as sleep was won,
And over the boy's bright eyes of brown,
The delicate lashes came drooping down,
Thro' the silvery eddies of moonlight mist,
There stole the shadow of lips that kissed
The stain from the childish soul away,
That sadly sinning, had deemed it — play!

KISS ME, KATIE!

KATIE, Katie, little Katie!
Mouth of rose and eyes of blue,
(Eyes that look one frankly through!)
When I'm absent don't you miss me?
Now I'm near you, come and kiss me!
Katie, little Katie, kiss me!
Katie, do!

Katie, Katie, pretty Katie!
Prettier far than Jane or Lu,
Madge or Margaret, Maud or Prue;
Graceful as a spring-born fairy,
Tuneful as your pet canary—
Katie, pretty Katie, kiss me!
Katie, do!

Katie, sly, deceptive Katie!
If you fly me I'll pursue.
(What though *corns* or *gout* should rue!)
Then, if I can overmatch you,
Running fast can clasp and catch you,
Captured Katie, won't you kiss me?
Katie, do!

"Katie, pretty Katie, kiss me."

Katie, mute, day-dreaming Katie,
If I tell your thoughts to you,
Guess your dreams and *make* them true,
Won't you cease your coy defiance,
Vanquished by such wondrous science—
Won't you kiss me, Katie darling?
Katie, do!

Katie, captious little Katie!
Why that quickly tapping shoe,
Ready shrug and scornful *moue?*
Can it be you mean to scout me?
Just because I'm *grayish*, flout me?
Are you muttering, "KISS HIM! NEVER!
No, I *can't!* and no, I *won't!*"
O, you petulant, changeful Katie!
Katie, *don't!*

CAGED.

YOU think he sings a gladsome song!
Ah, well, he *sings!* but only see
How oft on glossy neck and breast
His bright head droops despondingly;
Or note the restless, eager bird
When a *free* minstrel's voice is heard.

You think because he pecks his grain
With vigorous mien and active bill,
This long captivity has trained
To tame content his roving will.
But watch, as some wild pinion flies,
Flashed near his cage, from summer skies:

He lifts his crest, his eyes dilate
To yearning orbs of passionate fire;
His whole small body seems to thrill,
And vibrate to the heart's desire:
The deathless wish once more to roam
The broad blue heaven God made his home.

Mark, next, the weary pant, the sigh
Of hope deferred, that follows then;
Perchance your captive's pain is deep
As that which haunts imprisoned *men*,
Pining behind *their* cruel bars
For sunlight or the holy stars.

Come! ope the door! he owns a soul
As tender, sensitive and fine
As yours or mine—for aught *we* know,
And dowered with rights scarce less Divine;
Come! let him choose, at least, between
God's azure and yon gilded screen!

Freed! yet he flies not!—Wait!—his brain
Is dazed!—he comprehends not yet
How earnest is your proffered boon,—
How surely his the glorious debt
Of freedom and all free-born things:
Wait!—ha! he prunes his doubtful wings.

Hops, perch by perch, to gain the door;
Then, as if first conviction came,
Full-faced, and whispered, "*thou art free!*"
He darts without, a wingèd flame,
And soon from far, fair cloudland floats
The rapture of his grateful notes!

LITTLE LOTTIE'S GRIEVANCE.

MAMMA's in heaven! and so, you see
My sister Bet's mamma to me.
Oh! yes, I love her!—that's to say,
I love her well the whole bright day;
For Sis is kind as kind can be,
Until, indeed we've finished tea—
Then (why did God make ugly night?)
She never, never treats me right,
But always says, "Now, sleepy head,
'Tis getting late! come up to bed!"

Just when the others, Fred and Fay,
Dolly and Dick, are keen for play—
Card-houses, puzzles, painted blocks,
Cat-corner, and pert Jack-in-the-box—
I must (it's that bad gas, I think,
That makes me somehow seem to wink!)
Must leave them all to seek the gloom
Of sister Bet's close-curtained room,
Put on that long stiff gown I hate,
And go to bed—oh, dear! at eight!

Now, is it fair that I who stand
Taller than Dolly by a hand,
(I'll not believe, howe'er 'tis told,
That cousin Doll is ten years old!
And just because I'm only seven,
Should be so teased, yes, almost driven,
Soon as I've supped my milk and bread,
To that old drowsy, frowsy bed?
I've lain between the dusky posts,
And shivered when I thought of ghosts:
Or else have grown so mad, you know,
To hear those laughing romps below,
While there I yawned and stretched (poor me!)
With one dim lamp for company.
I've longed for courage just to dare
Dress softly — then trip down the stair,
And on the parlor pop my head
With "No, I will not stay abed!"

I'll do it yet, all quick and bold,
No matter how our Bet may scold.
For, oh! I'm sure it can't be right,
To keep me here each dismal night,
Half scared by shadows grimly tall
That dance along the cheerless wall,
Or by the wind, with fingers chill,
Shaking the worn-out window-sill
One might as well be sick or dead,
As sent by eight o'clock to bed!

A NEW VERSION OF WHY THE ROBIN'S BREAST IS RED.

Know you why the robin's breast
Gleameth of a dusky red,
Like the lustre mid the stars
Of the potent planet Mars?
'Tis — a monkish myth has said —
Owing to his cordial heart;
For, long since, he took the part
Of those hapless children, sent
Hadean-ward for punishment;
And, to quench the fierce desire,
Bred in them by ruthless fire,
Brought on tiny bill and wing,
Water from some earthly spring,
Which in misty droplets fell
O'er their dwelling of unrest,
While the sufferer's faces grew
Softer 'neath the healing dew!

But, too far within that hell
Venturing, some malicious fiend,
A small devil hardly weaned,
Seized bold Robin in his claw,
Striving thro' the flames to draw
His poor body, until fled
Sight of eyes and sense of head,
Scorched he lay and almost dead!

Then, a child whose tongue and brow,
Robin's help had cooled but now,
Clutched the baby-fiend in ire,
And in gulfs of his own fire
Soused the vile misshapen elf.

Fluttering upwards, scarce himself,
After all the pain and fear
Of his horrid sojourn there
In that realm of flame and smoke,
Lo! earth's happy sunlight broke
On the bird's dazed view at last;
But the ordeal he had passed
Left a flame-spot widely spread
Where the wind-blown feathers part
Just above his loyal heart.
So the robin's breast is red!

THE LITTLE SAINT.

At the calm matin hour
I see her bend in prayer,
As bends a virgin flower
Kissed by the summer air;
Oh, meek her downcast eyes!
But the sweet lips wear a smile;
How hard our little angel tries
To be serious all the while!

I tell her 'tis not right
To be half-grave, half-gay,
Imploring in Heaven's sight
A blessing on the day;

She hears and looks devout—
  Although it gives her pain;
Still, when the ritual's almost out
  She's sure—to smile again!

She shocks her maiden aunt,
  Who thinks it a disgrace
That, do her best, she can't
  Give her a solemn face;
She'll scold and rate and fume,
  And lecture hour by hour,
Until she makes the very room
  Look passionate and sour!

Alack, 't is all in vain!
  Soon as the sermon's done
My fairy blooms again,
  Like a rose-bud in the sun.
I cannot damp her mirth!
  I will not check her play;
Is guileless joy so rife on earth,
  Hers shall not have full sway?

I asked her yester night,
  Why, when her prayer was made,
Her brow of cordial light
  Scarce caught a serious shade.
"*Father*," she said, "*you love*
  Better to meet me glad;
And so I thought the Christ above
  Might grieve to see me—sad!"

A NEW PHILOSOPHY; OR, STAR SHOWERS EXPLAINED.

One luminous night in winter,
  All crystal clear and still,
A band of wondering children
  Were grouped by the window sill.

The window looked out northward,
  Where through the tranquil hours
The stars kept falling, falling,
  In a ceaseless shine of showers.

Ah! beautiful sight! those children!—
  As they gazed on the magic skies,
With their tiny hands uplifted,
  And their large, bright, marvelling eyes.

"What is it?" asked curly Alfred,
  Of his elder brother, Gus;
"Does you think it is coming nearer?
  If it comes, can it fall on us?"

"No, stupid!" (in tones determined,)
  But soon he was touched by doubt,
And wished, as the flames waxed brighter,
  Somebody would put them out!

For, indeed, the radiant sparkles
  Now poured from a grander height:
And filled like a conflagration,
  The hollows and gulfs of night!

Till at last they all grew frightened;
  And the small dark heads and light
Were in a closer circle,
  While still they watched the night!

All but one sturdy urchin,
  The smallest and shrewdest there,
Whose eyes like a pert cock robin's,
  Turned up on the northward glare,

As he lisped, with an air quite final,
  And with somewhat of scorn and scoff:
"*It's the Fourth of July up yonder,*
  And the wockets is whizzing off!"

BABY'S FIRST WORD.

We watched our baby day by day,
  With earnest expectation,
To hear his infant lips unclose
  In vague articulation.

But weeks, nay weary months, passed on;
  His last wee tooth had broken
From rosy gums, yet not a word,
  Not *one* had baby spoken.

"O Rol!" I cried, "it cannot be
  A child so quick and clever,
Who hears ('tis plain he hears our talk),
  Should thus stay dumb forever!"

Rol answered sharply, vexed and red,
"What wretched nonsense, Jenny!
I never could have dreamed, my dear,
You'd prate like such a ninny!"

(Yes, that's the term, I must confess,
By which, with judgment narrow,
He dared for once, just once, you know,
To call his "winsome marrow.")

But what cared I? since as I live,
True as my name is Jenny,
From out the cradle clear and loud,
Came back the bad word "Ninny!"

Thence uprose baby all aglee,
His peaceful slumbers routed,
And thrice that naughty, naughty word
He spoke, nay, almost shouted!

Rol, glancing at my startled eyes,
His mirth could scarcely smother.
But oh! to think the rogue's first word
Should thus abuse his mother!

THE CHAMELEON.

I KNOW that I'm *like*, yet I am *not*, a snake!
'Tis true that I glisten by boll and by brake,
That I dart out and in, can glide, quiver and coil
As swift as the lightning, but softer than oil,
Yet a creature more innocent never was drawn
From the gray of cool shadows to bask in the dawn!

If I pause by a brook the rock-currents divide,
I grow silvery-white as the foam of its tide;
If 'mid dew-freshened meadows at sunrise I pass,
There's a shaft of pure emerald shot through the grass.
When to gay garden-closes I joyfully turn,
'Tis mine with all hues, of their roses to burn;
I reflect each bright blush that the petals have won
Of their young virgin-flowers from the kiss of the sun.
My skin's a clear mirror, a glass of the elves,
In which all lovely tints can smile back on themselves!
Stranger still! for on ugliness mirrored therein,
Though it tarnish a moment, this magical skin,
On the dark and uncouth some slight beauty's bestowed;
Why, even that dull little hunchback, the toad,
I endow with faint outlines of sweetness and grace,
While the newt, glancing down on his lop-sided face,
Reflected, — in pity,— by softened degrees,
Almost dreams he was formed by kind Nature to please!

Ah, therefore, sweet maiden, shrink not when you see
My lithe body reposing by streamlet or tree;
But kneel down where I rest, and all mellowed behold
Your eyes of deep blue, and your ringlets of gold,
In my miniature mirror, my glass of the elves,
Wherein all lovely things can smile back on themselves!

FLYING FURZE.

AIRILY, fairily, over the meadows,
Over the broom-grasses waving and gay,
O! see how it shimmers,
How wavers and glimmers,
Flying, and flying away.

Hastefully, wastefully, over the copses,
Over the hedge-rows in scattered array,
See, see how 'tis curling
And twinkling and whirling,
Ever and ever away!

Merrily, cheerily, down the far verges,
Verges of fields growing misty and gray,
Still, still how it shimmers,
Grows fainter and glimmers,
Shimmers, and glimmers away!

THE NEW SISTER.

Phil. SAY, Pete, do you like her?
Pete. Like! love her you mean!
Phil. Ain't she jolly and red?
Pete. And hurrah for her! just think of her head!
Phil. As big as a pippin, and round as a bullet!
Pete. And bald! oh! as bald as a newly-plucked pullet!
Phil. Did you look at her eyes too?
Pete. Of course; they are blue.
Phil. Not a bit of it—black!
Pete. Blue, I tell you—ask Jack!
Phil. Jack! I've eyes of my own that see better than his!
Pete. Brag on! but for once they have led you amiss.
Baby's eyes are blue—very!
Phil. As black as a berry!
Pete. Blue, you ninny! but s'pose we come down to her nose!
It's as funny and fat with an end like—
Phil. Like a rose?
Pete. No! a small dab of putty just tinted with pink!
Phil. Now, stoo-pid! how can you! I'm sure that I think
Nothing nicer than roses so dumpy and smug—
Pete. Pshaw! you mean it's a boo-ti-ful, boo-ti-ful pug!
Phil. Well, you naughty old Pete! you can't laugh at her chin!
Pete. Oh, no, it's the nattiest, sauciest, sweetest—
Phil. The nicest, completest,
Of arch little chins, with a dimple put in,
That winks up like a sunbeam,
Pete. And then her wee throat!
Phil. Her throat like egg-foam, or a syllabub boat
On a lake of clear cream!
Pete. And her arms; they are nice now; there's nothing can beat them!
Phil. So plump, round, and soft! I'm most ready to eat them!
Pete. Of course, Phil, you kissed her?
Phil. Oh, didn't I!
Pete. Well!
Phil. Well, I put my mouth down; I had something to tell;
Ah! close whispered close in the shy little ear,
That seemed to turn up, Pete, half coyly to hear,
And again, as I kissed her—
Pete. You blessed the good Lord for so jolly a sister!
Phil. Yes, I did!
Pete. So did I!
Phil. And now, Pete, 'tis but right
We should go in once more and bid "Baby" good night!

HOP, SKIP, AND JUMP: A QUEER TRIO PERSONIFIED.

O! HOP is a sailor used up in the war,
With a single good leg to stand on;
And a face as dingy almost as the tar
He was wont to rest his hand on:
And he grumbles strange oaths in his hairy throat
Whenever he sees a fair vessel afloat,
Especially one with those staring round eyes
(Port-holes, you know)
Whence the hot shot flies
At a quaking foe;
For then his anger, it fizzles up

(Like the sputtering foam in a lager-beer cup),
And he hoarsely cries,
"May witches fly off with that fellow by whom
I'm reduced to the cruel, contemptible doom
Of tottering all day,
In an imbecile way,
'Twixt a single good leg
And this base wooden peg,
Far, far from the spume
Of the gay ocean-spray!
So, seize him, and scorch him, and fry him, I say!"

But Skip is a mincing lady fine;
She never was seen to breakfast or dine;
And how she lives, none knoweth;
Her waist is so very slender and thin,
You fear it must snap, and topple in,
At the first slight wind that bloweth.
Her favorite motion's an airy jerk,
With her eyeballs raised, and her chin a-perk,
And her little red ringlets bobbing,
Bobbing and hobnobbing,
In a friendly fashion, each to each;
And her cheek is the hue of a delicate peach
(That never a shade can vary);
"*Perpetual motion*" she's sometimes called,
And really, truly one feels appalled
To view her galvanized skipping,
Her dancing, wriggling, whipping
Of one skirt in and one skirt out,
Her general manner of going about,
Which lies, I ween,
Half pitched between
The twittering, fussy, old-maidish way
Of the restless jay,
And the airs of a sprightly canary!

Jump is a long-limbed sturdy boy,
With such strong muscles to back him,
That I hardly could wish the creature joy
Who should ever dare to attack him;
A four-foot fence he clears in a minute;
And if you bet from the cottage eave
(And a very tall cottage it is in sooth),
With your leave, or without your leave,
That he cannot jump
With a dauntless thump,
And a thundering bump, —
Be sure that he'll quickly win it!
And, to whisper the truth, — the fearful truth,
I believe if whale or dragon,
The one on sea, and t'other on land,
(The biggest that either could brag on),
Came floating, or crawling nigh,
That this marvellous boy,
With a ringing cry
Of fierce, exuberant, reckless joy,
Would, just for the fun of it,
Make a swift run of it
Right down the jaws of whichever dread vermin
The turn of chance or a thought should determine!

So here my song ends,
And ye, charming young friends!
Don't endeavor to pump
My dry fancy again;
'Tis enough I've made plain
As Tommy's big nose
Looming red o'er the snows,
Those impalpable ideas of Hop, Skip, and Jump!

DANCING.

Dancing! I love it, night or day:
There's nought on earth so jolly,
Whether you straightly glide with May,
Or madly whirl with Molly,
The country dance is smooth and sleek;
But waltzes (some call vicious!)
Bring one so near a rosy cheek,
That, Jack, they're just delicious!

At every chance, I'm bound to go,
  And join our "West End" classes,
With all about me *comme il faut*,
  To captivate the lasses.

I think they rather like me, Jack, —
  (Oh, dear! the pretty creatures!) —
One shyly praised — behind my back —
  She *did* — my *Roman* features!

"Dancing! I love it, night or day:
There's nought on earth so jolly."

Yet somehow, Jack, the loveliest she
  (I mean sweet Mary Whimple)
Has never, never turned on me
  A single charming dimple:
But when I try the least advance,
  Her smile is changed to sneering;
Three times she has snubbed me in the dance
  To please that odious Speering!

Ah! Jack, it makes my bosom swell,
  And all my life forlorner,
To think (while others like me well)
  She, *she* should be a scorner!
I cannot be revenged on *her*,
  Nor *would*, if able even;
But, oh! that long-legged Speering cur
  I wish he was — in heaven!

He has given my hopes a blighting touch
  Though lank as any mummy;
And as for *mind*, — I've seen as much
  In some poor pasteboard dummy:
But then the best of girls are queer —
  Titania loved a donkey;
So Mary airs her charms to snare
  This awkward ball-room flunkey!

Ha! now my steam is all blown off,
  Once more I'm pleased and placid;
If Mary Whimple still *will* scoff,
  Why should I too grow acid?
With jovial smile and heart in tune
  (Ill humor's best disarmers,)
See, Jack, if I don't figure soon —
  Adonis 'mid the charmers!

MOTES.

Up and down, up and down,
In the air the sunshine mellows —
Green or yellow, gold or brown,
See those gay capricious fellows!
Sparkling, glittering, frisking, dancing,
Now retreating, now advancing,
Livelier than the jolliest clown,
Tinier than the tiniest fairy
That e'er robbed a farmer's dairy
Of the luscious cream which floats
Round his frothed and brimming bowls
Buoyant, tireless little souls!
    Who can fold them,
    Catch or hold them?
Evanescent,
  Omnipresent,
    Shy eluders,
      Bold obtruders,
Past all joking, most provoking,
    Tricksy, whisky, frisky
      Motes.

Up and down, up and down,
Light in sunshine, lost in shadow —
Green or yellow, gold or brown,
Over hill and over meadow,
    Swiftly over
Rock-ribbed height and billowy clover,
    Still advancing,
    Still retreating,
    Glittering, fleeting,
Never dozing, nor reposing,
But forever dancing, dancing;
And in numberless quaint fusions,
And eye-dazzling convolutions,
    Deftly sped
      Overhead —
See (where happy sunshine mellows
All the air) those jovial fellows!
Ah! ye tricksome waifs and tiny,
Who may circumvent and bind ye?
Can it be such creatures antic,
Unrestrained, grotesquely frantic,
Are but small nymphs out of school,
Laughing at all graver rule?
Or loose sylphides, bent on sowing,
        Sowing,
          Sowing,
In their thoughtless mirth o'erflowing,
Naughty crops of wildish oats?
How they jostle, whirl and hustle,
Up and down, up and down,
Through the air the sunshine mellows!
Green or yellow, gold or brown,
All those gay, capricious fellows,
    Evanescent,
      Omnipresent,
        Shy eluders,
          Bold obtruders,
Past all joking, most provoking,
    Tricksy, whisky, frisky,
      Motes!

THE GROUND SQUIRREL.

Bless us, and save us! What's here?
    Pop!
    At a bound,
A tiny brown creature, grotesque in his
    grace,
Is sitting before us, and washing his face
  With his little fat paws overlapping;
  Where does he hail from? Where?
    Why, *there*,
    Underground,

From a nook just as cosy,
And tranquil, and dozy,
As e'er wooed to Sybarite napping
(But none ever caught him a-napping).
"Don't you see his soft burrow so quaint, lad! and queer?"

Gone! like the flash of a gun!
This oddest of chaps,
Mercurial,
Disappears
Head and ears!
Then, sly as a fox,
Swift as Jack in his box,
Pops up boldly again!
What does he mean by this frisking about,
Now up and now down, and now in and now out,
And all done quicker than winking?
What does it mean? Why, 'tis plain, fun!
Only fun! or, perhaps,
The pert little rascal's been drinking?
There's a cider press yonder all day on the run!

Capture him! no, we won't do it,
Or, be sure in due time we would rue it!

Such a piece of perpetual motion,
Full of bother
And pother,
Would make paralytic old Bridget
A fidget.
So you see (to *my* notion),
Better leave our downy
Diminutive browny
Alone near his "diggings";
Ever free to pursue,
Rush round, and renew
His loved vaulting
Unhalting,
His whirling,
And curling,
And twirling,
And swirling,
And his ways, on the whole,
So unsteady!
'Pon my soul,
Having gazed
Quite amazed,
On each wonderful antic
And summersault frantic,
For just a bare minute,
My head, it feels whizzing;
My eyesight's grown dizzy;
And both legs, unstable
As a ghost's tipping table,
Seem waltzing, already!

Capture him! no, we won't do it,
Or in less than *no* time, *how* we'd rue it!

ARTIE'S "AMEN."

THEY were Methodists twain, of the ancient school,
Who always followed the wholesome rule
That whenever the preacher in meeting said
Aught that was good for the heart or head
His hearers should pour their feelings out
In a loud "Amen" or a godly shout.

Three children had they, all honest boys,
Whose youthful sorrows and youthful joys
They shared, as your loving parents will,
While tending them ever through good and ill.

One day—'twas a bleak, cold Sabbath morn,
When the sky was dark and the earth forlorn—
These boys, with a caution not to roam.
Were left by the elder folk at home.

But scarce had they gone when the wooded frame
Was seen by the tall stove pipe aflame;

And out of their reach, high, high, and higher,
Rose the red coils of the serpent fire.

With startled sight for a while they gazed,
As the pipe grew hot and the wood-work blazed:
Then up, though his heart beat wild with dread,
The eldest climbed to a shelf o'erhead,
And soon, with a sputter and hiss of steam.
The flame died out like an angry dream.

When the father and mother came back that day —
They had gone to a neighboring church to pray —
Each looked, but with half-averted eye,
On the awful doom which had just passed by.

And then the father began to praise
His boys with a tender and sweet amaze.
"Why, how did you manage, Tom, to climb
And quench the threatening flames in time
To save your brothers, and save yourself?"
"Well, father, I mounted the strong oak shelf
By help of the table standing nigh."
"And what," quoth the father, suddenly,
Turning to Jemmy, the next in age,
"Did *you* to quiet the fiery rage?"
"*I* brought the pail, and the dipper too,
And so it was that the water flew
All over the flames, and quenched them quite."

A mist came over the father's sight,
A mist of pride and of righteous joy,
As he turned at last to his youngest boy,
A gleeful urchin scarce three years old,
With his dimpling cheeks and his hair of gold.
"Come, Artie, I'm sure *you* weren't afraid:
Now tell in what way you tried to aid
This fight with the fire." "Too small am I,"
Artie replied, with a half-drawn sigh,
"To fetch like Jemmy, and work like Tom;
So I stood just here for a minute dumb,
Because, papa, *I was frightened some:*
But I prayed, 'Our Father,' and then, and then
I shouted as loud as I could, 'Amen.'"

THREE PORTRAITS OF BOYS.

STURDY little form, of true
Saxon pattern, through and through;
Face as purely Saxon, too,
With a smile demure and sly,
Dimpled cheek and twinkling eye;
Robin head, with sideway perk,
O'er some cunning *ruse* at work;
Welcome, lad! of wholesome ways,
And true juvenile displays;
Now progressing at full speed
On your gay velocipede,
(Yet where'er it deftly goes,
Wronging no one's dress or toes);
Now, beneath the basement hid,
On a dwarfish pyramid
Toiling, with scarred bricks and stone,
After methods, all your own;
A small Cheops! scarce less shrewd
In your purpose and your mood,
Than that king of mobs and mud,
By the old Nilotic flood!
Or with flying scarf and hat,
Coursing some half-frantic cat,
Fraught with wrath, and words that rail,
Should poor Tabby save his tail!
For the "old Adam's" sometimes seen
In your actions and your mien,
But no more than *must* appear
In his undegenerate heir.

Grown from what seems nature's plan,
What will Henry be as man?
One of healthful, mental range,
Honored at the doors of 'Change?

Of a quick and eager mind,
At the rise of fortune's wind;
Shrewd! perchance with scores of friends,
And productive dividends?

On life's middle pathway still,
By extremes of good and ill.
Evermore unvisited,
Shall we see him safely tread?
Not ambitious of grand things,
Or the scope of eagle's wings;
But within the limits meet
Of his unpretentious feet,
A good man, perhaps a wise,
Who — (in ledger of the skies),
May — unsmutched by blots of blame,
Find, at last, his honest name?

MARION.

Urchin of the Syrian face,
And half melancholy grace,
With a look in your dark eyes,
Sometimes deep and overwise;
What shall be your mortal doom?
Desert blight, or healthful bloom?
Shall the lily, Virtue, shine
On your life, made thus divine;
Or Corinthian roses shed
Poisoned petals on your head?
Ah! the soul that dwells in you,
Heaven hath blent of flame and dew
Mixed by subtlest art together
In your nature's changeful weather,
Whence a lightning-glitter warm,
Now and then, portends a storm;
Such a storm of tropic strain,
Scathed by fire and big with rain;
All your being o'er and under,
Thrilled as if by spirit-thunder;
Till, exhausted at the source
Of its wild imperious course
Passion — like a blast that dies
Down the slowly brightening skies,
Thro' loud sob and weary moan
Falls to plaintive monotone!

Strange child-soul, but half unfurled,
Who shall scan its complex world?
Glimpsed 'twixt light and shadow dim,
Dare I prophesy of him?
Subtle, mystical, refined,
Seem the thoughts that haunt his mind,
While large forces play their part
On the boy's embattled heart,

Stubborn *will* — it irks to yield,
Always watchful — under shield;
Scorn of all who do him wrong,
Keen, implacable and strong;
Yet — toward the fair and just,
Love, that's crowned with generous trust;
And those graces, pure and high,
Born of tender loyalty!

With a firm and wise control,
Guide the currents of his soul!
Forceful are they, and must ride
Ever, with impetuous tide,
If to duty's strand they flow,
Fraught with all pure flowers that blow,
Or, the Syren's lotus-lea,
Fronting death's unfathomed sea!

HERBERT.

Ah! you tricksy little elf,
How you idolize yourself!
And believe the world was made
Like a gay-hued masquerade,
Just for you to sport and dance,
Ever, in a happy trance!
How I envy you the joy
Of such bright *abandon*, boy!
All your buoyant veins are rife
With the sunniest wine of life!
And if e'er a shadow strays
O'er your glad, elysian ways,
'Tis but like the doubtful mote
In the morning's eye afloat;
At the slightest breeze of fun,
Cloudless is your spirit's sun!

Still, my tricksy little elf,
Idolize your blissful self;
Dream you'll always be a boy,
And that life's a painted toy,

Just for you to hasten after,
Full of thoughtless mirth and laughter;
Soon, alack! how grim and grum,
Disenchantment's sure to come!
Life, with which you loved to play,
Slowly turns from gold to gray;
All its splendid tints are lost,
For, experience, cold as frost,
Dims the hues which undefiled,
Blessed the outlook of the child;
And we learn in mournful wise,
Earth's no longer — Paradise!

BIRDS.

THAT'S the dove, my darling!
Murmurous, soft and tender;
There! she's mooning, crooning,
On a pine-branch slender.
And ah! it's the dove, the dove, dove, dove,
That never can coo, but she pleads of love,
Of love, love, love,
In the shadows fair and tender.

That's the wren, my fairy!
With her wee love-pledges;
See her playing, straying
Underneath the hedges.
And oh! it's the wren, the wren, wren, wren,
That is never contented too far from men,
But lives, lives, lives
Secure in the field-side hedges.

That's the thrush, my beauty!
Hark! and let us hear her,
Yonder swinging, singing,
Higher, bolder, clearer,
And oh! it's the thrush, the thrush, thrush, thrush,
Whose loud song wakens the noon-tide hush,
The deep, deep hush
Of the meadows and wolds, to hear her!

That's the mockbird, sweetheart!
To all tones beholden,
Which are thrilling, filling
Glades of woodland golden,
And ah! it's a bird, a bird, bird, bird,
The sweetest that ever a mortal heard.
Ah! sweet, sweet, sweet,
In the sunshine, fresh and golden!

THE DEAD CHILD AND THE MOCKING-BIRD.

ONCE in a land of balm and flowers,
Of rich fruit-laden trees,
Where the wild wreaths from jasmine bowers
Trail o'er Floridian seas;

We marked our Jeannie's footsteps run
Athwart the twinkling glade;
She seemed a Hebe in the sun,
A Dryad in the shade!

And all day long her winsome song,
Her trebles and soft trills,
Would wave-like flow or silvery low
Die down the tinkling rills.

One morn, midmost the foliage dim,
A dark-gray pinion stirs;
And hark! along the vine-clad limb,
What strange voice blends with hers?

It blends with hers which soon is stilled!
Braver the mock-bird's note
Than all the strains that ever filled
The queenliest human throat:

As Jeannie heard, she loved the bird,
And sought thenceforth to share
With her new favorite dawn by dawn,
Her daintiest morning cheer!

But ah! a blight beyond our ken,
From some far feverous wild,
Brought that dark shadow feared of men,
Across the fated child!

It chilled her drooping curls of brown,
It dimmed her violet eyes,
And like an awful cloud stole down
From vague mysterious skies!

At last, one day our Jeannie lay,
All pulseless, pale, forlorn;
The sole sweet breath on lips of death.
The mocking breath of morn!

When just beyond the o'ercurtained room,
(How tender yet how strong!)
Rose through the misty morning gloom,
The mock-bird's sudden song!

Dear Christ! those notes of golden peal,
Seem caught from heavenly spheres;
Yet through their marvellous cadence, steal
Tones soft as chastened tears!

Is it an angel's voice that throbs
Within the brown bird's breast?
Whose rhythmic magic soars, or sobs,
Above our darling's rest?

The fancy passed, but came once more,
When stolen, from Jeannie's bed,
That eve along the porchway floor,
I found our minstrel . . . dead!

The fervor of the angelic strain
His life-chords burned apart,
And blent with sorrow's earthlier pain,
Broke the o'erburdened heart!

Maiden and bird! the self-same grave
Their wedded dust shall keep,
While the long low Floridian wave
Moans round their place of sleep!

THE LITTLE GRAND DUCHESS.

WHAT a pure and chastened splendor,
What a grace of joyance tender,
Like to starlight or to moonlight,
Melting into fairy Junelight,
Sleeps my little lady sweetly, —
In the air that answers meetly
With each soul-illumined feature,
Which the lovely, winsome creature
Lifts toward us so demurely,
That despite their candor, surely
Something of an elfish slyness
Sparkles 'round their shadowed shyness,
Though a *pose* that's sometimes stately,
(Baby brows thrown back sedately,)
Charms us by a look that such is,
She might be a wee Grand Duchess!

But anon that aspect changes,
Through all moods her spirit ranges.
Free and far as Ariel pinions
O'er a warlock's weird dominions;
Happy fields of dim romances:
Woods wherein an elve-troop dances
'Neath a noon of splendid trances,
Culling flowers, or chanting lowly
Songs of golden melancholy;
Or in stretch of wildest dreamings,
(Holding true their gracious seemings,)
Wafted into blissful vision
Of some rarer realm Elysian.

Well I know that mark the yearning
Through her snowy eyelids burning,
Shadowed by those midnight lashes,
(Quickly closed when aught abashes,
And as quickly flashed asunder,
When swift anger lightens under,)
How supreme the hidden forces
Blindly struggling at their sources
In her depths of nascent being:
Insight, but half-born to seeing,
Faint perceptions, intuitions,
And soft-murmuring admonitions,
Toned and mellowed down so finely
That their voices breathe divinely.

Ha! but see, our dainty fairy
Freed from thought, or dreamings airy,
All an embryo flirt's beguiling,
Wooes us in her roguish smiling,
Rippled into silvery laughter,
With arch glances levelled after,
Coy, coquettish, gay, capricious
Sprite! thy every mood's delicious;

Yet amid these spirit-phases
Whereupon thy poet gazes,
There is one that steals above thee;
Dewy pure from heavens that love thee.
'Tis not when thy heart is lightest,
'Tis not when thy glance is brightest,
But when sober Contemplation
Near thee takes her pensive station,
While a strange ecstatic quiet
Follows on thy childish riot.

Lo! her trifling fancies vanished, —
Lo! her baby bearing banished,
She has grown so sweetly earnest
That I'm sure the harshest, sternest
Cynic who should chance to meet her,
Must with fond caresses greet her!
Introspective, deep surmising,
Glow her eyes like moonbeams rising,
And across her face, where wonder
Seems with tremulous awe to ponder,
Smiles a glory, as if angels
Whispered her their soft evangels!

So that for the moment losing
Time and place while on her musing,
One might say, this eerie creature
Hardly owns our earth-born nature,
For she's changeling, fay and fairy,
In a word, all things that vary
Most in wizard transformations,
And the round of weird creations!

ROLY POLY.

Roly Poly's just awakened,
  Wakened in his cosy bed;
All his dainty ringlets tumbled
  O'er his shoulders, and his head:
Roly Poly's cheeks are rounder
  Than a dumpling duly done,
While they look as rich and ruddy,
  As a freshly-dawning sun.

Roly Poly's keen for breakfast;
  Ah! he stays, he tarries not,
But as soon as mother's breeched him,
  Rushes for his "hot and hot";

Such huge sups of oatmeal porridge
  Swallows he at lordly ease,
That I'm sure in stout digestion,
  He's an infant — Hercules!

Roly Poly rises briskly
  (When repletion bids him stop),
Shall he take his kite for flying,
  Or, go out with cord and top?
Not the faintest breeze is blowing,
  So, of course, the top's preferred;
Eagerly he hastes to spin it,
  Almost flying — like a bird!

But unlucky Roly Poly
  Chooses — since the ground is hard —
As the fittest place for spinning,
  Mother's well-stocked poultry-yard;
So, what time his mammoth "hummer"
  Circles on its nimble pegs,
Roly feels a rearward *something*
  Dabbing, stabbing at his legs!

Round he turns in vast amazement,
  Round, to find erect and free,
Ruffled, ireful, a great gander,
  Quite as tall ('twould seem), as he;
But brave Roly Poly battles,
  Knight-like, on his sturdy thighs,
Battles, till the treacherous monster
  Leaves his legs, to smite his eyes!

Then, must Roly fly affrighted,
  Fly, the sudden wrath beyond,
Of that ruthless, base aggressor, —
  But to tumble in — *a pond!*
Over head and ears to tumble
  In a dark, unsavory flood,
Bubbling, doubling, kicking fiercely,
  Plucking weeds, and grasping mud!

While — as pitiless fate *would* have it —
  Ponto, panting on the run,
Thinks that Master Roly Poly's
  Only sought the pond in fun;
So, he dashes in, exultant,
  Paws the boy, with bark and bound,
And instead of gallant rescue,
  Madly rolls him round and round: —

"Roly Poly 's just awakened,
Wakened in his cosy bed."

When a gasping groan and sputter
  Prove to Ponto, shrewd and true,
What is now the sacred duty
  That a faithful dog should do;
See, he tugs at Roly's trowsers,
  Tugs with steadfast might and main,
Till he brings our dripping urchin
  Safely to the shore again.

Ponto's teeth are sharp and potent,
  And impelled by need to speed,
They have made poor Roly Poly
  In no stinted measure bleed!
Therefore, with his gory garments,
  And his mud-bespattered knees,
He is like a dwarfish Sindbad,
  Sorrow-laden, by the seas!

Oh! to mark our roguish Roly
  Throw his fright and trouble off!
How he laughs at dangers vanished,
  With his merriest boyish scoff.
Decked once more in spotless trowsers
  How he makes the household ring:
Scours and scampers, shouts and dances,
  Domineering like a king.

Doubt not that at lunch and dinner,
  Fervid is the fork he plies;
Presto, how the mutton dwindles!
  Gone are sweetmeats; melted pies!
Not one drop of bygone trouble
  Bitter makes his cup, or can;
Roly! let us change our places —
  I, the boy; and you, the man!

THE IMPRISONED INNOCENTS.

[Or the Complaint of a Philosopher of Family !]

  One morning I said to my wife,
  Near the time when the heavens are rife
  With the Equinoctial strife,
"Arabella, the weather looks ugly as sin!
Observe, how those mists from the ocean begin
To creep eastward and blend
With the sickly street vapors fantastic and thin;
So, (*won't* you attend?) keep the children within,
Safe-housed from these damps of September!
For myself — as I'm studying '*Barret On Drainage*' just now — I'll go up to the garret,
And thus will be barred from all noises,
And tumults of infantile voices!
(Please listen, my dear! I am speaking, I *think*,
And put down your baby! he'll drink, and he'll drink
Warm tea till he pops!) so again let me say,
Keep the juveniles housed on this treacherous day,
May I trust you, for *once*, to remember?"

Then, with pain (for my limbs are rheumatic),
  I slowly climbed up to the attic;
  And all the 'mid-stories o'er passed,
  Reached the dismal old garret at last!
"Now," thought I, "no echoes of riot
  Can break my philosopher's quiet;
  Thank heaven! all luxuries scorning
  Of stuffed couch or sofa, — I'll settle just here —
(Though perhaps I would like a less imbecile chair)
And be deep in research the whole morning!"

Alack! for all bright expectation!
  While safe, as I fancied, from worry,
  For below me I heard,
  Ere my choler was stirred
First, a faint indefinable flurry,
Then, a deep roll, and thunder-like rumble,
With the shock of some terrible tumble,
  Which shook the whole house to its basis!
In a trice from my foolish elation
  I emerged with the blankest of faces,

And, well, I confess as a Christian I erred
But who, my good sir, or good madam!
Could have throttled, (just then), the "old Adam"?
I'm afraid that I muttered a something
That ought to have rested a dumb thing!
Yet before your stern censure you urge on,
Bethink you! the same term 's been uttered
Quite roundly, not stammered or stuttered,
By good men from Edwards to Spurgeon!
So, pray don't confuse me,
But kindly excuse me,
If once in a justified passion,
I followed their clerical fashion,
(Albeit much modified too!)
And whispered, not shouted, a d——n!

Of course, to the doorway I scurried,
And down the old stairs from the attic
(In spite of my twinges rheumatic),
Incontent hurried!
Having reached the back parlor, I trembled,
Alack! now, with fear undissembled,
For Jacky all spattered with gore,
Lay flabby and flat on the floor!
A pestilent urchin,
Who stood much in need of promiscuous 'birchin'
With his tricks and his manners unstable,
He had taken to tipping the table,
(A rickety table, though heavy as lead),
And succeeded, the mischievous elf!
In tremendously tipping himself!
And then the big board like an unloosened rafter,
Came sundering, blundering, thundering after,
Gave his pert shanks a majestical rap,
And one fat little thumb,
Round as a plum,
Caught — as in spite,
And held on to it tight,
As a new patent trap!
But worst of all, he had thumped his head,
Thumped his head and maltreated his nose,
(Hence, the sanguine stains that disfigured his clothes!)
And yet after all the ado,
We managed to rescue, and bring him to,
On his pipe-like pegs
Of ridiculous legs,
To set him up in the general view,
No longer flecked by a crimson hue,
But, a trifle black and a trifle blue!

Behold me, once more in the garret!
This time with the door barred fast,
And locked by a rusty key,
(As if one could banish trouble,
By making one's fastenings double!
"Here's peace," quoth I, "at last!
One row, and a row of such degree,
Is surely enough 'till twilight!"
And so, 'neath the garret sky-light,
Again I pored o'er my "Barret"
("Barret on Drainage," I've said),
With calmer nerves and a cooler head;
Determined to compass the topic,
In a mode most philosophic,
And launching a sudden shot,
Lightning-swift, and fiery hot,
Through an article terse and satirical,
Those foolish savants to bring down,
Who with theories basely empirical,
Had so startled and shocked the town!

Ah! soon in order beautiful,
To a masterly logic dutiful,
My thoughts were ranged for fight;
I was making here and there,
A note on the fly-leaves bare,
When horribly higher and higher,
Uprose the shout of "Fire!"
In a monstrous dumb affright,
I hardly walked, but fell,

(As it seemed), from the garret's height,
(Though how, I could never tell!)
I alighted beneath to find
In the parlor a spark half out,
Which the feeblest puff of wind
From the chimney had blown about
But the children still would shout,
And dance, and prance, and bellow,
In a deafening, demonish rout,
While as for their mother, low and limp,
She lay, in a faint, by the opened door,
With her eighteenth-monther, a restless imp,
Drawing and pawing o'er and o'er
The folds of her rumpled dress!
Somebody in years gone by,
Had pronounced her fainting *pose*
The *ne plus ultra* of loveliness,
As she lay like a sweet white rose;
But now! perchance, perchance,
I have lost my young romance,
For, unadmiring quite,
I gazed on the touching sight,
And (I'm a brute no doubt!)
But I let the syren lie.

Ah me, the vexations,
Exasperations,
And tribulations,
Confusions,
Obtrusions,
And endless affrays,
Which marked with dark tracing that blackest of days!
Don't tell me that children are angels,
All fraught with pure heaven's evangels,
And trailing — what is it! — from some mystic star
Bright cloudlets of glory. I know what mine are,
Not a whit worse I'm sure than the rest of young "fry,"
Whose natures are thoughtless and spirits are high;
But as for your "angels!" all that's "in my eye!"

To enter again
On that morning of pain:
I should wretchedly blunder
In counting the number
Of times I was harried
(My thoughts all miscarried!)
By yells of shrill laughter
Or dread cries thereafter,
By accidents seen or invisible,
And mishaps high tragic, or risible;
Young Tommy three window-panes shattered,
And, of course, cut his head in the process,
And an old silver heir-loom
That oft held the rare bloom
Of vintages mellow and lusciously fine
From the banks of Moselle or the banks of the Rhine,
A tankard four centuries old and no less,
By wee Janet was battered,
Disgraced,
And defaced,
Till the Bacchus Cellini had graven thereon,
Was broken and wan,
And the sweep of the vine, and the curve of the grape,
Were twisted hopelessly out of shape.

Then Harry fell down in the cistern!
With yells to be heard for a mile,
And in striving to fish him out,
(For the boy is portly, puffy, and stout)
Back would he slip, and slip, and slip,
E'en from the cistern's utmost lip,
Until with a wrench swift-handed,
The human gudgeon was landed,
Who made with a ghastly smile
The half-inarticulate pledge,
That never more would he tempt the edge
Of well or cistern, fount or river,
Although upon earth he should dwell forever!

And lastly, Cornelia, aged five,
(I marvel the child is still alive!
Contrived in the subtlest, deftest way,
From the surgery shelf, to steal, in play,
A box of my pills cathartic;
Enough (if swallowed at once) to slay
A bear of the regions Arctic!
How many she took I cannot say,
But thereafter for many and many a day,
Supine the suffering maiden lay,
And I scarce believe that her blood has set
To the shore of health that is perfect, yet!

What is the moral of this, my masters?
(To you that are fathers, I mean,
Fathers, and students as well?)
Tis easy enough to tell),
Would you 'scape all household disasters?
And be cosy, sweet-tempered, serene?
Then *never*, *never*, *never*,
Make the absurd endeavor,
Because the sky's not bluish
And the wind seems somewhat shrewish,
To pen a young regiment in,
Of heirs to Adam's sin!

Boston Stereotype Foundry, 4 Pearl Street.

www.ingramcontent.com/pod-product-compliance
Lightning Source LLC
LaVergne TN
LVHW020934110826
845150LV00004B/860